Literacy

Literacy

Reading, Writing, and Children's Literature

Gordon Winch

Rosemary Ross Johnston

Marcelle Holliday

Lesley Ljungdahl

Paul March

OXFORD

UNIVERSITY PRESS

OXFORD
UNIVERSITY PRESS

253 Normanby Road, South Melbourne, Australia

Oxford University Press is a department of the University of Oxford.
It furthers the University's objective of excellence in research,
scholarship, and education by publishing worldwide in

Oxford New York

Athens Auckland Bangkok Bogotá Buenos Aires
Cape Town Chennai Dar es Salaam Delhi Florence
Hong Kong Istanbul Karachi Kolkata Kuala Lumpur
Madrid Melbourne Mexico City Mumbai Nairobi
Paris Port Moresby São Paulo Shanghai Singapore
Taipei Tokyo Toronto Warsaw

with associated companies in Berlin Ibadan

OXFORD is a trade mark of Oxford University Press
in the UK and in certain other countries

© Gordon Winch, Rosemary Johnston, Marcelle Holliday,
Lesley Ljungdahl, and Paul March 2001

First published 2001

National Library of Australia
Cataloguing-in-Publication data:

Literacy: reading, writing, and children's literature.

   Bibliography.
   Includes index.
   ISBN 0 19 550671 5.

   1. Language arts (Primary)—Australia.
   2. Literacy—Australia.
   I. Winch, Gordon, 1930–.

Edited by Venetia Somerset
Index by Geraldine Suter
Text designed by Polar Design
Cover designed by Sylvia Witte
Typeset by Promptset Pty Ltd
Printed by Australian Print Group

Contents

Figures

Contributors

Marcelle Holliday taught for eighteen years in primary and demonstration schools in New South Wales and South Australia before beginning work on the assessment of reading as part of the Australian Cooperative Assessment Project in 1980. She has since worked extensively on a range of projects in literacy including curriculum development, teacher professional development, and the development of effective literacy assessment materials. From 1997 to 1999 she played a major role in the design and implementation of the NSW Department of Education and Training Literacy Strategy, having responsibility for the reading component of the strategy. As part of this process, a widely acclaimed 'balanced approach to reading' was developed and the structure of a 'daily literacy session' was refined and made available to all primary teachers in New South Wales. In 1998 she pioneered *Log on to Literacy*, a professional development program in the teaching of literacy that is delivered to teachers in isolated communities via the Internet. Furthermore, she has served as a council member of the Primary English Teaching Association, for which she has written and edited a number of publications, and has presented papers and worked with teachers and trainee teachers at conferences and in seminars in Australia, the UK, the US, and Sweden.

Rosemary Ross Johnston is the Director of the Centre for Research and Education in the Arts at the University of Technology Sydney, Australia, and has taught at all levels, primary, secondary and tertiary. In 2000 she was H. W. Donner Guest Research Professor with the ChiLPA (Children's Literature: Pure and Applied) Project, an international project at Åbo Akademi University, Finland, funded by the Finnish Ministry of Education. She remains as Expert Advisor with the project. She is secretary of the International Research Society for Children's Literature, and Assistant Secretary-General of the *International Federation des Langues et Litteratures Modernes*, both since 1996. She is also an International Board Member of the Montgomery Institute in Canada. She has been published in a number of national and international journals, including *Children's Literature in Education, Canadian Children's Literature, Bookbird, the Australian Journal of Language and Literacy*, and *Papers*. She is the editor of *CREArTA*, an international, interdisciplinary journal in the arts.

Lesley Ljungdahl is a Senior Lecturer in the Faculty of Education at the University of Technology, Sydney, where she has taught in subjects on approaches to the teaching of reading, writing, and children's literature. She began teaching in London after obtaining a BA(Hons) in Language and Literature in Sydney (UNSW) and later returned to work in Canberra and Sydney before being appointed to the William Balmain College of Advanced Education. Lesley is also a qualified librarian, holds a Master of Library Studies, and has worked as a secondary-school librarian in Canada. Lesley is a past president of ATESOL (NSW) and has given conference presentations on literacy-related issues at national and international conferences. She has presented numerous papers on literacy at TESOL conferences (Teaching English to Speakers of Other Languages) in the United States and Canada. Her major book publication, *A Week in the Future*, highlighted the work of Catherine Helen Spence. Dr Ljungdahl's current interests are in the teaching of language and literature with a particular focus on the needs of students from a language background other than English. Other current interests are in international studies with a focus on China and the Mandarin language.

Paul March began his teaching career in primary schools. He is currently a senior lecturer in the Faculty of Education at the University of Technology, Sydney, and Director of Publications for the Centre for Research and Education in the Arts. He lectures in primary English curriculum studies as well as child drama. Among his publications are several co-edited academic texts: *Writing and Learning in Australia* (Oxford/Dellasta), *Teaching Writing K–12* (Dellasta) and *The Teacher Is The Answer* (Centre for Reading, UTS). He has presented papers at international conferences in the UK and USA and has worked as an Adjunct Professor in Boston, USA. He is active as an adjudicator and examiner for speech and drama and has had extensive experience in devising syllabuses for the Australian Speech Communication Association. He has also been active on committees for the International Reading Association and the Primary English Teaching Association.

Gordon Winch was previously Head of the Department of English at Kuring-gai College of Advanced Education, now the Lindfield campus of the University of Technology, Sydney, and is currently a full-time author. He holds a Master of Arts degree in English, a Master of Education degree, both from the University of Sydney, and a Doctor of Philosophy in English and Education from the University of Wisconsin. Before entering the academic world he taught in primary and secondary schools in Australia and overseas.

Among his publications are a number of books for children, including a collection of verse; academic texts, such as *Teaching Reading: A Language Experience* with Valerie Hoogstad and *Give Them Wings: The Experience of Children's Literature* with Maurice Saxby. His educational books on literacy for children are sold around the world as widely as the Middle East, South East Asia, Great Britain and Ireland, New Zealand, Canada and the United States.

While working overseas in the 1970s he perceived the need for a professional organisation for primary school teaching of English and was one of the founders and the first president of the Primary English Teaching Association. It is now one of the largest professional organisations of its kind in Australia.

Foreword

There have been many books published on literacy and almost as many published on children's literature. However, there are far fewer that attempt to cover both literacy and literature, and even fewer that remember to include writing as part of literacy. But one might still ask, 'why another book on literacy?' The short answer is that there is still much to learn about literacy and the way it is used and developed as part of life. I want to congratulate the authors of this significant book for the scope, quality, and freshness of their work.

I have known the work of the writers for many years. Indeed, I have been part of the same community of literacy scholars as the authors for almost 25 years. I worked with Marcelle Holiday on literacy curriculum reform in the late 1970s. I first encountered Gordon Winch's work at the same time and have been an active participant with all the authors in a range of professional and scholarly organisations throughout this period.

I feel quite privileged to have shared this period of growth in our understanding of literacy and the development of the Children's Literature field in Australia. This has been a significant time. In the 1960s the word 'literacy' was hardly mentioned in curriculum documents, textbooks, and professional organisations. We spoke of reading, spelling, writing, handwriting, speaking, listening, and literature as if they were separate entities. Literacy was defined much more narrowly than today, and was seen as the combined skills of reading and writing. These 'subskills' in turn were seen as sets of cognitive skills to be mastered. This was a very narrow view of all that we now recognise as literacy.

Reading was dominated by a concern for the development of word recognition skills, comprehension, and study and reference skills, as if each were separate sets of abilities to be mastered. Writing was often seen simply as 'composition' and received little attention beyond the teaching of surface features and grammar within the framework of narrative discourse. In fact it was not until the mid 1970s that writing became a serious research pursuit and gained the interest from educators that it deserved. The explosion of 'process writing' under the bold and zealous leadership of scholars like Bob Walshe in Australia and Donald Graves in the USA, was one of a number of key events that changed the way we viewed the primary and secondary English curriculum in Australia.

When one considers the last 40 years it is possible to identify broad phases or themes in the teaching and research literature as well as in curriculum. In the 1960s the emphasis was on reading and writing as skills. The 1970s saw the emergence of process and meaning as twin concerns within the fields of writing and reading respectively, and an emergence in the latter stages of the decade of a concern for literacy as an integrated practice. In the 1980s we saw a strong concern among teachers and researchers to reconsider literacy as a linguistic phenomenon, a desire to make language form and structure more explicit to students, and the emergence of profiles and global assessment of literacy. The 1990s saw a concern for the sociocultural nature of literacy, and a desire to consider literacy not as a unitary skill but as multiple literacies, and finally, national action on literacy assessment and curriculum development becoming a reality. Throughout these four decades children's literature continued to develop and grow in its own way with an explosion of new literary genres, new authors, excursions into reader response theory, the first multimedia texts, and so on. Non-fiction emerged as an even more exciting genre with the boundaries between literature and factual genres being blurred. Indeed, the division between the traditional school reader and literature also began to break down, with literature finding its way increasingly into instructional programs. These were exciting times.

This book is a product of its times. The opening pages provide a definition of literacy that recognises that literacy is seen differently than it was 40 years ago—an integrated set of practices that require literacy users to draw on multiple sign systems to make meaning. The pages that follow provide a detailed overview of many of the key developments that have shaped literacy research and practice to the present day and a wealth of practical ideas for teachers.

The challenge for all of us as teachers and students of literacy is to expand our literacy horizons. As a literacy researcher I have found that the more I have learned about literacy, the more questions this has posed for me. As a practising cognitive psychologist in the 1970s, I tried desperately to understand how the mind constructed meaning. As I developed greater precision in 'getting at' the cognitive processes that represented reading, I discovered linguistic complexity that made my quest more elusive. As I increasingly explored sociolinguistic aspects of literacy, I began to see a social and cultural complexity to literacy that I hadn't recognised before. In the last ten years as I have explored the sociocultural dimensions of literacy I have continued to be amazed by new facets of literate practices that previously had not been visible to me. I have come to see that while it is important to understand the cognitive processes that allow us to engage in literacy, this cannot be done in isolation from literacy's role as a set of social practices that have the potential to empower or exclude, and indeed to shape the very human relationships that are the essence of our being. I have also come to appreciate that literacy offers the power to inform or deceive, to express love or hate—to have an impact on the human condition.

But being positive, literacy has the potential to open up 'other worlds' (Cairney 1991). In the last four years or so I have also been struck by the enormous impact that cyber text and multimedia texts are having on the way we experience and use literacy in our world. The next decade will be one in which literacy will ever increasingly be characterised by the use of multiple sign systems to make meaning. The boundaries between written, visual, and real-word texts will blur as we seek to make sense of our worlds utilising all that we have available to us. And yet, as I conclude my comments, I'm reminded that there is something inherently basic about literacy that will not change—the power of story. This is something that Harold Rosen constantly brought to our attention. Much of human experience and existence is lived out through narrative. As the children's literature chapters make clear, there is immense power in 'story' to teach, to share, and to express all human emotions. This is indeed timeless.

In his wonderful story *The Stone Book*, Allan Garner (1976) writes of his English ancestors. In this brilliant tale, Mary expresses to her father the desire to have a book—a prayerbook, to carry to chapel. This was a significant request to make of her stonemason father, a man not of letters but of stone. Her wish was indeed granted, her father presenting her with the book she wanted. Garner tells it this way:

> *'There,' said Father. 'That'll do.'*
>
> *He gave Mary a prayer book bound in blue-black calf skin, tooled, stitched and decorated. It was only by the weight that she could tell it was stone and not leather.*
>
> *'It's better than a book you can open,' said Father. 'A book has only one story. And tomorrow I'll cut you a brass cross and let it in the front with some dabs of lead, and then I'll guarantee you'd think it was Lord Stanley's, if it's held right.'*
>
> *...*
>
> *And Mary sat by the fire and read the stone book that had in it all the stories of the world and the flowers of the flood.*

In a profound way, the old stonemason had learned something that it has taken literacy scholars and teachers many years to learn. Books have the power to be used to tell but a single story, and yet all the stories of the world are at our fingertips in the multiple signs that fill our world.

I want to thank the authors for asking me to write this foreword. I trust that the book will enrich readers' understanding of what literacy is and how it is nurtured and used as we relate one to another.

Trevor Cairney
Professor of Education
Pro Vice-chancellor (Research)
University of Western Sydney

Preface

This book has been written to provide a suitable text for students in primary education and a resource for teachers. It places emphasis on both the theoretical and practical aspects of literacy and relates directly to everyday practice in the classroom.

Literacy: Reading, Writing, and Children's Literature is divided into three parts. Each part is written by different authors who explore the various aspects of literacy while giving attention to the obvious interrelationship among them. In doing so, the authors have provided day-to-day examples of classroom practice allocated specifically to the teaching of literacy in the school.

Gordon Winch and *Marcelle Holliday* take what they term a balanced view of reading. They see reading, and literacy generally, operating in a sociocultural context where readers take on a number of roles depending on the situation, the text-type, and the nature of the reader. They explore the research relating to a range of aspects of reading and argue that both reading and writing depend on the simultaneous interaction of phonological–graphological, grammatical, and semantic information operating in varying contexts

Practical outcomes of reading are viewed chronologically. For example, chapters dealing with the child before school, the emergent reader, the developing reader, and the independent reader are considered. Shared, Guided, and Independent Reading sessions are explored and assessment in reading is discussed in a range of possible types. The section provides the necessary amalgam of theory and practice that supports the underlying aim of the book.

Lesley Ljungdahl and *Paul March* consider writing in a sociocultural context also and see it developing in the classroom with other literacy skills. They feel that teachers should have a clear understanding of the nature of writing in society as well as a knowledge of ways it can be developed in the primary school years. Thus approaches and strategies for teaching writing are discussed, together with the skills of spelling, grammar, and punctuation and how they can be integrated to develop a polished text. The authors view writing as a process—a process over which students gain greater control as they progress through the grades. It is therefore important for the young teacher to have a grasp of the different stages of the writing continuum and to be able to assess students' writing progression in order to devise suitable teaching practices and assessment. Although the focus of this section is on the practical skills of writing and the ways they can be achieved, the authors emphasise that writing itself is a creative act and a source of wonder and joy.

Rosemary Ross Johnston believes that children's literature is part of a literature continuum and that serious study of its theory can inform and enrich classroom practice. She stresses the contribution that the study of children's literature can make to the multiple aspects of literacy, particularly critical literacy, and notes that children's books inscribe cultural attitudes and reflect in diverse ways the society that shapes them. She also stresses the importance, in a print-rich technological environment, of teachers modelling principles of lifelong learning and exposing children to books beyond their immediate needs and capacities. This must always be done with care and consideration for the young students. Children's literature offers diverse sites for practising and developing literacy skills (not only reading and writing but also speaking and listening), for philosophical enquiry and the exploration of social issues, and for learning about the new ideas of visual and cultural literacy. Children's literature is also a valuable resource in the multicultural classroom.

The section on children's literature has also been designed with classroom activities that provide examples of how theoretical ideas can be applied in teaching. There is a strong emphasis on picturebooks, which, in their modern form, can be sophisticated and complex and which are short and admirably suited to teaching practice.

Key features of the book

Literacy: Reading, Writing, and Children's Literature covers the spectrum of the theory and practice of teaching literacy in modern Australian primary schools.

Its structure allows students to focus on the various aspects of literacy teaching and its practical outcomes.

Students will be able to use the book over an extended period during their university courses and retain it as a suitable reference when teaching.

Each of the parts of the book, Reading, Writing, and Children's Literature may be accessed separately or be used with general courses on literacy.

Discussion questions and activities are provided in each of the chapters and further reading is included to augment the references at the ends of chapters.

A glossary of terms is provided and a full index with cross-referencing is located at the back of the book, together with appendices that point to locations of further information relating to literacy teaching in Australia.

The text is designed to be used in all states and territories, and reference is made to each curriculum and literacy practice, together with mail addresses and web sites.

In this book the problem of the gender-neutral pronoun has been dealt with by having the masculine and feminine pronouns used more or less alternately, whether of teachers or of students, unless a generic 'he or she' is needed.

For easy access to the content of every chapter an introductory *Focus* statement pinpoints the features of the chapter while a *Summary* of the content is provided at the end.

Scholarly comment on various aspects of literacy is included in separate sections within the text to add depth to the discussion or to elucidate significant points.

The three parts of the book stress the developmental nature of literacy and provide examples of literacy teaching strategies across the primary school. Some of the material, particularly in the children's literature section, will also be helpful to secondary teachers.

Literacy in Australia is considered in a world perspective and international research, theory, and practice are consulted throughout the text.

Acknowledgments

The authors would like to thank the Academic Publisher at Oxford University Press, Jill Henry, for her professionalism and unflagging support throughout the development and production of this book; Venetia Somerset, who edited the manuscript with unrivalled skill; and Lucy Davison, Mark Ralph and the Oxford University Press team who brought the book to fruition.

We would also like to extend thanks to the following people: Rhondda Brill and Gregory Blaxell for their work in the planning of the project; John Stannard, National Director of the National Literacy Strategy in the United Kingdom, for providing invaluable information; Professor Trevor Cairney, Professor of Education and Pro-Vice Chancellor, University of Western Sydney, for his scholarly research and foreword to this book; Ed Truscott, Past President of the Australian Literacy Educators Association, for informed advice; Associate Professor Barbara Poston-Anderson for her contribution to the early literacy section; Phillipa Morris and the staff of the library at the Kuring-gai campus of the University of Technology, Sydney, for their professional assistance; Rodney March, who contributed original art; Diana Parry, who took the photographs; members of the ChiLPA (Children's Literature Pure and Applied) Project in Finland; Annabel Robinson and Helen Cousens for research assistance; David Costello, Principal, and the staff and students of North Rocks Primary School for their help in the writing section; our colleagues, and the whole community of scholars in universities and professional associations who have contributed directly and indirectly in ways too numerous to mention.

The authors and publishers wish to thank copyright holders for granting permission to reproduce illustrative material and textual extracts. Sources are as follows:

ABC Books for extracts from *A is for Aunty* by E. Russell; Blake Education Pty Ltd for extracts from *Sal and Sam on the Farm*, *Danny Dolphin's Nose* and *Hot* by G. Winch and G. Blaxell; Cambridge University Press for the extract from *English as a Global Language* by David Crystal, 1997, Cambridge University Press; Childerset Pty Ltd for extracts from *Samantha Seagull's Sandals* written by Gordon Winch, illustrated by Tony Oliver; Christopher Little Literary Agency for the extract from *Harry Potter and the Philosopher's Stone* by J.K. Rowling, copyright © text Joanne Rowling 1997; Department of Education, Training and Youth Affairs, Canberra for extracts from *Mapping Literacy Achievement: Results of the 1996 National School English Literacy Survey (1996)* and extracts from *Australia's Language: The Australian Language and Literacy Policy, Companion Volume to the Policy Paper (1991)*; Education Department of Western Australia for the extract from *Overview of Writing Development continuum*, reproduced by courtesy of the Education Department of Western Australia; HarperCollins Publishers Australia for the extract from *The Bamboo Flute* by Gary Disher; Heinemann, Portsmouth, USA for the extract from *Bridges to Literacy* edited by DeFord, Lyons and Pinnell; Lothian Books for the extract from *Memorial* by Gary Crew, illustrated by Shaun Tan; Magabala Books Aboriginal Corporation for the extract from *Do Not Go Around the Edges* by Daisy Utemorrah and Pat Torres; Margaret Hamilton Books for extracts from *V is for Vanishing* by P. Mullins and *Rain Dance* by C. Applegate and D. Huxley; New South Wales Department of Education and Training for the extract from *Teaching Reading: A K-6 Framework*, 1997 and the extract from *Basic Skills Test (BST) 1997*; Office of the Board of Studies, New South Wales for extract from 'Reading Outcomes and Indicators', from *English K-6 Syllabus* © Board of Studies NSW, 1998; Omnibus Books for the extract from *Time for Bed* by Mem Fox and Jane Dyer, 1993; Pearson Education Australia for the extracts from *My Place* by N. Wheatley and D. Rawlins, 1987; Penguin Books Australia Ltd for extracts from *The Wolf* by Margaret Barbalet, illustrated by Jane Tanner, *The Fisherman and the Theefyspray* by Paul Jennings, illustrated by Jane Tanner, *Henry's Bed* by Margaret Perversi, illustrated by Ron Brooks, *John Brown, Rose and the Midnight Cat* by Jenny Wagner and Ron Brooks, *Hating Alison Ashley* by Robin Klein and *You and Me, Murrawee* by Kerrie Hashmi; Penguin UK for 'Ears for my Family' by Christine, from *The Language of Primary School Children* by Connie and Harold Rosen (Penguin Books, 1973) copyright © Schools Council Publications, 1973 and for the cover illustration of *Each Peach Pear Plum* by Janet and Allan Ahlberg (Viking, 1978) copyright © Janet and Allan Ahlberg, 1978; Random House Group Ltd for the extract from *Tidy Titch* by Pat Hutchins, *Zoo* by Anthony Browne, *Way Home* by L. Hathorn and G. Rogers and *The Werewolf Knight* by J. Wagner and R. Roennfeldt; Rondor Music (Australia) Pty Ltd for 'Telegraph Road' by Mark Knopfler;

Scholastic, Inc. for extracts from *Let's Eat* by Ana Zamorano, illustrated by Julie Vivas; University of Queensland Press for the extract from *Lisdalia* by Brian Caswell; Walker Books Limited for extracts from *Mousewing* text © 1987 William Mayne, illustrations © 1987 Martin Baynton, *Owl Babies* text © 1992 Martin Waddell, illustrations © 1992 Patrick Benson, *Out and About* © 1988, 1998 Shirley Hughes, 'Who dat Girl?' © 1994 Valerie Bloom, from *A Caribbean Dozen* edited by John Agard and Grace Nichols, illustrated by Cathie Felstead, *Chameleons are Cool* text © 1997 Martin Jenkins, illustrated by Sue Shields, *Beware, Beware* text © 1993 Sue Hill, illustrated by Angela Barrett and *Ginger* © 1997 Charlotte Voake; R.D. Walshe for the extract from *Writing and Learning in Australia*.

INTRODUCTION

hat can we take as a suitable definition of **literacy** for Australian children? Probably the most workable and encompassing is that of *Australian Language and Literacy Policy* (1991).

Literacy is the ability to read and use written information and to write appropriately, in a range of contexts. It is used to develop knowledge and understanding, to achieve personal growth and to function effectively in our society. Literacy also includes the recognition of number and basic mathematical signs and symbols within text.

Literacy involves the integration of speaking, listening and critical thinking with reading and writing. Effective literacy is intrinsically purposeful, flexible and dynamic and continues to develop throughout an individual's lifetime.

All Australians need to have effective literacy in English, not only for their personal benefit and welfare but also for Australia to reach its social and economic goals.

This definition includes most facets of literacy as we know it today; not only the basic view of literacy as the ability to read and write but also what are termed social literacy, critical literacy, mathematical literacy, and computer literacy. Essential to all aspects of literacy in Australia, nevertheless, is the ability to read and write in English.

The importance of literacy

Literacy is integral to modern society. It pervades almost every area of social interaction including work, leisure, communications, and business, and is a key component of the information revolution.

Literacy is crucial to young people's success at school. Competency in it is essential if an individual is to participate fully in a literate society, able to take part in the workforce, engage in the democratic process, and contribute to society. Students with effective literacy skills excel not only in English but in other areas of the curriculum. They tend to be confident young people who aspire to high levels of achievement in further education and employment and experience the pleasure that effective literacy can provide.

Students' overall school performance and their successful transition from one stage of schooling to the next depend on a well-developed foundation of literacy skills and positive attitudes to learning. Students need to have the necessary knowledge, skills, attitudes, and understandings to engage with all the literacy demands of the curriculum and communicate successfully in the wider society.

High literacy standards contribute significantly to the economic development of nations. The cost of low literacy standards is staggering. In Australia it was estimated in the early nineties at $3.2 billion annually in lost productivity alone and would have been much higher if such factors as industrial safety, poor product quality, and low mobility were taken into account (Commonwealth of Australia, *International Literacy Year Report* [ILY], *Putting Literacy on the Agenda* 1992). In Britain it has been estimated at over 10 billion pounds sterling per annum in lost business and other costs (Ernst and Young 1998). The current *National Literacy Strategy* in that country, which resulted from the *National Literacy Project* (1996), has been developed to produce positive literacy teaching and learning practices for all children. Parallel strategies have emanated from the *Research Council Report* prepared by the Committee on the Prevention of Reading Difficulties in Young Children (1998) in the United States. The Literacy Taskforce and its recent report in New Zealand (1999) is another case in point.

Literacy in Australia

As a part of a national collaborative project, the *Statement on English for Australian Schools* and *A Curriculum Profile in English* issued in 1994 provided an agreed national curriculum framework for use by state and territory education systems in the development of programs for the teaching of literacy. These documents identified a series of levels of outcomes in listening, speaking, reading, writing, and viewing expected to be achieved by Australian school students, thus providing a clear description of a continuum of learning for the school years.

The development of these documents was prompted by a desire to see more commonality in the curriculum across Australia, to ease the transition between systems for the growing number of students moving between states and territories, and to define clearly the results of schooling in terms of a continuum of outcomes as a way of mapping student growth.

Using these documents in different ways, state and territory systems developed a range of curriculum documents, support materials, assessment strategies, and teacher professional development programs to assist their teachers to work towards student achievement of the outcomes.

In the years since the release of the *Statement on English for Australian Schools* and *A Curriculum Profile in English*, state and territory systems have continued to focus their efforts on the attainment of improved standards in literacy to meet the growing demands for higher literacy levels that the modern world is placing on all of us.

In Western Australia the First Steps project has been developed to provide a clear framework of support for the assessment and teaching of literacy in the first years of school. In Victoria the Early Years project provides documents and teacher professional development support in the teaching of reading, writing, speaking, and listening (Prep to Grade 6). In New South Wales the State Literacy Strategy identifies key elements for the teaching of literacy and provides extensive teaching materials and professional development programs for teachers of students from Kindergarten to Year 8.

In 1997 all state, territory, and Commonwealth education ministers agreed on a national goal in Australia, which stated 'that every child leaving school should be numerate and able to read, write and spell at an appropriate level' (Masters and Forster 1997b). A subgoal stated that 'every child commencing school from 1998 will achieve an acceptable literacy and numeracy standard within 4 years'.

The report, *Mapping Literacy Achievement: Results of the 1996 National School English Literacy Survey* (1997) was prepared for the Federal Minister for Schools, Education and Training, the Hon. Dr David Kemp, by the Australian Council for Educational Research (ACER) under the direction of the Management Committee. The survey took place in government and non-government schools in all states and territories in 1996. This carefully wrought report is far too complex to analyse here but it represents the most comprehensive picture yet developed of the literacy achievements of Year 3 and Year 5 students in Australian schools. It highlighted, among other things, the wide range of literacy achievements among the sample and the resultant complexity of teachers' tasks in providing suitable literacy teaching and learning strategies. The top 10 per cent of students in each year are working about five year levels ahead of the bottom 10 per cent (*Mapping Literacy Achievement* 1997: v).

A further report written by Masters and Forster titled *Literacy Standards in Australia* (1997a), which resulted from the above survey, pinpointed specific key findings from the survey. Some of these are listed below:
- There was a wide range of student performance in reading and writing.
- In each aspect of literacy girls outperformed boys.
- Students from a language background other than English had, on average, lower English literacy levels than students from English-speaking backgrounds.

- Literacy achievement varied according to the occupation of parents. Children whose parents were from professional and managerial occupations fared better.
- Students in the Special Indigenous Sample had very low levels of English literacy achievement (three to four levels below students in the main sample).

Since that time a *National Literacy and Numeracy Plan* has been developed that provides a framework for literacy and numeracy improvement. Using the framework, each state and territory has developed a comprehensive plan to include assessment of all students to identify those at risk, early intervention, and the professional development of teachers. There is national reporting on student achievements and the professional development of teachers to support the key elements of the National Plan. Literacy benchmarks in writing, spelling, and reading for Years 3 and 5 were approved by education ministers in 1998, and all states now assess literacy and numeracy in the primary years against these benchmarks and report to the Commonwealth.

Australian literacy standards

The authors of this book take the view that there is no sudden crisis in Australian schools but that there are certain problems, particularly in specific areas, that must be addressed. Whatever the complexity of being literate in modern society—and particularly Australian society—may mean, it is nonetheless the achievement of a satisfactory level of reading and writing in English that underpins all literacy learning. We are mindful also of the rich diversity of languages in our country that does so much to enrich our cultural life.

Crystal (1997: viii), in his book *English as a Global Village*, points out that language diversity and the value of a common language are two sides of one coin.

- I believe in the fundamental value of multilingualism, as an amazing resource which presents us with different perspectives and insights, and thus enables us to reach a more profound understanding of the nature of the human mind and spirit …
- I believe in the fundamental value of a common language, as an amazing world resource which presents us with unprecedented possibilities for mutual understanding and thus enables us to find fresh opportunities for international cooperation …

In Australia we are in an extremely fortunate position as we have both sides of the coin: a rich diversity of language background in our people and our common English language.

As Beard (1998) points out, nations around the world are not witnessing a large and visible downturn in literacy standards. In modern society there is a bigger demand for greater literacy skills and increased complexity in the ways literacy is used. This places the teacher in a pivotal position to assist students in attaining the required levels and varieties of literacy they will need in the future.

Part I Reading

Gordon Winch and Marcelle Holliday

Reading is an integral part of literacy. Linked with listening, speaking, writing, and critical thinking it establishes the essential basis for literacy learning and literacy practice as they operate in society today.

Chapters 1 to 8 of this text are specifically devoted to reading and learning to read. In Chapter 1, the authors have taken what they term a balanced view of reading, arguing that there is no one way of teaching a child to read. The best teaching practice emerges from a confluence of a number of theoretical positions and their practical outcomes operating in sociocultural context.

Fundamental factors in reading and learning to read are considered in Chapter 2, including a discussion of the writing system of English, the nature of phonemic awareness and its importance in reading, the way the eyes operate while reading, the locus and importance of meaning, and the developing significance of the computer in literacy learning.

In Chapter 3 a model of the reading process is established which forms a basis for sound practice in the classroom.

Chapters 4, 5, and 6 deal with the development of reading in chronological fashion beginning with the child before school and ending with the student in the upper primary classroom. Examples of Shared, Guided, and Independent Reading are demonstrated to give a clear view of this practice in the primary school.

Chapter 7 explores the issue of assessment in reading, illustrating the many forms and approaches which will result in the most effective programming, teaching, and monitoring in the teaching-learning cycle.

Chapter 8 ties the practical strands of literacy learning together in the Literacy Session or Literacy Block. It considers actual classroom practice during a literacy session with particular emphasis on the teaching of reading.

All chapters conclude with practical tasks for students using this textbook. These are in the form of discussion topics and specific activities to be carried out in and outside the classroom.

The amalgam of theory and practice will provide a solid ground-work for students who are engaging in the task of teaching reading and literacy generally in the primary school. The vital interconnection of listening, speaking, reading, writing, and children's literature is illustrated in the above approach.

Chapter 1
A Balanced View of Reading

Focus

The nature of reading is discussed and the historical development of research and theory is outlined. Movements in the world are towards a balanced view of literacy and reading in particular. This is the position taken in this book.

What is reading?

Reading is the process of constructing meaning from written text. The text may be wholly print as in most novels, or contain visual elements such as illustrations, diagrams, maps, and graphs as in most children's books and many information books, magazines, and newspapers. Increasingly, the texts we read are presented electronically, and often interactively, and contain a mixture of screen print, graphic or visual elements, and even sound.

At the core of reading is meaning. Meaning is what we search for as we read (our goal) and it is also part of what we use to reach that goal (our guide). In constructing meaning from text, readers combine what they know about the world, the topic of the text, the grammatical structure of the language in which the text is written, and the way spoken language relates to the letters, words, visual elements, and symbols on the page.

Because reading is essentially a purposeful act, a reader seeks to fulfil some individual purpose by reading a text. Perhaps it is to enjoy a novel, or to find some information about plants for the garden. It may be to purchase a new car or to plan a holiday. Whatever the purpose, readers will bring to the reading task the skills and knowledge they have to fulfil that purpose. In the process they will learn more about what it means to be a reader.

Because reading is primarily a thinking task, readers relate what they draw from the text to what they already know about the topic, about texts of this type, and about the context. For example, when reading an information book about the wildlife of Kakadu a reader might hope to add to her knowledge about how climatic conditions and ecosystems relate to animal species and would expect to see illustrations, and perhaps photographs of animal and birds. The reader may look at the credentials of the author and/or photographer and consider what their purpose was in producing the book; perhaps the book has been produced by a mining company. And she would take the book's publication date into account when considering if the information was up to date. Reading, then, can be described as a process of literate thinking and can be further defined as *bringing meaning to and taking meaning from text in a social and cultural context*. This definition provides a balance between the reader and the text. It also defines reading in terms of the context in which reading occurs and places meaning at the core of the process.

But what really happens? What does research tell us about reading and the best methods of reading instruction? What are the essential features of a balanced view?

Research and the teaching of reading

Research has not provided a perfect alignment to practice in the teaching of reading (Beard 1998), and the way children learn and should be taught to read remain contentious issues (Scholes 1998).

Historically, there has been a sharp division among researchers and theorists about the teaching of reading. On one side stand those who stress decoding, phonics, and specific phonemic awareness training for beginning readers with heavy emphasis on word recognition in its various forms, on the alphabetical writing system, and on the subskills that are claimed to make up the reading task. This approach has been described in various ways, such as a '**bottom-up**' view of reading, a code-based approach, a subskill approach, and a phonic approach. It has been heavily criticised for its limited vision of what reading is, for its lack of emphasis on comprehension of the text, and its playing down of the input that the reader makes to reading.

The 'bottom-up' or skill-based approach can be found in the writings of many theorists, from the past to the present: S. Jay Samuels and Philip B. Gough, for instance, and more recently Keith Stanovich and Charles Perfetti. It is misleading and inexact, nevertheless, to place these writers in a neatly defined category as their work crosses a wide range of theory and research.

On the other side stand those who are often termed '**top-down**' or whole-language theorists. They stress meaning as paramount in any approach to reading and devalue code as a substitute for context in word recognition. These theorists have been termed 'top-down' because of their emphasis on what the reader brings to print and on the primary importance of meaning generally. They are opposed to the subskill approach and view reading from an holistic point of view. They have been criticised for their lack of attention to the alphabetical system of English writing, for their overreliance on context in word recognition, and for their refusal to look squarely at research that shows high correlation between phonemic awareness and learning to read.

The 'top-down' or whole-language approach is found in the writings of Frank Smith, Kenneth and Yetta Goodman, Brian Cambourne, and others, but again caution must be exercised in describing these researchers because their works reflect a much richer vein of educational thought than a simple category can indicate.

As recently as 1998, Scholes, who supports the 'top-down' view, has stressed his strong opposition to the subsyllabic (phonemic) segments of speech as factors in literacy acquisition, arguing that developing an understanding of subsyllabic elements is a limited consequence of acquiring literacy in an alphabetic script and that positive correlations between phonemic awareness and reading skill are based on a misguided definition of reading. He also argues that phonemic awareness is a *consequence* of acquiring alphabetical literacy and not an engine in providing for success.

Johnston (1998c) attacks Scholes on the grounds that children have to recognise the 'building blocks of literacy' even though the ultimate purpose of reading is comprehension. She argues for a reciprocal relationship between reading skill and phonological awareness and states that using a learned knowledge of the alphabetical system of English spelling eases the burden on learning to read. She argues further that what skilled readers may need is orthographic knowledge (knowledge of the writing system), underpinned by an adequate but not particularly precise awareness of **phonemes** (sound units) in spoken words so that we can recognise printed words with ease.

Stuart (1998) also disagrees with Scholes, setting out a multidimensional view of reading that allows for two intersecting dimensions: word recognition and comprehension. She looks for agreement between the two antagonistic positions, arguing that perhaps all can agree that word recognition is a necessary part but not the whole of reading.

Fortunately there has been in recent years an emerging view of reading and acquiring reading, both from research and from ensuing practice, which can be termed 'a balanced view'. Before considering the current position we shall look at some important steps along the way.

From the past to the present

In 1967 Jeanne Chall published a milestone text, *Learning to Read: The Great Debate*. The work was funded by the Carnegie Corporation in the USA and was written to draw some conclusions about current and past research on reading and learning to read. Chall put forward the view that learning the alphabetic code (variously termed by her as phonics, word analysis, decoding, and sound–symbol relations) was essential to beginning to read, although it was not all that was necessary. Other important factors were language, good teaching, and instructional materials at the appropriate level of difficulty.

At about the same time as Chall was completing her studies, another project, commonly known as the First Grade Studies, was carried out and published by Bond and Dykstra (1967). This work was sponsored by the US Office of Education and experimentally compared various research methods. The First Grade Studies confirmed Chall's conclusions.

Chall (1999) drew attention to these facts and to following studies that had supported her views, in particular, Anderson et al. (1985), Adams (1990), and Snow et al. (1998), which essentially came to the same major conclusion as *Learning to Read*. Chall also referred in her paper to the Follow Through Studies—a large-scale investigation of compensatory education that extended into Grade 3. Again, higher achievement occurred among those children learning from a direct instruction model with code (phonics) emphasis.

It should be noted, however, that Chall was eager to point out that many of her recommendations in *Learning to Read* and others of her writings included many of the practices that are commonly associated with whole language. She stressed that teaching only phonics—and in isolation—was not what she would support, that library books have an important place, and that children's writings should be incorporated into the teaching of reading. Likewise she warned against the overteaching of phonics, 'leaving little time for the reading of stories and other connected texts' (1967: 531).

Stanovich (1994), while making the point that Chall saw the teaching of reading much more broadly than has been commonly accepted, argued that some children in whole-language classrooms do not pick up the alphabetical principle through simple immersion in print and writing activities but needed explicit instruction in spelling–sound correspondences. He argued that this fact was borne out by voluminous research evidence.

Modern cognitive research as reported by Perfetti (1995) and Stanovich (1994; Stanovich and Paula 1995) has made a number of contributions to views on the nature of reading and its application to the way reading should be taught. The position taken is that skilled readers read more words than they skip, use phonology when reading, and rely very little on the use of context for word recognition. Children benefit from learning how their writing system works. It is also argued that comprehension and the use of context are not sacrificed by following the above tenets of reading teaching.

Stanovich (1994) makes the point that essentially the 'reading wars' that have wasted so much energy can be reduced to having both sides say simultaneously, 'Some teachers overdo phonics' and 'Some children need explicit instruction in alphabetic coding'. The matter may not be as simple as this, but a defusing of the issue and a rapprochement between the two sides is beginning to appear in the literature, as explained below. It is important to remember that many good teachers continued to use a balance of both approaches in their classrooms while the reading debate was raging in academic circles.

The emerging situation

At the risk of trivialising the issue or ignoring the enormous amount of research and carefully woven theory that is available, it is necessary in a book of this nature to move to the current situation in the light of national and international movements in the field, with special emphasis on their practical outcomes. It is valuable to look at some recent reports and publications that point to a middle way between the extreme positions taken in the past. While various researchers have argued strenuously for a reading program based exclusively on one or other specific approach, the evidence is now overwhelming that no one element holds the key to the successful teaching of reading. Each element is necessary but none is sufficient on its own.

Beard (1998) draws attention to the fact that recent research-based models of early reading and fluent reading suggest that reading is neither 'top-down' nor 'bottom-up' in nature. Instead, as Adams and Bruck (1993) in the USA point out, sources of contextual, comprehension, visual, and phonological-graphological information are used simultaneously and interactively by the reader. This is a similar bringing together, Beard argues, to that which operates in the composition of writing.

Substantial changes in how fluent reading is understood are incorporated in Beard's document, which refers to the British National Literacy Strategy. In particular, it draws attention first to the relationships between word recognition and context, and second to the role of phonological processing in reading. It is argued that fluent readers rely less on context for word recognition than was thought. They are experts at word recognition and are able to use their skills in rapid, effective reading, relying for comprehension on context and the knowledge they bring to print.

The hallmarks of skilled reading are fast word identification and rich context-dependent understanding of the text (Perfetti 1995). If we look at fluent, effective reading from a commonsense point of view, backed up as this is by a battery of research (Beard 1998), we realise that a balanced view is a logical and valuable one for the teacher of literacy. It opens the way to teaching children to read and write, bringing into play phonological-graphological, grammatical, and semantic information from a range of sources, and it allows teaching to be both balanced and focused on the needs of a child.

When it comes to working with fluent readers in a context that requires improvement in reading flexibility across a range of text-types, improvement in speed, skim reading, or reading in depth for highly specific and detailed information, the model holds up well: fluent readers are experts in word recognition, so much so that the process becomes automatic and higher reading skills can be taught through context and the use of improved strategies.

The role of phonological processing has been reconsidered, producing much more interest in the nature of the alphabetic writing system in English. Learning to read is not only learning to construct meaning from print but also learning how the writing system works and how it encodes the reader's language. Knowledge about the grammatical system of the language works in conjunction with phonological-graphological processing in fluent reading.

The Great Britain National Literacy Strategy has included these balanced findings in recommendations for practice in its Literacy Hour. Focus is placed on three broad dimensions of literacy: word-level work, sentence-level work, and text-level work, and each is incorporated in a structured hour of teaching.

An evaluation of the National Literacy Project was carried out by Sainsbury (1998) for the National Foundation for Educational Research. The test results showed that there was a statistically significant improvement in children's scores in the 250 schools that took part in the study, from autumn 1996 to summer 1998. This amounted to reading progress of between eight and twelve months above what was expected, with an equivalent rise in percentile rank.

It is important to note that effective teaching within the Literacy Hour was characterised by consistency, clear structure, high-quality interaction, and good pace, underpinned by thorough planning. Other aspects of the Literacy Hour and the balanced approach to literacy and the teaching of reading carried out in the project included a 30-minute designated period of whole-class teaching, 20 minutes of group and independent work, and 10 minutes of whole-class review, reflection, and consolidation. It was recommended that additional time may well be needed for reading to a class, pupils' own independent reading, and extended writing. The introduction of a special period for the teaching of literacy has become the desired strategy for improving literacy skills in many Australian schools, where it is often termed the Literacy Session or Literacy Block. The structure and presentation of such a session is described in Chapter 8.

The National Literacy Strategy recognised the need to provide well-designed, balanced models for teaching literacy and saw as a strategic task that schools would not be expected to 'reinvent the wheel' but would be informed about the best practice and be provided with the teaching skills to act on it.

Other factors seen as vital to the development of literacy skills included the need to exploit the reciprocal links between reading and writing. These links were recognised by Marie Clay (1972, 1991, 1998) and have been widely accepted. (See Chapter 12, pp. 197ff.) The value of the inclusion of non-fiction texts was now recognised and increasingly stressed. In addition, Shared, Guided, and Independent Reading approaches (see Chapter 8) were incorporated into literacy teaching strategies. An increased emphasis was placed on the importance of grammatical knowledge and standard spelling, while children's literature was seen as being fundamental in developing the literacy skills of children.

It is interesting to notice how the National Literacy Strategy was influenced by research, theory, and practice from overseas: the work of Marie Clay in New Zealand; Halliday Cairney, and Cambourne in Australia; Adams, Tierney and numerous others in the USA; and Stanovich in Canada. Special reference was made to curriculum work in Australia that led the field in many aspects of literacy development. In particular, it emphasised the importance of the various text-types, including non-fiction, that students should read and write; this variety in genres related to the social purpose of the text concerned. Beard's well-documented

Review of Research, however, can only touch on the sources and influences that come into play during the development of the National Literacy Strategy, although it shows clearly that the teaching of literacy has a significantly international flavour, particularly in this age of rapid and available communication.

The *Report of the Literacy Taskforce* in New Zealand (1999) also illustrates the emergence of an acceptance of commonly recognised principles and practice of teaching literacy. The document highlights the acceptance of a balanced model of teaching literacy and the general need for the highest quality teaching, the development of a culture of high expectations, close participation between home and school, and recognition of the need to cater for rising demands for literacy, especially with minority groups.

While New Zealand measures up well on international literacy standards, the report recognises that special intervention is needed. Its authors are also concerned about the polarisation of approach in the debate on phonics as against whole language. Some schools have moved to placing too heavy emphasis on teaching skills in isolation in reading programs, while others have moved towards an exclusively whole-language approach with no systematic teaching of phonological awareness. Nevertheless, decisions on how to teach literacy are traditionally made at school level in New Zealand, with official guidance being made only at national level.

The Literacy Taskforce recommends that a statement of best practice be drawn up and promulgated to schools. It is aware of the need to inform teachers of 'sound research that indicates that children should not rely on context as the primary or only strategy for working out unknown words, but should develop the use of word-level skills and strategies'.

In the USA also, there has been a movement towards a balanced view of acquiring literacy. A good example is the position statement of the International Reading Association (IRA) Board (1998) on phonemic awareness and the teaching of reading. The board makes the point that although phonemic awareness is the best single predictor of successful reading acquisition—few scholars would dispute this—there is considerable disagreement about what this relation implies for reading instruction. Most researchers advocate that we attend to the development of phonemic awareness as part of a broad instructional program in reading and writing, keeping in mind that different children require different amounts of this instruction.

The board notes that the relation of phonemic awareness and learning to read is reciprocal: interaction with print combined with explicit attention to sound structure in spoken words is the best vehicle of growth. The board emphasises that instruction in phonemic awareness must not overpower other important aspects of literacy instruction.

The five points for good literacy instruction that conclude the statement show how the balanced view that we have seen emerge in other countries is occurring in the USA:

- offer students a print-rich environment within which to interact
- engage students with surrounding print as both readers and writers
- engage children in language activities that focus on both the form and the content of spoken and written language
- provide explicit explanation of students' learning of the alphabetical principle
- provide opportunities for students to practise reading and writing for real reasons in a variety of contexts to promote fluency and independence.

In the USA the National Research Council's Committee on the Prevention of Reading Difficulties in Young Children in their document (Snow et al. 1998) looked first at mostly convergent, but sometimes discrepant, research findings to provide an integrated picture of how reading develops and how its development can be promoted. Two very interesting points were made: effective teachers seemed able to craft a special mix of instructional ingredients for every child they work with, and children with reading difficulties did not need radically different sorts of support but more intensive support. Excellent instruction was seen as the best intervention for children with reading problems.

The report points out that effective instruction in reading is built on a foundation that recognises that reading ability is determined by multiple factors; no prerequisite for success is sufficient by itself. The five requirements for initial reading instruction have perceived similarities with approaches discussed above:
- use reading to obtain meaning from print
- have frequent and intensive opportunities to read
- be exposed to frequent, regular instances of the spelling–sound relationship
- learn about the nature of the alphabetical writing system
- understand the structure of spoken words.

The crucial importance of excellent reading instruction was at the centre of the committee's recommendations: schools should be organised so that curriculum materials and support services function effectively.

Recommendations on detailed instructions are explicit in the report. They stress the careful teaching of words and their parts, the recognition of sight words as well as sound–symbol correspondences, comprehension by actively building linguistic knowledge, and the important link with writing. It encourages independent reading outside school and the use of libraries. The report also lists what are desirable accomplishments or **outcomes** at various grades, from Kindergarten to Year 3.

Such specific outcomes are being extensively used in Australia and provide a sound basis for assessment across a spectrum of achievement.

Reading outcomes and indicators in Australia

Literacy outcomes, which present clear statements of the expected results of teaching, are becoming the norm in Australian syllabuses. They are supported by indicators of behaviour, which contribute to the achievement of such results.

Reading outcomes are usually dealt with separately and, like other aspects of literacy, key into the National Literacy Benchmarks, which are used to report on student achievement.

Students should consult their particular State syllabus for specific statements of such outcomes and indicators across the years of schooling.

New South Wales

The *English K-6 Syllabus* in New South Wales refers in detail to desired outcomes and indicators for learning to read and learning about reading. A breakdown of the desired outcomes, and a wide variety of possible indicators, are given for grades K (kindergarten) through 6 and described in stages in the syllabus.

Indicators for the outcome *Demonstrates developing reading skills and strategies for reading books, dealing with print and comprehending texts* (Kindergarten), Learning to Read – Skills and Strategies, Early Stage 1, are 30 in number and cover a range of information relating to contextual, semantic, grammatical, graphological, phonological, textual, and computer aspects of reading. A sample of the types of indicators is given below.

- demonstrates awareness that print is an expression of meaning
- uses knowledge of grammatical structure of language to assist reading
- learns and articulates sound segments in words
- recognises sight words in printed texts
- hears and articulates sound segments in words
- recognises that words are made up of letters
- uses the illustration on the cover of the book to make predictions about what the story is going to be about when reading
- knows basic book conventions, i.e. can open book and hold book in correct way to look at pictures, can turn pages in correct order
- navigates through sections of computer software

Victoria

The Curriculum and Standards Framework (CSF II) in Victoria, although not a detailed syllabus, makes it clear what students should know and be able to do. It, too, presents outcomes and indicators of achievement for the various levels of schooling.

For instance, at Level 1 (end of Preparatory Year) in Reading, outcomes and indicators are provided for the reading of texts and aspects of language comprising contextual understanding, and linguistic structures and strategies. Although the actual wording and the terminology may differ slightly from that used in the New South Wales syllabus, there is—as one would expect—close similarity between the two sets of expectations.

For example, indicators at this level demonstrate that, among other things, the child does the following:

- uses title, cover illustrations, and knowledge of a text topic to predict meaning in texts
- reads aloud simple texts, which include some high-frequency words and oral language structures
- identifies frequently used words in context, such as *look*, *I*, and *me*
- uses context and graphophonic information to make meaning
- names the letters of the alphabet and identifies some sound-letter relationship
- uses illustrations to extend meaning
- reads from left to right with return sweep and top to bottom
- uses terms associated with books and print, such as page, author title, cover, illustrator
- reads and recalls simple messages, such as an electronic message.

A balanced approach to reading

In fact, across the Australian state and territory education systems there has been an adoption of a balanced view of reading and the way it should be taught. This statement is borne out in recent documents. The First Steps program in Western Australia (1994) states:

> A successful language program is one in which reading, writing, speaking and listening are integrated in a supportive and stimulating environment in which independent and reflective critical thinking is fostered.
>
> Children learn how language works when they are able to use it for purposes that are clear to them. They need to know that the purpose for reading is to make meaning. Some children believe that 'getting the words right' is the sole purpose of reading. These children are unlikely to be effective readers.

In Victoria the Early Years program in reading (Teaching Reading in the Early Years 1997) gives teachers clear guidelines for implementing a balanced approach to reading in the classroom. The program is based on the worldwide recognition of the significance of the early years of schooling to the acquisition of literacy. It was written as a result of extensive research into good literacy practice in Victoria and overseas and was informed by a wide range of literature relating to early literacy teaching and learning.

A positive reading environment is significant in encouraging students to value reading and in supporting their reading development. Readers learn to read best in a community of readers. Involvement in appropriate literacy tasks, access to a wide variety of texts, and regular demonstration and modelling of literate behaviours encourage students to develop their reading.

In New South Wales books in the Teaching Reading series (1997) provide teachers with theoretical underpinnings and practical classroom applications of a balanced approach to the teaching of reading. Students need a balanced reading program to develop:

- contextual knowledge
- knowledge about the sources of information
- skills in reading as code-breaker, text-participant, text-user, and text-analyst (see Chapter 3).

Teachers should ensure that every component of the reading program is covered explicitly and systematically. A balanced reading program enables students to develop as effective readers.

A balanced approach in this book

A balanced approach to reading is the position taken in this book. It is in keeping with emerging views about literacy teaching throughout the world and offers the best access to successful practice. It provides the best opportunity for all students to acquire the skills of effective reading.

The following are some essential features of such a position:

A balanced approach to reading

- places meaning at the core of all reading
- recognises the interaction between reading and writing
- recognises the importance of context in reading
- places equal emphasis on the development of semantic, grammatical, and graphological-phonological knowledge
- recognises the importance of students developing effective strategies for processing text
- provides for instruction across a range of fictional and factual text-types including public and electronic texts
- promotes a balance of Shared, Guided, and Independent Reading opportunities
- bases instruction on effective assessment of students' needs and abilities.

SUMMARY

Reading is bringing meaning to and taking meaning from text. It is a complex task. Research has been inconclusive about the ways children learn to read and should be taught. Sharp divisions have occurred but common ground is now being found. This is occurring throughout the world and is being documented in international studies and reports. This book takes a balanced view of reading in line with emerging theory and practice.

Tasks

Discussion

1. The beginning of this chapter puts forward a definition of literacy. Consider what *you* think is a suitable definition.
2. Discuss the two sides in the 'reading wars'. Attempt to isolate the main points of difference between a 'top-down' and a 'bottom-up' approach.
3. Consider how a balanced view of reading incorporates the best theory with the best practice in the light of eight essential features as listed at the end of the chapter. Are there others? If so what are they?

Activities

1. Read one or two of the papers listed in the references which support a particular side of the argument for a 'top-down' or 'bottom-up' approach. Write a critique of the article(s).
2. Write a brief statement supporting what is termed 'a balanced view of reading' in this book. Use some of the evidence presented in this chapter.

Chapter 2
Some Factors Relating to Reading

> **Focus**
> The English writing system is discussed and the notion of phonemic and phonological awareness is considered. The *locus* (place, location) of meaning is also considered and the nature of visual and non-visual information in reading. Eye movements when reading are explained. The dramatic growth in use of the computer in literacy teaching is discussed. Its importance in both reading and writing is considered with reference to the computer's wide and growing use.

THE WRITING SYSTEM OF ENGLISH

English **orthography** can be described as an alphabetical writing system. The written symbols, the alphabet, represent the sounds, or phonemes (individual speech sounds), that allow a reader to distinguish between words. For example in the words *cat* and *fat*, the two phonemes /k/ represented by 'c' and /f/ represented by 'f' allow the reader to distinguish the difference between the two words. There are 44–45 phonemes in English and because there are only 26 letters to represent them, the writing system presents special problems for the reader. To begin, some letters have to double up to represent the 44 sounds.

> Strictly speaking, 'phonemes' are abstract constructs and represent a range of actual sounds or phonetic realities called 'allophones'. There are great variations in dialects that contain a range of sounds representing the one phoneme. Take for example the different pronunciation of the /a/ phoneme in the word 'bath' in British and American English. Consider also the difference in the sounds representing the /k/ phoneme in *key, cup, cop*, which are slightly modified by the following vowel. These are allophones of the phoneme /k/.

To complicate things even more, English has borrowed from many different languages over its history and has kept many of the original spellings. As a result, we have different spellings of the one sound, such as in *pho*to and *f*oot. Added to this, some sounds in our language, particularly the long vowels, changed quite dramatically at some time in the 15th century, so that the written symbols in English writing came to represent different sounds in the spoken language. This change is known as the Great Vowel Shift. For example, the word *five*, which was pronounced /fi:f/ (something like *feef*) in Chaucer's time, had become /fai:v/ (five) by Shakespeare's.

If we consider also that many speech sounds in some dialects of English are different from those in other dialects, we have another mismatch between sound and symbol. Consider some vowel pronunciation differences found in American and Australian English. A real-life example makes the point. A mother of an Australian small child was visiting the mid-west American school that her daughter was attending. The teacher commented that the child was doing well with her spelling but insisted on beginning the word *octopus* with a *u*. Why? Why not? *Uktopus* is what the child heard her teacher say.

John Dewey (1971) calculated that for every 100 000 running words, English orthography averaged 9.1 spellings per consonant, and 20.7 per vowel. There is certainly no perfect match between symbol and sound is English spelling. Although graphophonic (symbol–sound correspondence) information is an important facet of reading, if it were the only source available reading would be both difficult and slow. Fortunately it is not the only source of information. Kolers (1970) says that if we did decode to sound for every written letter we would read no faster than 30–40 words per minute. Smith (1973) argues further, stating that our short-term memory cannot hold more than four or five random letters at once, so that by the time we reached the end of a long word we could easily have forgotten the beginning.

Regular features of English orthography

In spite of the limitations of orthography, there are features that are regular. They act as a valuable part of the available information we have when reading. For instance, although there is a poor match of symbol to sound in many spellings found in English, much of the written language is regular and predictable. Up to 80 per cent of symbol–sound relationships could be considered regular if we include the frequency of use of some of the letters that are used in English writing. The 26 letters of the alphabet, used as **graphemes** in writing, show considerable variations in consistency, but overall the correspondences between sounds (phonemes) and letters (graphemes) are very regular. A survey (Carney 1994) underlines this point: the phoneme /b/ is represented by the letter *b* 98 per cent of the time, the small exceptions being *bb* in words like *rabbit* (or *bh* in a few words imported from Hindi). The vowels show most irregularity: /ɪ/ as in *kid* is represented by the letter *i* only 61 per cent of the time, with varied spellings in other cases: *y* in *hymn*, *o* in *women*, *ui* in *build* and *u* in *busy*. Many common words contain these irregular spellings and cause problems in early reading—think of *are*, *were*, *come*, and *there*, for example.

The important point is that phonic instruction must be carefully undertaken to show both the consistencies and inconsistencies and allow the child to gradually develop an understanding of how the writing system works. Children learn, for instance, about the letter that follows *q* or the missing letter in a word like *walk...ng*. This extra information allows the child to reduce uncertainty and predict what the letter might be and what the word is.

English spelling is complicated in some of its instances, but it is not haphazard. Readers develop an expectation about the ways letters represent sounds and the order in which letters appear in English writing. George Bernard Shaw was not correct in saying that the letters in the nonsense word *ghoti* could spell *fish* (*gh* as in *rough*, *o* as in *women*, and *ti* as in *nation*) because the consonant cluster *gh* is not found in English initially as the phoneme /f/, and the *gh* spelling of /f/ and the *ti* spelling of /sh/ are fairly rare, with the latter never found at the end of a word.

The linguists Chomsky and Halle (1968) pointed out that there is another underlying regularity in English spelling that readers understand and use when reading. This is the deep-structure similarity of pairs of words such as *line/linear*, *compose/composition*, and *anxious/anxiety*. Readers ignore the surface–sound mismatch between the words because they recognise the similarity of paired words in meaning. Venezky (1967) drew attention to the bigger meaning-chunks of words that readers use when dealing with English spelling. The word *shepherd* is read as two meaningful chunks or 'morphemes', *shep* and *herd*, a *herder of sheep*.

Native speakers of the language carry the rules relating to the above facts in their heads and use them automatically, as well as with surprising rapidity, when reading. English orthography overall is remarkably effective as a writing system and is extensively used throughout the world. The important thing is that when a child is learning to read in English, or any other writing system for that matter, he or she must learn the writing system concerned, specifically how it encodes the language, and apply this knowledge to the reading task. The question of the relationship of the text to meaning is as fascinating as it is controversial.

> Writing systems throughout the world are products of human invention and vary in terms of how they operate. A child, learning to read in English or Italian, for instance, learns an alphabetical system which came from the Phoenicians and Greeks; in Japan, children learning to read Kana are dealing with a syllabic system, and Chinese children are confronted with a logographic script in which the writing units correspond to meanings or morphemes rather than to syllables or phonemes.

Olsen (1977), in an important paper, drew attention to the differences between speech, which he calls *utterance*, and written language, which he calls *text*. He argued that theories of reading and learning to read can be seen as expressions of the rival assumptions about the locus of meaning: whether meaning is in the mind of the reader or in the text. He argued further that the Greek alphabet, from which our alphabet developed, gave writing an explicit quality and an autonomy that allowed it to place the meaning squarely in the text. The student's problem, it is argued by some, is to find out how to decode that meaning through the gradual mastery of subskills such as sound–symbol relationships, the recognition of words, and later comprehension of the text (Chall 1967; Gibson and Levin 1975). The opposing view (Goodman 1967; Smith 1973; Scholes 1998) is that readers bring meaning to the text, which allows them to predict words in context. Recent thinking has placed emphasis on the nature of the alphabetical system in reading and writing and on the importance of context, including social context. In other words, in a balanced view of reading, the locus of meaning is in the situation, the reader, and the text.

The differences in oral language (Olsen's 'utterance') and written text in relation to reading have been well documented (Olsen 1977; Halliday 1979, 1985b; Winch 1988), but it is important also to note their interconnection. It is children's oral language that is a large part of what they bring to print, together with an understanding of the topic in question. Children use their oral language as a resource as they deal with written text and they do not confuse one with the other.

Scholes (1998) makes the point that viewing the English writing system as written speech is essentially wrong. (There are no truly phonetic writing systems, nor should there be.) It stems from the incorrect view (Bloomfield 1927) that to understand writing you must first convert it to speech. No, says Scholes. *Children are smarter than that—in a relatively short time most of them realise that writing is not like speech.*

As children increase their reading skills they become less willing to use phonological data alone to process writing. It must be noted, nevertheless, that this view does not contradict the view taken in this book—and increasingly throughout the world—that good readers are extremely good at word recognition as well as very good at bringing vital comprehension data to text. The point is, and it is Scholes' point also, that our writing system does not require pronunciation before comprehension, unless it is in the form of a linguistic joke, as in this Valentine's Day greeting: BEAM EYE VALE AND TINE BE COURSE ISLE OF EWE. This joke is, as Australian readers would readily recognise, the basis of Strine.

OW DUZZY REDIT, MITE?
OIM STUFF TIFF EYE NO!

PHONEMIC AWARENESS AND PHONOLOGICAL AWARENESS

Phonemic awareness and phonological awareness are important concepts in reading and learning to read. Understanding their meanings is significant for both theory and practice.

Some definitions

Phonemic awareness refers to an understanding of the smallest units of sound that make up oral language, taking into consideration that there is a range of precise phonetic differences in each phoneme depending on such matters as dialect and where a phoneme exists in a word. (See boxed discussion of allophones above.) Phonemic awareness is characterised by a speaker's ability to hear, segment, and manipulate sounds in speech, e.g. saying the first sound in the word *cat*.

Phonological awareness is a more general term and can refer to larger segments than phonemes such as **onset and rime**, as in *b-ike*, and syllables, such as *un-der*. Sometimes the two terms are used interchangeably, but more often phonemic awareness is made the generic term in research and other literature.

Scholes (1998) correctly makes the distinction between syllabic awareness and subsyllabic awareness, arguing that manipulating subsyllabic particles (segmental phonemes), often called phonemic awareness, is really phonetic awareness (because the actual sounds differ so much). He uses the term Phonetic Segment Awareness (PSA) for the ability to manipulate individual segmental sounds as in the three sounds that make up the word *ball*.

Phonics refers to the relationship between written letters and spoken sounds. When children are asked what letter makes the first sound in the written word *bat*, they are asked to call on phonic knowledge. It is a matter of the relationship between sound and symbol. **Phonic analysis** is a method of teaching word recognition by matching elements in writing with their corresponding sounds. This involves analysing *consonants*, *vowels*, **blends**, **digraphs**, and **diphthongs**. **Phonic synthesis** on the other hand is building up words from the sounds within them. There are many approaches to teaching phonics and a great deal of instructional material is available.

It should be noted some whole-language theorists have been opposed to the breaking up of words 'into bite-size but abstract little pieces' (Goodman 1986), which amounts to a disavowal of the value of teaching phonics out of the context of whole text. Others support it strongly (Stanovich and Paula 1995). Today there is widespread support for the inclusion of effective text-based phonics teaching in early reading programs. The National Literacy Strategy in Great Britain is a case in point. Phonics or any graphophonic teaching should not overpower the teaching of reading. It must sit beside other approaches to reading in a balanced program that combines such systematic code instruction with the reading and writing of meaningful texts.

The importance of phonemic awareness

It is an established fact that phonemic awareness is a successful predictor of reading success (Stanovich 1994). It is a better predictor than many other candidates, including a child's IQ. The question whether there is a causal link between phonemic awareness and learning to read is often debated without clear conclusions being reached. The important point is that there appears to be a strong reciprocal relationship between phonological segmentation and alphabetical coding skill and that these skills are mutually facilitative (Stanovich 1994). Lack of phonological sensitivity appears to inhibit the learning of the alphabetic coding system that underlies fluent word recognition. Although reading is essentially about bringing meaning to and taking meaning from print, it is also true that a child must learn the writing system and how it encodes his or her language.

The importance of phonemic awareness and phonemic processing is widely accepted (Beard 1998). Making the link with print through analytic and synthetic phonics (segmentation and blending) is the next step forward. For instance, 'Tell me the sounds in 'cat' (analytic); 'What do these sounds make when I put them together? c-a-t' (synthetic). The best way to develop phonemic awareness is making it part of a broad instructional program in reading and writing so that young children are involved in language activities that help them recognise such things as initial sounds, **rhymes**, and the distinct speech energy rhythms that produce syllables (as in (cat.er.pil.lar).

Children's phonological development appears to follow a clear pattern, from awareness of syllables to being aware of patterning in initial sounds (onsets) and rimes within syllables (*c-at*), to being aware of phonemes (Treiman and Zukowski 1996). Children will develop these skills at different rates and according to the focus of the teaching program. Rhymes, poems, songs, and shared books help to facilitate both phonemic awareness and reading through repetition, rhyme, and the pleasurable matching of sounds.

Although the precise relationship between phonemic awareness and learning to read may not be clear, its importance is nevertheless recognised. The best teaching practice leading to reading acquisition combines interaction with print and explicit attention to the sound structure of words.

Perfetti (1995: 112), in his discussion of cognitive research and its importance to reading education, states: 'The fact that literacy and phonemic awareness can develop in tandem has implications for reading instruction. Rather than stressing phonological training in isolation, phonological training and word reading can be effectively linked together.'

Recent increased professional interest in the nature of phonemic awareness and its role in reading and writing has occasioned focus on the subject at conferences in Australia such as the 1999 ALEA conference and the publications of discussion papers such as that of Freeman (1998).

How readers operate

Visual and nonvisual information

It is obvious that the eyes are important in reading—you cannot read in the dark or with your eyes shut (unless you are reading Braille)—but there is a severe limitation on the *visual information* supplied by the eyes. They represent, in fact, only the camera that takes the picture and sends the information to the brain. It is the brain that converts this visual information into meaning and allows us to read. It supplies the *nonvisual* information that makes reading for meaning possible.

It can be argued that there is a trade-off between the two types of information: the more nonvisual information you have when you read, the less visual information you need. The opposite also applies. It must be noted, however, that this point of view is contentious. Perfetti (1995) argues that skilled readers fixate on most words on the page when they are reading for most purposes, from over 50 per cent to 80 per cent, with *content* words (nouns, verbs, adjectives, adverbs) featuring more than *function* words (articles, prepositions, etc.). He also argues that along with this dense sampling of the text the skilled reader relies on phonology to recognise the words in question and does not rely heavily on context for word recognition. This view is supported by Stanovich (1994), who found that context in word recognition was used less by skilled readers than by less skilled readers.

There is no doubt that skilled readers are experts at word recognition, and their ability is both rapid and automatic. Word recognition, however, is not reading in itself. Comprehension of the text is an essential component, as we have stated above. The balanced view taken in this book is that recent research has added to our knowledge of the way skilled readers operate in terms of word recognition but does not alter the fact that reading is a very complex matter relying on cues from a variety of sources—graphophonic, grammatical, and semantic—and that the reader's understanding of the written text is primary in any act of reading.

Seeing and understanding

Smith (1978) has used an interesting example to show how much reading can be achieved in a single glance. He refers to one of the oldest findings in experimental psychology, that four or five letters constitute the upper limit of how much can be seen at a single glance in a line of randomly selected letters such as those below.

x j p r q n o y r t v p s l m w k j l h z s p j m

He adds the interesting information that when the same number of letters are arranged in words the brain can recognise twice as many letters in a single glance, although the amount of visual information is the same.

happy   give   when   improve   climb

If words are arranged in a sentence, the number of recognised letters in a simple glance is doubled again, so that the whole sentence is recognised. The visual information is made to go four times as far as with the random letters.

small seeds grow to tall trees

There are many factors associated with this finding. One is that the brain responds to the information arranged in a sentence more effectively than randomly arranged letters; another is that the **redundancy** in the language allows the reader to ignore much of the visual display and thus reduce uncertainty about the meaning; another again is the meaningful arrangement of the syntactic patterns of the words in example 3. It is also important to notice that the more the reader understands the meaning of the texts, the bigger the chunks of language he can recognise in a single glance.

Perfetti (1995) points out correctly that reading for gist or general understanding of a text allows readers to rely on fewer eye fixations when reading than if they were reading in depth, for detailed information (Just and Carpenter 1987). Winch, working with adults from 1990 to 1998 to improve reading flexibility and speed, confirms this. When reading for gist, skilled readers can be taught to read at more than 1000 words per minute with limited sampling of the text and effective use of strategies such as reading for main idea and finding the key to paragraphs in first and last sentences. Readers in this process skip large sections of text and certainly many words, but still read effectively for that particular purpose.

A large number of adult readers, many of them senior professional people in executive positions, Winch confirmed, read far too slowly, mainly because they tend to read everything at the same, often laborious, pace, failing to use **metalinguistic** knowledge relating to textual information that lies beyond the **lexical** level. In doing so they ignore the purposes for which they read.

How the eyes move during reading

Most people, when asked how the eyes move when reading, will answer that they move evenly from left to right. This is not the case. The eyes do not glide evenly along a line of print but proceed in a series of jumps (called 'saccades'). They jump and stop, jump and stop, during the reading process. The stops are called 'fixations' and are somewhat like the jumps and stops the eyes make when one looks around a room or watches a tennis match.

Fluent readers make about four stops every second, and the time taken in moving the eye from fixation to fixation is very brief (about 1/1000 to 1/10 second) depending on the angle through which the eyes have to travel. It follows that for most of the time the eyes are stopped. This is just as well because while they are travelling the print is a blur that the brain ignores.

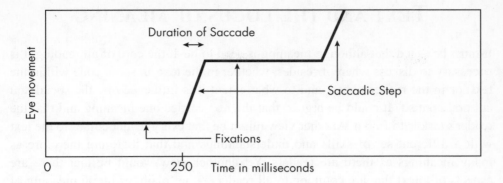

Fig. 2.1 Eye movement in reading showing saccadic steps

From this information we can see that reading occurs during fixations and that these occur about four times in a second. It is important to know that beginning readers and fluent readers change fixations at about the same rate. The difference is in what the brain processes during this time.

Fluent readers make more effective use of the cue systems: they use graphophonic information; they handle the grammatical system skilfully; and they bring much more to print in terms of the world knowledge they possess, the breadth of their vocabulary, and their overall skill at *prediction*. This information about the fluent reader gives us important guidelines on how we should teach children to read. The important thing to notice is that good readers are good thinkers; they process larger chunks of print and use a variety of cue systems to do so. They do not see more, they understand more.

In speaking of the dense sampling of text described above, Perfetti (1995) agrees that the amount perceived in a single fixation is limited to the extent discussed. He concludes from this that readers, limited as they are by the eyes' inability to see much in a fixation, must sample a lot of words to read effectively. He does not address the matter of varying reading speeds by the adoption of strategies that allow the skilled reader to process large chunks of text as discussed above. Not every reading act requires the fixating and processing of most words on the page.

Other eye movements during reading also occur. Readers' eyes 'rove' around the page before and during reading, depending on the reading purpose and the level of concentration. Readers look back over text read at various stages of reading. These regressions are important to confirm or correct what has been read. It is also common for good readers to browse print by skimming through the text or scanning to find specific points. The latter techniques or strategies are valuable assets to a reader and can be successfully taught.

TEXT AND THE LOCUS OF MEANING

It must be noted that although meaning is seen to be at the core of all reading it is necessary to discuss where it resides, whether in the text, in some code within the text, or in the reader's head, and to what extent it is influenced by the social and cultural context. It could be argued that the text carries one meaning and that the reader's task is to find it. Another view might be that every reader comes to the text with a different set of skills and understandings and that there are therefore as many meanings as there are readers. Yet another view would be that there are aspects of a text that are common to all readers—the 'plain' or literal meaning of a text—while different levels of meaning would produce varying amounts of difference depending on the input of the reader and the social and cultural context.

Bloom (1956) produced a **taxonomy** of educational objectives that defined comprehension as exhibiting three types of behaviour in ascending order of reader input. Smith (1978) developed a further taxonomy that, although similar in many ways, extended the reader's input. She specified a series of skills that has been used widely by teachers. Four levels of comprehension were included: the *literal* level in which a reader, among other things, identified, remembered, or recalled details and ideas; the *interpretative or inferential* level in which a reader concentrated on main ideas, further details, made contrasts, drew conclusions, generalised, and predicted; the *critical* level in which a reader judged, detected propaganda, analysed, and checked validity; and a final *creative* level in which a reader applied information to a new situation and responded emotionally. While these approaches appeared hierarchical, heavily cognitive, and skill based, they provided teachers with a framework for discussion and questioning and were widely used. They did not, however, give significant attention to the social context in which situations occurred or the cultural background of the reader and what she brought to print. One method that gives attention to social context while providing a framework for practice is the Freebody and Luke (1990) concept of the four roles of the reader (see pp. 43–4).

Sociocultural views argue that comprehension and literacy, generally, can be seen only in their social and cultural setting (Gee et al. 1996: 1, 3): 'Texts are parts of lived, talked, enacted, value-and-belief laden practices carried out in specific places and at specific times'. Reading is thus a plural notion, '*readings* rather than *reading*', and must operate as a social practice. This idea views literacy and thus meaning or meanings more in terms of ways of behaving and using literacy. It places emphasis on the language and literacy practices that a student brings to school from home and community, so that a teacher bases practice on how the individual is behaving and on what she already knows.

These practices are not neutral and may not 'fit' with those of the school. School literacy practices may advantage some and disadvantage others, or, to use the terminology employed by this approach, may 'empower' or 'disempower' particular sociocultural groups. Literacy practice can thus become a political enterprise. It 'not only constructs the way an individual can operate in the world but also the way different cultural groups and agencies are structured and operationalised' (Anstey and Bull 1996: 153).

The above view is not universally accepted. Oakhill and Beard (1999) argue that while cultural factors are important, they play a secondary role. Close attention should be given to the necessary skills of literacy, which will allow children to learn to read, write, and understand. They question the concept of literacies as pluralistic and argue that by equating literacies with various cultures and cultural practices there could be as many literacies as there are cultures. Their perspective is that 'teaching literacy is primarily about teaching the skills of reading and writing, which once learned can be applied and extended in many ways that cover the broad definitions of literacy' (1999: x). These skills are the essentials that enable people to decipher the writing system or systems that they need to use. Oakhill and Beard's view and that of the other contributors to their volume is deeply influenced by cognitive psychology and empirical research relating to reading and writing.

Literary theory and the locus of meaning

Literary theory also throws light on the locus of meaning in text. It places different interpretations on the place where meaning should reside and therefore how a reader comprehends. It also makes clearer how different approaches to reading have come to be.

Put simply, the varying viewpoints of linguistic communication can be seen from the following diagram, which has been modified from that of the linguist Roman Jacobson (see page 318).

WRITER	CONTEXT	READER
	WRITING	
	CODE	

The writer or *addresser* sends a message in writing to a reader or *addressee*. The message has a context and is sent through a medium, in this case writing.

Some literary theories focus on the writer's life or mind; others focus on the reader's experience; others focus on the nature of writing and the code; and others are more interested in the social context of the writing rather than the writing itself.

Some broad approaches to literature

It is too easy to oversimplify the complex world of literary theory and the above discussion touches only the surface. In Part III Rosemary Ross Johnston explores it more deeply in terms of children's literature. However, certain approaches can be kept in mind while following the discussion in this section.

Early critics, when talking of literature and meaning, focused on the writer's personal experience, the social and historical background of the work, the human interest and the imaginative thrust of the literature. They saw meaning as very much to do with the writer of the text.

Structuralist criticism, which places emphasis on the underlying structures or codes within the text, argues that the source of true meaning is found not in the writer or reader but in the system that governs the language. The Formalists, too, concentrated on the text as a special use of language.

Reader-oriented theories offer yet another approach. They argue that unlike Jacobson's formalistic model, which places meaning in the text, no text has any meaning until it is read. The addressee, the reader, is the active agent in the making of meaning. There are 'blanks' in the text for the reader to fill and the reader's experience is at the heart of meaning.

Marxist criticism and to some extent feminist criticism place the focus on the social and cultural context of the writing with a view to changing the existing political and social order.

It is not difficult to equate some of the approaches to meaning (cognitive-psychological as opposed to sociocultural) with the positions discussed above and to see how extreme positions can emerge. However, no matter how 'pure' a particular view of literary criticism may be, whether it is reader-dominated, code-dominated, or dominated by social context, no approach excludes the other entirely in explaining approaches to literary understanding and concomitantly to reading and the construction of meaning.

In the balanced approach to reading adopted in this book, the importance of the reader, the writer, the code, and the sociocultural context of the text are all considered as important in finding meaning and teaching children to read.

Applied to learning to read at school, this approach takes into account the varied experiences of language, world experience, and literary experience that a child brings to school. These understandings are included in the school's literacy program so that students can more readily bring meaning to and take meaning from text.

READING AND THE COMPUTER

In 1985 Jonathon Anderson wrote:

Microcomputers are beginning to be a regular part of most schools ... and imaginative teachers are finding a multitude of ways in which these new resources can promote learning. For reading and language teachers especially, microcomputers can be powerful allies. For a start they are highly motivating. More importantly, almost any interaction with micro-computers involves reading and writing of some kind. (1985: 203)

It is interesting to observe how prophetic Anderson's statements were, although he probably did not envisage the dramatic explosion of computer use in education that followed. He considered various aspects of computers in home and school: interactive software, including games; the computer and reading, writing, listening, speaking, thinking; simulation and database applications; the computer as a tool to develop reading skills; word-processing in its many aspects; and the potential of the computer for future literacy development.

Since that time and the advent of cheaper computers, the increased sophistication of the technology and its breathtaking rate of change, the World Wide Web and its many manifestations such as email, the availability of the CD-ROM, and the explosion in the software available for use, the computer is with us in full force. Many schools have their own considerable array of computers, not only in the classroom and the special computer area, but also in the library, where the monitor has replaced the card index and computer skills (particularly reading skills) are at a premium. Major references are on CD-ROM and that doyen of all resources, the *Encyclopaedia Britannica*, now comes to us in no other form than compact disk. Many schools now have their own web sites, students carry around their personal laptops, and homework is done on the home computer with all the embellishment that desktop publishing can bring.

Current syllabuses contain specific and detailed requirements in computer use. Computer technology sits beside handwriting, and basic desktop computer publishing skills are written into syllabus outcomes. As a consequence, textbooks are beginning to address computer skills and subskills as part and parcel of their content. The sophisticated level of computer knowledge and skills required in current syllabuses is illustrated by the following list of specific outcomes and indicators in the current NSW English K–6 Syllabus (NSW Board of Studies 1998: 43) at Stage 3, senior primary. To achieve at this level it is necessary that the student produces texts in a fluent and legible style and uses computer technology to present these effectively in a variety of ways and that she:

- uses computer software programs and associated technology to format a variety of texts
- locates and uses a **thesaurus**
- uses font and layout to suit particular audience and purpose
- chooses appropriate graphics to accompany text
- designs and organises information for a web page
- locates and uses columns or borders when appropriate
- adds graphics, changes spacing and style when publishing
- uses word-processing programs to design school or class newspaper, importing graphics and written texts from a range of sources
- uses multimedia authoring software to create published works incorporating text, graphics, sound, animation
- creates texts that incorporate graphics or tables when appropriate.

The above may seem highly sophisticated to a reader who is not familiar with computers or is unaware of the rapidity with which young students learn to use the computer and its many facets. Students seem to have added a new dimension to their learning of literacy skills.

The use of the computer illustrates how closely reading and writing are intertwined. Most syllabus statements related to use of the computer tend to focus on its writing or word-processing use, but it must be remembered that every writing act is also a reading act. No student who is unable to read can effectively use a computer except in the most limited sense.

Reading the written text is only one facet. Instructions and the applications of the various techniques of word-processing alone require considerable reading skills. The reading of computer icons adds an extra dimension and extends the concept of reading itself. Other skills, such as using computer software to find information and using **hypertext** and graphic materials effectively, are also examples of reading using the computer. The teaching of reading will more and more include the teaching of the 'grammar' of the computer and students will become increasingly able to navigate the complexities of electronic text.

As computers become more readily available students will become familiar with electronic mail and its reading and writing processes. Email itself is providing a different type of discourse to be read. A new genre of written material is becoming available and new reading approaches are needed to deal with it. New, interactive study programs are beginning to appear on the market. These combine online Internet access with dedicated CD-ROMs to create multimedia presentations, including sound and visual effects. They claim to be complete packages, even including built-in self-assessment in order to allow students, parents, and teachers to monitor progress. The rapid development of software available to help young children learn to read is another example of the use of the computer in reading. Software programs that assist in developing phonemic awareness, and interactive stories and games with a literacy base, are becoming increasingly common and of improved quality.

Electronic professional programs are becoming a reality at tertiary institutions, and education online now exists in some universities. In the first class of 2000 at the College of Law in Sydney, education in the electronic mode allowed students to access lectures, quizzes, and course materials as well as communicate with lecturers and fellow students via email. At the University of New England three-quarters of the 13 000 external students are doing some of their course online (Ho 2000).

William Crossman (2000) takes the view that the new technology and the talking computer will make literacy as we know it obsolete during this century. He argues that human society is moving away from a print culture to an oral culture. His reasoning is both interesting and persuasive, although it fails to recognise two fundamental factors, among others: that spoken language is comparatively very slow—a reader can read infinitely faster than a listener can comprehend speech—

and that written language is different from spoken language in many aspects. These differences have been discussed above. The power of written language, its distinctive quality, its richness and remarkable flexibility make it a vital part of being educated and, indeed, human.

The computer will sit beside the book in the future. Just as film and television sit beside the book now, and often support reading by building up semantic knowledge, so will the computer act as both supplement and complement to the book. Likewise, voice-interactive computers will convey oral language with increasing effectiveness and sit beside telephone technology. The survival of print material in its many forms is not at risk. Johnston discusses the survival of the book with reference to children's literature in Part III (pages 310–11). In no way does the new electronic age herald the death of the book.

SUMMARY

1. English is an alphabetical writing system and has regular and irregular features. It is important to understand the writing system when learning to read. Meaning is found in the text, the writer, and the reader. Writing is not just speech written down.

2. Phonemic and phonological awareness are important concepts in reading and learning to read and need definitions. Phonemic awareness is different from phonics. There is an important relationship between phonemic awareness and learning to read. Readers use graphological-phonological, grammatical, and semantic information when reading.

3. Readers use visual and nonvisual information when reading. It is interesting and important to be aware of what readers see and understand when reading. Readers need to read flexibly, using different strategies for different purposes. Eye movement when reading is not always understood: the eyes move in jumps and stops; reading is carried out during the stops. Other movements include those made by the eyes while skimming and scanning text, although the mind may be working during the jumps.

4. Literary theory throws light on the locus of meaning in text. Various critics argue that the meaning lies in the author, the author's intention, and the historical setting; others argue that it resides in the text and others again that it is in the reader. A balanced view of reading places importance on each of the three.

5. Computers are becoming an integral part of literacy learning. They are used in both reading and writing as well as listening, speaking, and thinking. Current syllabuses contain specific computer teaching. The computer will sit beside the book. The book is not 'dead'.

Tasks

Discussion

1. English can be described as an alphabetical writing system. What implications does this have for learning to read?
2. Discuss the concept of 'phoneme' in linguistics and the way a 'phoneme' differs from an 'allophone' and a grapheme.
3. Consider some of the strengths and weaknesses of our English writing system and discuss some reasons for its widespread use around the world.
4. Discuss in what ways the commonly held view that eyes move evenly from left to right when reading is wrong.
5. Discuss ways a teacher might develop phonemic awareness in a classroom during the first year of school.
6. If you take the view that reading is a plural notion (*readings* rather than *reading*), what would one say about reading a legal document such as a will or reading a train timetable?
7. Consider in what ways an indigenous child from the Torres Strait Islands might find it extremely difficult to read and respond to nursery rhymes that are common to English-speaking children. Take as an example:

A Week of Birthdays

Monday's child is fair of face,
Tuesday's child is full of grace,
Wednesday's child is full of woe,
Thursday's child has far to go,
Friday's child is loving and giving,
Saturday's child works hard for its living,
But the child that's born on the Sabbath day
Is bonny and blithe and good and gay.

8. Read the following excerpt from a recent book on literacy. Discuss the position that might be taken by these writers on the nature of literacy.

To illustrate the operation of power, we would like to share three examples from the research on language and social power. These particular three have been chosen not because they illustrate empowerment, but because they show individuals being disempowered in the interplay of power in literacy events in classrooms. We share them not

as a comment on the classrooms or the teachers, but as a comment on how power operates.
(Anstey and Bull 1996: 171)

9. The English literary scholar I. A. Richards wrote:

    In most poetry, the sense is as important as anything else; it is quite as subtle, and as
    dependent on the syntax as is prose; it is the poet's chief instrument ... and in the immense
    majority of instances we miss nearly everything of value if we misread his sense. (1929:
    191)

    He is talking about the 'plain meaning' of poetry. Where do you think
    Richards would place the locus of meaning of a poem: in the writer, the
    poem, or the reader? Give your reason and say where *you* think the meaning
    of a poem (or a piece of prose) resides.

10. Consider the ways the computer is used in *your* daily life. What uses could
    be described as part of literacy?

11. Use a 'crystal ball' to look into the future. Write a brief essay (about a page)
    on the way you think computers will be used to teach literacy in the school.
    Think about the library and the classroom in particular.

Activities

1. Test yourself on the examples on pages 25 and 26 by glancing at each one
    separately. See how much of each you can read with one glance per
    example.

2. Redundancy refers to the fact that much of the information in our written
    language is a matter of overkill—there is much more than we need. To give
    an example, read these two sentences. As you can see, not all the
    information supplied in the fully printed form is necessary for you to read
    the sentences.

    I r_n in t_e r_ce last y_r.
    I have two eyes and _____ ears.

    Make up some examples of your own.

3. Take a tiny test.
    · How many phonemes are in each of the following words: *chase, parked,*
      might, and *bough*?
    · How many syllables are in each of the following words: *plough, particle,*
      permeated, painted?
    Answers on page 471.

Chapter 3
Towards a Model of Reading

Focus
A model of reading is developed. It includes the various cue systems used, the global strategies employed, and the four roles of the reader when reading for meaning in social and cultural context.

Context

A reader reads the notices and prices in a supermarket for a specific social purpose: to make the most of the visit by obtaining the required goods at the best possible price. Another reader who reads the editorial of a newspaper has a different social purpose: to obtain news and to find out what the editorial writer thinks about a particular subject. As well, each reader reads differently in terms of her cultural background. Different cultural groups bring different purposes and understandings to print and therefore react in different ways to it.

Likewise, the text itself is subject to similar influences. The writer's social purpose and cultural background will affect the genre in which text is written: a church newsletter has a totally different social purpose from that of an instruction on how to build a model car. The cultural background of the writer would also be reflected in the text. *Bury My Heart at Wounded Knee*, a history of the American Indians from an Indian viewpoint, would likely be very different from a history written by a white American rancher.

These differences are often discussed in terms of **register**, which means the way a particular situation affects the language of a text or oral discourse and is reflected in the choice of vocabulary, grammar, and other features. Register is described as consisting of field, tenor, and mode. **Field** refers to the subject matter involved; **tenor** refers to the people involved and their relationship; and **mode** refers to the type of language use, whether written (in the case of reading) or spoken (in the case of oral language).

Social and cultural context must be built into any model of reading, because meaning is influenced by a number of factors relating to writer, reader, and text (see Chapter 2).

Different social and cultural contexts will affect the **genres** in which texts are written and each genre will have a different internal structure in terms of its grammar and its sequential makeup. A *report* is significantly different from an *instruction*; an *exposition* is significantly different from a **narrative**. Also, readers must access the necessary aspects of graphophonic information in a text; they must have grammatical information and semantic information, which includes word meanings and knowledge of the real world.

Genre or **text-type** refers to the way a text is structured to achieve a particular purpose. There are various categories of text-type and their names (and definitions) sometimes vary according to the person who describes them. A useful description for our purposes is that texts can be termed **literary** or **factual** with various subcategories.

Literary text-types include narrative, poetry, and drama although, obviously, many of these overlap. Factual text-types and some of their particular characteristics have been helpfully classified by Derewianka (1991):

Recount: an account of something that happened in the past.
Report: facts and information about a topic.
Explanation: an explanation of how things work.
Instruction (Procedure): a description of how to do or make something.
Argument (Exposition or Discussion): arguing a case.

Again, although it is understood that text-types overlap and we often find 'mixed' texts, these distinctions help teachers to focus on the different ways texts are structured and their characteristic language features.

The reading cue systems

The phonological-graphological cue system

The first cue system can be described as the *phonological-graphological* cue system. Although this cue system, and its relation to phonemic awareness, has been discussed to some degree above, it needs elaboration here as it is particularly important in word recognition.

There are two types of information at this level on which the reader will call: one is *phonological* information, which includes hearing the sounds, syllables, and morphemes in words and manipulating these sounds by exchanging and blending.

The next is *graphological* information, which includes knowledge of letters, letter clusters such as blends (*cl*, *bl*), digraphs (*ch*, *th*, *oa*), syllables (*syl.la.bles*), prefixes (*non-*, *anti-*), and suffixes (*-ness*, *-ation*). As well as these more common examples, graphological information includes concepts about print, such as spaces between words, **directionality**, punctuation, and book conventions such as page layout and **sight words**. There is some overlap here with the grammatical cue system because inflections such as past tense markers like *-ed* and other affixes have a grammatical role to play.

Graphophonic is a term often used to describe the relationship between the graphic units of the language and the sounds they represent (Goodman in Smith 1973: 25). Readers make generalisations about the letter–sound and letter pattern–sound correspondences when reading. They extend these correspondences through the use of analogy and build up their skills at decoding written text when reading and encoding words when writing. Smith (1973) made the interesting point that these relationships are not strictly grapheme–phoneme correspondences but what he termed morphophonemic (*morpho* relates to meaning-bearing chunks of words called morphemes, as *see-ing* in 'seeing'), operating quite often at levels above the individual sound, which varies among dialects. Readers do in fact decode by using meaning-bearing letter groups that relate to sounds when they are reading. They also relate to blends (*bl-*) and the segments found in onset and rime (*bl-ack*). Simply reading at the grapheme to sound level could often be confusing.

> In English as in other languages the spelling system is fixed and standard-ised. This means that correspondences will vary from dialect to dialect and that over time changing phonology will loosen the fit of even the tightest alphabetical system. (Goodman in Smith 1973: 25)

The phonological-graphological cue system as a source of information can be represented in various ways. A useful table is contained in the NSW Department of Education and Training document *Teaching Reading: A K–6 Framework* (1997). It contains examples of semantic and grammatical sources of information, which are discussed below.

Traditional approaches to word recognition recognised three categories of subskills: *phonics*, *structural analysis*, and *sight words*. Phonics was restricted to letter–sound correspondences; structural analysis included the rules of syllabification and the use of roots and affixes in words; and a basic sight vocabulary was usually built up from non-decodable function words like *there* and *through*. These subskills were often taught in isolation and were insufficiently linked with meaningful context.

Knowledge about the sources of information:

Semantic

Students need experiences which will enable them to develop:

- real-world knowledge about topics of interest and relevance to students including knowledge about everyday situations in the home and community.
- knowledge about topics being studied in all key learning areas.
- conceptual knowledge about the world, eg concepts of size, shape, position, height, direction, orientation and time.
- vocabulary knowledge:
  - world meanings
  - common expressions
  - subject-specific vocabulary
  - figurative language.

Grammatical

Students need experiences which will enable them to investigate:

- grammar at the text level:
  - connecting words and phrases
  - content word chains throughout a text
  - how events are linked in a text by connectives such as *because*, *so, and*.
- grammar at the sentence level:
  - types of words in sentences, eg nouns, verbs, adjectives
  - sentence structure
  - clause structure in sentences
  - subject-verb agreement
  - correct tense
  - plurals
  - word order in phrases and noun groups
  - word order in sentences
  - pronoun reference within sentences
  - connectives within sentences.

Phonological

Students need experiences which will enable them to develop:

- phonological/ phonemic awareness:
  - hearing the sounds in words (rhyming, alliteration)
  - separating the sounds in words (isolation, onset/rime, segmentation)
  - manipulating the sounds in words (exchanging blending).

Graphological

Students need experiences which will enable them to develop:

- knowledge of book conventions:
  - page and book layout
  - front and back cover.
- concepts about print:
  - spaces between words
  - directionality (left to right and top to bottom).
- sight vocabulary:
  - high frequency words
  - irregular words.
- letter knowledge:
  - individual letters
  - upper and lower case letters
  - letter clusters (syllables, prefixes/suffixes).
- punctuation:
  - capital letters
  - full stops
  - question marks
  - exclamation marks
  - commas
  - inverted commas
  - apostrophes
  - colons; semi-colons.

- Letter/sound correspondence:
  - awareness that sounds can be written down
  - difference between sounds and letter names
  - alphabetic principle (systematic relationship between letters and sounds)
  - making generalisations (use of analogy)
  - recognising that letters can represent different sounds.
- Blending:
  - Combining sounds (letters and letter clusters).

(NSW Department of Education and Training 1997: 20)

Fig. 3.1   Knowledge about the sources of information

The grammatical cue system

The second cue system can be described as the *grammatical* cue system, which relies on the reader's knowledge of the way sentences and texts are structured. Two examples illustrate this system:

> *She _____ the length of the pool using a backstroke style.*
> *He had one pet and she had two pet___.*

In the first case, a reader can predict that the word is *swam*, the past tense of the verb *to swim*; in the second, a reader can predict that the required **inflection** is *s*, so the word becomes *pets*. In each case the reader could easily supply the word or inflection without reference to the visual presentation of either. The fact that we can supply this information by calling on our linguistic knowledge of vocabulary and syntax (sentence structure) is also an example of redundancy in English: there is more information than we really need. Knowledge of the sentence structure of the language and word inflections such as –s and –ed is a vital component of reading. The grammatical cue system gives important cues to what sentences say and mean. Grammatical cues are particularly important in reading English because its structural system relies more heavily on word order than is the case in other languages (because for historical reasons its inflection system is largely broken down). Therefore the reader knows what type of word to expect next in a sentence.

Consider the example below:

> *When I _____ coffee I always add _____.*

In the first instance we know that the missing word should be a verb, something I *do*. In the second instance we know it should be a noun, a *thing*. It is our grammatical knowledge that tells us this. This knowledge helps readers enormously in predicting what *kind* of word will come next. We often then need to check only one or two letters to predict what that word is. In checking we might find the following.

> *When I dr_____ coffee I always add su_____.*

This is often enough to confirm what the words are. Only if meaning is lost or the grammar of the sentence disrupted will the reader need to check more closely. A reader might misread the sentence as follows:

> *When I drink coffee I always add sung.*

It is grammatical knowledge that will tell the reader that this cannot be right and that he needs to reread and to check more of the letters in the word.

Linguists have pointed out that grammatical cues are carried across sentences and not confined within them. Words are connected throughout the text by special links called **cohesive ties**. Chapman (1983), using insights derived from the linguists Halliday and Hasan (1976), has stressed the importance of these ties in reading. A simple example of one form of cohesive tie is shown in Fig. 3.2.

Kahli looked at the lion.
It stood near him in the grass.
Its enormous head and
jaws increased his fear of
the hungry beast.

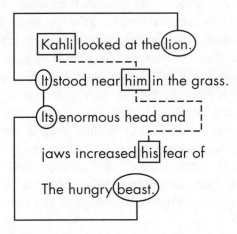

Fig. 3.2   Cohesive ties

These cohesive ties are called **reference ties** and this particular example is called *anaphora* because the ties relate back to the original reference. There are many different types of cohesive ties in English. Others include *substitution* (using a different word): 'My *fishing rod* is a good *one*'; *ellipsis* (leaving out words): 'Jim is tall and (*he is*) strong'; *conjunctions* (linking words that join phrases, clauses, and sentences): 'The boy *and* his dog'; 'He turned quickly, *then* he ran'; *related words*: 'The man was a *liar* and a *thief*'.

Added to this, there is a 'grammar' at the text level such as the way the text is structured with a beginning, a middle, and an end. Then there are the effects of text-type on grammar across the discourse. For example, **procedural texts** are in the present tense, narrative texts mainly in the past tense.

The semantic cue system

The third is the **semantic** cue system. This cue system refers to the meanings in the text and in the mind of the reader, which include word meanings, subject-specific vocabulary, and figurative language. Readers use semantic cues when they consider ideas, information, and feelings in a text. The more they call on their own knowledge that they bring to reading, the better they read. The subject under consideration, the meanings of the words in the text, and the reader's knowledge of common or colloquial expressions, vocabulary, and figurative language all affect the operation of the semantic cue system.

It is this cue system that provides the main guide or monitor to readers as they continue to ask themselves, 'Does this make sense?' It is by using their semantic knowledge that readers provide the answer to that question. It is usually when meaning is disrupted that readers go back in the text to check the grammatical and phonological-graphological cue systems to correct their earlier error.

It is the semantic cue system that enables the reader to link a new text to everything he already knows about the topic of the text or the setting of a narrative. This gives him tremendous power in unlocking the meaning of the new text since he already has a mental frame of reference for what is being described. In scientific or technical texts, where this is linked with subject specific vocabulary, the reader with a good bank of semantic knowledge is at an enormous advantage over the reader without such knowledge.

It is important to note that the act of reading itself is one of the best ways of increasing a reader's semantic knowledge. As students read they add new words to those they already know and develop new concepts and understandings that strengthen and deepen their current knowledge. Many well-written factual texts make a point of clearly describing the meanings of key terms, often with the use of diagrams and illustrations.

Consider the difficulty you encounter when trying to read a text when you know little or nothing about the topic. In particular, imagine you know nothing about computers and try to read the following:

> *To move or delete buttons when the customize dialog box isn't open, hold down ALT and drag the button to a new location or off the toolbar.*

Or the following:

> *In your Word toolbox, you can customize existing menus by adding or removing commands, or you can create your own menus.*

The actual process by which a reader accesses the cues in the text can be described in theoretical terms and applied to a model of reading. Readers operate with all of these cue systems when reading fluently and, it is argued, simultaneously. Good readers also read selectively: they do not attempt, for example, to laboriously decode every word or read every phrase or sentence if they are skimming a passage for gist or general meaning.

A diagram of the cue systems of reading discussed so far would look like that shown in Fig. 3.3.

Considering our case for a balanced view of reading, it is now possible to produce a model of the reading process. First it is necessary to look at the various roles readers take on when they read.

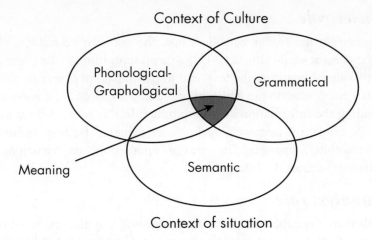

Fig. 3.3 A model of the reading cue system

The four roles of the reader

Readers read to satisfy a variety of purposes as they interact with a text. It is an active process during which they take on a number of roles, described by Freebody and Luke (1990). If these roles are included in a model of reading it helps us to understand how a reader operates and how teaching can be designed to address the various roles.

The code-breaker role

When taking on the role of **code-breaker**, the reader is concerned with the basic decoding of the visual information of the text. In this role she gives attention to letter–sound correspondences, sentences, paragraphs, grammatical information, punctuation, and word meanings. It is largely a word recognition role although it extends to understanding book conventions and concepts about print, such as paragraph layout. In the code-breaker role the reader uses phonological-graphological, grammatical, and semantic information to decode the text.

The text-participant role

In the **text-participant** role the reader is concerned with the overall meaning of the text, in particular what the text is saying in the context of the reader's own knowledge about the topic. Her primary concern in this role is to access the literal and inferential meanings of the text and understand how the text structure helps to find that meaning. The **literal meaning** is the 'plain sense' of the writing, often called 'reading the lines'. The **inferential meaning** is the inferred or associated meaning or 'reading between the lines'.

The text-user role

In the **text-user** role the reader considers how the text can be used to suit his purposes in the present social situation. This role prompts him to take some action, to interact with others regarding the text, and to participate in events in which the text plays a part, such as acting in a play after reading it or making a purchase in a shop after reading the information about a product. In this role a reader may use the text for a range of purposes such as enjoyment, finding information, purchasing something, engaging in spoken interaction, or participating in computer activities such as the Internet.

The text-analyst role

The **text-analyst** role is concerned with the underlying way the text positions the reader in terms of what the text might be trying to do to him, what line is being taken on the subject, and what the writer's point of view might be. In this role he reads critically by considering the author's opinion and the purpose of the text, compares different viewpoints, discusses points of agreement and disagreement, constructs alternative positions, and understands how the text structures portray, for example, different social groups or scientific positions. In the text-analyst role the reader detects propaganda and bias and weighs arguments—in essence, he thinks critically. This type of reading involves making a judgment about a text and could be called 'reading beyond the lines' or evaluating the text.

Code-breaker	Text-participant
How do I crack the code in this text?	What is this text saying to me?
Text-user	Text-analyst
In what ways can I use this text now?	What is this text trying to do to me?

The basic strategies of reading

Good readers have good strategies which allow them to read effectively. A major difference between good and poor readers—and, in some ways, beginning readers—is that good readers have efficient strategies and poor readers do not.

Strategies provide an overall plan to gain meaning from text. Often termed **metacognition**, these strategies include scanning the text, sampling, predicting, confirming, understanding, and correcting errors in meaning as they occur.

Strategies develop with age and experience, are important for effective reading, and must be taught. They might also include rereading parts of a text, changing reading speed, and questioning oneself during reading. A useful diagram that illustrates the basic operation of this **metacognitive** technique in reading is shown below in Fig. 3.4.

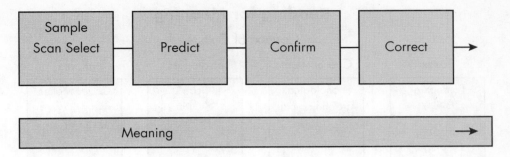

Fig. 3.4 The basic strategies of reading

The first strategy is to *sample* the text. To do this the reader *scans* it to obtain a quick overview of what it might contain, such as page layout, headings, or paragraph lengths. Then significant aspects of the writing are *selected* that will lead the reader to obtaining meaning.

Next, the reader uses the various cue systems to *predict* what the meaning will be, making use of phonological-graphological, grammatical, and semantic information. Finally, the reader *confirms* the meaning that has been gained and proceeds. If meaning has been lost the reader *corrects*, using the final strategy. This is done by going back along the line or up the page to find where the error occurred. In correcting, the reader searches for more information and often compares one source of information with another.

These global strategies illustrate that reading is very much a thinking process. Good readers are good and flexible thinkers and they use an array of available information to arrive at meaning.

Viewing the reading model

Reading, then, is essentially an interactive cognitive task in which the reader constructs meaning. In essence, good readers have the correct bases to read well. These include perceptual ability, language ability, and cognitive ability. They must make effective use of the cue systems, which rely on graphological and phonological, grammatical, and semantic information. And they must use reading strategies effectively. These include the ability to sample, scan, select, predict, confirm, correct. In this way they read for meaning, as shown in Fig. 3.5.

No diagramatic models are perfect, and this one has some limitations in that it appears to present a linear representation of the act of reading. In practice, all of the facets represented below operate simultaneously or in a coordinated way. The model shows, nevertheless, what the facets are, how they are all essential in the process of reading, and how they can be applied to teaching.

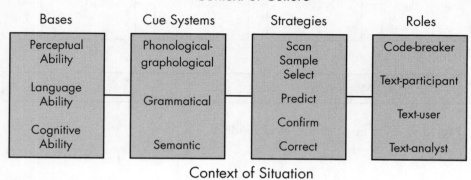

Reading for Meaning

Context of Culture

Fig. 3.5 A model of reading

SUMMARY

Reading requires the use of a number of cue systems: phonological-graphological, grammatical, and semantic. The concept of reading roles is also important: code-breaker, text-participant, text-user, and text-analyst. Good strategies promote effective reading. A model can be developed to describe the reading process.

Tasks

Discussion

1. The reading model Fig. 3.5 attempts to show how reading operates in terms of necessary bases, the cue systems, and strategies available, and the various roles readers take in certain situations. Consider:

(a) how a reader might use phonological-graphological, grammatical, and semantic cues in the code-breaker role while reading the following:

HOT

It is hot.
Sam is hot.
Dad is hot.
Mum is hot.
The cat is hot.
Sal is not.

(b) how a reader who was an environmentalist would use semantic cues in the text-analyst role if he were reading a piece about logging native forests.

2. What grammatical knowledge would you need to apply in order to work out the words that complete the following passage? (This is a cloze passage—see page 120.)

Thunderclouds

Thunderclouds _____made up _____three things: air, water, and ice crystals.

Inside a _____ there _____violent movements of air currents.

3. Select a children's book. Write down examples of questions you might ask a student to help her take on each of the four roles of the reader.

4. Discuss how any aspects of the model of reading described in this chapter could help you if you were teaching a child to read.

Activities

1. More than half of the visual information has been removed from this sentence. See if you can read it. In what way is this an example of redundancy in English orthography?

Reading is important to every child.

2. Practise increasing your own reading speed by thinking more effectively. Try reading the opening sentence only of each paragraph of a page of print. This will make you take bigger *jumps* as you read. It is a good skimming technique. See if you can get the gist of the passage by reading this way.

Chapter 4
The Child Before School:
The Beginning of Literacy

> **Focus**
> The importance of preschool literacy experiences is considered. The oral language of the child is shown to be of vital importance in later literacy learning.

Learning to read

Children begin moving along the road to literacy before they come to school. They begin the journey on the day they are born, from the first time they hear a human voice. Talk leads them into making a range of meanings with spoken language and it leads them into written words and into books.

As Meek (1988) points out, 'Most children come to school with a crop of reading-like behaviours and an awareness of what they expect reading to be like'. They have come into contact with multiple literacy experiences: road signs, advertisements on television, writing on food packages, and all the mysterious letters, journals, newspapers, and books that adults read as well as those electronic images that appear on computer screens. They have already discovered writing and have made, in most cases, their early attempts at it. If they have entered the world of literacy through adults who are interested in their development, they are a further step along the way.

To help them, young children have oral language, and when they come to school they are surprisingly sophisticated speaker-listeners: they can satisfy their own communication needs through their speech; they can use a wide variety of syntactic rules with increasing accuracy; they can understand and produce most of the important sound distinctions; and they can effectively handle the grammar of their language without explicit knowledge of how it works. This impressive array of language abilities is all the more significant if we bear in mind that it has been achieved without formal teaching. The way has been paved for acquiring literacy at school under the guidance of teachers who introduce explicit instruction in reading and writing.

Young children rely heavily on speech for communication. They share their experiences through talk with those around them. As well, parents, grandparents, and other carers introduce children to rhymes that are tiny stories in themselves, to language games, to songs, folk stories, and fables, and to books that have been written for children the world over. Indeed, young children live in a world of print and image, not only in the books that are read to them but in every social situation in which they find themselves: at home in the bedroom, living room, and kitchen; on the train; in the car; at the supermarket; watching television; looking at a computer screen; going to the beach; at the preschool or daycare centre; at a party—'public print', as Meek (1982) calls it, is part of the child's world of print 'and sooner or later he will notice it'. For young children these early experiences are important foundations on which the school can build. Print in the environment gives young children an awareness of how literacy is used in their community. This awareness is one of the most important things children can bring to school.

It is from books, nevertheless, that children gain the richest and most rewarding literacy experience. Books provide 'the essential link between learning to talk and learning to read, because they are a special kind of play with language that separates it from speech. The simplest answer to the question "How does a child come to know how print works?" is by being read a story' (Meek 1982: 38–9). As Clay (1991) points out, 'the most valuable preschool preparation for school learning is to love books and to know that there is a world of interesting ideas in them'.

Much-quoted studies by Durkin (1966) and Clark (1976) illustrate through research the importance of early exposure to books in the literacy development of the child. Clark, working with an experimental group of young fluent readers—children who came to school able to read—found that her subjects had certain factors in common: one was the early involvement of the parents and other interested adults in the child's progress. She did not find that the children's parents were all of a socially privileged group; on the contrary, some had left school early and had had no further training. What they had in common was time to talk with their children, listen to them, read to them, and encourage an interest in books.

The other factor was the important role played by the local library in catering for and stimulating the interests of the children. Accessibility of different types of reading material was common to the group. These parents did not set out to teach their children to read. Their role was sensitising the children to the features of book language, such as conventional openings to stories ('Once upon a time'). This, Clark concludes, is probably a more valuable preparation for school than attempting to teach the child phonics or a basic sight vocabulary.

Not all children come to school with a rich book experience behind them. It is the task of the teacher to build on the child's other early literacy experiences and to supply a rich diet of books in classroom and library.

The central role of literature is well documented in current publications (Beard 1998), the International Reading Association position statement (1998), and in ongoing curriculum development in Australia. The importance of literature in the achievement of literacy is seen by the authors of this book as so important that it warrants a special section of the text.

All those who deal with small children before school must capitalise on knowledge of the language development of children. We need to be aware that the period from birth to five years is the fastest language-learning time in a child's life. Vocabulary growth alone illustrates this: as a rough rule of thumb, a two-year-old controls about 200 words, a three-year-old about 1000, and a four-year-old about 2000. An average adult's vocabulary is between 4000 and 5000 words. 'With language growth goes intellectual growth because the two are intertwined: the more sophisticated the language, the more sophisticated the thinking' (Winch and Poston-Anderson 1993: 5).

Fig. 4.1 Stages of speech and language development (Winch and Poston-Anderson 1993)

The vital role of the parent must be realised as home and school develop a partnership in the child's literacy development. The parent or other carer as listener, speaker, prompter, supplier of information, asker and answerer of questions, co-reader, and co-writer, are all important before and during schooling.

The important transition from preschool literacy to school itself must be transparently clear to parent and teacher alike. Children, through their early association with books and other forms of print, have become involved in what they see before them. This interaction with texts provides the untaught lessons that children have before school that help them to find out 'how the book works, how the story goes' (Meek 1988).

The early literacy experience

As discussed above, the earliest literacy experiences that children bring to school are associated with their encounters with public print and quest for meaning from books. They react to street signs, advertisements on television, labels in supermarkets, and other forms of writing they see all around them.

They also carry out a quest for meaning from books that are read to them. They know that books carry stories within them; they have heard the stories read and they have investigated them in their private interactions with books and the reading-like behaviour they exhibit when they retell or 'read' the story in bed at night, in a quiet corner during the day, or out loud to an interested adult who has time to listen. Rhymes and language play are also important. They add enjoyment and help to develop children's linguistic growth. Their own rhymes in play make the value of this form of language growth apparent.

These early literate experiences include an interpretation of the mysterious lines of print and the pictures that either reinforce the story or add another dimension to it. These lines of print are not there to be deciphered in a linguistic sense. Children, by and large, are not engaged in the business of phonic decoding to sound before they come to school. It is wrong to expect them to do so for two reasons. The first is that while they can indeed use the phonemes that carry meaning in their oral language as they speak or listen, they find it difficult to do so consciously. That is, they are not yet phonemically aware; they are unable to segment the phonemes in speech (see discussion above). An effective way to develop phonemic awareness in young children is to involve them in language games such as *I Spy*. In this example ('I spy with my little eye something beginning with "c"') it is better to make the onset sound rather than say the letter. Many interactive computer software packages capitalise on this principle.

The second reason is that children have only primitive concepts about print. Very young children will probably not know that it is print that carries much of the meaning in the picture book they have before them, that to read print one moves from left to right with a return sweep at the end of a line, that words are entities within themselves, and that letters represent sounds in an alphabetic system of writing. To ask very young children to decode print is to ask something essentially beyond them. It is infinitely better to engage children in the delight of having stories read and told and to capitalise on the early literacy experiences that are pleasurable and rewarding to them.

It is interesting to note that 'real' books, which carry stories through words and pictures, build up a knowledge, implicit though it might be, of the nature and variety of written discourse and the different ways that language lets a writer tell, and the many and different ways a reader reads (Meek 1988: 21).

It is often sadly the case that when children come to school and they encounter stilted linguistic reading texts, they find the business of reading both difficult and uninviting. Consider the following text as an example of such dull and lifeless prose:

> *Sam. Pam.*
> *Hello, I'm Sam. Hello, I'm Pam.*
> *Hello, I'm Sam. I am six. Hello, I'm Pam. I am six, too.*

In such an example 'the language reads like no language the child has heard spoken and bears little affinity to the richly rewarding stories which have come from libraries and other sources of literacy material' (Winch 1988: 6). As Halliday (1979: 42) points out:

> Some of the failure in reading and writing of which we are all so conscious nowadays has been due at least in part to children failing to make the conceptual leap which relates writing to speech, never co-ordinating the new behaviour with an ability they already possess, the ability to speak and listen. The new experience never clicks into place alongside the old.

The point is made again by Ferriero and Teberosky (1982), who argue that the text of contrived reading books may look like real sentences but they take away the learnt predictive approaches used by children because the words do not correspond to any real language they know. Children attempting to read with this material must forget all they know about home language, as if written language and the activity of reading had no relationship to real language functioning.

Real books require very young children to bring meaning and language to the pages, to draw on their past experience of stories, rhymes, characters, and, of course, words. These books allow children to build up the types of early reading experiences they need in their encounters with books and other reading material at school.

It should be noted that not every child has had a rich exposure to books written in English before coming to school. These children will have had experiences in other languages and exposure to print in different forms. It is important that positive action be taken by schools to use the different linguistic backgrounds of children and that they be cognisant of the different cultural context of the home. In this way a partnership in the children's literacy development can be established between home and school (Cairney 1997).

The role of the parent in early literacy
Early literacy with books

Reading to a child

The parents' role in literacy development is extremely important, as pointed out above. It is wise to start sharing stories with young children at a very early age. Babies recognise and respond to the sound of a parent's voice whether or not they understand the exact meaning of the words. When we consider that the child's language learning develops most rapidly during the first five years of life, a child is never too young to begin sharing stories.

Although books themselves are the major source of the stories young children meet, the oral tradition is very important, too. Many stories are passed on by word of mouth, so storytelling provides another source. Stories should be read and told to the young child. There are significant differences in the two forms. Consider the beginning of the story of *Little Red Riding Hood*, first as it was read and then as it was told.

READ	TOLD
Once upon a time there was a little girl and her name was Little Red Riding Hood. She lived with her Mother on the far side of the woods. (Reader points to the picture of Little Red Riding Hood in front of her cottage.)	Once there was a little girl who was very much like you, except that she had a red cape. Do you know what her name was? (child responds) Yes, that's right—Little Red Riding Hood.

READ	TOLD
One morning her mother said to her, 'Little Red Riding Hood, please take this basket of good things to eat to your Grandmother.'	One day her mother said to her, just like this,
	'Little Red Riding Hood, please take this basket of good things to eat to your Grandmother.'
'Yes, Mother, I will,' Little Red Riding Hood replied. (change of voice)	'Yes, Mum, I will,' she said. (change of voice, nod of head)
Immediately she put on her red cape and started through the woods. The day was bright and she skipped happily down the path …	What do you think was inside the basket? (child responds) Little Red Riding Hood started down the path through the woods. The birds sang like this (twitter). The sun shone brightly and Little Red Riding Hood was so happy that she sang a little tune (hum).

(Winch and Poston-Anderson 1993: 11)

You will notice that when the story is read, the reader reads the words exactly as they are written. It is formal book language with little interruption and little dramatic action to support the text. Vocal expression is very prominent, however, and the child is encouraged to follow the pictures and the print as the story is read.

When the story is told without the book, the language is much less formal and the teller actively involves the child. There are frequent interruptions to allow for questions and replies; sound effects are added, and the speaker is free to dramatise the characters and the situation, using different voices, facial expressions, and body movements.

A modified approach that allows more interaction between the reader and the child can also be used. In this way the types of interruption that the straight reading of the text excludes may be introduced at different times to involve the child in the story:

'… please take this basket of good things to eat to your grandmother.'
What do you think might be in this basket?
'The day was bright and she skipped happily down the path …'
What sounds might Little Red Riding Hood have heard?

Interactive reading of this type, which can include discussion about the illustrations as well as the story, increases readers' understanding of the book and lets them take on the reader role of text-participant as they participate in constructing meaning from the text.

The best books

The way to provide the best experience for a child is to find the best stories and the best books. Here are some guidelines. If you are looking for books to read, select those with appealing illustrations. Young children like clear, uncluttered illustrations like those found in the books of Dick Bruna, John Burningham, and Pamela Allen, but they like other forms of illustration too. Find out which books appeal to the child.

Here are some further things to consider: Does the story read well? Is the language clear and well suited to a child of that age? Does the plot hold together and move at a lively pace? Are the characters interesting? Do they have special characteristics that make them memorable? Does the story stimulate the imagination. And, probably most important of all, do you and the child want to read the book together? If you are reading a factual book, consider answers to these questions. Is the language clear and suitable to the child's linguistic level? Do the illustrations support the text? Is the book a good example of a particular factual genre?

It is important to remember that a book, whatever else its attributes, must bring light to a child's eye. That is, it must provide enjoyment and satisfaction to a young reader (Winch 1991). There is another useful guideline: good books stand up well to rereading. They are often requested by children, to be read again and again.

The best stories to tell

These are usually the old favourites like *The Three Bears*, *The Billy Goats Gruff*, and *The Little Red Hen*. These stories seem to be just right for telling. This is not surprising, considering that they were more often than not passed down by word of mouth. This accounts for the fact that there are so many versions of each tale. A teller gave his or her special twist to the story depending on the audience, the occasion, and the storyteller's mood.

Good stories for telling can be found in classic collections such as *The Fairy Tale Treasury* by Raymond Briggs, but there are many good collections full of suitable stories in bookstores and libraries. It is important to include stories that relate to a child's social and cultural background.

Children whose first language is not English will hear stories that come from the culture and language of the country concerned. Aboriginal and Torres Strait children will hear dreaming stories told, in English or, often, in their native tongue.

When choosing stories, remember that a story must hold the child's attention through its plot, its characters, its action, and its humour. It must allow the child to participate through predictable words, phrases, and longer refrains.

Reading and writing

The child's early development in writing is closely intertwined with development in reading; the two are never really apart. Early motor skills come into play as the child puts pencil to paper in response to stories, heard and told. (See Part II.)

Early literacy in the community

Modern children meet print in their early years in a wide variety of ways, and parents and carers can take advantage of print exposure to prepare children for reading and writing at school. These experiences are invaluable if children are to develop necessary understandings about what literacy is and how it is used in the community in which they live.

When shopping in the local street or in a big store, such as a supermarket, children can have their attention drawn to advertisements on shop signs and labels on items of food and clothing. The child will easily predict the meaning of a word or phrase and will begin to associate the letters of the word with the meaning. Simple questions about the beginning sound of a word, or simply what it says, are examples of very valuable uses that can be made of public print.

In the kitchen at home, young children can share in the experience of preparing food and have their attention drawn to the labels on cans and bottles. Recipes can be read aloud with the child looking on, and instructions on and relating to appliances can be read aloud.

The arrival of the mail can be another literacy experience. Children will enjoy working out who wrote a letter, to whom it is addressed, and what its contents say. Junk mail has its place too. Young children become skilful at working out the gimmicks that advertisers use. Birthday and other greeting cards fill young children with delight as these examples of print and picture have a personal dimension.

The television program and the television guide are important to young children, and parents can draw their attention to the information this material contains. Television watching takes up a significant part of the day for many young children. Parents should direct them to programs that are introductions to literacy in themselves, e.g. *Sesame Street* and *Playschool*.

Instructional technology is having an increasing influence on people's lives, and young children are eager to have 'a turn on the computer' whenever they have the chance. Some computer games have literacy offshoots, and instructional software for children of all ages is appearing on the market. Because of the interactional features of the software programs, activities suited to early literacy are becoming more prevalent. Examples of possible exercises featuring onset sounds and rhyming words are shown in the following figures.

In Fig. 4.2(a) the child must move the cursor to the items and click the pictures that start with the sound made by C. This exercise depends on both phonemic awareness and the graphophonic skill of knowing that 'c' stands for the sound /k/ in the two relevant examples. In Fig. 4.2(b) the child must click the pictures that represent words rhyming with 'hat' in the box. The young child does not need to read the word to do the exercise correctly, although the caption is presented as an additional reference.

Technological change and the availability of computers at home and in school are both increasing rapidly.

Fig. 4.2 Interactional software exercises

SUMMARY

Children have made significant steps towards literacy before they come to school. Of particular importance is a close involvement with a caring adult, oral language, stories told and read to the child, and an awareness of print in the environment and the way literacy is used in his or her community.

Carlos is three and about to go to bed. His father tells him that when he is ready—teeth cleaned, face washed, and suitable goodnights made to Gran and Mum—he will read him a story. Carlos says he would like to hear a story in bed and he would like to select his own book. He selects *Bertie and the Bear* by Pamela Allen. 'You've had this story before', his dad said. Carlos insisted that he have it again. And he did.

Carlos watched as his father opened the book and began to read. He managed to get in 'There's Bertie' as his father paused at the title page. Carlos loved the noisy lines and repeated them, pointing to the repetitions in the speech bubbles or the lines in the text ('Shoo, shooo you monster YOU!'). He liked the noises of the trumpet, the gong, the drum, the horn and the flute, especially, and the yip, yip, yip … of the little dog. The big word IN-CRED-IBLE was a favourite. He kept saying it after his father had turned the page.

Carlos' father slowed the reading down when the bear 'stopped quite still, turned right around, and said, "All this for me? Thank you …" and bowed very low'.

When the bear stood on his head and turned a few cartwheels and danced, Carlos burst into roars of laughter. He pointed to the pictures again and again, laughing more and more. He liked the resolution of the plot and the happy ending.

'Time for sleep now', said Carlos' father.

'Please can I read the book myself', asked Carlos.

'Just for a while.'

Carlos 'read' the book by himself, making up the story as he went, while, surprisingly, repeating some whole lines accurately. He did this for some time until …

'Lights off now, Carlos. Good night!'

Tasks

 Discussion

It is a good idea to have a copy of *Bertie and the Bear* available or read the text before carrying out these activities.

Carlos chose Pamela Allen's **Bertie and the Bear**, the Children's Book Council Picture Book of the Year, 1984. Is it a good thing to have a child share a quality book with an adult, rather than a lesser text that may be a favourite of the child? Winch (1991) argues that it is not if the quality book does not bring light to the child's eye!

1. Here are some questions:
   - What is the advantage of reading the same book to a child, again and again, if the child wishes you to do so? What might be some disadvantages?
   - If you are reading a book to a child consider the importance of mentioning matters such as the information on the cover, the name of the author, the dedication (For Jessie Mary Allen), and the imprint page.
   - Carlos joined in with the reading of the book, particularly the 'noisy' parts. What advantages are there in having a child do this?

· Although Carlos is obviously carried away by the sheer vitality of the text (and the pictures), would it have been of value to have included some questions to develop his concepts about print? (Where do I start to read? What words say 'Shoo, shooo you monster, YOU!'? Where is that said again?) What other concepts about print and about books generally could be included? What ways could Carlos' phonemic awareness have been developed, using this book? (Think of the onomatopoeic words throughout the text such as BLAH! BLAH, TOOT-TOOT, YIP, YIP.)

· The word *incredible* is popular with Carlos. What would be some ways you might capitalise on his interest in this word? (Think of word meaning, the way the word is said, other uses of the word.)

· What are some things Carlos' spontaneous laughter tell us about reading books to children? (Consider enjoyment of reading, development of sense of humour, involvement with the story.)

· The pictures highlight the incongruity and delightful absurdity of the text. It also shows clearly where the crisis ends and the bear changes his attitude to Bertie. What features of the pictures illustrate the change in the bear? (Think of his expression, teeth, eyes, among other things.)

· Reading and writing are 'social things to do in any community where written language is part of our social function as human beings' (Meek 1988:4). What social functions did Carlos experience? (Think of the whole scene from the beginning to the end and how reading was part of it.)

· Carlos wanted to read the book by himself. What 'private lessons' would he experience? What are some things he might learn about the way a story goes?

· What does Carlos know about reading? What parts of the reading process can he already do? How do you know?

2. And some broader issues:

· Consider the case made for the importance of a caring, listening adult and of stories read and told for the preschool child on the road to literacy.

· What experiences with literacy in the community are important for young children?

· Consider how you would provide for a child with a disability (e.g. hearing or seeing). Read about Cushla, the multiply disabled granddaughter of Dorothy Butler, in *Cushla and Her Books* (1979).

· Consider how the information in this chapter might influence the way reading is taught during the early years of school. In particular, give attention to the children's language knowledge and book experience.

· Consider the choice of books for children from language backgrounds other than English. How would such a choice be made?

Activities

1. Sharing a book with a child
   - Select a well-known and popular children's picture book such as *Rosie's Walk* by Pat Hutchins. Make sure that you are familiar with the book. Read the story to yourself and look carefully at the illustrations, which form a vital part of the story. Rehearse the reading and vary your voice and facial expressions.
   - Now, talk to the child about the book before you start reading: the cover and its illustrations, the writing on it. What does the writing mean? What might this book be about?
   - Next, put into practice what you have rehearsed. Read the book to the child at a suitable pace. Slow down to enjoy the pictures. Allow time for the child to comment on what is happening, on what it all means. Make sure that the reading is a happy experience for you both. If your listener wants to become a 'reader', allow the child to do so. This reading-like behaviour is valuable as it allows the child to deal with story meaning in a different way. Children often like to engage in this activity alone and should not be pressured to perform in front of you.
   - Finally, record your responses to your experience. How did you gauge your performance? What did you do well? What could you have done better? What did you observe about the child's reactions?

2. Telling a story
   - Select a story to tell to a child. Practise the story and memorise its main sequences. It does not have to be perfect; just remember how the parts fit together. Practise using your voice: pause, volume, pitch, rate; your facial expressions; your gestures. Use props if they are appropriate. They can bring life to a story. These could include parts of costumes, musical instruments, pieces of furniture.
   - Now, tell your story and record your responses to the experience. Ask yourself the same questions as above: How did you gauge your performance? ...

3. Literacy in everyday activities
   - Plan an activity with a young child, such as shopping, cooking, or making a greeting card. Consider what literacy learning you can insert into the experience. Provide the child with opportunities to tell and show you what she has learnt about literacy.

Chapter 5
Learning to Read:
The Early School Years

THE EMERGENT READER:
AN EXAMPLE WITH SHARED READING

> **Focus**
> A particular example of teaching the emergent reader is considered in this section. A shared book experience provides a window to the classroom during the first year of school. (See also Chapter 8, pages 127–8.)

Jenny is working with her class of emergent readers. They are in their first year of school. The students come from a variety of social and cultural backgrounds and have had a wide range of different experiences with books and with print in their communities. They all display the eagerness of young children starting school, particularly an eagerness to learn to read and write.

Jenny looks at the little group sitting on the mat before her. They are on the way to becoming literate, although some will need special help before the end of the year.

How will Jenny achieve this? What does she know that will direct her teaching? What practices will she adopt?

The background of theory

As a professional teacher of some years' standing, Jenny brings both knowledge and experience to her task. She knows first of all that there is no single approach that stands out as the one way to teach a child to read. Research has pointed this out. Jenny will base her teaching on what she knows about the theory of the reading process and the teaching of reading, backed up with experience. She is well aware of the importance of writing, both in sitting beside reading and as a support for reading itself. (See Chapters 11 and 12.) Her approach, whatever methods she uses, will allow her to tailor her teaching to the needs of individual children.

Using the reading model

Jenny is aware that both reading and writing operate in cultural and social context and is sensitive to the varying backgrounds of children in her class. The bases of reading—perceptual ability, language ability, cognitive ability—will vary also. There may be some children who have a visual or auditory disability requiring special attention; those children who have little or no English will require extra work to build up their oral skills in what is to them a second language. There may be some children who experience difficulties and will need extra help to enable them to achieve success in the reading program. And, there will be some who will be able to achieve at a higher level than the rest of the class.

Jenny is aware that early readers use the same cue systems as mature readers, but most children will need to experience systematic teaching before they use them effectively. In particular, Jenny will make sure that she teaches an understanding of sound–symbol relationships in writing along with the exposure to a variety of meaningful texts. That is, she will teach children how to use the phonological-graphological cue system along with grammatical and semantic cues. Put another way, she will include code-based instruction with context-based prediction, using sentence structure and knowledge of the subject that her young readers bring to print.

Early readers need to learn to become increasingly phonemically aware. They need to learn how the alphabetic system codes the language and how letters represent the sounds in words. In working with a range of carefully selected texts, Jenny will give systematic attention to the sounds of letters, the way they are written, and the relationship of the two. She will give attention to the immediate recognition of words in context, to the prediction of words and repeated sentence patterns, and to the overall meaning of texts.

There is also a great deal her students will need to learn about how books work: what part of the page we read, where we start, how print travels from left to right and top to bottom, how pages follow one another in sequence, and many other concepts about print and books in general.

In her balanced approach to teaching reading, Jenny will give a suitable weighting to all aspects of the reading model, varying her approach for each child as required.

Theory into practice: Shared Reading

One practical application of theory Jenny will use frequently in her class of emergent readers is Shared Reading (also called Modelled Reading). This will usually involve the whole class and will allow Jenny to provide her students with structured demonstrations of what skilled readers do when they read. In the following example, Jenny has chosen a big book, titled *Sal and Sam on the Farm*. It is part of the Go Book series, published by Blake Education. There is ample scope in this text for teaching about graphophonic, grammatical, and semantic cues, about the basic strategies of reading and the various roles of the reader.

The Shared Reading lesson

Before reading

Jenny has prepared her students for a Shared Reading of the text by building up their semantic knowledge about the topic—life on a farm. She knows that children will find the text easier to read if they can form mental images to relate to words on the page and the illustrations. She has taken the class to visit a farm owned by a relative of one of the children—a very special excursion. The children, many of whom had not seen farm animals before, are now full of the experience. Some of the class have drawn pictures and 'written' about their visit. Jenny has also read them Pat Hutchins' picture storybook ***Rosie's Walk***, which proved a great favourite.

The first reading of *Sal and Sam on the Farm* is mainly for overall meaning and enjoyment. Jenny begins with the whole text before looking at its parts. As she has decided to adopt the approach of 'masking' the print on this occasion—one of various introductory techniques she uses—Jenny is ready to introduce the book.

She wants to make sure that the students enjoy the first reading and respond to the book's meaning before dealing with its parts. She adopts the rule of thumb 'whole-part-whole', always coming back to the full text at the end of a reading. For instance she has made up sight word cards of commonly used vocabulary found in the text. The words have been taken from the list of the most frequently used words conveniently provided by the authors on the inside back cover of the book. The words are then placed in sentences written on the board to show their use in context. Then the book is read again.

Introducing the book

Jenny sits her class on the big mat in front of her and holds the big book on an easel so all the children can see. She points to the front cover, with its bright, full-colour artwork, and asks the children what they think the book might be about. As the farm visit is fresh in their minds, the class is quick to point out that the book is obviously about a farm—just like the one they visited last week.

She then asks what the title of the book might be and where the title is on the page. Some children can read the title and there is talk about the children on the cover and their names. Jenny points to the names of the authors and the illustrator. There is discussion as to their role in the creation of the book.

The children then turn their attention to the title page and the fierce bull chasing Sal and Sam. Will this book be about a visit like the class's visit or will there be something else? Some predictions are made regarding the story line. It might be an adventure story. It might contain something scary.

Reading the text

The class is then led through the text with the print masked and asked to predict the story from the illustrations. Who is that man on page 3? What are the children doing on page 4? Where are they going on page 8? What might Grandad be telling them on page 9? What happens when the children wander off on pages 11 and 12? What might be happening on page 16?

They fed the hens.
Cluck! Cluck!

They fed the ducks.
Quack! Quack!

They fed the pigs.
Oink! Oink!

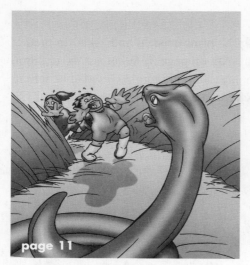

The masking paper is then removed from the text, page by page, and the story read to the children. Jenny takes special care to discuss the characters and the story line, allowing the children to predict what might be happening next and to confirm or revise the predictions they have made earlier. The last page is particularly interesting because Sal and Sam have not obeyed Grandpa and their faces tell a story that goes beyond the text, allowing the children to infer what the two characters are thinking.

Reading strategies: some examples

Jenny demonstrates the prediction strategy of gaining significant reading cues from the illustrations in the book. She uses page 4 as an example and asks the children the question 'What did Sal and Sam do on Grandpa's farm?' while pointing to the pictures on the page, one at a time. The children are quick to respond with 'They fed the hens', 'They fed the ducks', and so on.

She is then able to move quickly to the text on the page and link the text to the picture in each case. The important idea about print, that the words themselves tell the story, is reinforced in the children's minds. The illustrations are there to assist prediction and the actual reading of the text.

They fed the hens.
Cluck! Cluck!

They fed the ducks.
Quack! Quack!

They fed the pigs.
Oink! Oink!

The children are then directed to the words in bold type. What might these words say? Why are they in bold type? What are the sounds that the animals made? Point to the words that tell us what sounds the pigs made. Make those sounds yourselves.

Grammatical knowledge
Focus is placed on the use of the past tense in narrative:

*They **fed** the … They **picked** the … They **collected** the …*

The class is asked to tell Jenny some other things the children did:

*They **went** for a ride … They **ran** across … They **shouted** …*

Word meaning
Words that are difficult or interesting are given special attention. *Bellowed* and *charged* are discussed and drama is used to demonstrate these words. Synonyms for the words are suggested as alternatives.

Sight words
High-frequency sight words are given special attention. Words such as *said*, *the*, and *was* are held up on flash cards and then found in the text. They are then read in context. Sight word games are played with the flash cards.

Letter–sound knowledge
Initial sounds that are frequently used in the text, such as *s* as in *Sal*, *Sam*, *said*, *snake*, are emphasised. What sound does this letter make? Find me another word that starts with the 's' sound. Does anyone's name start with 's'? What letter makes the 's' sound?

Punctuation
Full stops are given focus on a browse through the text. Why are they there? What purpose do speech marks serve? What is happening each time speech marks appear?

Literal and inferential meaning

Jenny places emphasis on the literal meaning of the text (reading the lines) in the first part of the book. That is, what Sal and Sam actually do. The inferential meaning (reading between the lines) is raised in the later pages, particularly at the end when Sal and Sam are asked if they have been good. What are they thinking? What might they say? Jenny's class is very interested in the moral dimension of the story, and this is explored. Would the children tell Grandpa what they had done? Should they have wandered off? What happens when children disobey their parents or grandparents?

Jenny places emphasis on the four roles of the reader as she proceeds with her teaching: the code-breaker role (letter–sound knowledge, sight words, punctuation) in which her students are decoding the visual information of the text; the text-participant role (literal and inferential meaning) in which her students are involved in finding out the meaning of the text; the text-user role (what knowing about a farm means to me) in which students apply the text to their own situation; and the text-analyst role (what is this author trying to tell me about responsible behaviour?) in which the students work out what the text is doing to them—finding out the underlying assumptions in the text relating to the author's intention.

Rereading the text

Jenny rereads the text with her class. All the children are able to participate in making the animal sounds and reading the simple sentences, which contain repetitive structures: *They picked the apples. They picked the oranges. They picked the peas.* The dramatic sections are very popular and the class joins in to read them: *The big bull bellowed and charged.* **Roar!**

In subsequent readings of this text later in the same week, Jenny takes the opportunity to focus on a number of teaching points that her assessment shows needed further attention.

After the reading experience

Jenny uses the big book as a springboard into a range of varied activities for the children. These include making a language experience book with the class. It is built up by the teacher and the children and written by Jenny. The resultant 'story' is written on sheets of butcher's paper and later illustrated by the class (see Chapter 13).

As the big book is supported by ten small books about Sal and Sam (see over page), also published by Blake Education, Jenny is able to introduce these publications for Guided Reading with some groups in the class. The ten books are pitched at the emergent reading level and are suitable for instructional reading during the literacy session (see Chapter 8). During Guided Reading Jenny reinforces the teaching points on which she has focused, including specific letters, the full stop, and common sight words.

Jenny's students are reminded of the various skills they have learnt in their lesson and are told to look out for examples of these in the Guided Reading lesson they will be having at a later time. Sight words, examples of the 's' sound, and the past tense of verbs are noted.

The Sal and Sam Set

Assessment and Shared Reading

Jenny has developed an approach to independent assessment of each student in her class. She has placed focus on the outcomes and indicators in her state syllabus and has drawn up an independent profile in a reading portfolio for each student. She monitors the reading development of individuals by observation in the Shared Reading lesson, makes judgments, and places checks against indicators as children achieve them. This is done on a weekly basis (see Chapter 15).

For instance, indicators relating to a desired outcome concerned with reading and viewing texts for Shared Reading may include

- enjoys Shared Reading
- participates in Shared Reading lessons in familiar and imaginary topics
- recognises words in Shared Reading
- uses illustrations to assist reading
- reads text of a big book largely from memory.

SUMMARY

Using the reading model with children beginning school requires knowledge and imagination. Aspects of the model are discussed in the context of teaching practice and a shared book experience is explored with a class of emergent readers. An example is used in which a teacher is working with a class of children who are in their first year of school. Details of one approach are given.

TASKS

Discussion

1. Consider ways you might involve children who have oral language differences in a shared book experience. How would you maximise the benefits these children may gain? Consider having them say the word or words in their own language, giving them additional one-to-one assistance in Guided Reading ... and so on.

2. Discuss ways the progress of children could be monitored in a Shared Reading lesson. Build on what Jenny has done. Think of running records when the children begin to read, parental involvement, and teacher reports on progress.

Activities

1. Prepare a set of lesson notes for a Shared Reading lesson. Follow the sequence used in this chapter and add Shared Reading activities of your own.

2. Present your lesson to a class, group, or a single child. Write a comment on your lesson. Include ways you might improve the presentation.

THE DEVELOPING READER: AN EXAMPLE WITH GUIDED READING

> Focus
>
> In order to turn theory into practice, the technique of Guided Reading is illustrated by an actual lesson with a class in the second year of school. (See also Chapter 8, pages 128–9.)

1G is working busily during the literacy session. The class has now broken up into groups. John, the class teacher, is about to take Group 2 for Guided Reading. They are all approximately at the same reading level. Other groups are reading independently, reading to parent helpers, or engaged in literacy activities based on the shared text they have just read together.

After a year at school, these children are beginning to use a variety of strategies for processing text. Most can read simple texts of short duration containing two or three sentences per page; all students need to extend their reading skills with more sophisticated use of the cue systems and become more conversant with the four roles of the reader.

John has multiple copies of the book he has planned to use with Group 2. It is *Danny Dolphin's Nose*, one of a series of eight books about Danny the dolphin, and is pitched at a level that will allow the group to read between 90 and 95 per cent of the words in the text correctly. The book has been graded by the authors, but John has his own set of criteria that he applies to all books used in his classroom and he matches his students to their reading texts with care.

The Guided Reading session

Before reading

John makes sure that the rest of the class is working purposefully before he begins work with Group 2. The separate copies of *Danny Dolphin's Nose* are spread out on the desks in the group reading corner. John has a Guided Reading record sheet ready to record the progress of each child in the group.

Introducing the book

John lets the students 'warm up' before reading the new text by reading out aloud a text that they have already mastered. He then turns his attention to the new book.

He discusses the front cover, the title, the title page, the names of the authors, the name of the illustrator, and the Go Books logo that appears first on the top left-hand corner of the front cover.

John then discusses the topic at first generally to activate the students' semantic knowledge and build on what they already know. Dolphins are very popular with the children, as many have seen them in the ocean and in marine parks. The discussion is spirited. Talk turns to the specific title. Why Danny Dolphin's nose? Is it really a nose like their noses? What is its function? Is this nose something special? This 'mini-brainstorming' session builds up the information that the students bring to print. They develop a rich schema to apply when they are actually reading the book.

Next, the talk is about the type of text this book might be. Is it a story, a narrative? Is it a factual text? If it is a factual text, what type of factual text? They think it is a factual description, a book that describes Danny, a special dolphin. We'll see.

The students have their attention drawn to the word 'dolphin'. It is a difficult word. What is hard about it? Let's look at it in two parts, the way we would say it: *dol.phin*. What says /f/ in the second part? Do we know any other words that have a /f/ that is spelt *ph*? The students supply *phone* and *photo*. What are the big words that these words come from? Other words in the text that might cause difficulty are also discussed.

The students have now developed a range of knowledge that will provide a 'scaffold' or supporting context for the language and the meaning of the book they are about to read.

Reading the book

John tells the students to turn to the title page and asks them to read it with him.

Danny Dolphin's Nose

Gordon Winch & Gregory Blaxell
Illustrated by Luke Jurevicius

What is that hard word we looked at? What were the hard letters? What did they say? Why is that apostrophe there? Let's all read the title again. What is on the title page that wasn't on the cover? I wonder why that bottle is there. We'll come back to it later.

John asks the students to turn to the next page and selects a student to read.

Danny Dolphin's mouth
can open wide.

2

When the student needs 'nose' for 'mouth' John prompts her by saying, I know 'nose' makes sense here, but does it look right and sound right? Look at the first letter. The student reads on and self-corrects after picking up the meaning in context and confirming it graphophonically. She is also assisted by the pictures.

John monitors the reading of all students in the group. He keeps a record for each student on the Guided Reading record sheet and makes notes to assist him or her in future teaching sessions. The record sheet allows him to focus on specific indicators relating to desired outcomes in his state syllabus. This record sheet is included in each student's portfolio. For instance, the book *Danny Dolphin's Nose* has particular relevance to *drawing on an increasing range of skills and strategies when reading and comprehending texts.*

Specific Indicators include the following:
- draws on letter–sound relationship when reading unknown words
- uses different parts of a text to access information, e.g. title page
- reads a variety of literary and factual texts
- attempts to self-correct when meaning is disrupted
- identifies sentences in written text.

Each student is then given an opportunity to read in turn, a double-page spread at a time. As each student reads, John prompts with questions to help the student draw on what he or she knows in order to solve unknown words. At the end, John talks with the group about relevant aspects of the text: the meaning of the pages, what the illustrations tell the reader, and what might come next. To build up fluency and expression, he reads some of the pages himself, running his finger under the line of print. He involves the whole group also by having them read some parts of the book in unison, with emphasis on fluency and phrasing.

The students are pleased that they have predicted correctly and that the book is a factual description. One of them has predicted correctly that Danny is indeed a bottlenose dolphin and informs the group in no uncertain terms.

Danny is a bottlenose dolphin.

12

Working with the text
Overcoming difficulties

When a student has trouble with a word, John quickly identifies which cue system is causing difficulty. Is it phonological-graphological, grammatical, or semantic? As an example, does the student's problem stem from the fact that he or she cannot decode the printed letters with the correct sound–symbol relationships? Is the student failing to provide a word that fits the grammar of the sentence? Does the student provide a word that just does not make sense?

If the student is having phonological-graphological difficulty (e.g. the word the student reads does not match the sounds that the letters on the page represent), she is told to look carefully at the word and questions like these are asked: What letters do you see? What sound does the first letter in the word make? What might the rest of the word say? Can you see any letter patterns in the word to help you? (morphemes *bottle/nose*; syllables *dol.phin*; onset and rime *m-outh*). Say the letters in the word. Say the sounds they make.

John says the sounds with the student and helps her to blend them to get the correct pronunciation of the word. The word is constantly tested in context to see that the meaning of the text is maintained. For example, a reading of 'mouth' as 'nose' is entirely inappropriate in the context of the following: *Danny Dolphin's* **mouth** *can open wide. It has tiny teeth in it.*

If the student is making mistakes of a grammatical nature and losing meaning as a result, John asks the student such questions as: Does that seem right? Is that what someone would really say? Does that word really fit into the sentence? For example, if a student reads 'cat' for 'catch' in the sentence on page 5, *He can* **catch** *little fish with his mouth,* John asks the questions above and finally, Would we say 'cat' then?

Semantically, if a student reads a word that fits the sentence grammatically but does not make sense in that context, such as *It can catch a* **wing** for *It can catch a* **ring** John asks: Does that make sense? Would Danny really catch a wing? Look at the picture. What is Danny really catching?

John is careful to make sure that the students in the Guided Reading group are able to engage in the various roles of the reader in gaining understanding of the text. He asks literal questions such as 'What things could Danny do with his mouth?' He asks inferential questions such as 'Why do you think Danny is called

It looks like
the neck of a bottle.

11

a bottlenose dolphin?' (the text-participant role, which is concerned with the meaning of the text). He asks questions relating to the purpose of the text, such as: Since we have decided that this book is a factual description, what did we learn about Danny and about dolphins? What information did we gain? (text-user role). He asks questions relating to the author's purpose in starting out writing about Danny's mouth and then bringing in his nose. Did the author have any particular reason for saying that Danny's nose looked like the neck of a bottle and how did the illustration on page 11 help us to understand the last page, 'Danny is a bottlenose dolphin'? (the text-analyst role, which works out what the writer wants the reader to understand or feel).

After the Guided Reading session

The students in the group then form pairs and reread the text to each other. They are later allowed to take it home to read to their parents.

John has prepared a number of activities to reinforce the teaching points of the lesson. These include sequencing sections of the text, which he has written onto cardboard strips; matching high-frequency words on cards and teaching the students to play matching games with them. There is also published material to support the text. As there are seven other books about Danny in the set, John flags the fact that the group will be meeting Danny again soon.

SUMMARY

A Guided Reading lesson is explored in this section. The class is in their second year of school and the children are able to work effectively in group situations, reading and writing independently. Aspects of the Guided Reading lesson are explained and the teacher's approach to the session is discussed in terms of practice before, during, and after reading. A particular text is used during the session.

Tasks

Discussion
1. Guided Reading is a particularly important part of reading instruction. Discuss why this is so.
2. If you are engaged in teaching a guided reading group, it is necessary to manage the remainder of the class effectively. Consider the best ways you might do this.

Activities
1. Prepare lesson notes for a Guided Reading lesson. Follow the sequence used in this chapter and add guided reading activities of your own.

2. Present your lesson to a group. Write a comment on your lesson. Include ways by which you might improve the presentation.

THE DEVELOPING READER: AN EXAMPLE WITH INDEPENDENT READING

> **Focus**
> This chapter provides information on how Independent Reading may operate in a classroom. Its importance is emphasised. (See also Chapter 8, pages 129–30.)

2D consists of children with a range of reading abilities. They are in their third year of school. Most can read independently at some level. C Group is about to engage in an Independent Reading session while Maria, their class teacher, is working with B Group on Guided Reading.

C Group goes to the class library and makes a selection from the books that are at the appropriate level. These are on the C Group shelf. Independent Reading begins.

The Independent Reading session

Before reading

Maria has explained to the children the routine they are to follow during Independent Reading. They know that it is a special time and that they must use their own initiative for most of the period. She has introduced the children to three or so books from the C Group shelf, and has explained what each one is about and the way the books are arranged on the shelf.

Choosing a book

Maria has explained to the children in the group the best ways they might find books that would interest them during the Independent Reading session. These include choosing three books that they might find interesting; looking at the cover, author's name, the title of each book, and reading the information on the back; reading the first page of the book to see if it is interesting and testing the difficulty of the book by applying a rule of thumb (more than five unknown words on a page means that the book is too hard). It is important that the children find books that interest them and they are encouraged to return books to the shelves until they find one that does.

Special attention must be given to children who are new to the technique or are having difficulty with reading alone, and Maria does this while the Guided

Reading group is assembling. Simple texts must be selected that will ensure success, and encouragement and help are given when necessary.

Keeping a record

Maria requires that each student keeps a record of his or her Independent Reading. She has prepared a special sheet for the purpose and maintains an overall class progress sheet herself.

Independent reading

The students are allowed time to read and record their progress. The Independent Reading session gives them the opportunity to practise and consolidate the skills they have learnt in Shared and Guided Reading. It is also a very pleasurable period, because they are not only demonstrating their skills but are also reading to follow their interests.

Maria uses the Independent Reading session effectively by taking other groups for Guided Reading. She walks around the classroom, sometimes checking the independent readers, working with Guided Reading groups or commenting on the work of another group who are writing about their reading experience. Two parents are assisting Maria during this literacy session. They are listening to children as they read and filling in a checklist of skills that Maria has prepared.

The Independent Reading session is a development of DEAR (drop everything and read) and USSR (uninterrupted sustained silent reading). It is an integral part of the daily literacy session in Maria's class.

After reading

Maria has introduced various 'after Independent Reading' practices. These include dividing the students into groups of twos and threes and having each student tell the others something interesting from the book he or she has read; describing one of the characters from a narrative text; relating something of importance from a factual text; making a comment (with demonstration) on the illustrations in the book; offering an opinion of the author's purpose in writing the book; making a comment on the author of the book or series, where relevant; providing or a short reading from a part of the book.

Follow-up

Because the students spend most of their time working independently during this form of reading, Maria is careful to spend some time each week talking to each student about the books he or she has read. She uses the information to assist her in later work with the students in Guided Reading and to help her decide whether there is a need to change the difficulty or type of books used in Independent Reading, both in class and at home.

The variety and scope of books available for children in the class library must be constantly monitored, and Maria adds new titles as well as removing others every week. She consults the children about the selection and makes a complete change of books at the end of term or when the class is involved in a particular theme or unit of work.

This is an interesting book.

Matching books to children

It is important that children have a range of books of various genres available to them. The books must be arranged to suit the various needs of children at a particular time. For the best results the books must be arranged in a number of predetermined levels according to the degree of difficulty. This process is known as grading or 'levelling'. (See Chapter 7 for further information on how to grade or 'level' books.)

Next, the books must be matched to individual children according to their special needs. Children then proceed from level to level of book difficulty as their reading skills develop. Naturally, books for Independent Reading at school or at home would be of a lower level of difficulty than

Engrossed in Independent Reading

those used for Shared or Guided Reading. Wille (1996) makes the important point that matching books to children should be only a part of a balanced literacy program and that children should also have many opportunities to choose from a wide range of ungraded texts. (See also Chapter 8 for a further discussion of book matching.)

SUMMARY

Independent reading is an important part of the reading program and takes place in every literacy session. It is the third of the essential three strategies: Shared (Modelled), Guided, and Independent Reading. Independent Reading requires carefully wrought practice; it also requires planning, and considerable time spent in organisation.

Tasks

 Discussion

1. Independent Reading provides students with the opportunity to practise and integrate the skills they have learnt in Guided Reading. It also provides pleasure. Consider ways you might encourage students to spend more time reading independently, both at school and at home.

2. A range of text-types should be made available for students during Independent Reading, depending on the reader's interest and ability. Discuss the range of text-types you would make available for a particular class.

 Activity

1. Obtain a selection of books from a source such as a school or public library and place them in order of difficulty. Now divide the books into six levels. Remember that these are not Reading Recovery levels, which are much finer in gradation of difficulty. (See also the activity in Chapter 7.)

2. Practise matching a book to a student for Independent Reading. Remember that if a student is making one or two errors in each twenty words, the book is probably at his or her instructional level and too hard for independent reading.

3. Begin compiling your own children's literature collection by visiting a good bookshop and selecting two or three books you particularly like. Add to your collection over time as you see new books that appeal to you. Build a poetry collection by obtaining one or two good anthologies of verse, collections from your favourite poets, and photocopies of poems you wish to use with classes. (See a good collection of recommended poetry texts such as in Winch and Poston-Anderson 1993. See also Part III of this book for many examples of quality children's literature texts.)

Chapter 6
Learning to Read: The Middle and Later Primary Years

READING IN YEARS 3 AND 4

> **Focus**
> Approaches to teaching reading in the middle primary years are discussed and specific examples of practice in Years 3–4 are given in the context of the Literacy Session in the middle primary classroom.

The background of theory

As we have seen, children in the early school years build on their knowledge of the world and of the language that they bring to school to develop the skills and under-standings that will allow them to read and understand simple texts.

By the time children enter the middle primary years, Years 3 and 4, they have generally developed knowledge about meanings (semantic knowledge), about the structure of language (grammatical knowledge), and about sound and print relationships (phonological-graphological knowledge) to enable them to read a variety of texts. These include written and visual texts, both narrative and factual, on topics that are largely familiar to them.

They have also learnt to draw on and integrate their knowledge as they read. They can read texts of increasing difficulty automatically and fluently by using their growing knowledge flexibly and efficiently. When they meet an unfamiliar word, or temporarily lose meaning in the text they are reading, they can ask themselves such questions as: Does this make sense? Does this fit with what's gone before? Does this sound right? Would we say it like that? Does this look right? What words/sounds do I know that match the letters I can see?

As Clay (1991: 6) says,

> I define reading as a message-getting, problem-solving activity which increases in power and flexibility the more it is practised ... Language and visual perception responses are purposefully directed by the reader in

some integrated way to the problem of extracting meaning from cues in a text, in sequence, so that the reader brings a maximum of understanding to the author's message.

It is the task of the teacher in the middle primary years to assist children to increase the power and flexibility of their reading by increasing their ability to use and integrate the knowledge and skills they bring to the reading task and by broadening their experiences of unfamiliar texts. But it is important to remember that each child is different and in a Year 3 or 4 class a teacher can expect to find children with many different needs, abilities, and sociocultural backgrounds.

It is most important that the teacher begins the task of developing a reading program for the class by first developing a thorough understanding of the needs and abilities of each student. This is done by using a range of assessment practices, including, in particular, running records, to provide the necessary information on which to build an effective teaching program. It also helps teachers to identify those students who will need increased support in order to reach the outcomes of their particular stage of learning (see Chapter 7).

A reading program has three main areas of focus.

1. The teacher develops and extends each student in the three areas of semantic knowledge, grammatical knowledge, and phonological-graphological knowledge in order to increase their ability to solve unfamiliar and more complex texts. More importantly, the teacher helps children to learn to use this knowledge flexibly and efficiently as they read by using a variety of strategies, for example by reading on and referring back, by looking at words in context, and by crosschecking or comparing one piece of information against another (that word *looks* like 'house' but it doesn't make sense in this text).

2. The teacher develops in each student the skills to be able to adopt the four reader roles of code-breaker, text-participant, text-user, and text-analyst. The teacher uses a text several times and in doing so supports students in thinking about the text in different ways and for different purposes.

3. As the core of the program, the teacher extends the range and variety of texts students encounter, and uses these texts to help students develop and strengthen their reading skills, knowledge, and strategies. Emphasis is placed on phrased and fluent reading in order to assist students to maintain the meaning and flow of the more complex texts they encounter.

Developing knowledge

Semantic knowledge

In developing semantic knowledge teachers build students' real-world knowledge about topics of interest and about topics being studied at school in all learning areas. Teachers also focus on building students' vocabulary knowledge, which includes word meanings, common expressions, figurative language, and subject-specific vocabulary. This means that the teacher is specifically conscious of the knowledge students will need in order to read each new text. The teacher thinks about the texts she wants to use as part of each unit of work, perhaps a unit on the environment, and about the understandings and vocabulary knowledge that will be needed to make meaning from the texts. During the unit of work, the students will be using their growing knowledge and understandings to read the new texts and at the same time will be learning from the texts as they read them together and individually.

Perhaps one of the texts in the unit of work is a picturebook or a novel with an environmental theme such as ***Where the Forest Meets the Sea*** by Jeannie Baker or ***The Paddock*** by Lilith Norman. What do the students already know about this topic and how can they be helped to acquire the topic knowledge they will need to read the text? The teacher also thinks about the vocabulary that is used in the text. Are there any words that students might not know, such as 'ecosystem' or 'habitat'? Are there any expressions that might be unfamiliar to students, such as 'life cycle'? By using these texts as part of a unit of work on the environment, the teacher is developing students' abilities both to learn to read and to read to learn.

Teachers use a range of strategies to help students gain new semantic knowledge. For example, students may watch a video or use a CD-ROM on the topic of the text, such as the video of *Where the Forest Meets the Sea* or one of the many excellent wildlife videos. The teacher then follows this up with much class discussion and reinforces important terminology using the chalkboard and charts. During this early part of the unit the classroom will come alive with pictures, posters, books, and charts collected from the school and local libraries, brought to school by students and the teacher, or collected from local authorities such as councils. Students may also visit a location such as a museum, zoo, or nature reserve where the concepts and understandings are explained and demonstrated on site. Materials are brought back to school to add to the classroom displays and for further reference.

Often teachers will use the shared book session to introduce students to new concepts and terminology. By introducing a new big book and reading it in a shared way with students, the teacher can pause at critical points and, often referring to the illustrations, explain concepts and terminology that may be unfamiliar to students. By using the same book over several sessions, and by providing small versions of the book for students to read on their own or refer to when writing their own texts, the teacher maximises students' exposure to the new concepts and terminology. The new terminology becomes part of the everyday classroom talk and the new semantic knowledge becomes part of each student's own working knowledge.

It is particularly important for students who have reading difficulties to be helped to develop a strong bank of semantic knowledge about the topics they will encounter in their reading. This will give them a meaning base to decide whether their attempts at decoding a particular text make sense and it will help them to predict what might come next.

As students learn these new concepts and terminology, the teacher will provide opportunities for them to write, both in shared and individual sessions, so that they can use their new knowledge. In the students' writing the teacher will expect to see the new terms used with accuracy and confidence and will work with individual students if this is not happening.

Grammatical knowledge

In the middle primary years students encounter many texts whose grammatical structure is unlike the spoken English they are used to. These texts may be narrative or factual and their grammatical structure may present a challenge to students in the ways the phrases, clauses, sentences, and paragraphs are structured. Particularly for students from non-English-speaking backgrounds and for those with reading difficulties, these texts pose special problems. For example, a literary text might contain this passage:

> There once was a woman called Miss Gardenia, who lived alone in a little flat in a large block of other little flats just like it. Miss Gardenia liked her home, for it was little just like her, and folded round her like a flower. Not only that—because the building was tall, and built on a hill, and because Miss Gardenia lived near the beach, she was able to look out her window and gaze across rooftops and backyards and pine trees and see the ocean whenever she wanted to. (Miss Gardenia's View, Cassandra Golds, *The School Magazine*, 84(4) 1999)

This text presents the reader with complex sentences of several clauses, past tense verbs (who *lived* alone, and a sentence word order unlike that of everyday speech ('There once was a woman called Miss Gardenia ...')

A factual text might contain the passage:

> Mars has two moons, Earth has one, and Mercury and Venus have no moons at all. These last two planets are moonless because they are close to the sun, and the sun's powerful gravity would drag anything smaller than a planet towards itself. (Night Lights, David Hill, *The School Magazine*, 84(4) 1999)

This text presents the reader with generalised statements which use the timeless present tense (Mars *has* two moons) and a causal relationship represented through a complex sentence.

Both these texts could present problems for students trying to predict what might come next in each sentence. Their reading would be slowed down to word-by-word level as they attempted to construct the flow of each sentence. In order for all students to develop effectively as readers it is important that they develop a good knowledge of what to expect in the grammatical structure of the texts they meet. The use of 'sounding out' strategies will be insufficient to support their reading if their grammatical knowledge is unsatisfactory.

In developing students' grammatical knowledge, the teacher shows them how whole texts are structured and what to expect of certain types of texts. For example, the class might look at several different narrative texts such as *The Enchanter's Daughter* by Antonia Barber, *The Paper Bag Princess* by Robert N. Munsch, and *Wilfred Gordon McDonald Partridge* by Mem Fox, and discuss how each of these texts is structured.

They also look at the use of grammatical devices such as past tense and direct speech and how adjectives and adverbs are used to enhance meaning in each of the narratives. The teacher also helps them to think about how connections (cohesive ties) are made in the texts. For example, how pronouns such as 'him', 'her', and 'it' refer back to people or things already named in the text, and how grammar works at the sentence level, including recognising the subject of a sentence or clause, subject–verb agreement in person and number, verb tense, and plurals.

The use of narrative and factual texts in the development of this grammatical knowledge is essential. Students need to see how authors structure texts and use various grammatical features to achieve their desired meaning. Using real texts helps students to develop a 'feel' for the sound of literary texts and a familiarity with the way literary language operates. It also helps them understand the often complex and very compacted grammar of factual texts. Teachers incorporate the teaching of grammar into most aspects of the Literacy Session. By reading aloud many different texts to students, teachers cue them into the rhythm and sound of the language and can take the opportunity to discuss how the authors have used language to make meaning. (The Literacy Session is considered in detail in Chapter 8.)

In Shared Reading the teacher might point out the way pronouns are used to refer to the main character in a narrative, or might ask the students to find the subject of a particular sentence or clause. Students might track the use of past tense verbs in the text and contrast this with the use of present tense for direct speech. The teacher might read part of the text aloud, asking students to join in with appropriate phrasing and fluency to help them develop a feel for the flow of the language. Afterwards the Shared Reading students, in pairs, might be asked to complete a retelling of the narrative as a cloze passage in which the pronouns have been deleted, and to discuss their responses with another pair. Or they might be asked to reconstruct paragraphs from the text that have been cut up into sentences. Students might prepare a 'reader's theatre' presentation of the text (acting out the text with a minimum of props) to focus their attention on the events of the narrative and the speech of each of the characters.

In Guided Reading the teacher might prompt students when they meet an unknown word by asking them to draw on their grammatical knowledge. Prompts such as 'Read that again and listen to the way it sounds. Do you think we would say it like that?' invite students to draw on their grammatical knowledge to read an unknown word or correct a **miscue**. The teacher often takes a running record of a student's reading to assess the student's reading accuracy and to check on how effectively he is using particular knowledge and strategies. If a student is having difficulty with using grammatical knowledge it will be evident in the running record.

Writing plays an important part in the development and use of students' grammatical knowledge. As the teacher models each writing task for students she emphasises the particular grammatical features that are part of the text being constructed. Together, in a joint construction of the text, teacher and students discuss the language choices they make in terms of their grammatical effectiveness. The teacher focuses on the particular grammatical features she wants the students to incorporate into their own writing. Later, in talking with each student about his writing, the teacher looks for the way he has used grammatical knowledge to structure the text and will ask him to explain particular grammatical choices, e.g. 'Which noun does this pronoun refer back to?' (see Chapter 13).

Phonological-graphological knowledge

In developing phonological-graphological knowledge teachers also build students' knowledge of book conventions such as headings and page layout, especially those conventions relating to factual texts, where layouts may include tables, maps, graphs, and diagrams, as well as a table of contents and an index.

Teachers work with students to build the number of words they can recall automatically and to learn to read multisyllabic words by breaking them into chunks, such as syllables, onset and rime, or morphemes. Students learn and use a growing number of letter clusters such as *str* and *tion*, to improve their skill at working out unknown words.

In developing students' phonological or graphological knowledge, both reading and writing play a part. Instruction in this area takes place in the context of students' attempts to read and write real texts. The interrelationship of reading and writing is, of course, paramount in all literacy teaching.

For Shared Reading, teachers choose texts that demonstrate the particular text features and phonological or graphological items they want to teach. The teacher might display a book's table of contents and help students to work out how to find some of the items it lists. Students might study past tense verbs to see how the *-ed* ending functions as a past tense signal. Later the teacher will provide a writing task to enable students to practise using one or more of these text features.

The teacher usually introduces new sight words or unfamiliar letter clusters using the same shared text. New sight words might be listed on the board as they are encountered in the text and, at a later reading, students could be asked to find the words in the text by matching them with those on the board. These new sight words and words containing the new letter clusters often form part of students' individual spelling lists for the week, the level of difficulty of the lists being adjusted to each student's ability (see Chapter 13).

In Guided Reading, where each group of students works with a text at their instructional reading level, teachers identify specific phonological-graphological items to focus on with each group. These items are usually the same as those taught during the Shared Reading lessons of the week but will be modified to suit the reading level of each group of students. The teacher might ask students to find particular sight words in their text, and to practise writing these words quickly on small whiteboards. Using a whiteboard or the chalkboard, the teacher might write some new words using this week's letter cluster (e.g. for *str* the teacher might write 'string', 'strange') and ask students if they can use their knowledge of the new letter cluster to work out what the words say.

In Guided Reading the teacher prompts students by asking them to call on their phonological or graphological knowledge when they miscue or meet an unknown word. For a sentence such as 'There was no one to greet them', the student reads 'There was no one to get them'. A prompt from the teacher could be: 'You said *get* them. *Get* would make sense but does it match the letters you can see?' Invite students to call on their phonological or graphological knowledge to resolve a mismatch. Teachers also use running records to check how well students are attending to the phonological or graphological information in the text they are reading.

After Guided Reading, students may work with small plastic letters to make the words that occurred in their text or to use the letter cluster to make new words. Teachers also monitor students' writing to see how they are using phonological or graphological knowledge as well as other knowledge in spelling.

Developing skills

In teaching students to read fluently and for meaning, teachers need to help them draw on semantic, grammatical, and phonological-graphological knowledge simultaneously as they read. They do this by helping students to develop the skills to take on the four reader roles: code-breaker, text-participant, text-user, and text-analyst (see Chapter 3).

The role of the teacher

The role of the teacher in the middle primary years in helping students to develop the skills and knowledge necessary to become skilled readers is a complex one that has three main components: selecting texts, selecting teaching strategies, and grouping students. Each of these aspects is taken up in Chapter 8 and can be referred to when needed.

In the next section we will see how one Year 3 teacher incorporates a guided reading lesson for one group into the literacy session for the day.

A Year 3 classroom is in operation. How is the teacher working to develop each student as a competent reader? What can we see as we enter the door?

Classroom environment

In the classroom we can see tables and chairs arranged for small group work as well as areas for Independent Reading and Writing. There is an easel in front of a cleared space where children can gather for Shared Reading and Writing and for class discussions. On the walls are many displays of children's work as well as posters and charts that provide models of writing and help with spelling. The room contains a large number of interesting books invitingly displayed and arranged for easy access. The computer area is organised to allow for the cooperation of two or more students on a reading or writing task. There is a busy hum of activity in the room as students work on assigned or selected tasks individually or in small groups. In one corner the teacher is working with a group of five students using a text for Guided Reading.

Grouping of students

On looking more closely we can see that the students who are working with the teacher all have a copy of the same book, *Samantha Seagull's Sandals* by Gordon Winch. The teacher tells us that these students are all reading at approximately the same level and she checks this by doing a running record with each student fortnightly and by changing the groups if necessary. The other students in the class are similarly placed in Guided Reading groups and each group will also work with the teacher at least once this week on a text selected for their current stage of learning. Today students not working with the teacher are completing a variety of reading tasks independently or in pairs or groups. At other times in the Literacy Session students will work as a whole class to undertake a particular task

Samantha Seagull's Sandals

Written by Gordon Winch Illustrated by Tony Oliver

Teaching practice

Earlier in the day the teacher introduced the Literacy Session by reviewing some of the tasks completed yesterday and by reading with students the wall stories they had created. This was followed by Shared Reading in which all students participated with the teacher in reading *The Paperbag Princess* by Robert N. Munsch in big book form. The teacher began the Shared Reading by asking students what they would expect to find in stories with princesses, princes, and dragons in them. These predictions were listed for future reference. The teacher then reads the text with the class, stopping at each page to discuss the events and the illustrations and what these revealed about the characters.

At several points students were invited to make predictions about the way the narrative would unfold and to compare their previous predictions with the text. During the Shared Reading the teacher focused students' attention on the implied meanings in the text and on the author's purpose in writing the text, in particular the way it departed from many of the conventions of a fairytale narrative. The class also looked at the use of past-tense verbs in the narrative and compared this with other narratives they had read.

After the Shared Reading students were directed to a number of activities designed to build on the key aspects of the shared text. Some students worked in pairs to reassemble parts of the text that had been written on sheets of paper and cut up. Others prepared a retelling of the text in their own words by using strips of paper to recall the main events in the narrative and then arranging the strips in the correct sequence. Others reread the story using small versions of the text, while others listened to a reading of the text on the listening post.

As students finished the activities they moved on to Independent Reading, selecting a text from one of the class displays. This was the time the teacher chose to begin the Guided Reading lesson with today's group. If we move over to the Guided Reading group we can hear how the teacher introduces the text, *Samantha Seagull's Sandals*, to the group and how she supports students' reading of the text.

On the left-hand side of the table is the text and on the right-hand side is the student–teacher interaction. (It is advisable to have a copy of *Samantha Seagull's Sandals* available while working on the following table.)

Text says	Guided Reading
Scan of book cover	*Orientation to the text* T: This is our new book for today. What can we see on the cover? ST: There's a bird … T: What's the bird doing: ST: It's wearing big shoes. ST: It's at the beach. T: Let's read the title of the book together … Samantha Seagull's Sandals.

T: Does the title tell us what sort of bird this is?

STs: A seagull.

T: Yes, a seagull. And what is the seagull's name?

STs: Samantha

T: Do you think this book will tell a story about birds or give information about birds?

ST: Tell a story.

T: Why do you think that?

ST: Because the bird's wearing sandals and real birds don't wear sandals.

T: And the bird's name is Samantha. Birds in stories have names but in information books it just says what sort of bird they are, like a seagull or a kookaburra.

T: Now let's look through the book and see if we can find out what's happening. We'll see if we're right that the book tells a story.

(Teacher and students look through the book page by page and discuss what is happening in each illustration.)

T: Now let's turn to the front and start reading. Kim, will you read first?

A long time ago there lived a young, silver gull who wanted to be different "
Why am I the same as all the other gulls?" she asked Hector the Hermit Crab who was old and wise. "The same grey bill, the same grey legs. The same grey feet. I want to be different. I want to be different right now!"
"Ho, ho!" said Hector in a voice as deep as the ocean. "You will be different one day. Wait and see."

ST: A long time the ... there lived a young, silver gull who wants ... wanted to be different. Her name was Samantha.

T: I liked the way you corrected 'wants' to 'wanted'. How did you know to do that?

ST: I saw it ends with 'ed'.

ST: "Why am I the same as all the other young seagulls?"

T: Have a look at this word again. (Points to 'gulls') You said 'seagulls'. It makes sense and it fits the sentence but look carefully at the letters you can see.

ST: gulls? she asked H ... He..

T: We know this is someone's name because of the capital letter. How could you work out this word? Can you see any small words you know?

ST: Hec ... tor ... Hector the Her ... mit Crab who was old and wise.

T: Read that sentence again so that it runs smoothly.

ST: "Why am I the same as all the other young gulls?" she asked Hector the Hermit Crab who was old and wise.

"The same grey bill, the same grey legs, the same grey feet. I want to be different. I want to be different right now!"

ST: "Ho, ho!" said Hector in a v..v..

T: What would make sense here? What would Hector use to talk to Samantha? What letters can you see?

ST: It starts with 'v'.

T: Read the sentence again and get your mouth ready for the first letter.

ST: :Ho, ho!" said Hector in a … voice as deep as the …

T: Think about what would make sense here. Something very deep. What letter does it start with?

ST: o.. as deep as the o ocean. "You will be different one day. Wait and see."

T: Good reading. You looked carefully at the letters and thought about what would make sense in this story.

T:O.K. Let's find out what happens next. Lee, will you read from here?

But Samantha could not wait. She thought and thought until she had a bright idea. "I know what I'll do," she said to herself. "I'll buy some shoes. Then I'll be different."	ST: But S..S T: What do you think this word could be? What can you notice? ST: It starts with a capital. It starts with Sam..Sam an tha Samantha T: Good reading. ST: But Samantha could not want. . T: Do you think that makes sense? Look carefully at this word (wait). What letters can you see in the middle of the word? ST: a..i..ai w ai t wait. T: Read the sentence with 'wait' in it. ST: But Samantha could not wait. T: Good reading work. You really looked closely at that word to work it out. ST: She thought and thought until she had a br..bright i i T: Think about what would make sense here. If she thought and thought she might come up with a bright … what? Look at the letters you can see. ST: idea. a bright idea. "I know what I"ll do," she

said to herself. "I'll buy some shoes. Then I'll be different."

T: Look at these words here. (I will.) You said 'Then I'll be different.' That makes sense and it fits the sentence, but does it match the letters you can see?

ST: I will. Then I will be different.

T: Do you think it's a good idea for Samantha to buy a pair of shoes?

ST: No. She won't be able to wear them.

ST: They'll fall off when she flies.

ST: They'll get wet in the water.

So Samantha went to a shoe shop and bought a pair of high-heeled shoes. "How smart and how different I am," she said as she stepped onto the beach.

T: Let's continue reading and find out what happens.

ST: So Samantha went to a shoe shop and b.

T: What would make sense here. What do you think Samantha did at the shoe shop?

ST: she bought shoes

T: Yes. Do you think that word could be bought? Look carefully at the letters. What can you see at the beginning and end of the word?

ST: b t bought. bought a pair of

T: Read on to the end of the sentence. What can you see at the end?

ST: shoes

T: Yes shoes. Look at the picture and see if that can help you work out what kind of shoes.

ST: ladies' shoes .. with high heels

T: Good. Now look at the word with the hyphen in it. Can you see anything you know?

ST: high ... heel high-heeled .. high-heeled shoes

T: Read that sentence again so you can hear how it sounds.

ST: So Samantha went to a shoe shop and bought a pair of high-heeled shoes. "How smart and how d.. diff different I am," she said as she stepped onto the beach.

T: Good reading. I liked the way you worked out different. How did you do that.

ST: Well, I looked at the letters and I saw it started with 'diff' and then I remembered that she wanted to be different.

T: Good work. Do you think she will be different now?

STs: YES

The teacher will continue to work through the text, supporting each reader with the use of prompts. She will draw out the various layers of meaning in the text by asking questions about the characters, events and setting of the narrative and by focusing on the author's purpose in writing the text.

After reading, students in this group will work in pairs to complete a cloze passage of part of the text that focuses heavily on the use of past tense verbs. The teacher will take the opportunity to take a running record with Kim, who may be ready to progress to a higher reading group. After completing the cloze passage the group will begin Independent Reading while the teacher checks on the work of the rest of the class.

This will be followed by Guided Writing in which the teacher leads the class in a joint construction of a narrative, which they will later make into a big book. Students will then work independently on the narratives they are writing while the teacher works closely with four or five students in turn.

The Literacy Session will conclude with the students returning to work with the teacher as a whole class, reviewing some aspect of today's work and then listening to the teacher read aloud from their current novel.

SUMMARY

As children progress through the middle primary years at school the reading tasks they engage in become more complex and varied. They develop an interest in a wider range of print and media texts and they become familiar with many of the everyday and community texts that form part of our modern world. Each reading task requires the child to use and integrate a growing range of skills and knowledge in order to understand and use each text effectively. Examples of teaching at this level are given.

Tasks

Discussion

1. Imagine you are the teacher of a Year 3 class that is studying endangered animals. This week your focus is on Australian animals. How will you find out what your students already know about this topic? How will you build your students' knowledge of this topic (semantic knowledge), which they will need to read and understand the texts you have chosen for the unit?

2. Select an everyday text such as a biscuit packet, chocolate bar wrapper, or drink can. Answer these questions about your text:
   · Who wrote the text? Why?
   · Who is the text intended for? How do you know?

- Which word or words are most prominent in the text? Why do you think this is?
- Which word or words are least prominent in the text? Why do you think this is?
- What ingredients are in the product? Are these ingredients healthy? How do you know?
- How would the text change if it was intended for a different audience (e.g. a younger or older group)?
- What reader roles are you adopting when you answer these questions?

3. Look carefully at the transcript of the Guided Reading lesson in this section.
   - What do you think the teacher is trying to achieve in the 'orientation to the text'?
   - Can you find examples of where the teacher is prompting the student to call on semantic, grammatical, or phonological-graphological knowledge?
   - This is a picture book in which the illustrations combine with the print to construct the meaning of the text. How does the teacher help the students to attend to the illustrations?

How is the teacher helping students to take on the four roles of code-breaker, text-participant, text-user, and text-analyst?

 ## Activities

1. Select an example of quality Australian children's literature which you think is appropriate for students in the middle primary years. Read the book to a small group, showing the illustrations on each page as you read. Explain why you chose the book and why you think it would make a good text to use in the reading program for middle primary students.

2. Select a factual text that you think is appropriate as a Guided Reading text for a Year 3 or 4 class. Examine the cover carefully and list all the things you would cover with students in your orientation to the text. Consider all the print and illustrations on the front and back cover.

3. Photocopy a page from a text and white-out every fifth word. Ask someone else to try to write in the missing words. How many were correct? How many others were appropriate for meaning and grammar? What skills and knowledge do you think the person needed to fill in the missing words correctly? What does this tell you about how effective readers operate?

READING IN YEARS 5 AND 6

Focus
The changes from middle primary to upper primary are dealt with. Effective critical reading is beginning to take prominence.

The later years of primary school, Years 5 and 6, are important years for students. While the early years are crucial in building the strong foundation for future learning, it is the later years that lead to secondary school with its closer focus on separate subject areas and the literacy demands that this brings. It is in the later primary years that students will refine the understandings and ways of dealing with texts which will shape their success in the secondary years.

In Years 5 and 6 students continue to build on their earlier development of reading skills and knowledge. As they tackle more complex texts and seek to use them for a wider range of purposes, they extend and build on the knowledge and skills they have developed in earlier years. Students continue to engage in an extended Literacy Session each day, but now it is more likely that the texts they are reading and the tasks they are completing will be part of their study in curriculum areas other than English. They undertake tasks that often require them to think and work independently, to plan, research, and present information and ideas using several texts, and to study and compare texts from a range of viewpoints.

At this stage of schooling, most students have achieved a good knowledge of the basics of reading and will be able to read widely for a range of purposes. Their code-breaking skills will enable them to decode most texts written for primary-age students as well as some more complex texts such as information books and encyclopaedias. In these years it is the text-participant, text-user, and text-analyst skills that will see the greatest development.

The teacher in the later primary years will be aware of a wide range of abilities and reading competence in the class. Some students will be able to decode almost any text they meet and will be able to understand many of its literal and inferential meanings. There may be one or more students in the class who have not yet achieved the level of code-breaking skills necessary to read effectively at this level, or who may be able to decode the text but not be able to understand its meanings. For all students, accurate assessment of their reading skills and careful selection of appropriate texts for instruction will provide the basis of the reading program. For students experiencing difficulties, the type of Guided Reading lesson described in the previous section will help to provide the necessary 'scaffolding' to a higher level of reading proficiency.

For all students the most important component of reading development is an understanding of *how* to apply their knowledge and skills to a new text. They should understand what they need to do when they meet a text that they find difficult or a word they can't read. They need to acquire and refine a range of strategies for approaching a text and for unlocking its meanings. Most importantly, they should be able to articulate what they need to do in order to get to the meanings of a text.

In the later years of primary school the teacher of reading has three main tasks: to continue to develop each student's skills and knowledge as a reader; to broaden the range and types of texts students encounter and the ways in which they use those texts; and to develop students' abilities as critical readers. To meet the literacy demands that study in a range of curriculum areas places on them, students need to continue to develop skills and knowledge in the sources of information (semantic, syntactic, and phonological-graphological) and in the four roles of the reader (code-breaker, text-participant, text-user, and text-analyst).

Developing skills and knowledge

Semantic knowledge

Semantic knowledge is closely bound up with content learning in any new topic area. As students study topics in science, for example, their teacher helps them to develop concepts and understandings about the topic and they learn the terms that describe these concepts. A unit of work on space involves learning to be precise and accurate in the use of such words as 'planet', 'star', 'asteroid', 'orbit', 'solar system', 'galaxy', and many more.

Students increase their semantic knowledge by developing their understandings of topics in all curriculum areas and by increasing their vocabulary knowledge of word meanings, common expressions, and subject-specific terminology in these topic areas. Teachers do this through many real-life and lifelike experiences including excursions and field trips, videos, visiting speakers, use of artefacts, use of CD-ROMs and the Internet, and a wide range of literary, factual, and everyday texts. In the extensive classroom discussions and activities around these items, teachers provide students with many opportunities to use, practise, and learn the new terminology, to compare the ways different texts approach a topic, to explore, compare, and contrast the information provided by different items, and to become familiar with the new body of knowledge.

In Years 5 and 6 the Literacy Session is used more purposefully to build students' knowledge of each topic area they are studying and to learn how to read and write texts about the topic. The teacher ensures that a great deal of discussion occurs around the Shared and Guided texts that have been selected for the unit of work so that students come to understand the concepts related to the topic.

In a unit of work on space, teachers and students might visit the school library and local library to borrow an extensive collection of books, charts, posters, pictures, videos, computer software, and other items about the topic. They may have already written away for brochures and other useful information from an observatory and they will participate in an excursion to an observatory or planetarium where, as part of the learning experience, the staff will introduce students to many of the terms and concepts they will meet in the unit.

The teacher will ensure that learning in this topic starts with what students already know, because it is likely that many of the students will have an interest in this area or have studied it in previous years. Learning in the later primary years should provide students with opportunities to extend and deepen their knowledge and understanding of the topic. In particular, they will be expected to bring their growing maturity and critical judgment to their study; to think about what they read and consider it from different points of view. In this unit the teacher might decide to introduce material on UFOs and reports of extraterrestrial visits to Earth, and ask students to consider whether these reports can be believed.

The teacher will probably provide opportunities for students to read and discuss science fiction and fantasy novels, such as *A Wrinkle in Time* by Madeleine L'Engle, *Playing Beatie Bow* by Ruth Park, and *The Transall Saga* by Gary Paulsen, and will select some of these to read daily as class novels. Not only will this reading be interesting and exciting for its own sake, but it will also enable students to follow their own interests and to engage with texts at a level of difficulty that supports them as readers (see Part III). It will also allow the teacher to demonstrate clearly the differences between narrative and factual texts on the same topic. Readers' circles will be formed for students to discuss their favourite novels and recommend books to their friends. As part of the unit students will be encouraged to write their own texts, both narrative and factual, based on the knowledge they have gained through reading and study (see Chapter 12, pages 197–9).

Grammatical knowledge

By the later years of primary school most students have developed a good basic understanding of English grammar and will be able to use correctly and to name a wide range of grammatical features, such as nouns (including abstract nouns), verbs, adverbs, adjectives, prepositions, sentences, clauses, and phrases. They will be familiar with more complex sentence types and will understand verb tense, subject–verb agreement, and singular and plural nouns.

The teacher helps them to increase their grammatical knowledge by developing wider understandings at the level of text, sentence, clause, phrase, and word. They become familiar with a wider range of text-types and their grammatical structures and features and learn to develop control as writers over a wider range of grammatical structures at text and sentence levels. They look at the way authors use grammatical features to achieve the purpose of their text, e.g. the use of paragraphs and topic sentences. They discuss the appropriateness of the way information is presented, e.g. a time-line to present events in a journey or a table to present information about features of the planets of the solar system.

Students consider the way a writer's choice of grammar influences a reader's interpretation of or response to a text. For example, they look at the way the use of the passive voice tends to focus a reader's attention on the information in a factual text. They consider information that is presented in running text and compare it with that presented with tables or diagrams. They look at an author's use of adjectives and adverbs in a narrative text and consider how these add to the meanings being described (see Chapter 14).

PLANETS OF THE SOLAR SYSTEM

Name	Diameter	Distance from Sun	Time to rotate	Satellites
Mercury	4 880 km	58 million km	59 days	None
Venus	12 100 km	108 million km	243 days	None
Earth	12 756 km	150 million km	23 hrs 56 mins	1 (Moon)
Mars	6 786 km	228 million km	24 hrs 37 mins	2
Jupiter	142 984 km	778 million km	9 hrs 50 mins	16
Saturn	120 536 km	1 427 million km	10 hrs 14 mins	18
Uranus	51 118 km	2 871 million km	17 hrs 54 mins	15
Neptune	49 528 km	4 500 million km	19 hrs 12 mins	8
Pluto	2 400 km	5 913 million km	6 days 10 hrs	1

Fig. 6.1   Table of planets in the solar system

Phonological-graphological knowledge

Students increase their phonological-graphological knowledge by learning more about the layout conventions of a range of text-types, especially factual texts and the use of graphs, maps, tables, and diagrams. They continue to learn how to segment multisyllabic words into chunks to assist pronunciation and meaning. They also continue to add to the store of words they can recognise on sight and become more skilled at seeing the relationships between words with the same base, such as 'inform' and 'information'.

Development of phonological–graphological knowledge usually occurs during the study of a unit of work. In selecting texts for a particular unit of study the teacher will design opportunities for students to become familiar with a range of layout and illustration conventions and will also look at texts that present information in innovative ways. The unit will probably also include use of the Internet and CD-ROM texts. As part of the unit of work, students will have many opportunities to build their sight vocabulary, as new words are encountered. New words may be listed on the board or charts, made into cards for use in games and activities, and written onto labels to add to posters being constructed by students. These lists provide models of conventional spelling and become a reference point for writing during the unit. Many of these new words will be studied for their phonological or graphological features and will be incorporated into students' individual spelling lists. Students will be shown how to break the words into syllables, how to construct word families (e.g. planet, planets, planetarium, planetary) and how to break up compound words such as 'spacecraft' (see Chapter 13).

The role of the teacher

The teacher in the later primary years continues to develop students' skills and knowledge as readers, to broaden the range and types of texts they encounter and the ways in which they use those texts, and to develop their abilities as critical readers.

The Literacy Session continues to be the major focus of this learning but, increasingly, learning in other curriculum areas becomes highly literacy based. Students will increase their use of literacy skills to learn in all curriculum areas as they gather, interpret, and communicate information on a wide range of topics from both print-based and electronic-based texts.

By using the framework of the four reader roles, teachers can provide for the balanced development of reading skills for their students. This framework enables teacher and students to think about their purpose in reading and about the different ways they have of interacting with a text to fulfil that purpose. It provides ways of moving beyond simply decoding the print to an understanding of the text on several levels. It gives flexibility and assists students to move towards independence as readers as they use their knowledge of the semantic, grammatical, and phono-logical-graphological elements of a text to take on the reader roles. By using this framework teachers can identify those students who are having difficulties and who need extra support to achieve reading success.

The teacher helps students to learn code-breaking skills to read a wide range of text-types. They become skilled at drawing on and integrating information from all sources as they read, at monitoring their own reading for a mismatch between meaning and print, and at self-correcting when they make an error. They learn how to vary their use of reading strategies to suit the demands of the particular text and their purpose for reading. They learn how to use parts of a text such as the table of contents and index to locate information quickly, how to source information from a range of text structures, and especially how to bring what they already know about a topic to the task of decoding the text.

Students having difficulties in code-breaking need explicit and structured Guided Reading sessions regularly. They need frequent opportunities to revisit and practise their understandings and skills using texts carefully matched to their reading levels.

The teacher helps students to learn text-participant skills to build meaning from a range of literary and factual texts. Students bring their prior knowledge to the task of understanding a new text. They learn how to relate the text to their own growing knowledge and experience, to understand the literal and inferential meanings of the text, and to be sensitive to the various layers of meaning in the text. They learn how the structure of a text, whether literary, poetic, or factual, contributes to the way the text makes meaning and they learn to use illustrations and diagrams of all types to increase their understanding of a text.

The teacher also assists students to learn text-user skills to use texts for a wide range of purposes in all curriculum areas. They learn to use a range of texts for specific purposes such as following the steps in a procedural text when they want to make or do something. They learn to use, evaluate, and compare product information when buying something and they use texts as an integral component of interaction in a range of situations. In particular, they use a wide range of print and media texts to refine their understandings and add to their knowledge in all areas of the curriculum.

Students develop skills in effective reading for study. Skills such as skimming to get the gist of a text or section of a text, and scanning for a particular piece of information or fact, are practised and refined. The teacher will support students in the use of a systematic information-gathering process such as the one below.

Defining: *What do I want to find out?*
Locating: *Where can I find the information I need?*
Selecting: *What information do I want to use?*
Organising: *How can I best use this information?*
Presenting: *How can I present this information?*
Assessing: *What did I learn from this?*

Teachers help students to learn text-analyst skills to think about texts within the contexts in which they were written. They consider an author's purpose in writing a text, learn how to identify opinion and bias in a text and how to compare texts on the same topic from different points of view. They learn to think about why people might interpret a text differently and explore how the author's choice of words and text structure contribute to the way a text portrays different social or environmental issues. In particular, they compare factual texts written by different authors that present the 'facts' of a situation or event differently. How do we decide which account is true? How do we know who to believe?

As an example, a Year 6 class was studying Australian Aborigines. They had collected several texts that gave different dates for the earliest evidence of Aboriginal people in Australia. One text said 30 000 years, another 40 000 years, and a third 60 000 years. How could they decide which one was correct? The teacher encouraged them to look at the publication date of each text. The text that gave 30 000 years was published in 1975, the one that gave 40 000 years in 1983, and the one that gave 60 000 years in 1995. The students decided to accept the latest date as the one that was probably based on the most recent archaeological discoveries, but it alerted them to the fact that information in texts needs to be read with caution.

The teacher works to help each student achieve independence in reading and writing skills, and to be able to use these skills to access a wide range of texts. Even texts that are outside a reader's ability to read fluently may be used to gather information and to refine understandings. The teacher will use the Shared and Guided Reading lessons extensively to assist students in this area.

In Shared Reading the teacher presents many different texts, often more than one in each lesson, and 'walks' students through the processes of accessing the texts. Their purpose in reading will be uppermost as teacher and students make use of the text and its features to meet their needs. For example, using a table of contents and index of one text, they may locate the information they need, read it, and summarise it on a chart, before moving to another text to find information on the same topic for comparison. At all times the teacher is modelling or demonstrating ways of interacting with texts that will provide students with independent learning skills.

By careful questioning around a text, the teacher prompts students to draw on their knowledge and to articulate how they are using it to work out what a text is saying. For example, using a factual text on the planets of the solar system for Shared Reading, the teacher may refer to a table and ask questions such as 'Which is the largest planet? How do you know?' to prompt students to read and compare the diameters of all the planets listed in the table, or 'Which planet do you think would be the hottest? Why do you think so?' to prompt students to infer that distance from the sun determines temperature and to compare the distance of each planet from the sun.

In Guided Reading the teacher provides students with opportunities to practise for themselves the skills that were demonstrated in Shared Reading, supported and guided by the teacher. On a text at their instructional reading level their task becomes one of applying what they have seen demonstrated. Later, in Independent Reading, or as part of work in another curriculum area, students will practise the skill on their own.

In Guided Reading, the teacher continues to help students use what they know to work on the unfamiliar text. When students meet a word they do not recognise, the teacher may prompt by asking 'What would make sense here? Is there any part of the word you know?' to help them call on the knowledge they already have.

The teacher wants the students to learn how to work out unfamiliar words by using a range of monitoring and self-correction strategies, by integrating all the information they have about the word, and by trying different options. Because the text is at the students' instructional level there will usually be several words on each page that the students do not automatically recognise. The Guided Reading lesson is designed to give them ample opportunities to refine and practise their decoding strategies, supported by the teacher. If a student can read a Guided Reading text without error it is probably too easy to provide the necessary learning and a more difficult text should be chosen.

In the next section we will visit a Year 5 classroom to see how the teacher incorporates the study of a unit of work on space with the literacy demands this places on students.

In a Year 5 classroom the class is studying a unit of work on space. Together the teacher and students have gathered a large collection of texts for use in the unit, including both factual and narrative books, posters, newspaper and magazine articles, video and audiotapes, and a CD-ROM. Around the walls are samples of student work generated in the early part of the unit and many of the pictures, posters, and charts gathered for the unit. A large sheet of chart paper fixed to one wall contains a growing list of words associated with the topic, such as 'planet', 'star', 'solar system', 'galaxy', 'asteroid', 'meteor', 'meteorite', 'constellation'.

Earlier in the unit the class visited an observatory and students were able to talk with the staff about their work. They brought back to school posters and pamphlets and a three-dimensional model of the solar system. They also made an audiotape of an interview that a group of students conducted with one of the staff members. They have decided to focus their study on our solar system, and in addition, for each student to undertake an individual project of his or her own choosing.

The class has spent considerable time discussing and mapping what they aleady know about space. They have enjoyed looking at videos and other materials and exploring the separation between fact and fiction, and between fact and opinion. They have listened to an audiotape of Orson Welles' *War of the Worlds* and talked about the reactions of 'Earthlings' to a reported invasion from outer space.

The Literacy Session

In today's Literacy Session students will engage in a Shared Reading lesson in which they will analyse and compare three texts on the same topic, space exploration. The class will consider the texts in terms of the text-type, audience, and purpose, and they will talk about how the structures and features of the texts contribute to the way each text communicates its information.

Today's Literacy Session began with the teacher and the whole class reviewing aspects of work done yesterday. Groups of students presented to the class the work they had done on researching the ways people have over the centuries gathered knowledge about space. The findings of each group were entered onto a large table for further reference.

In today's Shared Reading lesson the class will look at three texts that describe various aspects of modern space exploration. The texts selected are *Postcards from the Planets* by David Drew (big book and small version); *Put a Ring Around It* by David Hill; The School Magazine, May 1999; *Touchdown* (multiple copies); and a news report of the launching of a space probe to Mars as an overhead transparency.

The teacher produces a large sheet of paper drawn up as a table and, together with students, labels the columns with the categories text-type, audience, purpose, and text features. The rows are labelled with the names of the three chosen texts.

The teacher begins by focusing on 'purpose' and displays each of the selected texts in turn. Students are invited to comment on the purpose of each text and to support their comments by reference to the text's features. As students discuss the texts the teacher begins summarising their conclusions and adding this information to the table. From time to time the teacher asks the class to review the information to ensure that they agree it represents their ideas.

The teacher works with students in this way to complete the remainder of the table. This takes quite some time and involves much discussion in which students are encouraged to support their opinions by referring to the text or by producing other evidence.

The class engages in animated discussion about which text they would select to locate the information they needed for a specific purpose. Most students realise that a combination of texts would be needed for completeness and accuracy, and others have indicated that they would check the facts in other sources.

The class then begins reading activities that include working in pairs to complete a table for a new text similar to the one completed during Shared Reading. The teacher checks that all students are working profitably, then begins Guided Reading with today's group. The text for Guided Reading is a factual text with which students will pursue the same questions they answered with the Shared Reading text. They will also have an opportunity to read aloud and to practise their code-breaker and text-participant skills, assisted by the teacher.

During Independent Reading students engage in reading the novels they have selected, many of which are on the theme of space travel. In one corner the teacher works with a small group in a readers' circle. Each reader presents her novel to the group in a different way. One delivers a short oral book review, another reads a short passage from an exciting part of the book, another describes the book's main characters and how they relate to each other, and the fourth talks about the book's author and other books he has written. Prompted by the teacher, the group engages in discussion about the four books, their similarities and differences.

During Guided Writing the teacher works with the class to prepare for the writing of an information report on the solar system. After listing the information that they already know, the students then decide what more they need to find out in order to write an effective report.

Using this as a model, students will then begin Independent Writing by selecting a planet on which to write a report and beginning to research the necessary information. The teacher will remind them of the information-gathering steps they should undertake and, together with the class, construct a list of questions to guide the research, such as How big is the planet? How far is it from the sun? What are its special features? Has it been explored by space probes?

Students will combine their individual reports into a big book, which they will publish using a new word-processing program.

The Literacy Session concludes with the teacher reading from the class novel.

SUMMARY

When children enter the later years of primary school (Years 5 and 6) they have already learnt a great deal about reading and have developed the ability to read and interpret a variety of texts. While the focus of reading in the later primary years will continue to be on reading for enjoyment, the skills of reading to learn in all curriculum areas, of finding and using information, and of becoming an effective critical reader will begin to take prominence. Examples of teaching at this level are given.

Tasks

 Discussion

1. Consider the teacher's purpose in the Shared Reading lesson? Do you think the choice of learning experiences will help her to achieve this purpose?
2. How would you build students' semantic knowledge of a topic such as the bird life of Antarctica, before and during reading a shared text? How would you prepare them for the subject-specific words they would encounter in the text?

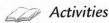 *Activities*

1. Select two newspaper articles on the same topic. Compare the features of each article that contribute to the way it presents the facts of the story. In particular, focus on headline, picture, and caption, choice of nouns, verbs, and adjectives. Do both articles present the story from the same point of view? Can you discern the opinion of the reporter?
2. Select an information text that you think would be suitable for students in Year 6. Does the text have a table of contents and an index? How would you teach students to use these effectively? What features other than connected text are used to convey meaning (e.g. tables, graphs, illustrations, maps, and diagrams)? What skills and knowledge would students need in order to gain meaning from these text features? How would you teach these?
3. Select two different cereal boxes. Consider each as a text and answer the following questions.
   · Who wrote the text? Why?
   · Who is the audience for the text? How do you know?

- What words or expressions are used to indicate the cereal is healthy? appeals to children? is slimming? is high in energy?
- What illustrations are on the box? What do they tell you about the intended audience?
- What are the four or five most common nouns and verbs used on the box? What does this tell you?
- Would you buy either of these products? Why?

4. Ask a Year 5 or 6 student to read to you from a book he enjoys. Ask him to begin by telling you about the book, what sort of text it is, and why it is enjoyable. As you listen to the reading, try to assess what particular reading skills and strategies the student is using; self-correction, sounding out unknown words, rereading when meaning is lost, breaking words into chunks. After the reading ask the reader some questions, e.g.:

- What do you do when you meet a word you don't know? (code-breaker)
- Why do you think the main character did ——? (text-participant)
- Would you recommend this book to a friend? (text-user)
- What do you think the author wanted you to think when he or she wrote this book? (text-analyst)

Chapter 7
Assessment in Reading

> **Focus**
> Effective assessment in reading is considered in this chapter. Such assessment is necessary to link programming, teaching, and learning. It provides important information for teachers, students, parents, schools, school systems, and governments about the achievement of students and the effectiveness of programs. There are many forms of reading assessment and selecting an appropriate form will depend on the purposes for which the assessment is being undertaken.

Nature and importance of assessment

Assessment is the process of identifying, gathering, and interpreting information about students' learning. The assessment process includes the following:
- gathering evidence of student achievement through a range of assessment techniques
- analysing the evidence to arrive at judgments about the achievement of the student in relation to expected outcomes or standards
- using the information arrived at for planning, programming, and teaching to promote further learning.

Assessment information can also be used to
- plan for ongoing teaching and learning
- report to parents about their children's progress
- evaluate the effectiveness of teaching programs
- evaluate the effectiveness of whole-school programs
- report to governments and education authorities about the effectiveness of school programs.

It is important that teachers constantly monitor the reading development of children in their classes through a range of balanced and varied assessment techniques. Coupled with this, teachers and schools must evaluate their own programs and teaching practices.

Assessment in reading is particularly important in schools and is becoming more so. Involvement in student assessment at state and national levels increased in the 1980s and 1990s. In New South Wales the Basic Skills tests in aspects of literacy for students in Years 3 and 5 have been in place for more than a decade and provide an example of assessment at a state level.

Beginning in 1999, schools and school systems throughout Australia were required to report to the Federal Government about the achievement of their students in relation to nationally agreed benchmarks in literacy. Schools and school systems were to gather assessment evidence to assist in making judgments about the achievement of students, the targeting of resources, and the effectiveness of programs.

Assessment practices of this nature are not unique to Australia. For example, similar procedures have been developed overseas in the UK, the USA, and New Zealand. Such a widespread occurrence may be explained by a movement towards greater accountability or a general pendulum swing of teaching practice away from what was perceived as the too loosely structured assessment practices of the past. There is no doubt that greater attention is being paid in Australia and around the world to levels of literacy, as has been discussed in the introduction to this book. Effective assessment and evaluation practices by teachers are therefore increasingly important.

Purposes of assessment

There are many forms of reading assessment available to teachers and those that are chosen for use in the classroom should be the ones that best suit the teacher's purposes. In selecting methods teachers should consider the following pre-requisites. Effective assessment

- should link directly to the teaching program, assess what has been taught in the program, and provide specific information for use in future programming and teaching
- should mirror classroom learning experiences and require the student to participate in authentic tasks to show what they know and can do
- should be comprehensive, balanced, and varied and provide students with multiple opportunities in a variety of contexts to demonstrate their literacy skills
- should be fair and provide all students with equitable opportunities to demonstrate their achievements, regardless of cultural and language background, gender, age, socioeconomic status, or disability
- should validly assess clearly defined aspects of student achievement and provide useful and meaningful information to teachers, students, parents, and others about the progress the student is making towards targeted learning outcomes.

Assessment in Australia today

It should be noted that the main purpose for assessment in reading is to provide information about students' achievement and progress to inform ongoing planning and teaching. While other purposes also need to be considered, it is this central purpose that most concerns teachers in their work with students.

Although there are various methods of assessment available, ranging from norm-reference testing to school-based assessment featuring **portfolios**, **cumulative files**, and **profiles**, a comprehensive approach is the most common practice in Australian schools. National and statewide testing provide valuable information for parents, teachers, and administrators, while classroom and school assessment provide the best individualised means of monitoring the progress of each child. Australian teachers are thus able to place emphasis on balanced literacy programs that give qualitative insights into the development of their students while satisfying the demands of external agencies.

Van Krayenoord (1996) has pointed to problems that exist largely in terms of the way external bodies such as governments use the information gained from **standardised tests** that provide standard instructions for administration, standard content, and standard marking procedures. Assessment practices such as the system-wide tests in Australia, as well as nationwide tests overseas, have been developed for accountability purposes that are external to schools and classrooms. She refers to Calfee (1994), who has commented that one important goal for the future will be to bridge the gap between curriculum, instruction, and assessment, which, are in the domain of the classroom and accountability for equity in educational opportunity, which is a government responsibility. There is also the growing sense of responsibility perceived by governments to provide for a literate society.

Fortunately, there have been important changes that have done much to overcome the problems reported above. Information about student achievement is now being gathered at all levels from classrooms to education systems. Whether this information is being gathered by governments to map the literacy achievements of students throughout Australia or by teachers to identify the learning needs of their particular students, the procedures and processes used are showing more similarity from one setting to another. This is because of the broad general agreement that has emerged about the complexity of reading and writing and the inadequacy of narrow tests that give a single score, age, or grade norm to describe a student's achievement.

An excellent example of this is the Masters and Foster (1997b) results of the 1996 National School English Literacy Survey. Although set up as a national program to gather data about student literacy achievement throughout Australia, the project's steering committee rejected the use of **norm-referenced** tests as inadequate even though these would have been much quicker and cheaper to implement.

The Introduction to the committee's report states:

It was agreed that the overall purpose of the Survey was to produce a consistent factual analysis of the existing situation to be used as baseline data to monitor national performance over time and to inform strategies to improve literacy in Australian schools.

The assessment methodology used for the Survey ... has produced the richest picture of the literacy achievements of school students to date in this country. This Report presents achievement data on a comprehensive view of literacy, including reading and writing together with speaking, listening and viewing. It draws on detailed and valid data for students demonstrating achievement across a wide range of literacy levels. The achievement data are enriched by an analysis of those home and school variables which appear to have a significant impact on literacy achievement.

The quality of the data can support a broad range of uses ... Currently the Survey data are being used to inform and facilitate the development of national literacy benchmarks at Year 3 and Year 5 ... System and school authorities also will be able to use the data to inform the development of literacy programs and to assist in the targeting of literacy resources.

...

At early meetings of the Steering Committee it was agreed that
• teacher judgement would be central to the methodology of the Survey
• the methodology would model good practice in assessing English literacy and enhance the professional skills of participating teachers in the assessment of student achievement in English literacy

...

The underlying aim of the Steering Committee was to develop an assessment methodology which had the capacity to link the richness and validity of classroom assessment practices into the framework of a reliable national data collection process.

...

The methodology shares some common features with a number of other assessment programs but is unique in the way it combines
• the central role of the teacher in the assessment process
• the collaborative assessment process involving teachers and external assessors
• the integration of the assessment process with normal classroom practice over the assessment period
• the degree and intensity of professional development for teachers and external assessors participating in the Survey

- externally set and moderated tasks and assessment criteria, and students' best work to assess student achievement.

Forms of reading assessment

In gathering assessment evidence to inform the decision-making process, a number of instruments and techniques are available—from tests to a range of more inclusive data-gathering procedures. It is important to remember, however, that any instrument or technique can provide only a certain level of information. It is the teacher's role to turn that information into a professional judgment about a student's achievement.

Norm-referenced and criterion-referenced tests

Norm-referenced tests allow an interpretation of an individual's test result by comparing his or her score with those of the group on which a norm was obtained. The most common outcome of norm-referenced testing is to provide a reading age for the child or a **stanine** or **decile** score. This score allows the teacher to compare the score of a student with the norming group which is considered as the 'standard'.

Criterion-referenced tests, or skills tests as they are often called, focus on a particular skill or reading criterion. Success in a test of this nature means that a student has achieved mastery over or competency in that particular reading skill. A mastery level is set, such as 80 or 90 per cent, and a student is deemed to have achieved success in that particular reading skill after attaining such a score. In recent times many criterion-referenced assessments are reported in relation to bands of achievement, with the characteristics of each band clearly described. The NSW Basic Skills Tests in Aspects of Literacy is an example of this. It should be noted that tests may be both norm-referenced and criterion-referenced. A score can be compared with a criterion or mastery level and a set of norms.

Norm-referenced tests do supply information about students' ability on particular tests in relation to others in a sample; criterion-referenced tests do supply information about a student's ability to perform on a set of particular skills. There are serious questions raised, however, about these types of tests as sole and suitable means of assessing students' achievement in literacy, and reading in particular.

In choosing to use a particular norm-referenced or criterion-reference test, teachers should ask themselves the following:

- Does it really measure 'reading' as it claims to do?
- Does an array of questions in a norm-referenced test cover the range of reading skills that are essential to reading?
- Is a particular skill being tested for mastery a vital reading skill?
- Does the test cover the skills being taught in the class program?
- Will the test provide the information that is required?

- Will the student's age affect the test result?
- Will the frequency of administration affect the test result?
- Will the student's language background affect the test result?

It should be noted that norm-referenced tests give no indication of a reader's specific strengths and weaknesses; nor do they indicate to the teacher the best course that might be taken to improve the student's reading.

More problematic is the fact that there is well-founded concern regarding the lack of relationship between the so-called essential skills of reading and the ability to obtain meaning from a text. Bussis (1982) described the case of a child who read effectively for meaning but performed poorly on an 'essential skills' test. Similarly, a child may master a range of so-called essential skills and still be unable to read.

Cambourne (1999), a long-time critic of what he would describe as one-off, group-administered, computer-marked, standardised tests of literacy, is particularly trenchant in his criticism. These tests, he argues, are based on quantitative measurement and view literacy as a single entity, ignoring its complexity. Added to this, the tests and their administration are not objective; the tests will not be similarly interpreted by those who take them; the tests place undue emphasis on outcomes or product and the results are not used by teachers and learners.

However, standardised tests are not in themselves intrinsically bad. The problem lies in the way such tests are used or if they are used exclusively. When standardised tests are given to provide some form of indicator of a student's standard or progress, they can form a useful part of overall assessment procedure. Standardised tests in Australia are developed by reputable scholars and research bodies, such as the Australian Council for Educational Research, and refinement of their procedure is continually being carried out.

System accountability

Because system accountability in literacy assumed prominent and increasing importance in the English-speaking world during the 1990s, it is not surprising that sharp focus was placed on accountability at national and state levels in Australia. The National Profiles point to Australia-wide standards, while the various states have developed curricula that derive from the profiles and are compatible with them. Desired achievement is generally described as a series of outcomes arranged in ascending order of difficulty. Assessment against the outcomes therefore provides information about the way the student is developing in literacy. It can also signal if a student is having difficulty in achieving the outcomes of a particular stage.

For example, Victorian schools are expected to structure their teaching around the Curriculum and Standards Framework (CSF). The four CSF levels are tied to particular age-grade expectations: Level 1 is the end of Prep, Level 2 is the end of Grade 2, and so on. Each child's progress is reported as Beginning, Consolidating, or Established within the relevant level. Victorian schools are required to list the CSF levels and sublevels of all children in their annual reports.

In New South Wales, the Primary School Curriculum, English K–6 Syllabus (1998), is organised in stages: Early Stage 1 relates to Kindergarten, the first year of school; Stage 1 relates to Years 1 and 2; Stage 2 relates to Years 3 and 4; Stage 3 relates to Years 5 and 6. A further breakdown to allow closer correspondence to grade levels refers to Mid Stage 1 and Later Stage 1, Early Stage 2 and Later Stage 2, Early Stage 3 and Later Stage 3. Another category termed Beyond Stage 3 is also included.

The NSW English K–6 Syllabus contains specific outcomes and indicators (statements of behaviour that students might display as they work towards outcomes). The outcomes state clearly what might be required of a student at a particular stage in listening, speaking, reading, and writing. Assessment in reading, for example, becomes *the process of collecting, analysing, and recording information about student progress towards achievement of syllabus outcomes.* Assessment procedures should relate to the knowledge and skills that are taught within the school program, and to the syllabus outcomes.

These examples illustrate the increased emphasis being placed on criterion-based outcomes by state departments. Similar movements are being made across Australia and the strengths of such a development in curriculum practice are obvious: goals are provided towards which schools may direct their teaching; there is ready accountability factored into the graded steps; classroom teaching and assessment are given a clear and uniform structure; reporting to authorities and to parents becomes much easier; and diagnostic assessment of an individual student's performance can more readily pinpoint areas of need. These and other advantages are important for the development of literacy.

School and classroom assessment

Outcomes-based assessment

As stated above, schools and teachers are increasingly structuring their programs and teaching towards the achievement of learning outcomes. These outcomes describe the knowledge, skills, attitudes, and values in each learning area that students will typically achieve at the end of a particular stage of schooling. The outcomes express the intended result of the teaching and learning programs provided for students. The set of outcomes in each stage provides a framework to help the school focus in a direct and specific way on what a student knows, understands, and can do. It provides a continuum of learning in each learning area and shows what students have achieved and where they are headed.

Teachers know that not all students will achieve the outcomes at the same time. Some students will need more time and support to reach a particular stage, while others will achieve outcomes ahead of their age-peers.

The use of an outcomes framework to describe the expected learning provides teachers with a strategy to monitor student progress. Teachers have clearly defined outcomes on which to base their planning, teaching, and assessing, students have detailed information about what they have achieved and what they need to learn next, and parents have clear information about their children's progress and how this relates to their stage of schooling. The use of outcomes-based assessment provides a clear and understandable framework that meets the needs of all parties involved.

Outcomes-based assessment is an integral part of a teaching cycle that includes the following:

- using assessment to identify what students already know and can do
- specifying the learning outcomes students need to work towards
- planning and implementing specific learning experiences designed to move students towards the targeted outcomes
- using ongoing assessment to identify when students have reached the targeted outcomes.

In using such an outcomes-based assessment framework, teachers are able to select and design assessment tasks for their students that meet the criteria for effective assessment described above. The National Plan assessment project in New South Wales produced a series of documents for teachers of Kindergarten, Year 1, and Year 3 that showed how this process could work. The project described assessment tasks that children could undertake as part of their normal classroom learning to demonstrate achievement of particular learning outcomes. The tasks were accompanied by indicators of behaviours that students might demonstrate as they completed the tasks. Teachers made detailed observations of students working on the tasks and were able to identify those students who had achieved the particular learning outcomes.

Authentic assessment

Assessment strategies, which use authentic or real-life literacy tasks and actual classroom procedures to obtain an overall picture of student achievement, are often called authentic assessment. These strategies stress an active engagement of teachers, students, and parents in the assessment process and explore new methods of collecting data. These include building portfolios of students' work, drawing up profiles of student attainment or progress, and carrying out running records of student reading. These procedures are essentially *qualitative* because they stress the quality of the particular student's reading efforts in actual literacy learning situations. Emmitt (1999) has drawn attention to tensions that may develop between the various stakeholders in education. This problem has largely been overcome, as stated above. The 1996 National Schools English Literacy Survey used a form of authentic assessment, moderated by external assessors, to provide its 'map' of student literacy achievement across Australia.

Authentic assessment values the input of the teacher, the student, and the parent. It places the emphasis on the professional in the field and can make a significant contribution to system assessment by cooperation with administrators at all levels. It places an enlarged responsibility on teachers and schools, however, and concern has been expressed at the time-consuming nature of its procedures. As Emmitt (1999) has pointed out, for authentic assessment to be successful, it must, among other things, work in the context of a clearly articulated policy. Added to this, it must be able to justify the procedures in terms of their accuracy, validity, and reliability (see Chapter 15, page 266 ff.); it must be rigorous and allow time to evaluate data. It must make sound judgments, it must include parents and students, and it must take into account the possible tensions with the assessment demands of administrators.

Portfolios, running records, informal reading inventories

Portfolios are collections of children's work that show significant aspects of development over a period of up to a year. A range of children's work and evidence of achievements can be included in the portfolio. With reference to reading, reading logs, literature responses, book reviews, reading interviews, reading profiles, running records, reading self-evaluation comments, and checklists are only some of the examples of a student's work that could be found in a portfolio. These, however, are merely collections of information or evidence. To be useful they must be analysed in the light of the outcomes to which the student is currently working in order to understand what the student has achieved.

Running records (Clay 1991) are a modification of Miscue Analysis and the Reading Miscue Inventory (Goodman and Burke 1972). In essence, a teacher takes a running record of the actual reading by a student of a particular piece of text. The selection of the text is important because the reading material, as a rule of thumb, should be sufficiently difficult for the reader to make oral reading errors (miscues), but not so difficult that the reader loses meaning. Miscues may be of a graphological, phonological, grammatical, or semantic nature, and an experienced teacher can gain important information from the results on the reading achievement and skills of the reader concerned. Interpretation of the results is of major importance; just counting errors is *to short-circuit a complex reading process* (Goodman 1997). An analysis of each error is necessary. The following running record is an example of one approach and is modified from Clay (1972).

The teacher may count the errors and or the words correct, but it is more valuable, as stated above, to analyse the types of mistakes or miscues. In the example that follows the reader is effectively using graphophonic skills to decipher most words, and is following the grammatical pattern and reading for meaning; reading *that* for *the* is not a serious miscue because it does not alter the meaning of the text in any significant way.

An effective method of checking the reader's understanding of the text is to ask him or her to retell the story. A teacher can easily discover from such an oral response if the reader has read for meaning.

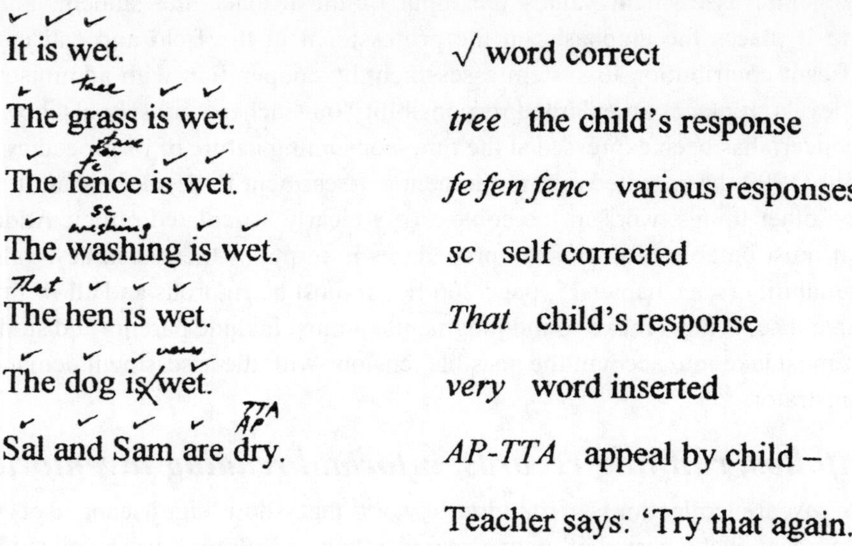

It is wet.

The grass is wet.

The fence is wet.

The washing is wet.

The hen is wet.

The dog is wet.

Sal and Sam are dry.

√ word correct

tree the child's response

fe fen fenc various responses

sc self corrected

That child's response

very word inserted

AP-TTA appeal by child –

Teacher says: 'Try that again.'

Fig. 7.1 A running record

Informal reading inventories are similar to running records in that a student reads a selected text and the teacher records his responses. Texts for reading inventories are divided into three levels of difficulty for a particular reader. Students progress to more and more difficult texts and the inventory serves as a rough guide to judge a reader's ability to read texts and to give clues to a reader's individual reading strategies. Criteria for judging the levels of texts are important in the informal reading inventory and texts are selected on the grounds of word recognition and comprehension. Texts are identified as Independent (requiring no teacher assistance); Instructional (requiring teacher assistance for instruction); Frustration (requiring so much assistance that the learning would be minimal). A rule of thumb such as the following is used:

Level	Word Recognition (%)	Comprehension (%)
Independent	99–100	90–100
Instructional	90–98	75–89
Frustration	less than 90	50 or less

Informal reading inventories are not criterion-referenced tests. The information obtained from them is to be used as a guide to aid teachers in monitoring the reading progress of their students. An important feature of this assessment procedure, however, is the emphasis placed on the grading or 'levelling' of texts. Teachers in mainstream classrooms are constantly placing levels on reading material to meet the needs of students in Shared, Guided, and Independent

Reading. The more structured informal reading inventory discussed above is giving way to a modified approach found in the Literacy Session.

Reading checklists, reading profiles, and cumulative assessment files

Reading checklists provide a useful procedure for guiding teacher's observations and recording the results of those observations. Their contents vary but they all contain two elements: the points of behaviour to be observed and a legend (a system for coding observations). Checklists can be used widely. They can be completed by teachers, parents, and students themselves. A simple checklist for basic concepts about print is shown below. The points of behaviour or indicators are often related to expected learning outcomes. This is one of many ways of recording student achievement of outcomes.

Concepts about print	Joanna	Pedro
The front of the book	c	c
Print not picture tells the story	c	a
What is a letter?	c	c
What is a word?	c	c
What is the first letter in a word?	a	c
Big and little letters	c	a
The function of the space	a	a
Use of punctuation	a	a

c = correct   a = attention needed

Fig. 7.2 A simple checklist

Reading profiles are lists of observable reading behaviour that are considered to map the desirable reading development of a child or children. State departments develop such profiles and some schools develop their own. An example of this is found at Moonee Ponds West Primary School, as reported by Davidson (1999). The school has arrived at a profile that takes into consideration a child's development from Kindergarten to Year 6. The indicators on their profile are objective observable behaviours and represent collective teacher beliefs about reading and information from curriculum documents such as the National Profiles, the Western Australian First Steps Reading Continuum, and the Tasmanian Pathways document. The profile has been refined and developed over the years and is used both as an assessment instrument and a reporting tool for parents.

Cumulative assessment files are collections of data relating to a child's reading development. They differ from portfolios in that they contain all the available data relating to this development. At their most sophisticated, they represent an example of authentic assessment and an alternative to standardised tests. The effective operation of assessment files as a sole means of monitoring students' reading development requires serious commitment from teachers. Criticism of such assessment has focused on such points as the danger of invalidity of the data; the time-consuming nature of the approach in the development and the implementation of the criteria-based tasks; reduction of the available time for teaching; and the tensions created by external requirements at national and state levels. These problems appear to be more obvious in the secondary school (see Moni, Krayenoord and Baker 1999). Again, such a collection of data is only useful if it is analysed to determine what it shows about the student's development of reading skills and knowledge.

Diagnostic assessment

Reports such as *Aspects of Literacy: Australia 1996* (Australian Bureau of Statistics 1997) and *Mapping Literacy Achievement: Results of the 1996 National School English Literacy Survey* (Masters and Foster 1997b) point to a number of interesting facts about literacy levels in Australia. As stated above, there is no general literacy crisis in Australia, although there are specific groups that are at risk. The most effective indicators are low socioeconomic status and language background. Among these groups, the worse performers are predominantly males. None of these findings is in itself surprising, but the fact remains that almost every classroom will have its share of students with difficulties. It is important that these students are accurately assessed that their difficulties are diagnosed, and that programs are instituted to improve their literacy skills.

A trial survey, carried out before the major study resulting in the latter report above, established the reliability of teacher judgment and recommended the best assessment procedure as combining portfolios with tests and having teachers work together with external assessors.

Most assessment practices will readily locate the student with difficulties. What is more important, however, is the provision of particular teaching procedures to overcome reading problems. Resource teachers, parents, and teacher-aids can supply additional assistance in the classroom, and suitable reading material for children with language difficulties or second-language problems can be used.

'Diagnostic assessment' is a term often used to refer to those assessment strategies that help the teacher identify or 'diagnose' the particular reading strengths and difficulties of a reader. Diagnostic assessment is often employed when an intervention program of support is planned in order to identify those areas on which the program should focus. An example of effective use of diagnostic assessment is to be found in the reading recovery program.

Reading recovery

Reading recovery is an early literacy intervention program developed in New Zealand by Marie Clay and designed for children who have made little progress in reading after their first year at school. The program provides individually designed and delivered lessons from a specially trained teacher. Generally, children in the lowest 20 per cent achievement range enter the program and most of these return to the mainstream and continue with normal progression. The remaining group (about 5 per cent of the program or 1 per cent of the age-group) are referred for special appraisal and long-term placement (Clay and Tuck 1991). Entry to the program is based on an early literacy survey, *An Observation Survey of Early Literacy Achievement* (Clay 1993). This test is composed of six tasks, administered individually. It contains a concepts about print test, a letter identification test, a word list test, a dictation test for hearing and recording sounds in words, and a writing vocabulary test over a ten-minute period during which a student writes all the words he or she knows. A summary of the results is then made to provide data for placement and guidance to help with planning a student's reading recovery program.

A cornerstone of reading recovery assessment during the program is the daily use of the running record described above. As Sale (1995) asserts, Clay's development of this observational tool—working out how to take a record of oral reading, how to analyse the behaviour it reveals, and how to best use this information—is probably her most valuable gift to teachers. Classroom teachers who are not trained in reading recovery may still use running records in their everyday literacy sessions in Guided Reading or with remedial work.

Grading texts

The matter of grading texts in classrooms (or 'levelling', i.e. placing them into levels of difficulty) is of primary importance as it provides suitably graded reading material for use by children as they progress and for teachers to monitor reading improvement. Reading material needs to be available for all students as they engage in Shared, Guided, and Independent Reading, and teachers must be proficient in selecting a range of interesting texts and placing them in ascending order of difficulty. (See also Chapter 8.)

The level of difficulty of a text, its **readability**, can be ascertained in a number of ways, but many of them are of little use to the busy classroom teacher. Such instruments as those arrived at by Flesch (1943), Dale-Chall (1948), Spache (1953), and Fry (1969) known as readability formulae, are cumbersome to apply and lack both validity and reliability when used extensively. They tend to make use of one or two-dimensional indicators, such as the number of long words, number of syllables, and sentence length, which often become inaccurate at lower levels of difficulty. Multidimensional indicators, which include amounts of repetition of words and sentence patterns, the number and function of illustrations, the nature of the language used in the text (e.g. whether oral or written) are some of the factors that affect the difficulty of a text. Then again, what is difficult for one reader may not be difficult for another. Language and cultural background, life experience, intelligence, and general reading ability, among other things, also play an important part.

The RIX readability scale, developed by Jonathan Anderson from Flinders University, South Australia, provides a similar estimation of a book's difficulty level. It is often used with other methods, described below, although its two-dimensional approach to readability has obvious weaknesses, particularly with texts at the lower levels of difficulty.

The cloze procedure

Another way of estimating the difficulty of a text is to use the **cloze procedure**. This procedure requires that words are omitted from excerpts of a particular text and a blank inserted. The student is asked to supply the missing words. Usually every fifth word is taken out, although this can be varied (e.g. to every tenth word). If a student cannot supply about 40–50 per cent of the missing words, or suitable synonyms, the text is too hard for reading with satisfactory comprehension.

> The word 'cloze' apparently comes from 'closure'. Psychologists call this filling in of blank spaces 'making closure'. Finishing half-uttered sentences and completing crossword puzzles are other examples of closure.

The cloze technique can be varied. For example, if it were applied to *Rosie's Walk* by Pat Hutchins, the book would need to be present and the words masked:

Rosie the hen went _____ a walk
across the _____ around the pond
over _____ haycock
past the mill _____ the fence
under the _____ and got
back in _____ for dinner.

The cloze technique can also be used for other purposes such as assessing whether a student has problems with predicting particular parts of speech. It is effective also as a class or group activity where children discuss which word or phrase is the most suitable, calling on grammatical or semantic knowledge. This is termed 'cooperative cloze'.

Of the many criteria that can be applied to the grading of texts the following ten, developed from Wille (1996), represent the most important features that appear to be significant.

> ### Criteria for grading texts
>
> *Subject matter:* from familiar objects to unusual fantastic happenings
> *Storyline:* from simple to complex, with elaborated episodes or events
> *Syntactic patterns:* from simple repetitive caption phrases and oral language structures to complex sentences and literary language

Vocabulary: particularly the number of words per page that might be difficult for the reader (long words, unfamiliar words)

Density of information: with particular reference to factual texts containing specialised vocabulary

Amount of print on the page: number of words per page and consistency throughout the book

Conventions of print: script type, size of print, layout, placement of print on the page and punctuation

Difficulty of graphophonic patterns: numbers of phonically decodable words and sight words

Illustrations: how much they directly support the meaning of the text and complexity of the illustration itself

Organisation of text: amount of variety of organisation according to nature and purpose of the text

Specific guides for grading

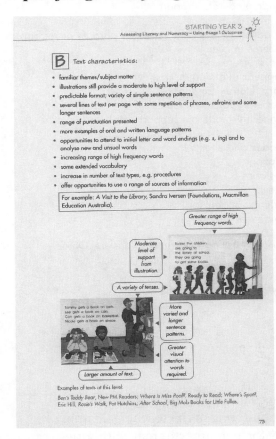

Fig. 7.3 Text characteristics towards end of Year 2

The above criteria have been included in guides that give specific detail for grading texts. One guide is the *Step by Step Booklist* (1994) published by the NSW Department of School Education. Another is the graded list of text characteristics developed as a joint project with the NSW Department of Education and Training, the NSW Catholic Education and Commission, and the Association of Independent Schools of NSW and published by the Commonwealth Department of Education, Training and Youth Affairs (1998). This project devised a continuum of six text levels to assist teachers of Kindergarten to Year 2. The example on the left describes the characteristics of text suitable for readers towards the end of Year 2.

Another guide was developed by Barbara Peterson (1991). This guide applies to the twenty gradations of difficulty required by the reading recovery program (the gradations are collapsed into five by Peterson) and can be modified for the classroom. It is a valuable and highly specific list of criteria for grading books for early readers.

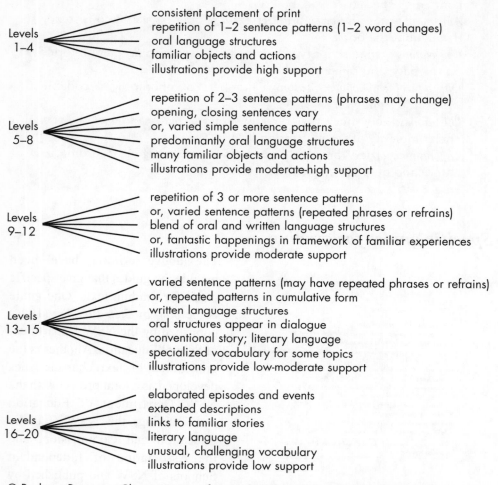

Levels 1–4
- consistent placement of print
- repetition of 1–2 sentence patterns (1–2 word changes)
- oral language structures
- familiar objects and actions
- illustrations provide high support

Levels 5–8
- repetition of 2–3 sentence patterns (phrases may change)
- opening, closing sentences vary
- or, varied simple sentence patterns
- predominantly oral language structures
- many familiar objects and actions
- illustrations provide moderate-high support

Levels 9–12
- repetition of 3 or more sentence patterns
- or, varied sentence patterns (repeated phrases or refrains)
- blend of oral and written language structures
- or, fantastic happenings in framework of familiar experiences
- illustrations provide moderate support

Levels 13–15
- varied sentence patterns (may have repeated phrases or refrains)
- or, repeated patterns in cumulative form
- written language structures
- oral structures appear in dialogue
- conventional story; literary language
- specialized vocabulary for some topics
- illustrations provide low-moderate support

Levels 16–20
- elaborated episodes and events
- extended descriptions
- links to familiar stories
- literary language
- unusual, challenging vocabulary
- illustrations provide low support

© Barbara Peterson, *Characteristics of Texts That Support Beginning Readers,* Ohio State University, 1988.

Fig. 7.4 Sources of predictability in groups of levels

Summary

Effective assessment of reading is necessary in classrooms to link programming, teaching, and monitoring in the teaching–learning cycle. It provides information for parents, external authorities, teachers, schools, and students themselves. There are many forms of assessment: standardised tests, graded lists of desirable outcomes and authentic classroom assessment based on a range of formal and informal instruments. These include portfolios of students' work, informal reading inventories, running records, checklists, profiles, and cumulative assessment files. Under-achievers require special assistance. Reading recovery, although not an assessment tool as such, is one specialist approach to providing that assistance.

Tasks

Discussion

1. Consider the matter of accountability in literacy, and reading in particular. Discuss whether authorities should set standards and assess students or whether assessment should be the sole responsibility of the teacher.
2. Is authentic assessment alone the preferred option for schools? What do you consider are its strengths and weaknesses?
3. What do you consider would be a balanced reading assessment program for a school? Consider the options and your preferences.
4. Why are running records valuable forms of assessment for the teacher? What are their strengths and weaknesses?
5. The ESL Scales from the NSW Curriculum Corporation set forth a special sequence of learning and assessment for children having English as their second language. Discuss the importance of such a program as it relates to reading and the approach to second language learners in your state.
6. Consider the purposes of assessment. How do they fit in with the teaching–learning cycle in the curriculum? Are outcomes the most suitable way to assess students as they progress through school.

Activities

Johanna has a new class of emergent readers and is setting about grading the supply of books she has available. Her students come from a mixed ethnic background and have varied control of spoken English. She needs graded books in multiple copies for Guided Reading; she needs graded books for Independent Reading; she needs to select big books for Shared Reading.

A committee has been formed in the school to establish guidelines for developing suitable criteria for grading books. The school librarian and a representative from each grade form the nucleus and provide assistance for all teachers. Johanna soon has things under control.

There are several readers in Johanna's class who are having difficulties. She provides special care for them, particularly with diagnosis based on running records, and has built up Cumulative Files of their work so that she can monitor the progress of each student. In this way, Johanna can both help the students and give ongoing reports to the Literacy Coordinator and the children's parents.

1. Develop your own scenario for assessment procedures in a class of your choice (real or imagined). What assessment instruments would you use? How would you keep records? Which books would you choose and how would you grade them?

2. Select a picture storybook you consider to be suitable for an emergent reader of your choice (brother, sister, child next door), preferably one beginning school. Read it with the child to see if it is at his or her level in the complexity of the concepts within the text, the vocabulary, the grammar, and the book's general appeal. Write a brief report on what you found.

3. From a library, or your private collection, select five early reading books. You may include a simple book or two from a series or reading scheme. Using Peterson's grading criteria above to help you, place the books into five levels, beginning from the emergent level (the first books a child learns to read). Briefly jot down your reasons for allocating a book to a level. If there is more than one book at a level, place the books in order of difficulty. Remember that you are not looking for the fine gradations you would find in reading recovery texts.

4. Now work with a buddy who has graded another set of books. Swap books and grade your buddy's collection. Finally, compare the results and have a discussion about any discrepancies. This technique works well in groups who are passing a set of books around.

5. Working with an older student, select a text that is at his or her Guided Reading level. That is, the student will not be able to read the text independently, but will not make more than one error in twenty words. Type or write out the section of the text on which you will record the student's oral reading. Double-space your copy of the text.

   Now, take a running record as your student reads from the book, using the technique described above. Make an analysis of the results and diagnose any outstanding problems. Suggest remedial action that might be taken.

Chapter 8

The Effective Teaching of Reading

Focus
The focus of this chapter is on effective teaching of reading in the classroom. Teaching strategies are outlined and methods of selecting texts for Shared, Guided, and Independent Reading are explained. Types of grouping for effective teaching are considered and the Literacy Session as a means of providing effective teaching of reading and other aspects of literacy are illustrated in detail and examples given.

Effective teaching of reading is a complex task and requires the careful orchestration of a number of components. Effective teachers understand the needs and abilities of their students and have a repertoire of strategies to employ in meeting those needs. They design programs and employ teaching procedures in response to what they learn about their students as they watch them grow and develop as readers. There is no one foolproof teaching method or packaged program that will work for all students. As teachers learn more about the teaching of reading they, too, grow and develop in understanding and skill. What kind of effective teachers might we see in the classroom?

We see teachers who have high expectations of their students and a belief that they will all learn to read effectively given the targeted program the teachers have designed for them. We see classrooms rich in print where students are encouraged to use reading and writing as part of their whole learning program. We see teachers who have planned for daily, systematic reading instruction based on careful assessment of each student's needs and abilities.

We see literacy taught in an integrated literacy session that lasts at least 90 minutes each day. The program is based on whole texts that cover a range of text-types. Teachers have an excellent understanding of how students learn to read and the reading program is well balanced across the three cue systems and the four roles of the reader (see Chapter 6).

Texts used in this literacy program are carefully selected and each student is matched to texts for Guided and Independent Reading. Students are flexibly grouped according to needs and abilities and the teacher uses the key strategies of

At work in a Literacy Session

Shared, Guided and Independent Reading in a range of whole-class, small-group, paired, and individual groupings. Students in these classrooms continue to make good progress as readers. The outcomes of the particular stage of schooling are a focus of the teaching program, and teachers monitor student progress against these outcomes. There is continuous assessment of all aspects of students' literacy progress and teachers use monitoring data to adjust the program and their teaching practice. Students experiencing reading difficulties are identified promptly and effective support is provided both in the class program and in consultation with specialist support staff. A congruence is evident between the language and literacy experiences of students' home cultures and that of the school. Teachers value students' home literacy experiences and use these as starting points for the classroom program.

Teachers accept responsibility for their own professional learning. They can articulate and reflect on their own beliefs and, as a result, classroom practice is continuously challenged and refined.

In the remainder of this section some of the key issues in the teaching of reading, which are evident in sound practice, are addressed. They are:
- how to select and use the most effective teaching strategies to assist students to make progress as readers
- how to select texts for various components of the reading program to promote effective learning
- how to group students to enhance their learning interactions and to enable the teacher to focus instruction to students' needs and abilities

- how to assess students' reading development to ensure that future learning experiences meet their changing learning needs.

Teaching strategies

An effective reading program uses the three important teaching strategies of Shared, Guided, and Independent Reading to provide students with a mix of demonstration, guidance, and opportunities to practise what they know. These three key strategies are usually incorporated into a daily Literacy Session or Literacy Block—a part of the day when the teacher provides a range of whole-class, small-group, and individual learning experiences structured around selected texts.

These three strategies help teachers to work with students on all parts of a balanced reading program in order to

- build an understandings of how texts relate to their contexts
- build knowledge in the three cue systems: semantic, grammatical, and graphological–phonological
- build skills in reading as a code-breaker, text-participant, text-user, and text-analyst.

Shared (or Modelled) Reading

This is called Shared Reading because it is usually done in a whole-class or shared situation. Shared Reading involves students in structured demonstrations of what effective readers know and can do. During it the teacher makes explicit the knowledge and skills needed to interpret a text constructed by someone else. (See also Chapter 5, pages 61–70.)

The students' purpose in reading will be uppermost as teacher and students make use of the text and its features to meet their needs. For example, a Year 1 class might be reading a big book of a narrative tale in which their purpose is to enjoy the story. A Year 5 class might be reading a factual text and using the table of contents and index to locate the information they need, then read and summarise it on a chart, before moving to another text to find information on the same topic for comparison. At all times the teacher will have particular learning outcomes in mind for the class and for individual students as he models or demonstrates ways of interacting with texts that will provide students with independent learning skills.

Teachers usually work with the same text for several lessons, and on each occasion a different teaching point will be addressed. At the first reading, the teacher shares with students the thinking involved in decoding the text and in working out difficult words. He focuses on relating the text to their current knowledge, in trying to understand the literal and inferential meanings presented in the text, and in understanding how illustrations contribute to the text's meaning.

The teacher models the way effective readers read; using phrasing and expression, and pausing at difficult or unfamiliar words to demonstrate the strategies needed to work out or 'solve' the word. These might include rereading the sentence, reading on to the end of the sentence, drawing on more than one cue system and comparing information from different cue systems against one another. (For example, 'This word looks like 'house', but it doesn't make sense in this sentence.) The teacher will articulate what he is doing and will ask for student input and suggestions. On subsequent readings of the text, students will join in reading with the teacher, attempting to use the skills and strategies they have seen demonstrated. In later readings the teacher will focus on particular grammatical or phonological– graphological elements in the text as specific teaching points.

It is in Shared Reading that students are encouraged to think critically about the text and to question the author's purpose and point of view. Because the teacher supports them, students can access texts in Shared Reading that are beyond their Independent Reading level.

Guided Reading

Guided Reading involves the teacher in working with an individual student or small group of students using a text at their instructional reading level. This is the level at which a student can read between 90 and 95 per cent of the text independently. As illustrated in Chapter 5, the purpose of Guided Reading is to enable the teacher to support and guide the students as they work to read the text, solve any words they don't know, and focus on the text's meaning. The teacher prompts and encourages the students to recall and use the knowledge and strategies that have already been introduced in Shared Reading or previous Guided Reading sessions. Teachers also use Guided Reading to draw attention to particular features of the text such as narrative text structure or sound–letter correspondences and to provide learning experiences that focus on these features. (See also Chapter 5, pages 71–8.)

In Guided Reading the teacher assists students to apply the skills and strategies that were demonstrated in Shared Reading on a text at their instructional reading level. By supporting and guided students as they read the new text, the teacher provides them with opportunities to practise and refine their text-processing skills and strategies. Students can later practise these skills on their own as they read independently.

In Guided Reading students work on an unfamiliar text. If the text has been carefully chosen there will be several words on each page that the student needs to work out because they will not be automatically recognised. This is where the teacher's prompts and questions help the student to draw on what she already knows in 'solving' the unknown word. The teacher will ask questions that prompt the student to think about what she knows and can see on the page which will help to work out the word. Prompts such as 'What would make sense here? Would that word sound right in this sentence? What does the word start with? Can you see any letters that you know?' all help to focus the reader on the cue systems that will provide her with information to solve the word. Prompts such as 'Read that part again. Get your mouth ready for the first sound' help the reader to focus on effective reading strategies.

The purpose of Guided Reading is to use each new text to teach students about the features of that text and the strategies they can employ to read it effectively. As students do this they increase their capacity to read more difficult texts and, over time, by continually moving to more difficult texts, they develop greater skill as readers.

Guided Reading provides teachers with opportunities to work with students in building their abilities to take on the four roles of the reader. As they work to solve the text, students are learning to take on the code-breaker role. Through discussion they will learn to participate in the meanings of the text such as the events in a narrative and what these reveal about the feelings and motivations of the characters or, perhaps, factors relating to environmental issues in a text such as those in *Where the Forest Meets the Sea* by Jeanie Baker. Here they are working in the text-participant role. They will become text-users by using texts for specific purposes both during and after the Guided Reading and they will be supported through questioning to think about text-analyst issues such as who wrote this text and what its underlying messages are.

While all teaching strategies play their part in assisting students to improve as readers, Guided Reading is the strategy that focuses most closely on each reader's particular stage of development and learning needs. It is a powerful strategy for improving students' ability to process a text and is particularly effective for catering for the learning needs of students with reading difficulties. As a general rule most students should be engaged in at least one Guided Reading lesson a week. Students with reading difficulties should participate in at least three lessons a week.

Independent Reading

Independent Reading provides sustained, uninterrupted time when students can read to themselves to practise and consolidate the skills and knowledge they have gained in Shared and Guided Reading. Most texts for Independent Reading are easier than texts for either Shared or Guided Reading, so that the student can read at least 95 per cent of the text independently, but more challenging texts should also be available to allow for exploration. (See also Chapter 5, pages 78–81.)

Independent Reading enables students to spend time enjoying reading and pursuing their interests. It is significant that students who engage with Independent Reading frequently and read a large number of varied texts make greater progress as readers than students who rarely read. The teacher's role in Independent Reading is to ensure that students have access to a wide range of quality texts from which to choose, to monitor each student's reading, and to assist in the selection of texts. An Independent Reading log is often kept by the teacher, or students themselves, to record what students have read and to provide opportunities for them to make comments. The log will often help in the selection of a new book, perhaps by the same author or on a topic of interest to the student.

As part of Independent Reading, students can form literary circles or discussion groups that allow them to share their responses to books with others. Students can be asked to prepare a short presentation on their text, to give a character profile, to compare this book to one they have read previously, or to read a short extract. Other students may then have questions for the presenter that will raise interesting issues for discussion. When the teacher joins such a group he or she is usually a participant rather than the leader, but can nevertheless model ways of questioning and discussing that will promote student learning. (See Part III for a wide range of classroom activities and discussion questions that will promote students' reading and thinking about literary texts.)

Selecting texts for the reading program

The use of whole texts is an essential component of an effective reading program, so careful selection of a range of quality texts is an extremely important part of the teacher's role. (See also Chapter 7, pages 119–22.)

Texts used in the reading program should include quality literary texts by recognised children's authors, quality factual texts in a range of curriculum areas, and texts used in everyday situations such as magazines and newspapers, posters, and timetables. They should also include a range of media and electronic texts such as audio and videotapes, CD-ROMs, computer programs, and texts presented via the Internet.

It is important to include a variety of texts of appropriate levels of difficulty to cater for the different learning needs of all students in the class, and care needs to be taken to match texts to the particular needs of students, especially for Guided Reading. It is also important to take account of students' cultural backgrounds and interests when selecting texts since students will be able to read texts more easily if they present ideas and situations with which children are familiar.

Texts will also provide students with access to information, ideas, and concepts beyond their current understandings. In using these texts the teacher supports students by showing them how to use the texts to find information and extend their knowledge and understanding of the world. Texts need to be selected for Shared Reading, for Guided Reading, and for Independent Reading, and different criteria are important for each purpose.

Selecting texts for Shared Reading

As stated above, in Shared Reading the teacher reads an enlarged text to and with students, involving them in the process of unlocking the text's meaning. The enlarged text might be a big book, either commercially produced or made by students themselves in previous lessons, or it might be an example of everyday text such as a poster advertising an upcoming event. It might be an overhead transparency or a series of overhead transparencies of suitable texts or it might be a text written on the chalkboard or whiteboard. In fact any text, whether it is in a book or some other form that can be seen by the whole class, is suitable for Shared Reading provided it meets the following criteria as a text.

- The text should present a good example of an effective text, whether a factual text, a literary text, or an everyday text (which may be either factual or literary). Carefully chosen texts create many opportunities for interesting and extended discussions, explorations, and activities that help children learn what it means to be a reader. Part III provides a wide-ranging look at the qualities of different texts that enable students to grow as readers.
- The text should be interesting to students and give them many opportunities to enjoy and participate in its many layers of meaning. Quite often, texts produced as part of reading schemes or series do not provide the richness and variety needed to meet this criterion.
- The text should be at a level appropriate for the students in the class. Because the teacher supports students in their reading of the shared text, it is not necessary that the text be able to be read independently by all students in the class. Rather the ideas and information presented in the text and the opportunities it provides for taking on the four reader roles should be uppermost in the teacher's mind when selecting it. As the text is read and reread over several days, students who initially found the text quite challenging will be able to access it more easily.
- The text should provide examples of the teaching points the teacher wants to present to students. These may include the type of text and its structure, the way it presents information or tells its story, its use of illustrations, maps, and tables or particular grammatical and phonological-graphological elements, and punctuation features. The teacher will be interested in how the text relates to the particular unit of work presently being undertaken by the class and what information or ideas will be added by this text.
- The text should provide opportunities for the teacher to demonstrate 'how to be a reader', how to use reading strategies such as predicting and self-correcting when reading, and how to take on the four reader roles.

Selecting texts for Guided Reading

In Guided Reading the reader works to 'solve' the text, bringing to bear all her knowledge and skill to work out the words she doesn't know and to construct meaning from the text. The teacher supports students as they do this, prompting and questioning to help them to draw on and integrate their semantic, grammatical, and graphological-phonological knowledge. It is important that the text for guided reading is easy enough for the student to read most of the words unaided so as to maintain meaning, but difficult enough to present about one word in ten that the student has to 'solve', since this is how the lesson promotes the student's learning.

In recent times a great deal has been said and written about the grading of texts for Guided Reading and about matching books to students. The reading recovery program has devised a system of reading text levels for the Year 1 students who are in the program. But these levels are often too finely graded to be really useful to classroom teachers and the system reaches only to about an average Year 2 level.

Some schools have worked collaboratively to grade their texts and have used these grades for their Guided Reading program. Many commercial reading materials provide a statement of 'reading level' or even 'reading recovery level' on their texts.

It is important to remember that these mechanisms are only a guide to teachers. In the end it is the teacher's professional judgment about the suitability of a particular text that is the deciding factor and this is based, more than anything else, on how well the student can handle the proposed text. The level of difficulty of a text for a particular student will be influenced not only by the difficulty of the text but also by its topic (whether it is a topic familiar to the student), its use of illustrations such as maps and tables (whether the student knows how to read these), the language structures (whether the student is familiar with these), the student's interest in the topic, and how relevant the text is to the student's cultural and social background.

Selecting texts for Guided Reading, then, involves two processes:

- putting the class Guided Reading texts into levels or groups based on teachers' professional judgment about what seems hard or easy and testing this over time with students
- considering the needs and abilities of students and selecting texts for them that are at an appropriate level and also meet the other criteria mentioned above. This will mean the student reading the text aloud to the teacher and, if possible, the taking of a running record to ascertain the student's accuracy level on that text.

Over time, teachers will come to recognise which texts their students find particularly easy or difficult and how to gauge what will be effective texts for them. As with Shared Reading, texts for Guided Reading should be good examples of effective texts, should present students with many opportunities to enjoy and participate in their meanings, and should provide examples of the teaching points that the teacher wants to teach with that particular group of students.

Selecting texts for Independent Reading

In selecting texts for Independent Reading the teacher should spend some time finding out about the interest of her students and in involving them in the selection of texts. It is often possible to find several texts on the same topic, and students will enjoy making comparisons between them. When particular authors become favourites with the class, or when the unit of work being studied is an author study, a selection of books by that author can be included in the Independent Reading collection. Students can be invited to include some of their own books in this collection.

The texts selected should cover the range of reading abilities in the class and should be numerous enough to provide a wide choice. Texts that have previously been used for Shared and Guided Reading are also suitable for Independent Reading since students often enjoy revisiting old favourites. The selection of

Independent Reading texts should be added to frequently and changed completely every three or four months.

Grouping students

Effective teaching of reading involves the use of a range of ways of grouping students in the class. Teachers provide opportunities for students to work individually, in pairs, in small groups, and as a class. This flexibility allows teachers to

- cater for the learning needs of students with a range of abilities
- provide opportunities for students to develop self-directed learning skills
- provide opportunities for students to develop collaborative learning and social interaction skills
- observe and assess students over time and in a range of situations
- use limited resources efficiently
- deliver the program in the most time-efficient manner.

Ways of grouping students are determined by the purpose of the lesson and students' ability to participate effectively. At all times teachers should ensure that all students are helped to gain the most from their learning experiences through the support, collaboration, and guidance of others, as well as being given opportunities to practise on their own and to demonstrate what they can do.

Working individually

Students work individually during such activities as Independent Reading and Independent Writing. This enables them to take responsibility for their own work and to concentrate on the details of the text they are trying to read or write. Teachers or assisting parents often work with individual students to assess their knowledge and skills by, for example, taking a running record of a student reading aloud or by engaging him in a writing conference. Students having difficulty with reading may need extra individual support from the teacher in the form of individual Guided Reading lessons.

Working with an assisting parent

Working in pairs

Teachers will often ask children to work in pairs so that they can use the process of discussion to help them come to new understandings. In pair work, where one partner is helping another, both the 'learner' and the 'teacher' benefit. Children often read in pairs, helping each other with words they don't easily recognise. Pair work is also useful in reading activities where students could, for example, reassemble a cut-up story or add to a list of words that contain a particular letter cluster. Pairs can consist of students reading at approximately the same level or a more able student working with one less able.

Paired reading

Working in small groups

Small groups can be formed in a number of ways:
- similar ability groups
- mixed ability groups
- friendship groups
- interest groups
- random groups.

Small groups can be formed with students who share particular learning needs or with students of diverse needs and abilities. Grouping together students of similar ability enables the teacher to target instruction to the needs of the group—

A group at work

particularly useful for Guided Reading. Grouping together students with varied abilities enables students to help each other and to harness a range of viewpoints and abilities; this is especially useful in creative arts such as playmaking and drama and music performance. When forming groups for Guided Reading, teachers assess the achievement of each student using an assessment device such as a running record, and place together students of similar ability. It is important, however, to monitor the progress of students in each group and to keep the membership of each group flexible. Students should be moved to another group if their performance indicates that they are progressing at a different rate from the other group members. Small groups are used not only for Guided Reading but also for many other activities during the Literacy Session where group interaction will promote student learning. The oral interaction that occurs during group work is an extremely important part of the literacy program and should be fostered every day. Group work enables the teacher to work closely with one group for Guided Reading while the rest of the class is profitably engaged in other literacy activities. This ensures that the teacher can work with each group, and therefore each student, over the course of a week.

Working with the whole class

There are times when working with the whole class serves an important function in the literacy program. For example, whole-class grouping allows students to participate in a shared experience such as an excursion or watching a video, which then becomes the basis for further discussion and learning. Whole-class grouping is useful for Shared Reading because it allows the teacher to build a common experience over several days. Reading a novel is often done as a whole-class experience because participation and enjoyment does not depend on an individual student's reading ability. Whole-class groupings are also useful for the sharing of individual, pair, or group projects with the rest of the class.

THE LITERACY SESSION

Many teachers find that the most effective way to cover all the elements of a comprehensive literacy program is to organise a daily session. A daily Literacy Session enables the teacher to

- provide a balanced literacy program
- focus the day's activities around whole texts
- include listening, talking, reading, and writing every day
- ensure that all students receive effective Shared, Guided, and Independent experiences in both reading and writing
- provide a range of individual, small-group, and whole-class learning experiences
- group students effectively for Guided Reading
- cater for the learning needs of the range of students in the class
- establish an effective and workable routine where students know what is expected of them and can work purposefully on tasks
- assess and monitor students' progress as part of the routine of the session
- allocate time for handwriting practice and acquisition of computer skills.

Most importantly, the Literacy Session enables the teacher to organise the flow of classroom activities so that there is enough time every day to take one or more small groups for Guided Reading while the rest of the class is purposefully engaged.

Some fundamentals

The Literacy Session or Literacy Block is being widely used in Australia. Although there are many ways of organising and carrying out such a session, certain fundamentals need to be present.

Classroom organisation
The classroom must provide a print-rich environment with, for example, wall displays, charts, word lists, labels, and samples of children's work. There must be a class library containing books of many genres in graded levels covering a range of key learning areas. There must be spaces for Shared, Guided, and Independent Reading and Writing. There must be prepared material for reading and writing activities, prepared by the teacher and/or published.

Shared reading in a print-rich environment

The students

Students must be familiar with the routines of the Literacy Session. They must be cooperative and share responsibility for carrying out and completing tasks. They must be familiar with assessment procedures, such as portfolios, checklists, profiles, and tests and be ready to talk to their teacher about their work. They must

Working
together
on a task

be able to engage in paired reading (a stronger and a weaker reader together) and be confident to work in a group focused on a particular task.

The teacher

The teacher must be able to teach flexibly and be able to move readily from task to task in the Literacy Session: from Shared to Guided Reading; from group teaching to supervision of individual students; from teaching to assessing progress. The teacher must be able to read orally with feeling and, above all, display enthusiasm about students' efforts.

An effective Literacy Session usually has the following elements:

Session introduction

This is where the teacher introduces the day's session and provides a starting point for the session to follow. During this part of the session the teacher often rereads or revisits previous activities that link to today's activities and reviews previous skills and knowledge in order to help students make the connections that will allow them to succeed in today's activities.

Shared Reading

This is where the teacher for example, shares an enlarged text with the class, demonstrating what effective readers do when they read. The same text is usually used for several days. Each day the teacher engages students in reading or rereading part or all of the text, and uses the text as a teaching focus for specific reading skills. Over a week he ensures that the reading skills dealt with will cover a balance of all four reader roles.

Reading activities

After Shared Reading students engage in a range of reading activities that allow them to practise the specific skills that have been part of the Shared Reading. They work individually or in pairs or small groups, sometimes using small versions of the enlarged text or with specially prepared task sheets or activities. It is important that the exercises or activities designed for this part of the session link to the specific focus of today's shared text if they are to be an effective learning experience for students.

Guided Reading

During this part of the session, while the rest of the class is engaged in reading activities, the teacher works closely with a small group of four or five students who have a similar reading level. Each student has a copy of today's text, chosen because it is at the students' instructional reading level. The teacher provides specific reading instruction as students read the text together or one at a time, and supports each student's reading by helping him activate his knowledge and skill to 'solve' the unknown parts of the text. Today's text will be reread as a familiar text at this group's next Guided Reading session. Over the week the teacher will expect to work in this way with all students in the class as part of a Guided Reading group.

Independent Reading

During this part of the session students read independently for enjoyment and to practise the skills they have been learning. Texts for Independent Reading are usually easier for students than their Guided Reading texts, although sometimes students will want to try a 'hard' book for fun or because they are interested in the topic. The teacher ensures that there is a wide range of inviting books available for Independent Reading and that they are arranged in levels to support students' selection. Guided Reading may continue with another group while Independent Reading is in progress.

Guided Writing

In Guided Writing the teacher involves students in a joint construction of a text to demonstrate how effective writers put a text together. With the teacher or one of the students acting as scribe, teacher and students solve the problems associated with the text's construction, discussing possible alternatives and contributing ideas. The discussion centres around models of this text-type that students have previously studied, often in that day's Shared Reading session.

Independent Writing

This part of the literacy session provides opportunities for students to create their own texts, using the Guided Writing text as a model. As they write, students practise what they already know about writing and work to gain control of an increasing range of text-types. Although students write independently, they share their drafts with the teacher and each other in their efforts to create an effective text. Although Independent Writing is usually part of every day's Literacy Session, students may work on the same text for several days to bring it to publication stage.

Teacher reading

As part of every day's literacy session the teacher finds time to read aloud to students. The text chosen will be a quality example of children's literature or a factual text that relates in some way to the unit being studied. If it is a long text the teacher will read it as a serial story over several sessions. This part of the session allows students to enjoy hearing a range of texts, to listen to models of effective language use, and to experience texts that may be beyond their ability to access independently.

Session conclusion

The literacy session usually closes with the teacher bringing the class together to share some part of the day's activities, and perhaps to allow students to present some of their work to others. Students are encouraged to think back over the day's session and to share what they have learnt.

Although teachers often make changes to a session depending on the unit they are teaching and the particular needs of their students, it is important to remember that no matter what changes are made, the key elements of Shared, Guided, and Independent Reading and Writing should be included every day.

Session introduction—*Whole class 5–10 minutes*

· introduce the day's activities
· review previous work
· build on prior knowledge

Shared Reading—*Whole class 10–15 minutes*

· read an enlarged text with the class
· module effective reading process
· demonstrate reading strategies
· focus on specific teaching points

Guided Reading—*Small groups 20–30 minutes*	**Reading and writing activities**—*Individual/small groups 1–20 minutes*
· read text at the group's instructional level	· involve students in purposeful reading and writing activities
· provide support for individual students to read the text	· provide opportunities for students to share their work
	· use students' work to assess reading development
· use the text to develop code-breaker, text-participant, text-user, and text-analyst roles	**Independent Reading**—*Individual 10 minutes*
	· involve students in independent reading
· assess students' reading development	· provide opportunities for students to share their responses to literature

Guided Writing—*Whole class 10–15 minutes*

· demonstrate how to construct a text
· involve students in making decisions about the text's construction

Independent Writing—*Individual 15–20 minutes*

· involve students in constructing their own text
· provide detailed feed back and support
· provide opportunities for students to publish their texts

Teacher reading—*Whole class 5–10 minutes*

· read text aloud to students
· encourage students to comment on the text

Session conclusion—*Whole class 5 minutes*

· review the day's learning
· encourage students to share their successes

Fig. 8.1   A Literacy Session format

Planning the Literacy Session

Teachers can use the following planning sheet to coordinate their Literacy Sessions. It is a useful guide that can be readily adapted to suit specific purposes.

Literacy session:
Daily planner

Week: _____ Day: _____

Session introduction
Shared reading

Guided reading group...	**Reading activities**
Guided reading group...	**Independent reading**

Guided writing
Independent writing
Teacher reading
Concluding the session

Fig. 8.2   The daily planner

A Literacy Session in action

Kindergarten/Prep

In the early weeks of Kindergarten children are learning about the routines of the classroom and how to adapt to the new school environment. The Literacy Session plays an important role in settling a new Kindergarten class into the types of classroom practices they will encounter in later months. By introducing whole-class, small-group, and individual literacy practices from the first week of Kindergarten, the teacher is able to

- set up expectations for classroom behaviour within a familiar routine of enjoyable activities
- provide a link to children's literacy learning in the years before school
- gain a good understanding of what each child knows and can do, on which to build the literacy program.

In the first weeks of Kindergarten the Literacy Session will run in a modified form until the class is familiar with the routines. In Week 3 or 4, after carefully observing students and their interactions with text, the teacher can begin to form Guided Reading groups. The first group will be composed of the four or five most able readers. Over the next four or five weeks the remaining Guided Reading groups will be formed one at a time. By the end of Term 1 all students will be placed in an appropriate Guided Reading group and will work with the teacher at least twice a week.

At the beginning of Kindergarten a unit focused on 'starting school' is often a good way to begin. Children can use the shared experience of starting school as the basis of many effective listening, talking, reading, and writing experiences. There are also many books on this theme, such as **The Kinder Hat** by Morag Loh, **Timothy Goes to School** by Rosemary Wells, and **Lucy and Tom Go to School** by Shirley Hughes.

The unit extract provided here shows Day 1 of a two-week unit on starting school and is designed to be run in the early weeks of Term 1. At this stage of the year the Literacy Session will not include Guided Reading, but all other components of the Literacy Session are included.

During the unit the teacher will carefully observe each student's interactions with text and will begin to establish an understanding of the learning outcomes each has achieved. This will enable the teacher to develop a learning program for the class which ensures that each student engages in learning experiences to enable him or her to achieve the next stage of learning outcomes.

Over the two weeks of the unit students will engage in creating and exploring text in various ways.

A Kindergarten/Prep Literacy Session

Starting School: Day 1

Session introduction

Read *Timothy Goes to School* by Anthony Wells. Talk about what happens in the book and what it feels like to start school. Ask children what they liked and didn't like about the first day. Ask what they would tell a little brother or sister about starting school.

Shared Reading

Write a sentence on the board to record some of the discussion, e.g. 'We like playing at school'. Read the sentence aloud, pointing to each word. Ask children to read with you. Focus on one word, e.g. the word 'school'; ask students to read it with you. Say the word slowly and emphasise the first sound. Ask if anyone's name starts with that sound. Write the name on the board and compare the shapes of the initial letters.

Reading activities

Provide each pair of students with seven or eight captioned pictures of children doing activities at school and at home (e.g. going to bed, playing in the playground). Provide a large sheet of paper with two clearly labelled sections (at school, at home). Ask students to discuss each picture and then paste it onto the paper in the correct section. Ask them to consider what they will do with activities done both at school and home (e.g. eating lunch, putting on a raincoat). As each pair finishes they can begin Independent Reading.

Independent Reading

Ask children to choose a book from the class library and begin 'reading'. At the end of Independent Reading show students how to return their books to the shelves nearby.

Guided Writing

Tell children you are going to write about something we do at school. Discuss what you might write, e.g. 'At school we eat our lunch under the trees'. Ask children to help you write. Keep rereading the sentence as it is built. Talk about the need for a capital letter to start and a full stop at the end. Read the sentence together when it is finished.

Independent Writing

Provide a sheet of paper for each child with the sentence beginning 'At school ...' at the bottom. Ask children to draw something they like doing at school. While they work, move around the class, asking each child to tell you what their picture shows and helping them to compose a sentence and write it under the picture. Write the sentence accurately on each child's page.

Teachers' reading

Read aloud to the class *The Kinder Hat* by Morag Fraser.

Session conclusion

Ask two or three children to share their picture and writing with the class. Assist children to read their writing aloud. Collect all children's work and staple into a book. Tell children the book will go into the class library.

Fig. 8.3 A Kindergarten/Prep Literacy Session

Year 1, Term 3

This Literacy Session takes place towards the end of the year. The classroom is an ideal place for literacy work, providing a colourful, print-rich environment with ample resources. Both the children and the teacher are well versed in the routines required for a Literacy Session to operate successfully, and parents are on hand to give assistance. Books used in this classroom have been carefully graded by the teacher, with the assistance of a specially trained reading recovery teacher.

Setting the scene

The class is sitting on the floor and the teacher has a copy of the big book **Bernard Was a Bikie** by Val Marshall and Bronwyn Tester (1988) on a display stand ready for Shared Reading. The class has been working on a unit called Leisure Time. The class begins by reciting the known poems 'Barbecue' by Anne Le Roy and 'Cubby-House in a Garden' by Lydia Pender. The students talk about some of the work they completed in the previous Literacy Session. They then launch into the big book they are going to share today.

Shared Reading

The teacher follows the Shared Reading sequence described above, stopping some way through the book. The question is, What happened next?—a mystery that will be solved during the next Shared Reading session.

Big Book, *Bernard Was a Bikie*. What happened next?

Guided Reading

The class now breaks up into groups; some move off to reading and writing activities associated with the leisure theme; the five students of Blue Group go with the teacher to the Guided Reading section of the classroom.

For guided reading with Blue Group, the teacher has chosen **Mr Gumpy's Outing** by John Burningham. This picture storybook is pitched at the instructional level of the children and has been carefully graded by the teacher and her peers. Its language is sprightly and original. The book is about outdoor activities and is a very good fit for the leisure theme. The teacher follows the Guided Reading steps described above and the students are allowed to take one of the multiple copies home for further reading after the session. Every student in the group is heard by the teacher and reading progress is monitored.

Reading and writing activities

Some students complete their leisure time writing tasks and add them to the display; others place work in their portfolios; others are busy with work sheets. The main point to note is that every student is fully occupied in systematic literacy tasks.

Independent Reading and Writing

Students read material in a variety of text-types. They access the class library and move to their desks. Some engage in paired reading or work with a parent. Additional reading material, such as the Poetry Box, as shown on page 147, is available and popular with students.

Leisure-time writing

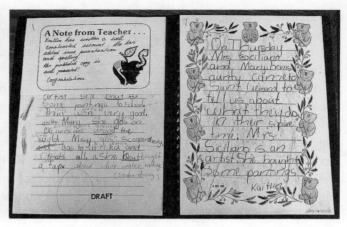

Benjamin's portfolio   A portfolio entry

Assessing student achievement

Apart from individual student portfolios that contain progressive examples of work, the teacher keeps records on each student for various aspects of literacy work. These can be readily collated and used for reporting and diagnostic assessment and teaching. The following examples are useful guides for setting up such record sheets.

Guided reading record

Name:.. Group:............................

Date	Text	Book box no.	Comments	Work needed on

Independent reading record

Name:......................................

	Title	Author	Date finished	Comment
1.				
2.				

Fig. 8.4   Reading record sheets

My poetry box

Teacher reading

The teacher begins reading Bob Graham's **Greetings from Sandy Beach**. This delightful, witty book proved a big hit with the students, who could hardly wait for the next Literacy Session to hear the rest of it. The Disciples of Death bikies, who turned out to be most helpful, were particularly popular.

Conclusion

Students reported to the class about their work during the session. The teacher noted those needing further assistance. All material was returned to its proper place before children went out for recess.

SUMMARY

Teaching reading effectively is a complex task. There are certain aspects that must be involved. Those include key strategies such as Shared, Guided, and Independent Reading, variable grouping in classrooms, the careful selection of texts, and suitable assessment. The Literacy Session is fast becoming common practice in Australia and has its equivalents around the world. The Literacy Session has various essential components, although it can take various forms. Two Literacy Sessions in action are then provided, one in Kindergarten and another in Year 1.

Tasks

Discussion

1. Phonic activities for reading need to be included in the Literacy Session. Consider where these would be placed and how they would systematically taught and monitored.

2. Consider the place of published English language books in classrooms and in the Literacy Session in particular. Is there a place for them as individual activities in handwriting, grammar and usage, spelling, modelling of text-types, and phonic activities?

3. Assessment is important in the Literacy Session, in the Guided Reading activity for instance. How would a teacher successfully monitor each student's progress over a period of time? Consider some of the tools outlined in Chapter 7.

4. Computer skills are becoming increasingly important in literacy development. Consider how the computer might be successfully incorporated into the Literacy Session.

5. The Literacy Session includes three types of strategies: Shared, Guided, and Independent. How does the role of the teacher change in employing these strategies? What role do students take when teachers employ these strategies?

6. In the Literacy Session the teacher works to help students take on the four reader roles of code-breaker, text-participant, text-user, and text-analyst. What activities could be used to help them do this? What questions can teachers ask to prompt students to take on each role?

7. What are the qualities of an effective teacher of reading? What would you see and hear in a classroom where the Literacy Session was operating effectively?

 Activities

1. Develop what you consider a suitable literacy session for a Grade 1 or 2. Make sure that you have included the basic and essential components as shown above.

2. What would be some valuable sources of reading material for students in a Literacy Session? Consider the class collection of books (the class core library), and posting of samples of print around the walls. What else?

3. Select a theme or unit of work. Plan how you would use this theme in a series of literacy sessions in a Year 1 or 2 classroom.

4. Using the information from Chapter 7 on assessment, describe what assessment processes you would follow in a literacy session (a running record for a student, development of portfolios, class and individual student records, etc.).

Part II Writing

Lesley Ljungdahl and Paul March

Writing involves making visual marks on paper, other surfaces, or through the new electronic media. It is in fact the other side of the reading coin and is very closely linked with speaking and listening. We can communicate with each other through the medium of writing, whether it be simply to jot down some items to remember to buy at the supermarket or to express our innermost feelings about an issue. Writing has many diverse social purposes and so can take on many different forms. Children learn most effectively when writing is used for real purposes—to inform, to entertain, to persuade, to clarify thinking. Above all, children need to regard writing as an exciting activity that is both functional and an important part of the learning process.

Chapter 9 examines the nature and role of writing in our society and presents an overview of the development of writing as a semiotic system through the ages. Chapter 10 focuses on the importance of writing as a learning tool, its place in the classroom, its power in the learning and thinking processes, its imaginative potential, and its place in the artistic process. We also discuss the way different text-types are used for different writing purposes in our society.

In Chapter 11 we explore the way writing develops throughout the grades and look at writing as being a lifelong process. Chapter 12 has useful suggestions as to how writing can be managed and taught within the classroom. Different approaches to the teaching of writing are discussed and a functional approach is recommended.

Chapters 13 and 14 focus on the skills of handwriting, spelling, grammar, and punctuation as having an important place in the writing process. They are a means to an end and must be seen in the context of the whole writing process as essential tools in the communication of meaning.

Chapter 15 explores the many ways of assessing writing. Portfolio assessment is discussed at length, with practical advice on the planning and design of language portfolios. There is a balance between theory and practice throughout the chapters, highlighting the important idea that the process of writing is part of the larger picture of literacy as a whole.

Chapter 9
The Role of Writing

> Focus
> This chapter examines the nature and role of writing in our society. In particular, it looks at writing as a social phenomenon that all children in a literate society need in order to be able to function adequately. The chapter also explores the development of writing as a semiotic system through the ages.

Writing is a phenomenon invented by humans to help in the communication process—it has become, indeed, a social and cultural practice in most societies today. Children need writing skills in a literate society. There is a close relationship between speech and writing, each reinforcing the other in the process of language development in children. Written language is organised differently from spoken language, and the world as seen in writing is different from the world as heard in speech. For Halliday (1986: 6) this is a positive feature because 'we get two complementary, mutually reinforcing, pictures of the world', both of which are vitally important in the learning process. He also sees them as different ways of meaning embodied in a common system we call language. Writing in fact evolved not to duplicate the functions of spoken language but to carry out the new functions that arose in advancing cultures. A consequence of this was that writing brought language into consciousness in a new way. Learning to read and write makes it possible for children to reflect on language in the process of their learning.

Language is integral to culture and cultural process:

> Some ideas/forms of language seem to exist in one culture and not in another. Language and culture are very closely interwoven; social structures and linguistic form are intimately intermeshed. This is so across larger cultures, much as it is the case in the social and cultural diversity within one society. (Kress 1988: ii)

Lankshear takes these ideas further and sees people as capable of making sense and meaning out of their experiences because they 'learn to do so through sociocultural processes of socialisation and education which initiate them into, or apprentice them to, what have variously been called "forms of life", "domains of social practice", or "discourses"' (1996: 19). Like Halliday and Kress, Lankshear sees language as central to education because it is both a necessary condition for cultural process and an outcome of that process. It has the ability to empower or disempower children at school, depending on their ability to access the many forms of texts used by our culture.

The power of language

A social-functional approach to language focuses on the power language can exert in children's lives. Because writing is a social and cultural practice, children must be given access to a wide range of discourses and practices so that they can participate fully in the society in which they live. They need an understanding of writing as a social construct, and practice in using language so that they can express themselves with confidence.

'Competence in English will enable students to learn about the role of language in their own lives, and in their own and other cultures. They will then be able to communicate their thoughts and feelings, to participate in society, to make informed decisions about personal and social issues, to analyse information and viewpoints, to use their imaginations and to think about the influence of culture on the meanings made with language.' (Board of Studies NSW 1998: 6)

It is interesting to note that although there are approximately 9000 languages in the world, only 300 of them are written. Languages such as Arabic, Chinese, English, French, German, Hindustani, Italian, Japanese, Portuguese, Russian, and Spanish all have strong written traditions. Historically, while both written and oral forms of a language pass on the knowledge and traditions of a society, the written form is a more 'permanent' record, not reliant on the presence of someone who has memorised the information. English has emerged as an important *lingua franca* among speakers of other languages partly because of its written heritage, partly because of US dominance of the computer hardware and software industries.

The evolution of language

How does a written language evolve? For the cave dwellers who produced the earliest known forms of written language in the shape of painted pictures on their cave walls, it seems that these pictures served as a mnemonic device to help in the recall of stories. The pictures apparently served this purpose very well, but problems arose when people wanted to travel. Hence the need for more portable mnemonic devices. For example, in the Inca empire, some used a *quipu* (pronounced 'key-poo') to help them remember tribal stories and to pass on

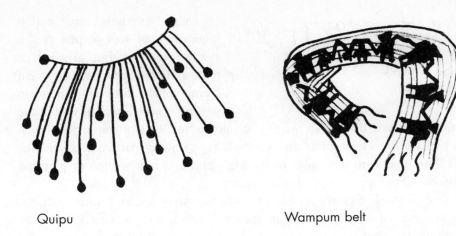

Quipu   Wampum belt

information such as the number of lifestock. The *quipu* was a cord with a series of coloured strings and knots that could be worn as a necklace. Different-coloured strings, different positions, and sizes of the knots all had meaning for the storyteller or recorder. The knots (using the decimal system) could record crop information or population counts. North American Indians used a wampum belt in much the same way—different-coloured shells were shaped into beads and woven into a sequence to tell a story or record an event. In many cases the colours represented different ideas: red was for war or anger; black was death or misfortune; white was peace, health, and riches; yellow was gold or tribute; purple was grief or sympathy. The number of beads used, their colour, and their order would help the teller remember the story or information.

Drums were another portable mnemonic device. In fact most memorisation techniques are based on sound or vision. Hearing a sound like a drumbeat or seeing a coloured bead can help the memory. There are some memorisation techniques that do make pictures that others can 'read'. The pictures may not tell the whole story but they give clues that even a stranger can understand. The Sioux Indians of North Dakota, for instance, made this kind of mnemonic device, called 'Lone Dog's Winter Count', a chronicle of 71 winters starting from the year 1800. A symbol or picture of the most important event of each winter was drawn on a buffalo hide. Even if you are not familiar with the Dakota tribe, you can guess at many of the events represented and you can follow their sequence. This is a great step forward in the art of writing—for a stranger to be able to understand when you are not there to say it. *Writing does what speech cannot*—it goes beyond the barriers of time and space.

Writing has undergone many transitional stages, one of which is the pictogram stage, where pictures represented objects. Many different cultures have used pictograms. Some are easy to understand while others are unrecognisable until you know the code. Some languages, such as Chinese, use written or pictorial symbols intended to represent a whole word.

他们正在做什么

Chinese symbols

These symbols are called **logograms** or **logographs** (i.e. a symbol representing a word or phrase). Other forms are Egyptian hieroglyphics and early cuneiform writing systems such as that of the Sumerians. However, no known writing system is totally logographic; all such systems contain both logograms and symbols representing particular sounds or syllables. The **ideogram** is similar to the logogram and is a written or pictorial symbol intended to represent an idea or concept.

Today we often use pictures instead of words to convey messages. International symbols are used at airports and train stations to help travellers find their way around, no matter what language they speak. Pictures also feature on some maps where writing might not fit or be as appropriate.

The mythology and symbolism of Aboriginal cultures in Australia were often expressed in rock art. Thousands of 'galleries' survive across the continent with millions of individual designs. The art holds a key to understanding the origins of the regional variations that characterised Aboriginal societies. 'Aboriginal worldview was a spiritual one and many values were expressed by the scars on their bodies … and the total array of their decorative art …' (Mulvaney 1987: 112). Much of the surviving rock art can throw light on what life might have been like many thousands of years ago.

Media such as television, the Internet, and computer games all rely on a knowledge of symbols representing language. Signs, symbols, and icons communicate messages without a printed message. The logo of a television station, a shopping trolley symbol on the World Wide Web, an icon representing a folder in word-processing software, the image of Super Mario, road traffic signs, and community symbols—these are designed to be easily recognised by the target audience. Language is conveyed through signs and symbols.

Another set of symbols

Semiotics is the study of systems of signs or symbols and how they have evolved. It comes from the same Greek word conveying 'sign or meaning', as in 'semantics' and 'semaphore'. Both mathematicians and musicians write texts that employ sign systems.

Origin of the alphabet

The English alphabet developed gradually over thousands of years. Most civilisations start with pictograms, then progress to ideograms and phonograms, which become their written language. Some cultures, however, have bypassed the pictogram and ideogram stages and gone straight to a 'syllabary'.

A **syllabary** is a list of the set of written symbols, each of which represents a syllable (i.e. an element of speech) of the written language. This happens when someone who knows about the idea of writing comes along and meets a group of people who do not have a written language. For instance, a syllabary was invented for the Cree Indians of North America by James Evans. The Cree writing system that he invented to do this used fewer than 50 signs, so it was very easy to learn and their knowledge of writing spread very quickly.

The letters we use today do not look like pictures any more but they were developed from pictures used by writers who lived in the Middle East thousands of years ago. For example, we get the shape of the letter 'A' from the Phoenicians, a group of people who lived in the Middle East about 3000 years ago. The Phoenicians had a letter shape called *aleph*. When letters were pictures, *aleph* meant *ox*. It was drawn like a picture of an oxhead: ◁. The Phoenicians were great sailors and traders and when they started trading with the Greek people, the Greeks adopted the basic Phoenician letter shapes. ◁ in Phoenician became △ or △ and finally **A** in Greek. The Greek letter is called *alpha* (from the Phoenician *aleph*), which in Greek means the beginning—the beginning of the alphabet.

Eventually the Greeks were conquered by the Romans, who changed the alphabet to suit the sounds in their Latin language, and this actually became our alphabet, a system in which the sounds in our language are represented by written symbols.

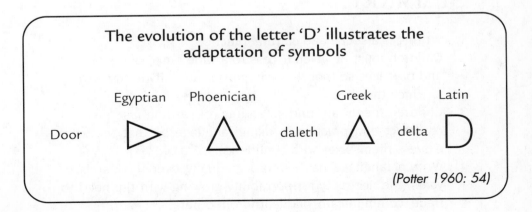

The evolution of the letter 'D' illustrates the adaptation of symbols

Door   Egyptian   Phoenician   daleth   Greek   delta   Latin

(Potter 1960: 54)

The Romans conquered most of the Mediterranean region and some of Europe, including Britain, over many years about 2000 years ago. They consequently taught their subjects the new alphabet. They carved it in stone on buildings, archways, stairways, statues, and signs. The Roman alphabet had at first only 21 letters, ABCDEFGHIKLMNOPQRSTVX, later adopting YZ for spelling foreign names. Early Roman writing was always in capital letters and only with the use of a cursive hand did the shape of our modern *u* develop from the earlier *V*. Roman *V*, when a consonant, was pronounced as modern English *w* as in *wall*, and when a vowel, could be long as in modern English *rude*, or short as in modern English *put*. Our letter *w*, originally written *uu* as the name implies, is a representation of the Roman consonant, and was first written as *w* by Norman scribes.

The 26 letters of English are used throughout the world today. The world's longest alphabet, Cambodian, has 74 letters and the shortest is 'Rotokas', from the Easter Islands, which has only eleven letters. The functions and uses of literacy vary greatly across literate cultures and historical periods, and in this sense reading and writing are not 'natural'. There are still cultures that operate without writing systems at all, and children, left to their own devices, will not 'necessarily organically or spontaneously develop or "invent" reading and writing' (Luke 1993: 26). But if children grow up in a literate culture, they will encounter, use, observe, and imitate functions and uses of literacy in everyday life.

In our contemporary society, literacy skills are increasingly important because they enable people to interact and satisfy their needs. English is an important language internationally because it is used by large English-speaking populations in the UK, the USA, and Canada, but also because it is used in other countries for international commerce and in communicating scientific knowledge. The spread of computer literacy may sweep English to increased popularity, although developments in voice-activated technology may change this. Even though many people do not use the written format to gain information, knowledge of writing is still a prerequisite to full participation in society. Writing is an integral part of our culture and it is generally the school's task to teach and develop it.

SUMMARY

1. Writing is a social and cultural practice.
2. Children must be given access to a wide range of discourses and practices so that they can participate fully in the society in which they live.
3. Children need an understanding of writing as a social construct and practice in using language so that they can express themselves with confidence.
4. Written language has evolved gradually over thousands of years, the necessity for portability growing with the need to trade, communicate, and learn from others.

5. Modern media, including computers, use a variety of symbols to represent language.
6. The school is the place where most children gain a knowledge of writing (an alphabet system) as well as a knowledge of symbols as a prerequisite to full participation in our culture.

Tasks

Discussion

1. Discuss the kinds of writing 'events' or experiences with print that children in our society are likely to have had before they come to school. Consider the diverse experiences that children from different social and cultural backgrounds might encounter, for example Aborigines or Torres Strait Islanders, immigrants, children from the city or from the country.
2. Discuss the implications for classroom teaching of the possibility that children on entering school have had a range of literacy experiences. Suggest ways of linking school experiences with children's preschool experiences.
3. Explore ways of capitalising on the experiences of children whose first language is not English. For example, ask them to talk about their country of origin in regard to language, certain customs, different sporting activities, dress, and foods that may be different from those they are currently experiencing. Devise projects that will involve the class in learning about the writing of other cultures.

Activity

What are your experiences of writing in a typical day? In a small group, brainstorm and list the many times throughout the day that you are likely to encounter writing. Children may use a variety of technologies, but forms of writing can be found when accessing the telephone, television, notes between friends, textbooks, books, films, computers, even when telling the time on a clock.

Chapter 10
The Importance of Writing in our Society

Focus

This chapter examines the enormous potential of writing
- as a learning tool
- its place in the classroom
- its power in the learning and thinking process
- its imaginative potential
- as one of the artistic processes.

It describes the range of ways in which writing operates in our society, including a discussion of various text-types along the developmental continuum from the 'most spoken' to the 'most written' form.

The philosopher Karl Popper wrote in his autobiography that learning to read and write is 'of course *the* major events in one's intellectual development ... the three R's ... are, I think, the only essentials a child has to be taught ... Everything else is atmosphere, and learning through reading and thinking' (1976: 12).

By 'atmosphere' he means the rest of the curriculum with its many and varied subjects—all of which are dependent in some ways on learning *through* reading, writing, and thinking. We learn by doing: through action, experimentation, and practice. Similar views are put forward by the Russian educator Vygotsky, who states: 'writing has occupied too narrow a place in school practice as compared to the enormous role that it plays in children's cultural development. The teaching of writing has been conceived in narrowly practical terms' (1978: 105).

While the surface features of writing (spelling, handwriting, keyboarding, grammatical correctness, punctuation) are important *means* to the end product, it is that final product, that collection of clarified ideas, that is at the heart of our intellectual endeavours.

Writing, however, is not merely a tool for learning. This view undervalues what writing is and does. Writing is (or can be) learning itself—it is the protracted synthesis or coming together of our human thinking and language competence, handling a range of problems that cannot be satisfactorily managed by mental reflection or talking.

The excitement of this excursion for a Year 3 student is abundantly evident in her written response to an outing.

Excursion to Botany Bay

On Monday 25th 1997 3J and 3M went to Botany Bay. I left home at 7.50. I was very excited. Mr Brownlow talked to us about our manners. I couldn't keep quiet. I was so excited. We went on Baxter's coach. I sat with Bethany. We had the best parents with us. There was Mrs Johns, Mrs Masterton, Mrs Kable, Mrs Holder and Mr Thoms. It took an hour and a quarter. We went to the La Perouse Museum. It was very windy. The guides were David, Steven and Siobhan. I had David. He told us the museum used to be an old cable station. They used morse code in World War 2. Then it was used as Nurses' quarters, then used by the Salvation Army, and now it is used as the La Perouse museum. La Perouse came from the middle class. He was in love with a girl in the middle class too, but his father wanted her to be someone from the upper class. So it took ten years for his father to say yes to their marriage. La Perouse was a captain at 20 years of age. He was kind during the war with the British, he left the supply store. Many men had scurvy. They got rashes, lost hair, their teeth fell out, and black rings around their eyes. A priest died in Australia. The aborigines kept on throwing the plaque away. La Perouse vanished in the Solomon Islands. The natives were wearing French jewellery. They found the cannon and the anchor. La Perouse's men built a raft and sailed away and vanished.

Elouisa

In retrospect and through a personal and factual recount text-type, Elouisa has been able to convey the mood of this learning experience and reinforced the knowledge gained through the medium of writing. Elouisa's account of the history of the La Perouse Museum has given the reader a good insight into what she has gained from the excursion and also those aspects of the excursion that particularly interested her and formed part of the learning. Through writing, she has been able to clarify, order, sort, and express ideas from an occasion that was obviously worth recalling and thinking about. Elouisa is still learning to control material to present a more organised structure, but this will develop as she becomes more familiar with different text-types and their purposes.

Writing, then, is a great collector of ideas. In fact it has been said (Walshe et al. 1986: 164) that the chief impulse that led to the invention of writing was the need to collect and store information. This complements its value as a means of communicating from a distance. Writing, whether it be through handwriting or computerised word-processing, can collect and store ideas that arise from reflection and talk. We can then access this stored information through reading obtained from various sources such as libraries and the Internet. Since it is possible to store great amounts of information on a compact disk, some children may access encyclopaedias through the compact disk form rather than the hard print version. Elouisa is able to recall her experiences at any time because she has written them down for posterity. By writing down these experiences she will more likely remember the knowledge she gained and be able to recall it at a later date (Wray and Medwell 1998: 6–7).

Students like Elouisa can use writing about an event such as an excursion to sift out the essential from the non-essential information and develop ideas that have an impact. Obviously Elouisa was affected by quite diverse pieces of information: on the one hand the young French captain, La Perouse, and the problems he had with marrying out of his class, and on the other hand the problem with scurvy on the voyage.

A major advantage of writing is that it is a wonderful clarifier of thinking. A writer takes the myriad ideas in the mind, orders them, and puts the relevant ones down on paper. In this way it objectifies thought so that we can peruse it, modify it, enrich it, refine it—in general, *revise* ideas continually so that they become the best thoughts we are capable of. Thus the invention of writing introduced a huge potential for learning into human culture through its ability to collect and clarify ideas.

When children write, they learn to be selective with their information, their choices reflecting their way of thinking and their personality. Children will also often put thoughts into writing that they will never say out loud. In this way writing becomes an important communication channel for the child.

Learning through writing

When the child writes, many kinds of learning are taking place.

Physical considerations

First, there are the elemental aids to thinking that cluster around the physical act of writing, especially four activities that promote concentration:

> *handling—the physical manipulation of pen or pencil on a page; the computer keyboard and use of the mouse*
> *depicting—handwriting, spelling, punctuation*
> *scrutinising—the constant reading back before writing on*
> *restating—the so-called 'shaping at the point of utterance', which is really our earliest form of editing, the editing of inner speech.*

> (Walshe 1986: 165)

Freedom and time lead to creativity

The act of writing actually frees the writer from social distractions and allows time to rethink and choose thoughts and words carefully. For the child in the classroom, however, this can happen only if time and opportunity are given to write without undue constraint and to experiment with words, phrases, sentences, and texts so that writing and reading become natural and integral to classroom activity. Peer sharing of writing develops over time and is a very rich outcome of a supportive atmosphere.

Quality process

A sensitive teacher can lift the quality of thinking to higher levels during a writing activity through emphasising quality preparation and, once a draft is achieved, the limitless potential for pondering, cutting, extending, putting aside, returning, revising again, and so on until it is right. Accordingly, writing can produce a deeper kind of thinking, but this can be achieved only if children are encouraged and challenged to revisit an initial draft with a view to modifying it. Many teachers find that students will more readily engage in a revision process if they can access computers and word-processing programs. Students like manipulating the icons of 'cut',' paste', and 'copy' on these programs. The classroom should not become a forum for repetitive, non-challenging, mundane writing.

When readers write

Writing can be used as a tool to enhance readers' learning about texts. Students can use writing to engage in an understanding of literacy processes, in meaningful, contextualised comprehension strategy use, and in extended and sustained opportunities to develop thoughts, knowledge, and positions (Raphael and Boyd 1997: 69; Clay 1998: 131ff.). You will find that wide readers import language and ideas from their reading into their writing. Reading expands their range of writing practices.

Writing as a creative process

Writing is a creative process. The table on page 162 compares some major models that have contributed over the centuries to the humanities, sciences, and technologies. The four processes parallel one another closely and are part of a 'creative process'. As cognitive theory cannot easily differentiate between thinking and learning, or learning and problem-solving, or problem-solving and scientific inquiry, all four processes can be viewed as learning behaviours. A common sequence of thought and action runs through them. In particular, writing offers its *thinking or learning* power for use in any classroom learning and is a powerful tool across the subject areas.

Writing, then, is more than simply a tool, markings on a page, or just a tedious service skill for writing down ideas about a subject—it is an 'offspring of the creative process', a 'learning behaviour', a 'sequence of thought and action'. Writing is truly integral to learning.

Tables like this one seldom show the full picture and this one is no exception. The table is almost exclusively concerned with verbal thinking or learning—it omits reference to feeling and emotional influences and it does not treat the non-linguistic 'intelligences' such as the six analysed by Howard Gardner in *Frames of*

Learning At Its Best

	Problem	Investigate	Get Insights	Express	Refine	Announcement	Reaction
ARTISTIC PROCESS	Experience Feel challenged Decide on project	Absorption Engagement Study/research 'Imagining'	Illumination Inspiration or revelation/ 'flash'	Drafting e.g. in painting, preliminary sketching or 'roughing'	Developing Working out Crafting 'Finishing'	Communication Show to intimates Exhibit widely	Response Appreciation Criticism Evaluation
SCIENTIFIC PROCESS	Problem Define as question Plan the inquiry	Observation Exploratory stratagems Data collection	Illumination e.g. methodical generalisation; or inspiration	Hypothesis Draft precisely	Experiment/test Verification or falsification Final writing	Publication Perhaps first to associates, then more widely	Response Acceptance or criticism
PROBLEM-SOLVING PROCESS	Problem/puzzle Define as question Plan the inquiry	Investigation Collect data Review alternatives Think laterally	Illumination 'Ah-ha' insight(s)	Formulation of best solution	Checking Error elimination Critical review	Report Demonstration Performance	Response Appreciation Criticism Evaluation
WRITING PROCESS	Experience Decide to write Define writing-aim Early broad plan	Pre-writing Idea-recollection Research Brainstorming	Illumination 'See a pattern' 'Limit the subject' 'Get a lead'	Drafting Plan, or further brainstorming; then first draft	Revision Self-editing Redrafting Proofreading	Publication Show to another Read to others Circulate widely	Response Appreciation Criticism Evaluation

(Walshe et al. 1986: 166)

Mind (1983): the logico-mathematical, spatial, musical, body-kinaesthetic, intrapersonal, and interpersonal intelligences.

Feeling and emotional influences are very important in the writing process because it is these which can be a crucial driving force behind a piece of writing. Note Elouisa's excitement about her excursion—it is this excitement that drives the piece of writing:

> ... I was very excited. Mr Brownlow talked to us about our manners. I couldn't keep quiet. I was so excited. We went on Baxter's coach. I sat with Bethany. We had the best parents with us ...

Elouisa is obviously eager to share her experiences with others. It is common to find emotional words or expressions in a recount of this kind of experience. While Elouisa goes through various cognitive processes to complete her recount—she needs to sort out the events of the excursion into a logical order, which she does, and she also needs to make choices about what information she will include in her work—the choice of words, phrases, and sentences is also governed by emotional considerations. The use of emotive words such as 'very excited', 'couldn't keep quiet', 'so excited', and 'best parents' is indicative of her state of mind about the excursion. In responding to Elouisa's writing the teacher could highlight these positive aspects.

Writing means the bringing of one's inborn thinking and language *competence* to the process, and it also means the potential, the opportunity, for that *deeper thinking* that is created by the visibility of the thought-on-the-page. This is why this incredibly complex process cannot be reduced to 'x' number of 'skills'.

SUMMARY

1. As writing is one of our tools for learning and communicating it is important for students to be genuinely interested in it. Thus it is important for teachers to be able to motivate students to write and to write often.

2. Writing is a great collector of ideas, a clarifier of thinking, and is a major aspect of learning itself—it is the protracted synthesis of our human thinking and language competence, handling a range of problems that cannot be satisfactorily managed by mental reflection or talking.

3. Writing can produce a deeper kind of thinking, especially when texts are being revised and edited.

4. Writing can be used as a tool to enhance readers' learning about text and to engage in an understanding of literacy processes.

5. Writing is a creative process and offers a powerful thinking and learning engagement for use in any classroom learning and is an important tool across the different subject areas.

Tasks

 *Discussion*

Read the following piece of writing:

A Day To Forget

One moment it was fine and sunny and the next the rain poured down. It was the wet kind of rain, the type that sou'westers and gumboots wouldn't keep out. It seemed as if the heavens had opened. It squelched at every step and my clothes stuck to me like flies to a flypaper. After some time I came to a bus shelter. I ran for it, but inside was my old enemy Joe Harper. I stood transfixed for a second or two and then bolted out again, into the rain. As I sauntered along I came across an old friend of mine James Story. 'Nice to see you,' I said (inwardly I thought differently for James was boredom in human form). We walked along for a while, James nattering on as usual. The rain frequently drowned his voice. Presently when he realised I wasn't listening the talk began to wane rapidly and then *silence* at long last. A dead rat floated along the gutter frequently being pushed underwater by hailstones.

Hailstones!?! It was not until then that I had noticed it was hailing. Suddenly I broke into a run. My hair stuck up in points leaving the astonished James wondering what was the matter with me. In another shelter I sank down in a heap. A bus came along, I caught it and away we drove.

Susan, 11

---

1. What is the overall tone or mood of this piece of writing? What words or phrases contribute to creating this tone? How do you think Susan is feeling? Are her feelings made clear in the writing? If so, how?
2. Use the surface features, the organisation, and the content of the two samples by Elouisa and Susan to decide which is the more advanced piece of writing. Justify your choice.
3. Could you give Susan any advice as to how she might make the writing clearer and/or even more interesting to the reader?

Activity

Examine the ways feelings manifest themselves in the following:

Last week daddy came home with four tickets for the circus. daddy are we going to the circus I said yes we all are said daddy we are going to night. Oh terrific I said. lets hurry and get ready now my mummy said So off we went. At the circus people were coming in and sitting down, then a lady said the acrobats It was good fun looking at them next it was red nose the clown with his pet monkey They was very funny the circus was good I said and my mummy said it was good to ...

Kate, 9

1. What is the child trying to do with this piece of writing? Is it largely a narrative, a recount, an information report, a combination of some or all of these? Why?
2. From an initial reading of Kate's writing, list the surface features such as punctuation and spelling that may need attention. How do you balance the importance of surface features and content in a piece of writing?
3. From a close reading of the piece, list the words and phrases that carry emotion and comment on the overall tone of the piece of writing.
4. Make some suggestions as to what a teacher might do to help Kate write more clearly and expressively.
5. Now see if you can write a couple of paragraphs about a recent event that you felt strongly about. Pay attention to how you will structure your recount and the kinds of emotive words and phrases you will use. Take into consideration your targeted audience. Share the writing with a small group.

Chapter 11
The Writing
Developmental Continuum

> **Focus**
> This chapter focuses on writing as a developmental process. The processes, skills and strategies are acquired over many years and students go through various *stages* of development. In fact the art of writing is a lifelong process in that we continue to learn new aspects about writing for as long as we are able to read and write. The chapter gives an overview of what writing looks like at various stages and gives some pointers to look for in the writing to help place it at a developmental stage in the process.

Before school

Before starting school children are exposed to many kinds of literacy (see also Chapter 4). They enter school with a vast array of literacy backgrounds. Some will already own many picture books and will be accustomed to the reading of books by members of the family, in the preschool environment, at the local library, or through television programs. Most households with preschoolers watch children's educational television programs and these can be valuable learning motivators.

Parents and carers play a key role in children's language acquisition since they have the opportunity to interact with children by fostering reading and writing at home. Shared language experiences promote children's confidence and self-esteem, which are important factors in promoting literacy awareness before they come to school. Through the provision of books and materials in English, and languages other than English, adults can develop children's linguistic awareness and language ability. Young children pick up their language learning in everyday situations (e.g. in verbal interaction; when parents point out and read signs, especially at places such as the supermarket; when they tell stories or read picturebooks to their listening children). Many preschools have rich language learning environments where the enjoyment of shared lullabies, stories, and rhymes fosters language ability. The encouragement of listening and speaking skills in preschoolers is very important for the later acquisition of reading and writing skills.

Many children live in a literacy-rich environment with many print-carrying messages where they can practise the language skills of listening, speaking, reading, and writing from a very early age. Other families rarely buy newspapers and many do not buy books but, most importantly, they still highly *value* literacy. The emergent reader will choose books, perhaps with the help of an adult, but there is no magical 'readiness' age when they should be introduced. In fact books should be introduced to children from birth, as Dorothy Butler has advocated in *Babies Need Books* (1995). The students' writing skills emerge as they progress from 'scribbling' to more purposeful and meaningful communications. Students' opportunities to develop literacy practices may be determined by their socioeconomic background—if reading and writing are seen as important skills then this will be passed on to the students.

At school

The role of the school should be to try to build on the knowledge and skills that children bring to school. In this way schools can achieve success with children from all backgrounds.

What is it we look for in students' writing? What are the kinds of things we can say about a piece of writing, and how does writing change as the student develops through the different stages? As you work through this section observe how the various pieces of writing under discussion exhibit different structures and language features as the purpose varies and the audience changes for whom the pieces are written.

Different syllabuses and programs contain writing samples and indicators of what to look for in children's writing. For example, the First Steps (1994) program from Western Australia uses the following useful continuum, which shows indicators telling us what to look for in texts. A glance at Fig. 11.1 can give you some idea of how writing develops during the primary years.

The NSW *English K–6 Syllabus* (Board of Studies NSW 1988a) has similar outcomes and indicators but divides the continuum into four stages—Early Stage 1, Stage 1, Stage 2, and Stage 3. Each stage has its own outcomes, and support documents give examples of different text-forms with discussion of indicators of achievement. These models are all helpful in giving a good idea of how writing develops.

Wilkinson (1980) produced a model (after the UK 'Crediton Project') that is still useful in discussing students' writing on a developmental basis. He and his team analysed different text-types of children aged between 7 and 13 and developed some useful categories for commenting on the development in the writing. They were not only concerned with linguistic features such as sentence complexity but also with qualities of thought, feeling, and moral judgment. He states that these assessment aspects arose from an 'interaction between our perceptions of the written materials, teachers' judgments and theoretical considerations' (1980: 65).

PHASE 3: Early Writing

Children write about topics which are personally significant. They are beginning to consider audience needs. They have a sense of sentence but may only be able to deal with one or two elements of writing at one time, e.g. spelling but not punctuation.

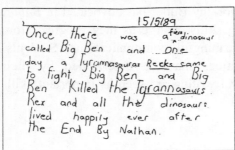

PHASE 4: Conventional Writing

Writers are familiar with most aspects of the writing process and are able to select forms to suit different purposes. Their control of structure, punctuation and spelling may vary according to the complexity of the writing task.

The Writer:

- uses a small range of familiar text forms
- chooses topics that are personally significant
- uses basic sentence structures and varies sentence beginnings
- can explain in context, some of the purposes of using writing, e.g. shopping list or telephone messages as a memory aid
- experiments with words drawn from language experience activites, literature, media and oral language of peers and others
- begins to develop editing skills
- attempts to use some punctuation
- talks with others to plan and revise own writing

The Writer:

- uses text forms to suit purpose and audience
- can explain why some text forms may be more appropriate than others to achieve a specific purpose
- writes a range of text forms including stories, reports, procedures and expositions
- uses a variety of simple, compound and extended sentences
- groups sentences containing related information into paragraphs
- is beginning to select vocabulary according to the demands of audience and purpose, e.g. uses subject-specific vocabulary
- uses proof-reading guide or checklist to edit own or peers' writing
- punctuates simple sentences correctly
- uses a range of strategies for planning, revising and publishing own written texts

Major Teaching Emphases:

- develop an awareness that writing is purposeful
- talk about the differences between oral and written language
- read, write and discuss a range of different forms of writing for different purposes and audiences
- teach planning and revision strategies
- show how sentences are linked to form a cohesive paragraph
- show how paragraphs are linked to form a whole text
- teach strategies for learning to spell new words
- continue to help children develop word banks using topic or theme words
- discuss the selection of words to enhance meaning
- model the use of appropriate linking words
- introduce a proof-reading guide and encourage children to use it

Major Teaching Emphases:

- teach children to plan and write both narrative and informational texts
- help children to adapt their writing to suit the intended purpose and to explore alternative ways of expressing ideas
- discuss linguistic features of basic text types
- teach children appropriate use of organisational markers such as topic sentences, paragraphs and headings
- show different ways of linking paragraphs to form a whole text
- encourage the use of a variety of linking words
- encourage children to take responsibility for their own learning
- teach revising, editing and proof-reading skills
- discuss and foster 'personal voice' and individual style in writing
- teach children the conventions of language (punctuation, grammar and spelling) in context

Fig. 11.1   Overview of writing developmental continuum

PHASE 5: Proficient Writing

Writers have developed a personal style of writing and are able to manipulate forms of writing to suit their purposes. They have control over spelling and punctuation. They choose from a large vocabulary and their writing is cohesive, coherent and satisfying.

> *Our Heritage*
>
> Many of the people who want to save the trees talk of history and heritage. The tree was a meeting place, a place of happiness, a source of shade on burning summer days after a refreshing swim in the nearby river. But then the traffic built up the river became a murky passage of sludge. The children grew up and had their own children but their children knew nothing of this once peaceful place.

The Writer:

- selects text forms to suit purpose and audience, demonstrating control over most essential elements
- can explain the goals in writing a text and indicate the extent to which they were achieved
- writes to define, clarify and develop ideas and express creativity, e.g. stories, poems, reports, arguments
- writes a topic sentence and includes relevant information to develop a cohesive paragraph
- organises paragraphs logically to form a cohesive text
- uses a variety of simple, compound and complex sentences appropriate to text form
- uses a wide range of words that clearly and precisely convey meaning in a particular form
- edits own writing during and after composing
- demonstrates accurate use of punctuation
- takes notes, selects and synthesises relevant information and plans text sequence.

Major Teaching Emphases:

- provide opportunities for students to analyse, evaluate and structure an extensive variety of forms of text, both narrative and informational
- discuss the specific effect of context, audience and purpose on written texts
- extend students' knowledge of correct use of writing conventions
- teach students to analyse mass media
- discuss and foster a sense of 'personal voice', e.g. individual style, tone, rhythm, vocabulary
- extend the students' range of planning and revision strategies
- encourage students to use writing to reflect on and monitor their own learning
- encourage students to read as writers and write as readers

PHASE 6: Advanced Writing

Content, Organisation and Contextual Understandings
◆ controls effectively the language and structural features of a large repertoire of text forms
◆ controls and manipulates the linguistic and structural components of writing to enhance clarity and impact
◆ generates, explores and develops topics and ideas
◆ may choose to manipulate or abandon conventional text forms to achieve impact
◆ maintains stylistic features throughout texts
◆ makes critical choices of tone and point of view to suit different purposes and to influence audiences
◆ writes exploring and developing abstract ideas
◆ makes informed choices about the linguistic features, organisation and development of ideas and information according to audience and purpose
◆ deliberately structures sentences to enhance a text and according to audience and purpose
◆ develops ideas and information clearly, sustaining coherence throughout complex texts
◆ conceals personal bias where appropriate

Word Usage
◆ selects and manipulates words, phrases or clauses, for their shades of meaning and impact
◆ successfully involved the reader by the use of literary devices such as metaphor, simile, onomatopoeia
◆ uses abstract and technical terms appropriately in context

Editing
◆ modifies and restructures phrases, clauses, paragraphs or whole texts to clarify and achieve precise meaning

Language Conventions
◆ controls the conventions of writing but may make a deliberate choice to break them to enhance meaning.

Strategies
◆ takes responsibility for planning, revising and proof reading to ensure that writing achieves its purpose
◆ reflects on, and critically evaluates own writing to ensure that content and organisation suit the purpose for writing and the audience
◆ evaluates and synthesises information from a variety of sources to support view.

Attitude
◆ responds to a compulsion to write
◆ reflects on, critically evaluates and critiques own writing and that of others

Phases

PHASE 1: Role Play Writing

Children are beginning to come to terms with a new aspect of language, that of written symbols. They experiment with marks on paper with the intention of communicating a message or emulating adult writing.

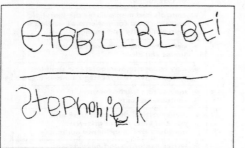

PHASE 2: Experimental Writing

Children are aware that speech can be written down and that written messages remain constant. They understand the left to right organisation of print and experiment with writing letters and words.

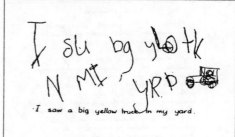

Key Indicators

The Writer:

- assigns a message to own symbols
- understands that writing and drawing are different, e.g. points to words while 'reading'
- is aware that print carries a message
- uses known letters or approximations of letters to represent written language
- shows beginning awareness of directionality; i.e. points to where print begins

The Writer:

- reads back own writing
- attempts familiar forms of writing, e.g. lists, letters, recounts, stories, messages
- writes using simplified oral language structures, e.g. 'I brt loles'
- uses writing to convey meaning
- realises that print contains a constant message
- uses left to right and top to bottom orientation of print
- demonstrates one-to-one correspondence between written and spoken word
- relies heavily on the most obvious sounds of a word

Major Teaching Emphases:

- demonstrate the connection between oral and written language
- demonstrate that written messages remain constant
- demonstrate that writing communicates a message
- focus on the way print works (print concepts and conventions)
- demonstrate that writing is purposeful and has an intended audience
- use correct terminology for letters, sounds, words
- encourage children to experiment with writing

Major Teaching Emphases:

- model brief, imaginative and factual texts and explain the purpose and intended audience
- help children build lists of high-frequency words from their reading and writing
- demonstrate the one-to-one correspondence of written and spoken words
- discuss how writing can be used to communicate over time and distance
- encourage children to talk about their experiences
- help children understand how written texts are composed in sentences
- help children develop a stable concept of a word
- help children relate written symbols to the sounds they represent
- talk about letters, words and sentences

At all phases:

- model good English language use
- model writing every day
- encourage students to reflect on their understandings, gradually building a complete picture of written language structures
- ensure that students have opportunities to write for a variety of audiences and purposes
- encourage students to share their writing experiences

When commenting on children's writing, it is sometimes the case that readers or teachers look at the stylistic features and make comments about the surface features such as punctuation and spelling and take little notice of what the writer is actually trying to say. It is here that Wilkinson's model is particularly helpful:

- *cognitive:* the writer's awareness of the world: one's ability to describe, interpret, generalise, and speculate
- *affective:* the writer's awareness of emotions and feelings of self and other people including the reader and one's environment and awareness of reality
- *moral:* the writer's awareness of a value system, attitudes, and judgments
- *stylistic:* the writer's awareness of **syntax** (the way words are organised), verbal competence, text organisation, **cohesion**, awareness of reader, and appropriateness of text

In recent years, language syllabuses have tended to focus on the way texts are organised and there has been emphasis on getting students to conform to a certain

Text structure	**An Excursion to the Rock Pools**	*Language Structure*
Orientation introduces the time, place, and characters in the event.	On Friday the 23rd of March our class went to the rock pools near Bondi Beach. We boarded the bus at nine o'clock.	Use of word families to build information e.g. rock pool, beach
Record of events.	When we arrived at the beach we went over to the rock pools. We walked around. The teacher told us to examine the shells and other sea life in the pools carefully. After a while we found a sheltered area to have morning tea.	Use of action verbs e.g. arrived, walked, found. Use of complex sentences e.g. "When we arrived we went"
Record of events, including evaluation.	We made lots of sketches of the shell-fish and other living things in the rock pools. We were all amazed at how many different kinds of animals and fish live in rock pools.	Use of past tense. & connections to sequence events in time e.g. when, after, then, next.
	After lunch we were allowed to explore some sand caves. We then had a game of tip on the beach.	Use of reported speech e.g. "...teacher told us..."
Re-orientation and evaluation.	We all took lots of good notes. We boarded the bus and returned to school at two o'clock. It was a really fun day.	Use of adverbial phrases of time and place e.g. "On Friday", "at the beach", "in rock pools".

Fig. 11.2   An example of a recount

text-form. This has the danger of children losing creativity or thinking that their writing must follow rigid structures. For example, when the Kindergarten child is learning to manage a recount, it might be structured in this way:

Orientation	*Yesterday I went to Grandma's place. She was sick.*
Record of events	*Mum cooked some food for her, then she cleaned the house.*
Reorientation	*Then I went home.*

By the time the child has reached the middle to upper primary grades, a recount would be more complex in sentence structure and idea but would contain the same overall structure. An example of a recount from a middle primary (Stage 2) student could look like the one in Fig. 11.2.

While the overall textual structure of these two pieces is similar, there are major differences in sentence complexity and sentence type. Much more information is included as the student's awareness of the world (ability to describe and interpret) has increased as well as awareness of self and others and an ability to make an evaluation ('It was a really fun day'). As the writer develops, there is an increasing ability to make meaning, which means that language choices become more complex and appropriate as the context for the writing becomes better understood.

Characteristics of early writing

Children in the preschool years may be able to write certain words, such as their name or *Mum* and *Dad*, with accuracy and a knowledge of what they mean. Their teacher may have repeatedly put their name on drawings and belongings so that they learn to identify the word with their own possessions or work. Writing at the preschool stage is characterised by random marks on a page ('scribbling'), which gradually begin to form a pattern.

Children in the early years (K–2) may find writing a difficult task. Indeed the physical act of representing all of the associated qualities of speech (tone, intonation, pause, emphasis, gesture) in a complex system of marks on paper is daunting for the beginning writer. At this stage writing activities should be short but frequent, and students should be allowed to use a variety of media for writing and/or making marks on paper. Students need something to write about, so lots of stimuli, including children's literature, excursions, picture study, and class talk about happenings and books, are important.

Writing can become laborious physically—it can take a 5–7-year-old a long time to form the words. Young students tire easily and are inclined to do one draft only. That is, the first draft often becomes the final product. The teacher may find that the computer will provide a welcome relief from the physical tedium of writing, especially for young students. Computers enable the editing process to be completed much more easily and they can make the publishing process much more satisfying for children.

The way the writing is constructed can be a challenge. Narrative or recount seems to be the easiest to do when one event follows the other in some kind of chronological order. Young writers often want to include what may appear irrelevant detail to the reader without getting on with the main events in the narrative or recount. The recount often tends to be disjointed. There is often mention of familiar rituals such as getting out of bed, having meals, watching TV, and going to bed. Students can use these to mark out the day, as is evident in Gary's writing:

> I had a great day last Satiday. I got out of bed I found some prsnts on my bed it was my bithday. I opened them and found some cricket ger. I knew it was my bithday I went downsters and had brekfast I played cricket all day with my frends. For tea I had a party with frends. I watched TV and went to bed. It was a grate day.
>
> Gary, 7

Notice how this is written from the focused view of the child. There is little awareness of others and when there is, there is little explanation about others. But the recount does have an orientation, a series of events, and a reorientation to conform to the overall structure of this particular text-type.

Students use narrative more easily than analytical writing. They find it a challenge to objectify in order to see the effects of their writing on others. Many stories at this stage have elements of the fairytale structure, which is a result of their own reading or of listening to parents or teachers sharing such tales with them. The 'once upon a time' opening and the 'lived happily ever after' conclusion can be readily found, as in Loretta and James' writing, and occasionally there is a cause–effect relationship expressed, as in Dale's writing:

> If the stadium was burnt down I would be sad.
>
> Dale, Yr 1

> Once upon a time there was onle one bird and it was calde a vilet and it was a pritey purpul. One day it had five eggs. When the eggs hatch there was a bird with pink with yellow with brown and with red blue perpull. and they lived happaly ever after.
>
> Loretta, Yr 1

> Once there was an old house in the woods. It was haunted and very scary.
>
> James, Yr 1

The writing of young children often omits information that might give the reader important background in order to conceptualise the context of the writing in time, space, and place:

> Wuns there lived a countree. It wos so hot No wun wanted to live ther. All of the tres wer folen down.

> Jacinta, Yr 1

It is a mark of development when awareness of the reader's needs—a sense of audience—is apparent in the writing.

The written style in these early years is often the spoken style. Obvious links such as 'and', 'then', and 'so' are used. There is wide use of common verbs such as 'be', 'have', 'go', 'say', 'take', and 'put'. Spelling is often close to pronunciation (e.g. *wun* = one). Nouns can be general (man, lady, policeman), often without qualification such as the use of adjectives. Concrete rather than abstract words are used. (There is not much about abstract concepts like bravery, honesty, fear, happiness, but realistic situations occur where these qualities are apparent). Sometimes direct speech is used but usually without the punctuation marks:

> At Saterday I am going to jason house and jason bruther had a prte he was turned satnen and his perns gav sum presns to ruj. and jason sed to ruj happy bithday.

> Joel Yr 1

Many of the above examples show evidence of 'temporary' or 'invented' spellings, which are a common feature in the early years. One of the best ways for students to learn to spell is to learn words by using them in real writing contexts rather than learning to spell by rote. The more students are presented with real writing models and the more they get to use words in writing, the closer their spellings will get to the correct form.

Sometimes writers in the early stages show evidence of approximating the standards of the writer in higher stages—a fact that highlights the individual nature of development. Students will progress at different rates and this will necessitate the teacher having different expectations and understandings for each student in the class. Here is a Year 1 writer producing a text that is more akin to that of a middle primary school writer:

> Last holidays I went to Warragamba Dam where our water comes from. When we put our tap on hard all of the water comes rushing down the river. It is very very deep. People would drown at the bottom and die but I was too scared to look down.

> Then after we went to a good view. Then I felt I could see all of Australia. It was so beautiful. We were on a cliff and I saw mountains that were so high and it was so peaceful and I had to be careful. You could see the water from the bottom on the way back. We had to go on a rocky road and it was a long way back.

> When we were on a dirt road we saw a cow, like a cow but just a calf which was out of the gate. So my mum stopped the car and took me over to

the calf but it was very very scared if I walked over to it. It would walk away from me eating grass. When we walked over to the car it went 'Moo, moo.' Then we went home.

Chris Yr 1

Students at all stages enjoy experimenting with new forms, phrases, and words—playing with language can be fun. Sally (Year 2) was asked to write about a topic using the letters of the word 'winter' to start her sentences (an acrostic):

Winter is cold and cloudy.
In winter we drink hot chocolate
Never go in the coldwater.
The sun is often not shining in winter
Everywhere it is rainy and misty.
Read books in front of the fire.

Hale (Year 2) chose to write her piece inside the outline of a fish drawing:

If stars were trout
They would glitter through the
ocean of darkness, Swaying their
jewelled tails behind them.

Emily (also Year 2) was motivated by something she really likes and suggested some ideas about ice-cream:

Ice cream
Its wriggly and smily
Smooth and creamy
and sweet
Nice

Tasks

Discussion

1. Read the following comments by teacher trainees about their early writing experiences and discuss in a small group your own memories of early writing:

The foundations of my writing career are etched deeply in my mind. I was terribly distressed with my kindergarten teacher on the first day of school as she had not attempted to teach me how to write. Much to my parents' amusement, I conveyed my distress and I'm certain that this tale will be shared at my 21st party.

K.

My earliest memory of writing was in Kindergarten with those orange folders that you used to put words in to make sentences. I remember that I would make the longest sentences in the whole class.

T.

2. Responding with encouragement to children's work is a very important part of the writing process to give the child early positive experiences in writing. Suggest teaching methods that might overcome any problems these students encountered. Discuss your own experiences in response to these comments by teacher trainees:

I can recall one moment of glory in Year 2 when the teacher gave me the highest mark in the class for a very long-winded creative writing story I had written. Not only had this mark made me happy, the teacher also asked me to read the story at the parent–teacher night.

K.

I think it is very important not to criticise anybody when they write their own things, as I was sometimes criticised when I was little. I think that children should be provided with more time to write and express their own feelings and ideas. When I was little we had themes to write about that were always marked. We did not really have time provided at school when we could write anything we wanted that wasn't going to be marked.

V.

Writing for me always feels like a chore ... My first and lasting memories of writing are from second grade. My teacher began each day of school by handing out a writing topic. I was always so confused over how to go about writing a story. From this time onwards I have always dreaded writing.

M.

Activity

Compare the following two pieces of writing about koalas from Year 2 writers: Kara's poem and Simon's text.

1. Comment on how the texts reflect the different stages of writing for each child.
2. Decide what their different purposes are, list the positive features of the texts, and note whether they are effective in communicating information and feelings about the koala.

Koalas

Koalas eat leaves high in trees.
They may have fleas,
They like the breeze.
The mother's pouch opens at base,
It is not made out of lace.
Koalas are rarely on the ground,
It's in trees the koala is found.
They don't make much sound.
Some have fluffy hair and,
Some have scruffy hair.
Beware of their claws and wide jaws.
Their feet are small and not fat at all.
When the baby is born it has no hair,
But it doesn't care.
When the koala makes a noise at night,
It might give you a fright.

Koalas

Koalas have two thumbs. They have two thumbs to make it easier to hold onto things. When the babies are born they are nearly as small as a baby bird. When the baby is born its mother licks a path for the baby to crawl up the pouch. The mother licks a path so it is easier to crawl up. I said crawl up because the Koala's pouch opens from the bottom of her. Koalas are marsupial. They eat gum leaves. They live all their life in gum trees. They are nearly all gone because of bush fires. It is very hard for Koalas to get away from bush fires. The mother or the father Koalas mixes gum leaves and waste together like cereal that we eat. Then she or he feeds the baby Koala the cereal. Some Koalas are nice to cuddle because some Koalas are very well trained. But some are NOT cuddly because they are not used to being cuddled at all.

The developing writer

By the middle primary years students are becoming quite adventurous and can experiment with a variety of text-forms (narrative, recount, information report, procedure, etc.) with a good understanding of a targeted audience. They are generally receptive to editing their work and see the sense in trying to improve their writing or in making it more appealing and meaningful for the reader as they are developing a better understanding of the concept of audience. The student will now have a store of words that can be spelt automatically, especially common words.

Strategies for getting many unknown words right or nearly right, including sound–letter knowledge, use of rules and use of analogy, will be developing. Also, legible handwriting and keyboarding skills will be evident by this stage. Students will be better at talking about the grammar of texts by this stage, especially when referring to how meaning can be enhanced by the use of adjectives, adverbs, phrases, and clauses.

The narrative form is still common at this level, but much longer stretches of text are written. There is less use of time markers such as getting up and meals. The student can generally begin with a significant incident without irrelevant events and without starting at the beginning of the day:

> There once was a mean drooly guard dog. He had shiny black fur with patches of brown on it. He guarded the museum which had models of cars inside. He was treated very well. He refered himself as the king of dogs and expected everyone to obbey him. Some people thought of him as a dog eater that only came out at night.
>
> One dark quiet night a female poodle passed the gate of the museum. She had luster white fur with beautiful blue eyes and she walked exactly like a show-of, dog would walk. When the museum people found out about her, they gave more love and care to her, and less to the guard dog.
>
> Two days later, the poodle was walking along the park with her owner. The poodle then saw a male poodle across the road, with fluffy brown fur. She got so carried away, that without thinking, she ran straight across the road, and got run over by a coming car. Much sorrow went around the museum. When the dog found out, he thought, 'maybe its good she died after all'.
>
> Carol, Year 4

- More adjectives are used, together with more complex sentences and phrases ('shiny black fur with patches of brown'; 'the museum which had models of cars inside'; 'When the museum people found out about her, they gave …'; 'She had luster white fur with beautiful blue eyes …').
- Also notice how Carol is able not only to advance a story with complex events but also to comment on the actions by making judgments: 'He was treated very well.'; 'Some people thought of him as a dog eater …'; 'Much sorrow went around the museum.'; 'maybe its good she died after all.'
- Carol uses dialogue to heighten interest or to further the narrative.
- Spelling: obey, show-off, it's = it is.
- There is more awareness of location and more description of setting.

Some students go through a stage of writing stereotypical language:

> … We left a note for mum and dad to say gone to get the paper and to go along the sea front. We did not wake my brother up. When we got out it was a lovely day with the sun shinning and a cool breeze. We went out of the

camp site and down onto the sand. We took our sandles of and went into the sea it was cold but refreshing.

Sandra, Year 4

The viewpoint is in many cases still egocentric and there is little comment on emotional aspects. There is more attention to other people but usually at a single dimensional level—with little attempt to enter into the mind of the other person.

Tasks

Discussion

Discuss the implications of these two statements by trainee teachers about their writing experiences in Year 4. Share ideas about what a teacher could do to overcome negative attitudes towards writing. Consider suggestions such as varying writing tasks so that boredom doesn't set in, or giving students more choice so that they can feel more in control of what they write.

I remember that in Year 4 we had to keep a daily journal. I loathed this chore. I often used to write lists, for example: 'Things I like, 'my favourite food', etc. Often I would simply state, 'I don't know what to write' or 'I can't think of anything'. I would also often try to be late for school as journal writing usually occurred in the morning ... I still don't necessarily enjoy writing but it doesn't frighten me quite as much as it used to.

S.

I received the highest mark in the class so my story was read to the other 4th grade. I was so proud. Throughout that year I continued writing my very best. After 4th grade my writing skills went for a dive ...

A.

 Activity

Ask students in the class to write a review of a book they have enjoyed and would wish to recommend to others. Use Tim's review of Roald Dahl's **George's Marvellous Medicine** as a model.

You may discuss with them the positive aspects of this response to a popular children's book. Consider structure, stylistic features (such as spelling, syntax, cohesion, verbal competence), and reader awareness:

George simply has to do something abut his miserable old grandmother. She's always grouching and griping and she has the nastiest eating habits in the world. Most old ladies are nice and like to eat cream cakes; not George's grandmother. she likes caterpillars and slugs with cabbage, and earwigs with celery. She's so horrible that George decides to do something.

He thinks of some clever ways to shake her up: bangers under her chair, snakes down her neck—but no! He decided to concoct a special magic brew that will either make her much nicer or make her disappear altogether. His marvellous medicine has everything in it from hair-remover to anti-freeze. Read the book to see what happens.

Tim, Year 4

The proficient writer

Upper primary students are beginning to manage a range of text-forms with appropriate registers; they have a better awareness of appropriate language for different types of texts. They are more aware of language that is colloquial, humorous, formal, dramatic, and so on.

They make extensive use of outside models (i.e. literary, newspaper, television, etc.) Students are more in control of the narrative and have more confidence in adjusting the chronological order. The capacity to write extended prose is one of the characteristics of a proficient writer. They may surprise you with their choice of a gruesome topic (in your eyes) and by their facility with words, often echoing— faintly or strongly—the novels that they have read or the television stories they have watched. The following effort, titled 'Noise in the Night', is the opening paragraph in a longer story and makes good use of punctuation for effect:

I woke with a start and heard the stealthy footstep in the passage outside my door. I dived under the blankets and gave myself a pep talk 'Listen this is when you become a hero don't be a chicken!' Reappearing from under my quilt I quietly slid back my blankets and listened. Had I given myself a pep talk for nothing? Wait!!! I heard it. The step was muffled by my shut door but I heard it. I slid off my bed and tip-toed over to my closet (with teddy in my hand) and eased it open. SQUEAK!!! I stood frozen with fear. What if the person belonging to the footsteps heard my closet squeak? After what seemed like hours I moved again. Seizing my cricket bat I padded to my door. As I slowly turned the handle I found out that my body was covered in goosebumps and I was sure they weren't there because of the Arctic climate in my room. Steeling into the hallway I raised my bat.

Betsy, Year 6

Proficient writers are much more aware of the reader and can experiment with ways of developing interest and tension by keeping the reader guessing.

Karen's (Year 6) writing is the first chapter of a book titled 'Insights into the Past':

Chapter 1. It was an ordinary day

I was 12 when it happened. No one expected it. It was just one of those ordinary day things.

I was always down and nothing could cheer me up. I was comforted by my friends and family, then grew tired of all the fussing being done about me and told everyone to back off, but they just wouldn't listen.

I would sometimes just have to lock myself in my room, as it would drive me insane to keep hearing Simone are you okay? Simone, do you want something, Dear, to keep you happy or Simone you've just got to stop sulking. Keeping me happy or sulking was not the issue, they simply didn't understand.

Before the tragedy I was living a normal life. I was happy and I was sad when I needed to be, instead of always being down and depressed.

My parent told me to strive high, but I couldn't think. I couldn't look at myself in the mirror. I could just see me the girl who has nothing to strive for. I wish they were still here. I miss them more than anything.

To explain how it felt is very hard. It's not just like a pet dying , because when they die you shed a few tears and that's about it, but when someone close to you dies you don't shed a few tears but a lot, and it takes time to get over them. I wish they would come home, but it will never happen.

Certainly there are still aspects of structure and ideas to be worked on here, but it can be seen how good communication is beginning to be developed. There is an awareness of *self* and of *others* as psychological beings—a movement away from egocentricity. The student shows good use of varying sentence structure to communicate ideas.

As witnessed in Neil's story about Kotic the seal, at the moral level there is an awareness of fairness and intention, and a less stereotyped method of portraying virtue and vice, good and evil, right and wrong:

Kotic was a seal. He had a big scar on his back. When he was two years old he was driven to the fur farm inland. One man said fire and in a few moments Kotic could not recognise any of his friends. They had all been skinned. Kotic just ran as fast as he could back to the beach but he could not. Desperately he ran round trying to get out, then a man walked up to him. Seeing the scar on Kotic's back the man flung him carelessly out of the enclosure. At that moment Kotic fainted.

When he came to his senses Kotic was in great pain. He had broken his flipper. Very soon as he lay on the beach dieing he thought that men could have taken his skin anyway because they will probably take it when I am dead.

Neil, 11

While Neil is having some challenges with tense and direct/indirect speech-forms, he is nevertheless able to empathise with others and convey a powerful moral message about the senseless slaughter of seals. Text-forms often become mixed at this level as further experimentation takes place. The boundaries of narrative, recount, explanation, and so on can become somewhat blurred as the writer struggles with ideas and emotions.

At the level of the proficient writer there is a much more confident choice of syntax, words, and literary devices such as repetition, parallelism, irony, and disjunction (i.e. expressing an alternative, expressing choice between two words):

> It is with some fear and apprehension that I relate to you the adventures my friend, Kerry Welsh, and I had with Spooky, the ghost, for I am rather afraid that the spirit of Spooky might come back to torment me. 'The spirit of a ghost?' I hear you ask me sardonically. 'Well,' I will answer you, 'you never know with ghosts!'
>
> Into the dark alley cautiously walked the affluent man. His huge, bulging bag was clutched tightly in his arm. Looking warily ahead, he then stepped uneasily in to the darkness, every now and again peering carefully behind him. Deeper and deeper he ventured, until he was a tiny dot in the distance.
>
> Josie, Year 6

Students have much more command of technical language, as witnessed by Carolyn's attempt at the procedural text of how to take a good photo. Terms such as 'wind the film', 'arrows', suitable subject', and 'telescopic lenz' are all associated with the act of taking photos:

> You first have to select the film, either black or white or colour and put it in your camera. Wind the film from the outside of the camera until the arrows reach no. one. To take a picture you have to find a suitable subject and maybe use a telescopic lenz for best results. When taking the photo, do not move the camera. I advise you not to take fast moving photos if you are a beginner. Good luck!!!
>
> Carolyn, Year 6

Sometimes the writer's eagerness to write well can produce an impression of 'insincerity' where the language seems stereotyped and second hand, and the emotions expressed appear exaggerated or overwritten. However, the experimentation with assonance and alliteration in the following piece produces some interesting effects:

> We started out on a beautiful morning with a bright sky above us and a cooling south wind. Nature was in her full glory, the air smelt sweet, birds were singing loudly, squirrels scampered up trees at our approach and rabbits' tails disappeared down burrows at our presence. Lambs jumped around friskily tormenting their mothers for nourishment. Cows lay lazily chewing their cud among the buttercups. A little foal galloped alongside her mother on its spindly legs. In another field a ploughman plodded along behind his horses furrowing the field. Butterflies fluttered from flower to flower.

And so our journey went on in the presence of Nature's glory. Oh what a wonderful thing to be alive!

At Langham we refuelled ourselves and continued our journey.

John, 12

Different aspects of writing develop at different rates as the student struggles with ideas, forms, syntax, choice of word, literary devices, and so on. One of the key factors influencing writing development is the teacher, who must provide appropriate experiences to motivate and stimulate, demonstrate appropriate models, and be a sensitive facilitator who guides, nurtures, and encourages writing across a range of subject areas.

 Activity

Collect at least three samples of writing from different classes and see if you can assign them to stages of development. Use your Syllabus to look for indicators. What does each piece tell you about the student as a writer? This activity would be best done in pairs or a small group.

SUMMARY

1. Literacy begins well before the child comes to school. The presence of books and print media in and around the home, and the attitude of parents and carers, are important influences on the child's literacy development.

2. Speaking and listening play a crucial role in the development of literacy before school. The child should be exposed to a rich variety of language in a variety of contexts, and be allowed to use and experiment with language in a variety of ways.

3. The school needs to use and develop the language the child brings to school.

4. As students progress through the grades they should gain greater control over their writing as they become more aware of purpose and audience.

5. When commenting on or assessing students' writing, the following aspects can be useful: stylistic features; surface features such as grammar, punctuation, handwriting, and spelling; cognitive, affective, and moral aspects; and text structure.

6. A helpful way of looking at the K–6 developmental continuum is to see the students' writing falling into three broad stages: early writing, developing writing, and proficient writing. All lines of demarcation are arbitrary as students may be at different stages for different aspects of their writing.

Chapter 12
Teaching Writing in the Classroom

Focus

This chapter looks at the sociolinguistic, genre, and process approaches to the teaching of writing, focusing on the social or functional model of language. The importance of critical literacy is stressed. The chapter looks at the many factors that contribute to making the writing process successful: motivation, the importance of speaking and listening, and the importance of planning, drafting, conferencing, responding, and publishing. These aspects are considered within the framework of Shared, Guided, and Independent Writing.

The teaching of writing in the classroom should focus on the effective use of language, bearing in mind the purpose of the writing and the audience for whom it is intended. The teaching strategies of modelling the writing process and imitating written texts, guided writing or joint construction of texts (with peers or the teacher), and practice in independent writing, will assist the child to become a confident and accurate writer. The modelling of text-types (or genres) can guide students in how writing is produced for different purposes and audiences. There must also be time for students to compose their own texts creatively, encouraging them to experiment with language.

A sociolinguistic approach

A number of theoretical approaches can assist teachers to help students gain the understanding they need of the different aspects of literacy. The **sociolinguistic approach** emphasises the strong link between language and social contexts. It emphasises that the communicative purpose of a text determines the appropriate structure, grammar, layout, typeface, language, and vocabulary to achieve that purpose. For example, a letter to a friend has a different structure and language from a letter of complaint about an unfair practice. A personal letter may be somewhat idiosyncratic in shape and structure but it still contains features that distinguish it from other kinds of letter writing such as a formal letter of complaint. The two kinds of letters have different functions and the writer chooses an appropriate language style to facilitate communication.

The register of a piece of writing or speech reflects in its vocabulary the sociocultural context in which the words are used. For example, the language children use in the playground when talking to their peers is usually more colloquial than the language used when talking to their teachers in the classroom. It is important to teach students how language appropriate for a particular context can lead to more effective communication. Familiarity with the conventions of language in different contexts and the different genres of writing will improve students' ability to make effective choices about language usage when they read, write, and speak.

Genres

Within the context of writing, **genre** refers to different textual types that have recognisable characteristics, such as narratives or reports. These distinguishing characteristics, however, change over time. In literary terms, genre refers to a type of artistic creation such as the drama, novel, or poetry, and various kinds of writing such as biography or the sonnet. In the 1980s *genre* was applied in the field of education to literacy. The concept of genres or 'generic types' is based in the systemic-functional theory of language made accessible through the research of Halliday and Hasan (1976). Various researchers have classified genres: Martin and Rothery (1981), Kress (1982), and Christie (1989).

Martin's definition of 'genre' in *Children Writing: A Reader*: 'Genre refers to any staged, purposeful cultural activity, and this includes oral language genres as well as written language genres. A genre is characterized by having a schematic structure—a distinctive beginning, middle and end.' (1984: 25)

Genres make explicit the linguistic choices that people make when they read and write, helping to explain why we choose a particular tense, or structure a text in a certain way. This should not imply that there is a fixed or 'correct' version since the conventions for a particular genre can change, either subtly or dramatically. Context and social relations are important factors that influence linguistic choices.

It is important to provide students with examples of a broad variety of textual types, mainly because models enable them to make more informed choices when they are using language. The issue of equity is central to genre theory in educational contexts. For this reason, a knowledge of different genres in a broad curriculum that is reflective of society gives children 'the possibility of the use of the resources of representation which makes possible the full participation in all aspects of the cultural and social life of a group' (Kress in Anstey and Bull 1996: 65). The types of texts selected in the curriculum should be useful and relevant to school life and society. Students can be introduced to the following text-types:

narratives, personal responses, information reports, explanations, expositions, discussions, procedures, factual descriptions, factual recounts, and literary recounts.

Features of the genre-based approach

- explicit teaching of the function, structure, organisation, and grammatical patterns of a particular genre
- discussion of several models of the genre and how effectively they use the text features to meet their purpose
- joint contruction of a text to illustrate features of the genre that students are learning to write
- critical analysis of a text to show how communication is governed by social and cultural context, purpose, and audience
- class discussion about how students' own texts might be written to reflect the broad genre and to meet their imaginative and creative needs
- further library research to develop range and depth of writing
- individual writing of texts by the students.

The importance of genres

'Learning to handle and manipulate the genres of the various school subjects, adapting and modifying them for different purposes, is important not only because it is a necessary part of learning the content of the subjects, but also because it is a necessary part of learning the ways of reasoning and organising the different aspects of experience that are characteristic of the different subjects.' (Christie and Rothery 1990: 188)

Genres are not 'fixed' and the divisions between different textual types of writing are not hard and fast but change in different contexts. A writer may choose to vary the standard format of a piece of writing and the desired format may also change over time. Even so, the reader and writer share assumptions about the linguistic features, the shape, and structure of a genre such as a recount, expecting particular characteristics to appear. The schematic structures and linguistic features of text have multiple ways of organisation. Divisions between different genres are often arbitrary because of the mix of linguistic features.

Even so, it is possible to see broad categories if not clear demarcations. Sometimes it is appropriate to organise material chronologically, for example when writing down the steps of a recipe or giving directions for the progress of a game. Illustrations can add to the meaning of a text but can also add to the blurring of genres.

Language features are open to change in the genres: changes eventually become acceptable, or a powerful elite of language users can exert an influence. Email, a form of electronic correspondence, may appear in several genres (recount, information report, explanation, etc.); it has affected the writing of memoranda and letters and shows how language is a social practice dependent on a particular setting. There is variety in email messages: some may be brief, yet the speed and efficiency of communication can also lead to long-winded replies. It is therefore useful to see genres as on a continuum and the blending of genres as common.

Knowledge about language

Knowing how language works is, of course, useful to knowing how to use it better. Explicit teaching about the structure, organisation, and grammatical patterns of different textual types is an important contribution of the genre approach (Hammond 1996: 211). Children need a language for describing how a text communicates its meaning. Talking about what makes a particular piece of reading and writing effective will help them to become more perceptive readers and writers. Just as knowing the meanings of words such as 'climax' and 'characters' will allow children to talk with more clarity about the books they read or the television programs they watch, knowing grammatical terms and understanding how to apply this knowledge will assist their writing development. Practice in comparing patterns of language and rearranging the order of texts can reveal what works best communicatively.

The terminology of traditional and functional grammar helps in describing how texts are organised, providing both teachers and students with a shared **metalanguage**. Familiarity with common sentence patterns, clause and paragraph construction, and the functions of different parts of speech help children to write with additional clarity and to analyse written texts. (See Chapter 14.)

Critical literacy

The development of a critical literacy helps children to understand and to share their likes and dislikes and also encourages them to form better judgments about what they read. For example, discussing truth and accuracy in advertising is something that Kindergarten children can grasp—they know what an advertisement for new toys is trying to do to them and to their parents. Comparing their own writing with other models develops a deeper understanding of what works well in communicating ideas and meaning. (See Chapter 18.)

> *Critical* is used in the special sense of aiming to show up connections which may be hidden from people—such as the connections between language, power and ideology ... Critical language study analyses social interactions in a way which focuses upon their linguistic elements and which sets out to show up their generally hidden determinants in the system of social relationships, as well as hidden effects they may have upon that system. (Fairclough 1989: 5)

As students progress through the school grades they can be exposed to an increasing range of printed media (advertising brochures, literature of all kinds) and other media (TV, the Internet) in order to develop critical faculties to determine the degree of manipulation and the 'hidden effects' of such materials.

Here are some suggested questions that may help to get students thinking about critical literacy and how they might respond to media and texts:

- *Who* has produced the text? What is their point of view? Who is the intended audience?
- *Why* has it been written?
- *How* is the material presented? Are there other ways of writing about it?
- *Where* is it distributed? Who sells it?
- *What* is the piece about? What information has been left out?
- *When* was the text written and is this significant?

Luke, Comber and O'Brien (in Bull and Anstey 1996: 38) point out that interconnected strategies can be followed with texts:

1. Talk about the institutional conditions of production and interpretation.
2. Talk about the textual ideologies and discourses, silences and absences.
3. Discourse analysis of textual and linguistic techniques in relation to (1) and (2).
4. Strategic and tactical action with and/or against the text.

The reading of a diversity of genres from a broad range of texts can provide the context for the children's writing. There are many different types of writing that have evolved to suit individual authors and to meet the needs of different audiences of writing.

Some texts may deliberately subvert expectations and break conventions to communicate a message or to create a certain effect. Advertisements may set out to attract the interest of the reader by painting incongruous images or deliberately mixing and blending genres. Authors often play with conventions by subverting the expected pattern of language usage. The final paragraph in Frank McCourt's novel *Angela's Ashes* is the brief *'Tis* (this word became the title of his next book). In this context, where most readers might conventionally expect a longer paragraph, *'Tis* is entirely apposite. Playing with the conventions is not new. The English novelist Laurence Sterne (1759–67), the author of *Tristram Shandy*, played with all kinds of eccentricities in his novel, using a blank page, writing unfinished sentences, and using all manner of typographical confusions. It can be argued that children need to know the appropriate usage before they can turn it upside down. But even without this knowledge, through their own creativity they can amuse the reader by subverting expectations. The definition of generic types of writing allows the writer to see with some transparency the different textual choices that can be made.

The process approach

The 'process' approach, deriving from the work of Donald Graves (e.g. 1983; see also Calkins 1983; Cambourne 1988), emphasises writing as a systematic series of actions leading to the composition of a text:

- Writing is a process involving pre-writing (planning), writing (drafting, editing, revising), publishing, and post-writing (response).
- A regular time for writing is allocated to allow for planning, writing, and editing—writing is done often, preferably every day, and at different times throughout the day.
- Discussion (or conferencing) among teachers and students or among students is encouraged to help the writer formulate ideas, to provide a reaction to the writer, or to seek information.
- Ownership of topic. Usually the child chooses the topic about which to write and makes the decisions about how it should be written, taking responsibility for the final version of the text.

The process and the genre approach can be complementary. Both advocate the need for drafting and editing in writing, both are in favour of discussing and talking about the language chosen, both help us to understand what to teach and how to teach. Both approaches can be brought together using the three teaching strategies of Shared Writing, Guided Writing, and Independent Writing. Whatever approach is used, there should be a broad and balanced selection of factual and narrative genres so that children can become familiar with different kinds of writing. Although the emphasis of both approaches is on a meaningful 'whole' text and extended pieces of writing, there is still the need for explicit and individual instruction about linguistic features such as verb tense or other grammatical features at the sentence level.

Writing can be a rapid process if the imagination is crowded with ideas or if the task is found to be easy. Even so, those children who appear to write effortlessly can usually make improvements to their writing at the drafting and editing stages. Children will vary in their writing capacity and temperament, some quickly writing down the main ideas, others labouring over the choice of words, just like some adult writers. The French writer Gustave Flaubert (1821–80) took seven years to write his classic *Madame Bovary*. Looking for the right word, the *mot juste*, can be an exacting business. Charles Dickens (1812–70), on the other hand, wrote quickly and prolifically.

Ways forward

Language syllabuses, not only in Australia but also in the USA and the UK, are adopting an approach that recognises *a social view of language*, which is concerned with how people use language in a variety of social contexts. The use of computers and technology has revolutionised the way that people communicate, in commerce and many other contexts.

Language choices made are dependent on the social context in which a text is produced. There are many social contexts but, broadly speaking, the home, community, and school form the basis for most children's language experience. These social contexts will provide most of the text-types that students will be engaged in. Recognition of a sense of purpose and audience is a crucial consideration when composing a text. Teaching strategies will include the macro-strategies of Shared, Guided, and Independent Writing (see Chapter 13). At the same time students will be engaged in basic textual analyses as they explore typical features of the type of text they are writing. Texts are often multi-model. They will be exploiting a typical text creatively and using a critical awareness (reflecting on the socially constructed meanings they are reading and writing). Inevitably, the ways forward will include elements and best practice from previous approaches to the teaching of writing.

Computer or technological literacy

The impact of the Internet will doubtless increase the importance of student-centred learning and help to change how we view literacies. The interactive multimedia on the Internet offer written text, graphics, and sound, pointing to how students might wish to communicate in the future. The non-linear text is already with us and there is now the possibility of composing texts that have visual and auditory components.

At present we are mostly concerned with print literacy, but the children of the future need to have computer literacy and word-processing skills. They may increasingly rely on the computer for their language development, closing the gap between speech and writing and further blurring the boundaries between different genres of writing. Voice-activated computing may revolutionise how we view writing and possibly negate the need for typing skills.

Email

Through the Internet there is the opportunity to send messages in seconds around the world. The new media of audio, print, software, and print publications, as well as CD-ROM formats, give children an almost inexhaustible supply of information. Newsgroups on specific topics, mailing list discussions, and chat lines all have the potential for encouraging writing and communication as respondents can send messages to many recipients at the same time.

Writing on the Internet has already introduced changes to communication. Because formatting is secondary, email emphasises *words*, although attachments also allow images to be sent. For brevity, emoticons (emotional icons) are used to convey emotion, e.g. -o = shock. Asterisks may be used for *emphasis* instead of inverted commas, underlining or italics. Intentional misspellings may be made to amuse or to draw attention to words. Some of the Net acronyms highlight the brevity and simplicity of many messages, e.g. GDM8 = G'day mate, LOL = Laughing out loud. On the other hand the Internet may encourage writing output because it is so quick and because recipients often reply promptly. Children may therefore become more productive.

What follows explains what a good writing classroom and best practice could look like.

A case study

Ears for my Family

'I'm coming'
Wind pushing and tugging at me
hugging my hair
scrabbling my clothes
'I want my tea'
But all is quiet
I stand straining my ears—
not moving in case I miss something
It's like a ghost house
only a creak of the stairs
and a stretching of the floor boards
I am fixed to my Sea—
my ears large
The gravel path scrunches under heavy feet
A scratched key scuffled in the lock,
stamping, coughing—it's dad:
Heavy shopping bags thump on the floor
Tins clank together. I wait for mum's deep sigh.

Christine, 11 years (in Rosen & Rosen 1973: 105)

Christine probably had many rich, varied language experiences before she could sit down and write a poem as sensitive as this one. The poem shows that Christine has developed an acute sensitivity to the world around her—she understands her father's familiar 'stamping' and 'coughing' and her mother's tiredness at the end of a shopping session; 'I wait for mum's deep sigh' expresses many possibilities, and in true writerly fashion leaves things unsaid.

The honesty of expression and creativity in use of language in such phrases as 'hugging my hair', 'scrabbling my clothes', 'straining my ears', 'stretching of the floor boards', 'my ears large', 'key scuffled in the lock' indicate that Christine's senses of touch and hearing in particular have been developed to such an extent that she is able to appreciate deeply the world around her and to empathise with the feelings of others. But writing like this can take many years to develop. Parents and teachers will provide many opportunities in the home, community, and school that contribute to sensitising their children to the world around them in such a way that the children will be able to communicate a part of that world to others through writing that is fresh, creative, honest, original, and exciting.

Not all writing that children do, however, is of this creative type. In fact a lot of children's writing is factual in nature and comes in the form of recounts, writing procedures, summaries, and so on. Teachers must help students to introduce creative writing into their repertoire. Students may encounter the following text-types during their primary years:

Text-types (oral and written)

Literary	*Factual*
Literary description	Discussion
Literary recount	Explanation
Narrative	Exposition
Observation	Factual description
Personal response	Factual recount
	Information report
	Procedural recount
	Procedure

It is clear that these text-types are somewhat idealised for teaching purposes and that in real life we often find 'mixed' texts. They should therefore not be seen as 'straitjackets' but as starting points. It is not until students understand that
- different types of text exist
- texts serve different purposes
- texts are typically structured in particular ways
- texts have characteristic grammatical features
- factual writing can still be creative

that they are in a better position to experiment with combining elements in a purposeful way (Board of Studies NSW 1998a: 66–7). The teaching of writing in these primary years, however, is not merely concerned with making sure students' writing conforms to particular forms. A major thrust should be to ensure that students are engaged in real writing for real purposes and that they are motivated to write and find it an exciting engagement with language rather than a task. It is very important, then, for the teacher to create an appropriate *writing climate* in the classroom.

Tasks

Discussion

1. Here are some comments by teacher trainees on their school experiences of writing:

Consider their implications for the infants and primary school classroom and discuss what could be done to make writing an enjoyable and meaningful activity. Discuss, in particular, the kinds of topics that might stimulate good writing.

Writing has always been a pleasure of mine. I regard it as a very important part of my sanity in life at times. From a very early age I was taught to write creatively and to use my imagination to its full capacity. My first recollection of writing was in Year 2. Our class had just come back from an excursion to Shark Island. My teacher had asked us to write a recount of what had happened and then conclude the report by drawing a picture. There were many of these experiences throughout my primary schooling years that I can recall. I still have some of my trusty 'botany books' at home somewhere.

I have kept several journals since 1992. These have kept me sane and often let me reflect over my life problems at the time. I have maintained this diary writing to present date. I enjoy writing in it, as it is my true feelings and life as I know it. No one reads it or ever will.

Writing is important to me. I find it relaxing.

N.

When I was in Year 5 I won a competition for a story about being stranded in the middle of the ocean. I can still remember what I had written (I loved looking in the newspapers, dictionaries, thesaurus etc for new and exciting words). I remember my main character scissored her legs through the water and her salt parched lips were burning.

S.

My only memories of creative writing in primary school were making poems and rhymes about the teachers and handing them out to friends.

S.

My history as a writer is a very feeble one. I have never gone out of my way to write something off my own bat so to speak. I remember when I was participating in the Duke of Edinburgh Award Scheme and after one of the hikes I had been on I had to write a log of all the events. This was probably the best thing I have ever written. I suppose it is probably because I was there laughing and crying at the events I was writing about. Since that time I suppose it has always been a philosophy to make sure that the children experience things they are writing about.

I would love to have the ability to pump out witty pieces of literature, but that is simply not a talent I possess.

C.

2. What was one of your more memorable writing experiences at school? How did you deal with it? How would you handle a similar situation in your own classroom now? What can you learn from it as a teacher?

The writing classroom

One of the major challenges for the thinking teacher is to develop a 'community of writers' (Smith 1982; Graves 1994). That is, to develop a classroom climate in which children want to write and want to share their writing in order to enrich their experience of the world. Writing is a social act in so far as most writers write for audiences, whether it be the imaginative, creative type of writing or the more factual type. The nature of the audience often determines the shape and formality the writing will take.

The teacher's role is to
- create an atmosphere where children will want to write and can write
- to establish a climate where both teacher and pupils are sharing their writing
- to provide conditions for 'real' writing for 'real' purposes
- to teach different language structures
- to give children equal access to writing forms and text-types which society values.

A good literacy session has the advantage of linking the activities of reading, writing, and speaking, giving the child plenty of opportunities to revisit writing. It can focus on language in use as well as some explicit understanding of how language works.

Conditions for effective writing

Time for creativity

One of the major problems teachers have is to organise their program so that students have sufficient *time* for writing. Many schools assign a block of time—usually during the morning periods—to a Literacy Session in which various activities involving talking, listening, reading, and writing take place within a framework that includes Shared, Guided, and Independent Reading and Writing. During such a session writing will often occur as a natural outcome of a response to a reading activity. For example, a teacher may be presenting a 'big book' to the class such as ***Possum Magic*** and may invite the children to respond to the story by rewriting the ending or innovating on the text (i.e. retaining the same overall structure of the text but inserting local names and/or events) or doing character analysis and/or plot-mapping activities. (See also Chapter 8.)

Sometimes a particular subject area lends itself to a writing activity. The class may be on an excursion to a rock pool or rainforest and be required to list from observation then to categorise and/or summarise the material listed. Science experiments might need to be written up using specialised formats. For the learning area Human Society in Its Environment pupils may need to write a dramatic scene to recreate events and roles from history or to respond creatively to an issue of local importance at the school or in the community. The important point is that writing is often done as an *integrated activity* and arises naturally from other subjects or other areas of the curriculum—the writing then becomes purposeful and realistic. There *is* time for writing if it is integrated into the curriculum in this way. Children need time to write and to practise written language skills at various points throughout the day. Nevertheless, some children will always find that they can do their best writing alone and uninterrupted at home.

Choice

A good writing classroom will often give children an opportunity to choose their own topics and formats for writing. One of the ways of developing 'ownership' of a piece of writing is to give children the responsibility of choice. Even if the class is focusing on a particular text-type (e.g. writing a recount or narrative) there can be choice within the topic. If the curriculum imposes a particular format, the teacher can usually encourage a degree of freedom of choice of topic and purpose *within* the format. A degree of ownership will then develop.

Student writers will be more likely to pay more attention to a piece of writing if there is a sense of ownership—it is their writing, not the teacher's. There may be an element of 'negotiation' where the teacher helps or allows the writer to choose the topic and the purpose of the writing exercise.

Control of the process can very easily be assumed by an over-anxious teacher, who may prescribe extensive revisions or even physically write 'corrections', show disapproval through body language, try to hurry the writer, or not listen to the writer's explanations. The teacher's art is to know the appropriate time for and the degree of intervention. It is better to have fewer but better interventions—then the writer's vital sense of ownership, responsibility/control is respected:

> I never really liked writing at school. I couldn't think of what to write about when given a topic and couldn't think what to write about when I wasn't. Often my stories ended up being a recount or slightly varied version of a TV show or book I had read recently.
>
> K.

If the child invariably chooses the topic there may be a disposition to follow a particular text-type such as the recount or narrative genre. Children need to practise and become familiar with a broad range of text-types. These should be introduced and explicit instruction given about them by teachers. The writer relies on various sources of information and inspiration and may need to use the resources of the library and the knowledge of others. For many kinds of writing, authoritative sources are needed to provide and substantiate information.

Sheer fright may set in about writing, as a student attests:

> Primary school writing, as I recall, was very formulaic. You had to write about a specified topic and you were given a set period to do it in. I can still recall the terror which at times would overwhelm me, when the teacher would come in after lunch and demand that we produce a two-page story on a certain topic and constantly reiterate to us that it had to be correct, with correct grammar and spelling. Despite such constraints I was a competent writer.
>
> K.

Another teacher trainee wrote:

> If only we could all make up what we wanted [instead of set tasks], then I could be a free spirit!
>
> T.

Teacher-dictated topics can still engage children's sense of ownership if they are balanced with topics of their own choice. Children will often find ways of making topics interesting. For example, a simple procedure of 'how to' do some activity could be applied to 'how to make and keep friends'.

Even if children have chosen their topic, teachers will often need to 'scaffold' or provide a framework for texts so that children can be guided to make appropriate language choices and gain control of different constructions. Individual choice of topic does not necessarily negate explicit teaching about language features.

'What are you going to write about?' To the child who answers 'nothing' there is the challenge for the teacher to motivate the child to explore the range of writing that is possible. Children can find out that in the most mundane of experiences there might be something unique and worth communicating. Writing that grows out of experience is usually the best—whether that experience is an activity the child has done out of school or whether it is part of the shared environment of the classroom. Children can use their imaginations to invent stories. But there are other kinds of writing where strict accuracy is needed and the writer needs to impart specific information.

Integrating the language skills

There is a close relationship between the different language skills of reading, writing, listening, and speaking. Understanding and proficiency in one area can contribute to these skills in another. Knowing how to scan a text when reading has similarities to writing the headings for a first draft. Analysing how authors convey meaning through word choice, cohesion, and punctuation can provide models for children's own writing. We must give children as much practice as we can with language, allowing them to be playful and imaginative and at the same time giving them experience of the formalities of language so that they become familiar with the possibilities of language use.

Teaching children to write creatively and with clarity is a complex process. It requires planned activities that will present opportunities for children to write in a wide range of contexts for different purposes and for a variety of audiences. The use of strategies such as 'mindmapping' (Wycott 1991) and Edward de Bono's (1970) creative thinking can help release children's imagination. Children will obviously gain a great deal of linguistic awareness from the practice of writing itself but they also gain from exposure, as listeners and readers, to particular kinds of writing. Through listening to a story or a variety of models they will begin to understand how a writer achieves a particular effect, and reading it independently will consolidate their understanding. Talking about it with their classmates, teacher, and parents will deepen a knowledge of

- how a writer achieves a response in a reader
- the different responses evoked by different kinds of writing
- how individual language skills can be improved.

There are many advantages to integrating the processes of reading and writing: recognition of models and knowledge of how texts work reinforces children's ability to write their own. Reading allows them to make sense of the print, while writing can consolidate understanding. It is important to integrate reading and writing early on, in the first years of schooling. As students strive to get down their meanings on the page they listen to the sounds of the word they want to write and attempt to record those sounds using the letters they know. Through this process they are developing the sound–letter knowledge that is crucial to their reading development. Communicative ability in speaking reinforces proficiency in other modes of language such as reading and writing, and encourages children to transfer successful learning strategies from one mode to another.

Links between reading and writing

Teachers who are engaged in best practice have always recognised the strong links between reading and writing. The following principles are relevant to students engaged in literacy activities. They need to:

- **Understand the purposes of literacy so they can appreciate and enjoy literacy in their lives.**

Young children need to have early experiences with print in the home context so that they can learn what print is and how it works. The preschool and Kindergarten classroom is often saturated with print in the form of different models of writing, labels, captions on posters, and lists of things to do. In the early years many opportunities are given for children to *listen* to stories read aloud and to *talk about* the stories in informal discussions; more formal situations come in the later years of primary school.

- **Hear written language so they can learn its structure and take in new information and ideas.**

The importance of speaking and listening in the literacy process cannot be overestimated. Although there are common vocabulary and sentence structures in oral and written versions of English, there are important differences between the oral and written modes of language, especially in grammar. The interjections, omissions, shortened forms (I'll, we've etc.), and incomplete sentences of speech are not always found in the more formal structures of book language. Pinnell and Fountas make a very strong point here:

> Children who know how to 'talk like a book' are fortunate because they have had opportunities to hear the books read aloud. As they hear the same story many times, they can 'absorb' the stories and make them their own. (1998:4)
>
> (See also Chapter 2, phonemic awareness.)

- **Become aware of the sounds of language in order to enjoy those sounds and to use this knowledge as a tool in becoming literate.**

Young children love to experiment with familiar and unfamiliar sounds through rhymes and games. It is this playing with sound that is the beginning of phonemic awareness—the ability to hear the individual speech sounds in words. Understanding sound–letter relationships is crucial to learning to read, spell, and write, but the understanding begins in spoken language.

It is especially important for children learning English as another language to have experience in a wide range of speech activities. Repeating and expanding phrases and sentences in a natural way, so that English structures are heard again and again, are important precursors to using them with confidence. Visualisation, using pictures and concrete objects, is a useful tool in the comprehension process. Reading and rereading favourite books give children a chance to internalise the patterns of the English language.

In these early stages of language learning, children can benefit from books with understandable, repetitive, and conversational English language. A classroom and a home rich in picture books, rhymes, and folktales are therefore advantageous to children's language learning.

- **Have many experiences with written symbols.**

It is not easy for the young child to distinguish one letter from another (Clay 1991: 266). A whole network of knowledge surrounds each letter. It has a shape, a sound, a name, it can be connected to other letters in a word, and it can appear in different ways—large, small, in colour, in different print, and so on. As well as recognising letters in isolation, children must also recognise them when the letters are embedded in print. Accordingly, lots of alphabet or letter games in both the oral and written modes should be played. Children need to see letters in a variety of print media; they need practice in writing the letters in isolation, with other letters, and in real words and phrases.

- **Explore words and learn how they work.**

Some children build a network of understandings around their names. The following concepts can develop from this: their name is a word; a word consists of a sequence of letters that go together; letters in a word progress from left to right; words have meaning and are written in the same way each time; words have blank spaces on either side; sounds go with letters in a word; some words start like their own names; words have meaning when put together with other words, and so on.

The Kindergarten teacher will engage in considerable Shared Reading and Writing experiences so that the children build up their visual and auditory knowledge about letters, words, phrases, sentences, and clusters of letters or patterns that are connected to sounds.

- **Read and write continuous text to expand their knowledge.**

Reading and writing develop together. Not all the letters of the alphabet need to be known before beginning reading and writing. Once a start is made, lots of experimentation will occur as the child goes from the known to the unknown and learns about letter–sound relationships and print conventions. Semantic, grammatical, and graphophonic knowledge increase as engagement with text increases. The classroom teacher needs to involve the children in a wide range of language activities both at text and word level. Talking and listening activities are very important here too as experimentation with known and new sounds increases.

- **Develop flexibility and fluency to enhance comprehension and enjoyment of reading and writing.**

Being a good reader and writer means more than simply being able to decipher letters or put them together to make words. It means being fluent and flexible with words, phrases, sentences, and text. The beginning writer needs to be able to let thoughts flow onto the page without being restrained by a lack of knowledge about how words are spelt and how phrases and sentences are put together. Pinnell and Fountas (1998: 11) say that fluency in writing is enhanced when children

- know a large core of words and can produce them quickly and automatically
- understand useful spelling patterns they can use to make many more words
- can associate letters and sounds quickly and easily
- can let their writing flow because they are not too distracted by the laborious processes of writing the words.

Once fluency is developed, flexibility in reading rates and in writing text-types can be gained as the child's knowledge of appropriateness to audience and purpose increases. Good readers and writers increasingly gain *control* over their medium.

Response: the writing conference

A good writing classroom invites response to children's writing so that they can be encouraged to write further, or improve what they have written, or prepare their work for publication. Response can come from the teacher, from parents, or from peers and may be in the form of an appropriately encouraging casual comment or a more extended response, often called a 'writing conference'. This usually occurs when a child wants to share writing with the teacher or peers in order to get some useful feedback. The best response often comes when a child writes for a real purpose that 'works'—for example, doing a poster advertising an event to which people actually come, writing a narrative that is published in a book format and put in the school or class library, or writing a procedural text that others follow to make or do something.

A good writing classroom will foster an environment that encourages children to share their work openly. If this is done from the Kindergarten years, then by the time students reach Year 6 it will form a natural part of the writing process and will greatly contribute towards the 'community of writers'.

Writing conferences are an ideal way of supporting a child's writing development. The teacher shows interest in the students' ideas and the way they express them by commenting or giving guidance or by answering requests for help. In a conference, each step of the writing process can be discussed and explained. The key to effective conferencing lies in the kind of questions asked by the teacher. There is no specific structure for conferencing as there needs to be openness and spontaneity in the sharing session, but teachers should try to get the child to take the lead and avoid imposing comments or a rigid structure. Questions may be *process* questions that focus on the line of development of the writing, *development* questions that focus on the quality of ideas in the writing, or *structure* questions that deal with key ideas and the overall shape of the writing. As Ernie Tucker says:

> The CONFERENCE is to be seen as an element in the process-of-writing: a potential in the teacher's hands to encourage confidence and perhaps add something to the student's thinking-discussing-drafting-revising-polishing-rewriting. Conferences are shorter when students really feel they are in control of their own writing. They work best when students have learnt to ask their own questions. (1986: 198)

A conference gives the learner a chance to get help from the teacher on structuring or language aspects such as word choice and syntax.

The teacher's opening remarks are very important. They should show interest in the student's work and give a chance to focus on aspects of difficulty or success. For example, remarks like 'Well, Sam, how is your writing going?' are more likely to get a positive response than 'Well, Erin, you haven't written much yet', which may well render the student silent. The positive remark elicits comments from the student like 'I just can't think of a suitable ending' or 'I'm not sure if this paragraph is in the right place'. When the student responds then the teacher has a starting point for discussion.

Help the student to make the first statement. Sometimes a focus on the content of the writing helps rather than a focus on the spelling, grammar, or punctuation—this can come later. If the teacher's opening remark does not succeed in eliciting a response from the student then the teacher should resist the temptation to start talking, advising, or cajoling. The conference really begins only when the learner speaks. To stimulate that speech the teacher may need to ask the right question.

Begin simply. Try not to attempt too much too soon. The teacher needs to be patient and to learn how to accept silences—the student may need time to respond and also may need to get used to the idea of talking while the teacher listens. The teacher needs to show an interest in the student's thoughts and writing and have an expectation that a final product will emerge in time.

Remember that your questions will vary according to the type of text the student is writing. Factual texts will need questions that focus on the accuracy and completeness of the information, while narrative texts will require questions that focus on the story. Different types of conference questions help children develop writing skills:

1. How do you like your story?
2. Does your title fit your story?
3. Do you have more than one story in your piece?
4. Can you add more feeling to it?
5. Is there more you could add?
6. Tell me in detail what happened.
7. Are there too many extra things in it that you don't really need?
8. Are you going to keep working on it?
9. Have you enjoyed writing it?

(Calkins 1983: 125–6)

Here are some other questions the teacher might ask:

- What is your purpose in writing this text?
- Who is your audience?
- How did you gather information or knowledge for your text?
- Do you think your text moves in the right sequence? What have you put first? What comes next? How does it end?
- Have you told the reader the most important information?

There are several other ways of framing specific questions:

Opening questions: 'Where are you up to, Lauren?', 'How is it going, Elisha?', 'Tell me about all of this interesting work, Clare'.

Open-ended questions: These help the student to keep talking about their writing. 'That was a really interesting part—how can you bring this other information into it, do you think?' or 'Tell me more about what happened during the storm'.

Process questions: These help the student to keep a line of development. 'How will you start then?', 'Where will you go to from here?', 'Why did you change what you had?', 'Do you think your description is clear enough?', 'That's a really long passage—could you break it up more?', 'How do you think you will end the story?', 'Are you ready to end it now?'

Questions that reveal development: 'Do you think this is a better piece than last week's?', 'Is there a part you aren't happy with?', 'Why is this a better ending?'

Questions that deal with structure: These help the student to focus on the structure of the piece. 'Where is the key idea ?', 'Have you created enough tension?', 'Go through the main steps in the story', 'Does this particular part move quickly enough?'

The teacher's role is crucial in conferencing—the kind of question asked determines the kind of student response and the kind of learning that is taking place. The teacher not only assumes the role of a *questioner* but also becomes an *instructor* when some aspect of the writing needs special focus, such as spelling, grammar, or punctuation, all of which need to be handled sensitively and not overemphasised.

Demonstration

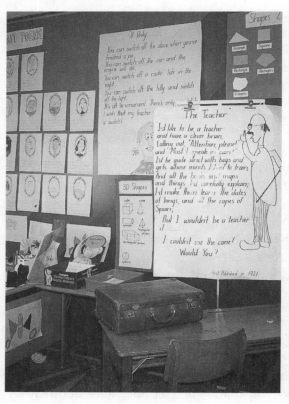

The classroom can be rich in language

A good writing classroom has a teacher who is prepared to help children by providing them with appropriate models of text-types. Children need to see good models of writing if they are going to emulate language patterns and structures found in their community, whether it be verse, fiction, or non-fiction texts, or texts from the media, including computer technology. Models of writing can be oral or written; both provide a structure that children can emulate. The models can come from many different sources: children's literature, popular newspapers, information books, journals, magazines, pamphlets, emails, or the Internet. The teacher may have many examples of such texts around the classroom.

Think in terms of filling the classroom with texts—on noticeboards, mobiles, curtains, walls, display areas, interest corners, or wherever appropriate. Displays of texts need to be changed frequently so that they are always fresh and 'alive'.

Modelling texts for children is an integral part of the writing process and should enrich the children's knowledge of the kinds of texts that abound in their community and help them to better select appropriate forms for their own personal writing efforts.

The teacher as writer

As well as providing writing models, it is important for teachers to demonstrate their own writing. This can be done on the chalkboard, chart paper, or overhead projector and can be very effective in demonstrating writing techniques and showing drafts in progress. Artists, ceramicists, and sports people demonstrate their crafts. Writing is also a craft and needs to be demonstrated, from choosing a topic to finishing the final draft. Children need to see the teacher searching to get the right form, connections, word, or phrase. They need to realise that they are not the only ones who find the art of writing challenging.

Expectation

Just as the family has an expectation that the young child will learn to talk, so too do the family and teacher have an expectation that the child will learn to write. High expectations will increase the possibility of a high standard of writing.

Physical considerations

Displaying students' writing can provide a rich stimulus

Children must feel that they can write with ease in the classroom. Apart from a warm, supportive teacher, the classroom itself should make it easy for writing to take place:

- Writing should be an integral part of daily classroom activities.
- Procedures for sharing or conferencing should be clearly established.
- Appropriate space should be provided for the writing act, with student desks arranged suitably.
- Procedures need to be in place to cope with issues such as noise or how to work with others.
- Writing folders need to be easily accessible for the children.

Assessment

Assessment generally focuses on how well the students are achieving the outcomes towards which they are working. A good writing classroom will encourage children to assess their own writing. Once again, the teacher can demonstrate here by assessing her own writing and by analysing samples of student writing (protecting anonymity if necessary). Using carefully selected questions, she can guide the child through a self-evaluation process. This process can be aided by children being able to use the language of evaluation—that is, children can be given a metalanguage that helps them to describe what meanings are being made in their writing. The terminology of a functional grammar and/or traditional grammar may assist in this process. Children can be encouraged to question their writing at all stages of the writing process. Expertise will take time to develop, but if started in the early years of writing the children will be quite adept by the time they reach Year 6. (A longer discussion of assessment can be found in Chapter 6.)

Motivation as a key factor

The classroom should be no different from the real world in that the need to write should spring from a real purpose or need. If the need is there, this is a strong motivation. We all know about the child who can't get started, who doesn't know what to write about, and who hasn't any ready ideas. The key to the problem is *motivation*. Some have the ability to write an imaginary story from very little or no teacher input, although many who do this may be drawing heavily on their past experiences, or from their reading of imaginary stories, or from TV programs they have seen.

The onus is on the teacher to provide the child with something authentic to write about, a real purpose for writing—not simply giving the child a *topic*. This could arise from many different kinds of motivating experiences, many of which may come from the Key Learning Areas:

- a response to a book—fiction or non-fiction—shared by the teacher, e.g. a summary, a character profile, plot mapping, writing a different ending
- a recent TV program, e.g. information report from a *Behind The News* program, personal response to a cartoon or 'soapie'

- an excursion that the class has just had, e.g. organising notes from observations, thank you letter to a park ranger, further reading and writing about the place visited, emotional response through poetry-writing, summary of events, critical appraisal of what was observed
- a visitor to the class, e.g. an adult sharing aspects of their occupation with the children, visitor from overseas, a sportsperson, an artist, or a writer
- response to a cultural visit, e.g. a live performance
- a sporting event, e.g. a swimming or athletics carnival, a netball or football match
- a visit to a local community facility such as a park, library, factory, shopping centre, museum
- a classroom science experiment, art or craft activity
- a holiday to a new and exciting place
- a visit, or travel in Australia or overseas.

The very best writing comes from a desire to write from a real experience that has developed the child's sensory perceptions—let the child feel the tree, smell the tree, taste the tree, see the tree, and hear the tree! Engagement with something or someone makes for active rather than passive learning. Thus many factors contribute towards a good writing classroom. Probably the most important 'condition' for effective writing is motivation—once the right atmosphere has been created, children can write with confidence and in the full knowledge that there will be a time for writing and sharing, that there will be opportunities for making choices, that writing will be for real purposes, that experimentation will be valued, that appropriate modelling will occur, and that there will be a positive expectation that their writing will be appreciated and will improve over time.

Task

Discussion

1. Creating the right conditions for writing may develop children who become lifelong writers. Discuss in a small group the following characteristics of lifelong writers and examine the teacher's role in the process. Having a reason to write is a most important characteristic.

   The following is a summary of Graves' characteristics of a lifelong writer (1994: 155):

   · initiates writing—chooses to write in order to recount, then understands experience
   · has a sense of the power of writing—understands its functionality
   · has a sense of history and of the future—the child senses where he has been and sees the past as basically healthy and foundational to the future
   · has a sense of audience
   · initiates writing at home and to affect others
   · senses the appropriateness of writing in a variety of genres

What are some other important characteristics of writers? Give reasons.

2. Read the article 'Discourses on Gender and Literacy: Changing the Stories' by Pam Gilbert (in Muspratt et al. 1997) and discuss ways in which children might gain more equal access to literacy practices in the community.

3. Make a list of the positive and/or negative influences on your own writing. How do they relate to the conditions for a good writing classroom described in this chapter? Consider the role of the teacher, the role of the home, and the classroom environment as important factors.

4. Consider the classrooms you have visited and design your own reading or writing classroom incorporating the best ideas you have seen and/or read about.

Drafting and editing

Some children find the drafting stage difficult. They are reluctant to revise, or feel they never reach a 'finished' product. Beginning writers are often unaware that professional writers may experiment with wording and edit their work constantly, searching for a more meaningful phrase or a more imaginative word or deciding that the structure of a text needs to be changed:

> In writing essays at school I tended to write as I spoke with no full stops, commas, correct spelling or grammar. This meant I always seemed to be on the rough draft, everybody else on their final copy.
>
> T.

Another teacher trainee remembers from primary school:

> Each week we would be asked to write a story, a piece of creative writing. These were due on Fridays and had to be nicely presented. A lot of these stories were selected by the teacher in regards to the topic and more often than not they were, 'My life as a something'. These were a huge task, but completed anyway, first as a rough copy, and then a final copy.
>
> J.

Here are some efforts in improving writing by using editing skills from a fourth-grader:

> ... Sudenly this hand groobed her leg and puled it in. Half of her body was in the bule crical. She said 'help me!' Then the bule cirlal was slowly closing up.
> Sarah said 'lets get help.'
> Blake said 'There is not enough time. We have to jum in!'
> 'But we might die,' James said.
> 'We have to take the risk' Blake said.
> 'I'am jumping in.'

'So am I'. Sarah yelled.
'Wait for me' James said.

Through substitution of vocabulary and changes in spelling and punctuation, the writer adds clarity:

... Suddenly this hand grabbed her leg and pulled it in. Half of her body was in the blue circle. She said 'help me!' Then the blue circle was slowly closing up.
Sarah suggested 'Let's get help.'
Blake answered 'There is not enough time. We have to jump in!'
'But we might die,' James shouted.
'We have to take the risk,' Blake exclaimed. 'I am jumping in.'
'So am I,' Sarah yelled.
'Wait for me,' James wailed.

Students should be encouraged to edit their own writing for content, organisation, grammar, punctuation, and spelling. Individual editing checklists can be supplied as well as useful wall charts to remind students of particular features. Selected proofreading marks may be used to familiarise students with editing, e.g. symbols for

insert	⋏
change to capital letter	*caps*
change to lower case	*l.c.*
transpose characters	*trs*
begin new paragraph	*n.p.*

Disincentives to writing

These comments from teacher trainees provide some warning signals about what not to do when teaching writing. For many people, writing or composing is a fairly difficult task. Few of us can put pen to paper or words on the screen with total ease.
Lack of interest in the topic:

I remember hating having to write compositions—yes I was around then. Writing was always a very personal form of expression for me and I was very insecure about having it marked or even read by the teacher—I still have that problem today.

M.

The problem may be handwriting:

I really did try to be a pretty writer, but I received blows to my confidence ...
I was one of the last children in Year 4 to get a pen licence, even after many of the naughty boys. For years I tried to conceal my real writing, but

university liberated me from the confines of childhood and now I have found the real me.

G.

Shyness or the desire for privacy may discourage sharing of writing:

> At school, I never particularly enjoyed writing. I remember feeling very concerned about other people reading my work. In Year 6 I tried to keep people from reading my work by writing very small.

S.

Lack of confidence is a common problem for the novice writer:

> S. as writer. These two things don't really go too well together. I have a habit of writing in a style that no one really understands except for me. This lack of confidence in writing good material makes me want to write as little as possible on most occasions.

S.

Some don't have the urge to write until high school:

> I guess that the pivotal moment in my life when I actually enjoyed writing was during Year 11. I had been placed into the top English class, with a brilliant teacher who I really looked up to. Ms H— not only made writing interesting and enjoyable, but she gave me the confidence to try different styles. Now, as an 'adult' (well, I think you can call me that) I enjoy writing plays and songs, short stories, letters of complaint, letters to my friends.

T.

Some children find inspiration for writing much later:

> I was never into writing as a child. I could always think of other things to do, especially when it was homework. I am not a creative writer. I would say that I am more a researcher. I love to read and critically examine old sources.

M.

> I was once in a musical and changed the words of the songs to form a poem which I would relate to all my friends. I am proud to say that it was the best piece of creative writing I have ever done.

M.

> I would prefer to read than write. The exception to this would be personal letter-writing.

J.

The reluctant writer

There is no magical solution for the child who says 'I can't write anything now'. Try to give a real purpose for writing so that a child will want to write and will very likely know what to say. Start 'small'—do not be overambitious. Get the child talking, preferably about things that have happened in very recent times—events that have been experienced at home, while shopping, at sporting fixtures, at the cinema, and so on. Either the teacher or the child can write down in the child's own words something that was enjoyable or significant about an experience—just one or two sentences will do. This is the beginning of many more encounters with the child, gradually increasing the number of sentences being recorded so that the student will eventually experience a sense of having compiled a real story or having recalled events and feelings. Work towards the student doing the writing rather than the teacher. This method relies on the one-to-one situation but is time well spent. Confidence and self-esteem will grow as well as a desire to write.

Selection of texts

The choice of texts available to children in the classroom is crucial since the selection of different text-types reflects a model of society and mirrors what the teacher considers to be important. The texts chosen should reflect the curriculum in all its aspects and include information and storybooks relevant to the different areas of knowledge explored at school. Literacy is developed as children listen to texts, as they read and discuss them and use them as models for their own writing. A teacher's selection policy for choosing texts is based on a wide variety of factors:

- the kinds of writing the teacher expects students to do at different stages of their development
- textual features that will serve as models, preparing children for the kind of writing they will need in the classroom and in the wider society
- whether the texts will stimulate children to write for themselves and for others
- the clarity and accuracy of information transmitted
- the inclusion of real people and real situations
- an appeal to the imagination and creativity of the children
- texts relevant to the curriculum
- texts that contain examples of different kinds of English, e.g. standard English, Aboriginal English, formal and informal English, regional dialects
- gender-inclusiveness
- texts that reflect a culturally diverse society.

Transmitting knowledge from a single perspective or choosing texts from a powerful elite will not allow students to make balanced assessments of what they read. For example, issues of social justice such as the rights of indigenous people require texts that represent a broad range of views at a level that children can understand at their stage of literacy development. The plethora of written texts makes it necessary to be selective.

The importance of planning

To produce writing that is clear and logical, planning is essential, not only at the beginning but also throughout the process. The amount and detail of planning varies from writer to writer and also from text to text. The amount of planning just done in the head or jotted down on paper will also vary. Early planning may involve the collection of information because the shape the writing will take may not be worked out until research and note-making have taken place. Children may need information and/or experiential input before a plan of the writing can take shape. Be careful, however, about prescribing planning methods since individuals prefer to work in different ways.

Some prefer to detail the steps of the writing very carefully so that when they do begin to write they know where they are going and will probably reach the end more quickly owing to the detail of the preparation.

Others prefer to plan as they go so that their writing may diverge in any direction depending on the whim of the moment or a desire to follow and explore a suitable lead. Some people prefer to think as they write so that they are not constrained by a determined direction, plan, or model. It must be remembered, however, that the purpose of the writing may predetermine, to an extent, the steps of the writing.

The reluctant writer may need a lot of teacher help to get started and it may be only through very careful questioning by a teacher and appropriate models that this kind of writer will be able to organise ideas and get started.

Once the topic has been decided, the writer needs to make some kind of *investigation* of it. This may include reflective thinking, observing, talking with someone, a little reading, or a great deal of research—any of which may require the taking of notes.

As the writer wrestles with this initial input, insights will occur as ideas are discovered and connected. The mature writer will scribble them down for use when the real writing begins. This, of course, is a skill that develops as the child moves through the various school grades and syllabus stages of writing. When insights are not readily forthcoming or writer's block sets in, writers do many different things—they doodle, pace the floor, talk to others about it, brainstorm, or just start writing down whatever comes into their heads in the hope that good ideas will come.

Once the investigation and insights have developed sufficiently, it is time to do a *first draft*. Mature writers really appreciate an insight that gives them 'a good lead', or an opening that will focus the reader's attention and initiate a flow of well-sequenced ideas. This draft can often command the greatest concentration of any part of the process because it is the time when initial selection from all available ideas (content) is made and when the basic shape of the form or text-type is made. This draft is often best done uninterrupted and free from the constraints of 'correctness', which can be concentrated on later. With Kindergarten writers the first draft at this early stage of a student's writing development becomes, in fact, not only the draft but the final product. That is, the concept of *revising* the draft is a developing one and should not be adhered to rigidly with beginning writers who have not yet developed the desire or the skills to 'revisit' what they have written. Very young writers are often so pleased with their initial efforts that they want to share or display them as soon as the initial effort is complete.

A more mature writer will revisit the first draft once it is finished, or even revise during the drafting itself—a lot of rereading and reshaping may occur. One of the hardest parts of the process is to get children to revise their writing. In the early stages of development, writers may attend to only the surface features during revision, such as spelling and punctuation. As a writer matures, a deeper revision will develop—revision of sequence and structure, of pace, and of elements of evidence and logic.

Once the final revisions have occurred, the writer has a *product* which can be *published*. In the classroom context this means making the writing available for others to see and read. If others are going to read the text, then it needs to be presented clearly and legibly, maybe even word-processed and illustrated. There are many different ways of publishing the end product:

- in class writing books, which are large and accessible to the children
- around the classroom walls—on charts, noticeboards, posters, writing focus boards, or corners
- on mobiles suspended from the ceiling or lines strung across the room
- in individual folders that others can have easy access to
- as part of Shared Reading time with the class, groups, pairs, and so on
- as texts sent to a real audience such as invitations to parents or letters to the local newspaper
- emails to friends; participation in chat rooms.

Response to the product or the creative work is important. When others read our writing it is encouraging to get positive, helpful comments. In a classroom, the teacher needs to work hard at getting the children to respond positively to others' writing. Sharing writing during the process is just as important as sharing the final product. If this approach is nurtured from the very early stages then by the time the child reaches the upper primary grades, sharing and commenting will be a natural consequence of writing activities—children will get better at it and will even want to do it. In this way a positive attitude to writing will be developed.

However, young writers must not be locked into a process that contains a set number of immovable and inflexible steps. Such a process might contain: experience or problem (decision to write); pre-writing; draft; revising and editing; product and publication; reader's response; writer's attitude. The process must remain flexible: not all pieces of writing need to be polished and published; the writer may not always want to revise a piece of writing; a writer may be wise to abandon a piece halfway through, and so on.

SUMMARY

1   Approaches to the teaching of writing in recent years have all made useful contributions to our understanding of what needs to be taught and how we should go about teaching it.

2   Having a metalinguistic knowledge can help in understanding and describing what is happening in texts.

3   A major thrust in classroom teaching should be to ensure that students are engaged in real writing for real purposes for real audiences or readers. Children should be motivated to write and should find it an exciting and interesting engagement with language. It is very important, then, for the teacher to create an appropriate writing climate in the classroom.

4   Teaching writing effectively needs time for the students to write, a degree of choice of topic and text-type for the students, integration of language skills, adequate response to the writing, appropriate demonstration by the teacher, an expectation that writing skills will develop over time, motivation, and an appropriate classroom setting.

5   Writing could be considered as a process that has definable stages such as pre-writing, writing (drafting, editing, revising), publishing, and post-writing.

6   There is no magical solution for the reluctant writer. Try to analyse the reasons for the reluctance. Quality one-to-one time may need to be spent with the student to motivate and develop confidence and self-esteem.

7   There are strong links between reading and writing. Children gain a great deal of linguistic awareness from the practice of writing itself and also from reading and listening to particular kinds of writing. Activities in writing, listening, reading, and speaking are best integrated to raise students' understanding of how language is used in a variety of contexts for different purposes and audiences.

Tasks

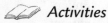 *Activities*

Children usually have excellent innovative ideas and approaches for writing. Encourage their interests and motivate them to write more and write often. Examine the following ways literature can be used in classroom writing sessions and talk about ways of using the children's literature you are familiar with.

1. Concentrate the attention of the class on the features of, for example, fairytales, and then ask them to look for other texts that have similar distinguishing characteristics. After collecting various examples, further analysis can be made to see how closely they fit the distinguishing features of a genre or subvert that genre. With further assistance from the teacher, the student can eventually construct his own fairytale, using the collected texts as models.

    A variation of this might be to collect different versions of a folktale such as *Cinderella* and analyse what makes them different and why they might appeal to different audiences. Share your findings with a small group.

2. Generate interest in creative writing through directed discussion of popular fiction with Years 5 and 6. Examples from Paul Jennings' ***Undone! More Bad Endings*** illustrate the variety of openings to short stories, encouraging the reader's interest:

    *   *'A stone with a hole in it. A sort of green-coloured jewel in a leather pouch. Just lying there in the beam of my torch.' (Batty: 1)*
    *   *'I, Adam Hill, agree to stand on the Wollaston Bridge at four o'clock and pull down my pants. I will then flash a moonie at Mr Bellow, the school principal.'*

        Who would be mad enough to sign such a thing? Suicide—flashing a bare bottom at Mr Bellow. (Moonies: 18)
    *   *Think of honey. Think of rotten, stinking fish. Put them together and what have you got? DISGUSTING COD-LIVER OIL. That's what.*

        'The nonsense you have just read was not written by me. My grandson Anthony wrote it. Silly boy.' (Noseweed: 31)
    *   *'I am never eating meat again,' I yelled at Dad.*

        He just smiled at me as if I was crazy.

        You might think I'm crazy too. I mean most people who live on farms eat meat. So I'll tell you what. You be me for a while and see how you feel about it at the end.' (Thought Full: 61)
    *   *'I'm undone.*

        Yes, I know. I'm a fink. A rat. A creep. Nobody likes Eric Mud and it's all my own fault.

        But I don't deserve this.' (Clear As Mud: 78)

3. Make mini autobiographies or autobiographical notebooks. Provide each child with a folder or cardboard sheet on which is placed a self-photograph or drawing. Involve the child to find out various likes and dislikes, for example a favourite song, favourite leisure time activity, favourite TV show, animal, book, saying. The format will vary for different ages. This activity allows the children to find out more about each other. In retrospect, when the child becomes older, it can be revealing and often amusing to look back on earlier preferences and thoughts. The writing can be collated in book form and/or displayed in the classroom.

4. Introduce children to the Griffin and Sabine trilogy by Neil Bantock (1997) to encourage their interest in writing letters (some may already have pen pals via email). The children can produce original postcards, cards, and letters which will help develop writing skills.

5. Involve the children in their own learning by getting them to edit and proofread their work. Provide a checklist of what to look for, such as is the message clearly conveyed? Make sure they know how to use the spell check on the computer and how to use a dictionary and thesaurus. Write in front of the children (e.g. on the board or on an overhead transparency) so they can observe by your actions and running commentary how you compose your thoughts—perhaps you will hesitate, cross out a word, or rephrase a sentence. Let them know that editing and re-editing is usual and necessary even for experienced writers.

6. Encourage children to be observant writers with a curious eye. Ask them to keep a writer's diary or a notebook in which they can write about particular events or activities that impressed them or affected them in some way. These trainee students remembered writing personal diaries.

I have kept my diaries from previous holidays and get much enjoyment at looking back and seeing what I was doing at the time and my general outlook on life ... Writing is a great way to express how you feel.

I.
—

Once I romanticised and thought I'd try to keep an accurate diary like Anne Frank—that didn't last long. I was very undisciplined, and I found myself too boring, unable to write interestingly or comically.

M.
—

The only time I can recall writing on my own initiative is when I kept a diary. I was about 9 at the time and this diary was something I completed every night. Mind you, it was one of the most boring diaries in the world—I'm sure. I simply wrote down exactly what I had done during the day, detail by detail, including about what time I got up and what TV shows I had watched—I even included the fact that I had written the diary article for the day—as if people wouldn't realise that by the fact that there were words and sentences on the page, done in my handwriting!

E.
—

I have always enjoyed writing. It allows me to express myself clearly, directly, capture thoughts, memories and ideas. I value words on a page. When I was younger I used to get homesick when my parents went away on business trips or when I stayed at a friend's house. I consulted my dear 'nanny' on this problem and she encouraged me to write my thoughts, feelings, day's events etc. in a journal. This method helped her when she was my age and experiencing similar problems. From that day, I have always recorded special events, special feelings, moments etc. in a pink diary hidden away in my cupboard. In fact, it is the same diary that my nan bought me many years ago and although it is not an everyday diary and is not written in too regularly, it contains some of the most precious moments and memories of my life.

K.

7. Expand children's vocabulary by asking them to find synonyms for different words and phrases or common expressions. Display these where they can be viewed and highlight how they can be used as appropriate choices in an extended written discourse.

He's nice. She's nice.

Try these synonyms:

likeable, attractive, beautiful, handsome, good, helpful, kind, lovely, friendly, generous …

Find synonyms for the following:

It was great. I thought it was fantastic.

8. Publish children's writing. Give them time in class to start writing chapters that can develop into a book. Help the children to make a class book of their writing. They may want to collect items on similar topics or have a medley. The book may be bound and photocopied or made accessible on computer disk. Encourage individual writing at home and on the computer, and find a way for these efforts to be recognised or published.

Discussion

What can you learn about the purposes of writing from the following comments by teacher trainees? What implications do these views have for the classroom?

I don't write many stories these days. However, my writing is purposeful in expressing my views and feelings. I'm a person who often finds it difficult to verbalise my opinions/views and feelings. Writing helps me to do this … Writing for me is easier than talking.

T.

I've always wanted to be a good communicator and recognised that writing is the key. The really crucial judgements about outcomes are made in the HSC, other examinations and written assessment.

C.

My problem is I'm very emotional and often my writing, like my speech is 'everywhere', haphazard, disjointed and quite often ending too abruptly.

M.

Chapter 13

Writing Skills in the Classroom: Handwriting and Spelling

> **Focus**
> This chapter gives an overview of some of the basic knowledge that students need to acquire in writing skills. Legible handwriting and accurate spelling in the writing process are means to an end. They must therefore be seen in the context of the whole writing process as essential tools in the communication of meaning.

The teaching of skills

Handwriting, spelling, punctuation, and grammar are simply the visible surface beneath which lie the ideas or meaning that writers struggle to compose. Sentences carry significant meanings—experiential, interpersonal, and textual. Writers need to get the conventions right so that ideas can be conveyed with clarity, and as a courtesy to their readers. They need to master the elements of English **orthography**, which consists of the alphabetic and writing systems but mainly refers to spelling. Teachers need to have a policy for teaching handwriting and spelling, keeping the following general principles in mind:

1. The language skills of reading, writing, listening, and speaking are inextricably linked. The skills learnt and practised in any area and the growing knowledge of semantic, graphophonic, and syntactic information can contribute to overall language ability.

2. The main responsibility of a good teacher of writing is to get the students to want to write clearly on topics of their choice over a wide range of text-types. Students can *learn to write by writing* (with reinforcement from their reading).

3. Shared, Guided, and Independent Writing activities will help students to write more confidently.

4. The teacher should assist where advice is most likely to be noticed and acted upon, namely at the individual student's point of need. This will probably be when the student is actually engaged in writing and can occur at any point in the process. This is why the writing conference is so important—the student

can be helped individually—and given assistance not only with the conventions of writing but also with ideas and text-types.

5. Encourage a habit of self-correcting when students write. Writing partners can assist when checking needs to take place.

6. Writing intended for readers must finally be proofread—that is, scrutinised for conformity with standard written English. However, forms of writing such as diary entries, notes, free writing, and trial drafts, not usually intended for readers, need not be subjected to such rigorous checking.

7. Apart from conference sessions, either individual or group, teachers can give occasional whole-class demonstrations for common language features and/or problems.

The 'skills' of writing should never be neglected, but they need to be considered in perspective. Writing needs to be approached in a way that will encourage students to write freely and encourage them to want to write—not in a way that will stifle creativity.

Here is the first draft of a student writing about what it means to be an Australian. While spelling and punctuation may need attention, the message is communicated and he has used an appropriate word, 'ancestors'. The teacher must decide where intervention is necessary without discouraging him:

> My family background. My pop cam for england and my great nan came from there. And my anstisers came from Island.
>
> Daniel, 8

HANDWRITING

Legible handwriting is a necessary skill so that writing can be understood by others. Handwriting should not, however, be taught in isolation from other language features. To do so can make writing a meaningless task. Recognising and memorising the shapes of letters (both upper and lower case) can be linked with lessons on

- literature and the reading session
- pronunciation
- spelling (e.g. letter combinations to make words)
- punctuation
- graphic design: distinctive shapes communicate different meanings (e.g. the letter x can symbolise many different meanings)
- the texture of typefaces, showing that different choices result in different kinds of communications.

Examples of typography

See the different results that can be obtained by the application of selected fonts, sizes, styles, and special effects which a word-processing program can provide. Remember that there are myriad additional choices to be made from computer programs. Encourage students to experiment.

Fonts	*Font styles*
Century Gothic	**Bold**
Geneva	*Italic*
New York	Regular
Times	

Font size	*Special effects*
10 point	Shadow
12 point	CAPITALISE
24	SMALL CAPS
36	Outline

The quick brown fox jumped over the lazy dog.

This is written in Times font, in regular style, 12 point, with no special effects.

Encourage students to see how different typography can be used e.g. Century Gothic, bold and italic, 24, shadow:

The quick brown fox jumped over the lazy dog.

Teaching handwriting

Children often learn the shapes of letters through alphabet books and may be taught how to write their name before they reach formal schooling. But most students need to be taught how to write legibly from Kindergarten onwards. At first handwriting movements are practised, then the letter shapes are taught, and later the letters are joined for a script, popularly called 'running writing'. As Royce Holliday points out, 'The teaching emphasis is not on the shapes of letters but on the movements that produce them ... Each letter is not seen as a separate phenomenon ... but is taught as a member of a group of letters related by common movements and patterns' (1988: 102).

The Foundation style

The style of handwriting preferred by education departments varies. For this reason it is important to consult the relevant state syllabus as a guide. The Foundation style adopted in New South Wales is designed to involve three basic movements that reflect 'natural' drawing:

sloped downstroke as in l, b, d
sloped clockwise ellipse as in b
sloped anticlockwise ellipse as in d.

Fig. 13.1   Sample of Foundation handwriting style with movement of pen strokes

The small letters

abcdefghijklm
nopqrstuvwxyz

The capital letters

ABCDEFGHIJKLM
NOPQRSTUVWXYZ

The numerals

0123456789

Fig. 13.2 Sample of handwriting style used in Victoria

Classroom practice

Teaching handwriting in a particular style may sound very prescriptive, but students will still develop their own individual styles in the way they form the letters, space them on a page, pay attention to layout, or even how they hold a pen. Even so, students need to be taught the rudiments of how to write and it is worth teaching aspects of handwriting such as how to hold the pen or pencil and how to sit at ease while writing. On no account should students who naturally write with the left hand be forced to change writing hands; nor should students who already write legibly in a script other than Foundation be told to change styles. Different parts of the country may advocate different styles of handwriting, but the basis of all should be that the style chosen is relatively easy to imitate (and teach) and that the final result is legibility.

Advice on the physical aspects of handwriting is designed to make the task of writing easier for the student. It would be a futile exercise, however, to insist on advice that does not suit an individual student. Basically, the pen or pencil is gripped with the thumb, index finger, and middle finger. The preferred position for handwriting is to sit comfortably at a stable writing surface with the pen held at a constant angle to the page. Textbooks exist for practising handwriting through the grades, and these are a useful ancillary to the classroom teacher.

Practice in handwriting is not only confined to committing writing to paper. At first, students are helped by practising the broad movements of the shape of a letter by whole arm movements or by tracing the shape of the letters. They can be helped to recognise letters visually by isolating individual letters or groups of letters in print. Attention needs to be paid to the correct formation of the letters, words or lines in regard to

- size and proportion to one another
- alignment
- slant
- spacing.

Handwriting is a physical exercise and there are various activities that will help students to write legibly:

- practising where to start on a page
- making sure that print moves from left to right
- using ruled lines and slope cards for mastering spacing conventions
- practising 'patterns' that can help with fluency.

Now that so much writing is done on the computer, learning to touch-type is a skill that should be acquired in the primary school classroom. Even so, students still need to be able to handwrite on those (many) occasions when a computer is not available, just as arithmetic cannot always be done on a calculator.

Handwriting is best taught in the context of normal school work, but regular practice sessions in the early years are definitely required. In the later grades practice sessions can be used when needed. Making this practice interesting and meaningful is a challenge. For example, on a worksheet relating to ***Charlotte's Web***, in answer to the question 'Who is Charlotte? Tell me something she did', Daniel (8) wrote:

Charlotte is a spider. She made some words in her web like some pig, terrific, and radiant. These words saved Wilboor from being turned into Christmas ham.

Here the main task is to encourage the student to think about the novel *Charlotte's Web*, but handwriting is practised coincidentally.

 Activity

This idea, borrowed from Chenfeld (1987: 385), will help students recognise how different styles of handwriting can achieve different effects:

> *The Seven Dwarfs' Handwriting: 'Would Grumpy's handwriting look the same as Bashful's? Would Happy's handwriting look exactly the same as Sleepy's?'*

Challenge the student to choose one or all the dwarfs and show samples of their writing in signatures, journal pages, letters, poems, or stories.

SPELLING

Knowing how to spell accurately is acquired through increasing recognition of the patterns of words through

- phonology (how words sound)
- sight (how words look in print or writing)
- **morphemes** (how words are constructed from meaningful elements)
- **etymology** (how words are derived; word origins).

Spelling knowledge may be gained by practice in all these areas and through Guided or Shared Writing sessions. Phonemic awareness is particularly important in the early years of gaining spelling skills so that students learn about

- **segmentation** (e.g. words are separate units)
- isolated sounds (e.g. the first sound in a word)
- discrimination (e.g. similarity or difference between first sounds, as in *thin, fat*)
- substitution (e.g. making up new words by substituting letters)
- alliteration (e.g. same sound recognition).

Encourage students to see accurate spelling as a worthwhile goal. Some people look back to a time when they think 'students knew how to spell' because of weekly spelling lists and spelling drills. Some believe that there is only one 'correct' way to spell a word and see spelling as fixed and not subject to change. The spelling of words such as *colour/color* or *program/programme* can cause controversy that appears out of proportion to relative importance. Unlike issues of cohesion or structure, it is usually evident whether a word is spelt correctly or not. Inaccurate spelling is seized upon as a key indicator of a 'poor' writer, yet this is not the case.

At one end of the spectrum are those who say that facility in English spelling is simply acquired by wide reading and that explicit teaching is unnecessary because students will eventually 'pick up' conventional spelling. This raises the ire of those teachers, parents, and researchers who notice that some students have not picked up conventional spelling at all. Explicit instruction about spelling strategies should be taught within the context of the school curricula.

Five spelling strategies are advocated by Bean and Bouffler (1997: 17):

1. Spelling as it sounds (this may lead to 'invented' spelling)
2. Spelling as it looks (from a student's 'sight' vocabulary)
3. Spelling as it articulates (may also depend on the student's pronunciation)
4. Spelling as it means (e.g. *thankyou* written as one word because it is seen as a meaningful unit)
5. Spelling by analogy (borrowing from how other similar sounding words are spelt).

Vocabulary that arises from class discussion in various subject areas may be listed on the board, in the students' books, or on a general list collated by the teacher. To some extent the 'list' is an arbitrary collection that will therefore be inappropriate for all children—some will find the vocabulary beyond their reach and understanding; others may consider it a waste of time. However, relevant lists can aid vocabulary development and be used to develop spelling skills.

Here is a list of words used during the day from a Grade 2–3 composite class. It includes words from an Italian lesson learnt in the school:

niece	*nephew*	*uncle*	
sulk	*bulk*		
should	*would*		
slave	*slaving*		
ferried	*ferry*		
carried	*carry*		
playing	*playground*		
bambino	*ciao*	*Napoli*	*bene*

This list, which includes sentences, is from a Grade 3–4 class after news of an earthquake disaster:

Japan, Kobe, Tokyo, tremor, earthquake, shock wave, after shock, crust, island
The capital of Japan is Tokyo.
Kobe had an earthquake.

Students need to know which strategies can help them to spell better (e.g. by using spelling 'rules', by sounding out words, or by using the dictionary) and when and how to apply these strategies. The teacher's role is to introduce students to a range of strategies and give them practice in using them. In this way students can select those that suit their own personal learning styles and that work for them.

Learners respond positively to a wide range of strategies. Some learn more effectively through the phonogramic mode while others have a kinaesthetic or visual preference. Different words might require different recognition strategies.

 Activity

1. Help students visualise the shape and pattern of these words by highlighting particular letters (e.g. all the vowels) or by drawing a box around a selected letter or letters.

   questions   students   ask

   Lead on to similar patterns that other words make.

2. Make up crosswords or acrostics on a particular theme to aid visual recognition. Acrostics are easily done on a computer or can be invented by the students. Acrostics can be formed in lines or verses from the first, the last, or other letters to form a word or phrase.

3. Names: make simple acrostics of students' names, e.g. Chris:

   Cheeky
   Happy
   Rowdy
   Impish
   Strong

The stages of spelling development

Spelling development varies from student to student and should not be regarded as a rigid sequence that must be followed. These are some broad stages of development in spelling that parallel the language–learning continuum as the student moves on to become an independent, effective communicator (see Winch and Blaxell 1992: 7–9).

The precommunicative stage

Although a child's writing development begins when she first begins to use a writing tool, the first stage is usually not readable. There are usually random strings of symbols that include letters, numbers, and invented shapes. Upper and lower case are used indiscriminately. Example:

Although this early stage is a real attempt to reproduce words, it does not conform to left-to-right progression or indicate any real knowledge of sound–letter relationship. Sometimes, however, a striking feature in a word, such as a sound, will lead to the writing of that letter in order to spell the word:

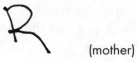

(mother)

No clear age guidelines can be given for each developmental stage, as each child learns to spell at his or her own rate. This early stage often corresponds to a period between 2 and 4 years old.

The pre-phonetic stage

At this stage children have begun to make sound–letter correspondences. Spelling is appreciated with only two or three letters representing a word such as in TL (table), HT (hit), BRD (bird). Vowels are often introduced, sometimes incorrectly as in BET (bat) or LADE (lady). The important point is that children are making the connection between sound and symbol and are recognising the left-to-right arrangement of words and correct word segmentation, as in TD Z MDA (Today is Monday):

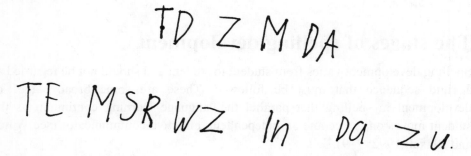

The monster was in the zoo.

The pre-phonetic stage usually covers a period between 3 and 6 years of age.

The phonetic stage

During the **phonetic** stage the child uses an almost perfect match between sound and symbol, even though the spelling is not standard. A trained reader will find a child's attempt at writing both readable and meaningful.

Examples:

I was only three.

> *when I waz sic I staid in bed.*

When I was sick I stayed in bed.

Children are usually at school during the phonetic stage, which covers the period between 5 and 7 years of age. It is at this stage that children are developing word knowledge quickly. They are experimenting with writing and should be encouraged to write freely without penalty for errors. Their spelling mistakes reflect a growing awareness of English spelling and they will become increasingly accurate.

The transitional stage

In this stage, which usually covers the period between 6 and 8 years of age, children are moving away from the purely phonetic strategy and rely more on visual and morphemic modes. As writers progress through this stage, an increasing number of words are spelt accurately.

Children now include vowels in every syllable and begin to spell digraphs such as w*ai*t and s*ee*d. Digraphs are the single sounds made from a combination of two letters, either vowels or consonants, e.g. *ay*, *ea*, *ie*, *th*. Although the visual mode is more in evidence, children have yet to consolidate this strategy and tend to use incorrect spellings such as rec*ee*ve, bl*ea*d, or monst*or*.

Examples:

> *We went out of the biulding.*
> *I ware wite shose on Satarday.*

We went out of the building. I wore white shoes on Saturday.

The correct spelling stage

Between 7 and 11+ years of age, students become more accurate in their spelling, depending on the difficulty of the words and the general level of discourse.

Now children can spell most words they meet, develop a knowledge of the various spelling modes, and attain a spelling 'conscience'. In particular, writers at this stage can deal with morphological structures, including prefixes and suffixes, contractions, compound words, derivatives, and silent letter sequences. They use the dictionary to check their spellings. A large body of words is spelt automatically. Students develop a mastery of uncommon and irregular spelling patterns and recognise when a word looks incorrect.

Example:

We used to thro throw the ball strate straight at him.

It is vital to emphasise that because the stages overlap and individual differences are great in any group of children, development to the 'correct' spelling stage will vary greatly among children.

English orthography

There is much that is regular in the English writing system. If there were not, we would not be able to spell. There cannot be a one-to-one correspondence of sound to symbol, however, because, to begin with, there are only 26 letters to represent the 45 meaning-bearing sounds or phonemes that make up our speech. Second, we have taken so many words from different languages that additional variation has been included. Fortunately, there are other aspects of language that produce similarities: they are the morphemic, syntactic, and semantic elements.

English orthography *is* manageable if we take into account the various ways it is put together. We need to teach sound–letter relationships that are regular, as well as morphemic relationships, letter patterns and sequences. Students need to learn that words in different sentences are spelt differently in different contexts.

> *Their home is over their.*
>
> *Their home is over there.*

Children must be allowed to rely on phonetic strategies, on the meaningful relationships among words, and on the visual images the words present. In this way spelling ceases to be a mystery and becomes a remarkable tool for effective and accurate writing.

If students are to know how to spell accurately, they need different kinds of spelling knowledge. This includes knowledge of different features:

- *phonological* (how words sound)
- *visual* (how words look)
- *morphemic* (how words change form)
- *etymological* (how words originate).

It is wise for a teacher to explore these different kinds of knowledge so that students can practise different strategies that suit their learning styles and consolidate their understanding of how spelling works. It is clear that instruction about spelling by sound, by pattern, and by meaning is necessary at all levels. Making sense of spelling requires thinking strategies, not simply a knowledge of phonics or a good memory.

Phonological knowledge

Linking a word with its sounds is essential in the early years when students are learning how language works. Use the sound–symbol relationships in conjunction with other semantic knowledge about language. For example, the words *break*, *freak*, *beard*, and *heard* have the same symbol but different sounds.

In the *pre-phonetic stage* the student is beginning to recognise links between sounds and letters or words. The student may easily recognise signs and symbols and frequently seen words that are meaningful.

At the *phonetic stage* the student recognises sound cues but may still make errors, e.g. *bik* instead of *bike*. Also at this stage
- words are usually spelt as they sound, e.g. *dark*
- commonly seen words are spelt correctly, e.g. *the*.

Teaching spelling is really teaching students about words, their patterns and regularities. We can encourage students to take an interest in how words are formed and the many unusual changes words can make in different combinations. It is remarkable that the 26 letters of the alphabet can be moved around in different spaces to create so many different words and meanings. Think of the variant pronunciations of 'ou': *tough*, *bough*, and *dough*, which are pronounced phonetically /tuf/ /bau/ /dou/. Consider also *cough* and *plough*. It is no wonder that there is confusion because, although words may look alike, they do not always sound alike.

Incorrect *pronunciation* is often the cause of incorrect spelling. Work on phonemes, blends, and digraphs is therefore extremely important. Find out how students pronounce words and listen for added syllables and/or incorrect substitutions that may affect their spelling ability. For example, the following words are often mispronounced in various ways:

aitch (H)	*Australia*
burglar	*going to*
congratulations	*library*

Clear articulation can be practised through songs and poems that reveal the importance of pronunciation in particular. Idiosyncratic pronunciation leads to misspellings.

At the Kindergarten level it is helpful for students to illustrate their sentences with drawings so that they can demonstrate meaning:

The bill was $10.
I am going to fill up.
I ran on the hill.
The pill was good.

- **Phonemes** are the smallest distinctive group or class of sounds ('phones') in a language. For example, *cap* consists of three different phonemes or sounds and differs from *sap*, *map*, or *cat* simply by changing one sound or phoneme.
- **Blends** are formed when different phonemes come together as in *str*eet, *bl*ue, *cr*ow, *scr*atch, and *pl*ay. Note that blends can be two or three letters in length.
- A **digraph** is a pair of letters that corresponds to a single sound, e.g. *ch* as in *chief* or *ee* as in *meet*. There are vowel and consonant digraphs.
- A **diphthong** is a sequence of two vowels produced in such a way that they are perceived to belong to one syllable, e.g., in Australian English, h*o*pe, w*i*de, b*ee*r, b*ea*r.

A knowledge of phonics will help students to spell accurately so that a focus is needed (especially in the early years) on the oral work of pronunciation. Clapping out the sounds of syllables written on the board can help students hear the different number of syllables and help their spelling, e.g.:

one syllable:	*dog*
two syllables:	*teach/ er*
three syllables:	*tel/ e/ phone*
four syllables:	*tel/ e/ vi/ sion*

Visual knowledge

Good spellers can often see if a word looks 'right' on the page or computer screen. They can remember from previous reading and recognition of word patterns what a word looks like. Spelling is heavily dependent on our visual memories of words and their parts. Students who read a lot will have the visual reinforcement of seeing the writing of common words many times, but those students who do not read widely or for pleasure need extra opportunities.

There are some students who have an inability to see spelling errors. As Gentry and Gillet explain:

> The visual coding mechanism is elusive and complex. It is not simple visual memory or a learning style. Undoubtedly, it works in parallel with other processing mechanisms related to spelling. Certainly phonemic, semantic, and etymological associative linkages function in parallel with it, allowing the mind to consider input on different levels and to look for overlap and connections. (1993: 54)

A 'sight' vocabulary is very important and can be encouraged by techniques such as *Look—Cover—Write* and games with flashcards. For example, words such as *find*, *kind*, *mind*, and *wind* have *ind* in common.

Morphemic knowledge

The morphology of words refers to their form or structure, and the meaningful units of which they consist, such as word bases, prefixes, and suffixes. Students can be taught the morphemes which make up a word. For example, the word *spelling* consists of two morphemes: *spell* and *ing*. Here, the morpheme *spell* can stand alone but the morpheme (or unit) *ing* is bound to another word. Correct morphemic division is important, as well as the ability to put a word into its syllables. Students vary in their abilities to do this and it can be confusing that the pronunciation of words does not always correspond with the morphemic division, e.g.:

> *res/ig/na/tion (syllables), is pronounced resig'nation, but it is composed of three morphemes: re/sign/ation*

If students can recognise patterns in words, they can become better spellers.

At the Kindergarten level, recognising the beginning letters of words, and how the main vowels are pronounced, needs to be practised, in context and with illustrations if possible, e.g. rain, read, ride, rose, rule. Students at the early levels will need much repetition in various guises as well as explanation to help them memorise and 'ingest' the information.

Bases of words

Knowledge of a base word will often help the student to decipher its meaning and correct spelling, and to understand that words often belong to 'families'. For example, *learn, learner, learning* have a similar base. Grammatically, the base of a word is a morpheme that can be expanded by grammatical **inflections** (word endings) or by prefixes and suffixes. For example, *child* is the base of *children, childlike, childproof, childhood, childless, childishness*. Recognition of base words will help students become good spellers as they see the extensions and derivates that can be built from them, such as the *ed* past tense ending, and the *s* or *es* of plurals.

Activity

Students can make up card sets of some of these words and play a game of 'Snap', locating the base of a word. Many variations can be made of 'Snap' to illustrate different elements of spelling. For example the card pack contains words from which compounds can be made, 'snap' when a compound word occurs, e.g.:

> *Word bases with suffixes: friend = friendship*
> *Compound words: child + proof; childproof, boardroom, landmass*

Make up a chart of words with Greek word elements, e.g. geo- is a word element from the Greek, meaning earth. From this, additions to a 'Greek' chart can be made:

> *GEO (Gk) = EARTH*　　　　　　　　　*geography, geology*

Word base	Origin	Meaning	Examples
bi	Latin/Greek	two	bicycle, bimonthly
sex	Latin	six	sextet, sextuplet
bio	Greek	life	biography, biology
ology	Greek	the science of	biology, palaeontology

Prefixes

Good spellers can recognise the syllables that make up a word. They can integrate this information with other language knowledge such as the recognition of prefixes and suffixes. Students can be taught to identify prefixes, i.e. those letters put before a word that add to or qualify its meaning. Thus *un* before a word affects its meaning, implying the opposite condition. For example, *un*, as in

unkind means not kind
unlike means not like or not similar
unbolted means not fastened
unprejudiced means not biased.

Students will come to recognise the link between sound and meaning, e.g. in understanding various prefixes or suffixes. A recognition of parts of words, e.g. prefixes *super-*, *trans-*, *circum-*, and suffixes *-er*, *-ing*, *-ish*, *-ly*, can help students to spell better if practice is given in their use and meaning.

Suffixes

Common English suffixes are: *-able*, *-ery*, *-ese*, *-ing*, *-ish*, *-ism*, *-ite*, *-let*, *-like*, *-ling*, *-ness*, *-ship*, *-tion*. Suffixes are a little complicated because they can alter the spelling or grammatical status of a word, e.g. the addition of *-ing* changes the word *love* into *loving*. 'Rules' for adding suffixes can help students with spelling, e.g. *y* changes to *i* before *-ed* (a suffix beginning with a vowel) so that *satisfy* becomes *satisfied*.

Suffixes

No change at all:
appear, appear*ed*, appear*ing*, appear*ance*
Some changes:
satisfy, satisf*ying*, satisf*ied*
It is very rare to see double *i* (*ii*) together in words of the English language.
The silent *e* is dropped:
dance, danc*ed*, danc*ing*, danc*eable*
love, lov*ed*, lov*ing*, lov*able*.

Activity

'Word webs' can be formed to help students build up their bank of vocabulary. For example, the morpheme *-ing* or *-ed* is commonly used for participles and the teacher can indicate how some of the past endings change.

Present (with -ing)	Past (-ed or other)
playing	played
looking	looked
flying	flew
reading	read
sleeping	slept
running	ran

Etymological knowledge

Etymology is the study of the origin and history of individual words, the language they derived from, and how the meanings and forms have changed over time. Knowing the history of a word can sometimes stimulate interest in its meaning and encourage students to remember its spelling. For example, the word 'robot' was first used in a play, *R.U.R.* written by the Karel Capek (1890–1938) and came from the Czech word *robotnik* meaning a serf.

Activity

Charts can be made to reinforce etymological knowledge, encouraging students' interest in language, e.g. the derivation of the word *electric* from the Greek *elektron* (i.e. amber, a substance that can be used to create electricity from friction). A word bank can be built up using words that are commonly used with *electric*:

electrical engineer
electric blanket
electric current
electric eel
electric fence
electric field
electric guitar
electrician
electricity
electric jug
electric light
electric shock
electrify

Many words in English are derived from other languages. Ask for suggestions, especially from multilingual students. Most English words are derived from Greek, Latin, or French words but increasingly there are new words or phrases that are added from other languages or simply made up.

Construct different charts that can have words added to them as students find etymological derivations from the dictionary. Charts can be made of words or phrases of

- *slang* words: Which are current? Which have dropped from use? Do Australians still refer to people as 'blokes' and 'sheilas'?
- *acronyms*: words formed from the initial letters of other words, e.g. Anzac (Australian and New Zealand Army Corps), AIDS (acquired immune deficiency syndrome), MIRV (multiple independently targeted re-entry vehicle),
- *neologisms*: new words or new sense of old words (beatnik, Internet)
- words from other countries (blitz, junta).

Learning styles and spelling strategies

Teachers can observe and record their students' strategies in learning how to write and spell. A record of how students actually behave when writing will allow the teacher to build on the strategies that work for the students and introduce them to others that might be helpful. Observations can be made on how students

- sound out words and then write them down
- look up words in a dictionary (or picture dictionary)
- use others (such as a peer or aide, or the teacher) to find out the spelling or meaning of a word
- have a knowledge of how words are segmented and how syllables form words
- are willing to try to spell a word
- attempt to proofread
- edit.

Students do not spell randomly but use reasoning processes to judge how a word is spelt. Asking why they have spelt a word in a certain way will often reveal the cause of a misspelling. Their spelling may be the result of visual memory of how it is spelt. If it is a new word they may borrow strategies from their previous knowledge, e.g. a commonly used ending such as *-ion* may help them to spell a word such as *action*; or they may rely on how it is sounded out.

Remember that knowledge about spelling is often drawn from a combination of factors. A student who tries to spell an unknown word may draw on all kinds of information, including phonological, morphological, and visual knowledge (sometimes for the same word). In writing the word *schools*, the student may be quite confident about the s and the *oo* sounds; he may realise that the word has a plural ending and register the unusual beginning of *sch* from a sight vocabulary. The word *school* has many dictionary definitions, mostly related to educational instruction. It is pronounced /skul/. The word is mainly used as a noun and can be used colloquially, as in *a two-up school*. Its derivation comes from Middle English, Old English, Latin, and Greek words, e.g. Greek *skhole*, Latin *schola*. *School* originally meant 'leisure' but it has changed meaning over the years to denote how we might spend our leisure, i.e. in studying.

Here a student has misspelt words but clearly knows the message to be communicated.

Original	Student Correction
I here the bell ring.	I hear the bell ring.
I were the boots.	I wear the boots.

Spelling strategies are diverse. A common strategy often used by the poor speller is that of 'avoidance'. If unsure about a word, students may try ignoring it altogether and trying to find a different way of expressing meaning. Students must be encouraged to 'have a go', perhaps with a special book in which they can record their attempts so that the teacher can observe on what basis they spell a word.

'Have a go' books

Students need to be taught to try out their best version of spelling, to 'have a go'. 'Have a go' books encourage risk-taking behaviour, which is important for students to progress in their writing and spelling. They are often divided into four columns:

Student's 1st attempt   2nd attempt   Spelling check   Personal dictionary

These lists provide a record for both student and teacher to monitor progress.

 ## Activity

Encourage students to think of the most appropriate strategy to discover how to spell a word. Write down various words students have struggled with and build up a chart of what strategies or key features to help in spelling. Students may find their own idiosyncratic ways of memorising, perhaps with a mnemonic:

Words	Strategy to remember
accommodation	double c and double m and three o's
separate	don't get separated from your parachute or you could be paralysed
tripod	tri means three
breakfast	two words break and fast form a compound word that means breaking your fast.

Correct spelling matters

While students are engaged in the creative process of writing, it can be argued that they do not really need to know how to spell every word. This is especially true at the early level where students have the oral vocabulary to express their ideas but not the formal knowledge of transcription. However, once others want to read the text and if it is 'published' in some form, then there is a need for accuracy. Correct spelling is needed for the text to communicate its meaning since readers are easily distracted from the meaning and the message by surface features of idiosyncratic or indecipherable spelling. While 'invented' spelling is part of the developmental continuum, the aim is to progress towards conventional spelling as quickly as possible. Identifying spelling errors should be regarded as an essential editing practice after the completion of writing. Editing can be done with the teacher's help, alone or with peers.

Independence and risk-taking

Accurate, independent spelling comes about with risk-taking behaviour. If students feel they are in an atmosphere where they can try out words without being criticised, they are more likely to become good spellers.

Spelling lists

Rote learning of spelling is not a useful technique for encouraging students to spell, basically because words out of context are difficult to remember. While avid readers become familiar with words and learn to spell without much explicit instruction, many students do not register this skill and remain keen readers but poor spellers. All students need to be taught how to recognise and be aware of how words are spelt, to know when a possible misspelling occurs, and to be able to consult a dictionary. While isolated words out of context might be difficult to spell, useful lists of commonly needed words or phrases can be made which can help the student. More meaningful lists can be compiled from

- lists of words related to work done in the classroom in connection with a theme or a topic from a particular subject area
- words centring on a topic discussed
- words which have similar features, e.g. the -*ing* ending
- word families
- class or personal dictionaries made by students as they come across new words.

Some of these 'lists' can become wall charts so that students can check spelling as they are writing. Commercial word charts may also be useful, e.g. of the sounds of English, blends, and digraphs.

Editing

A caveat about teaching spelling: spelling should not be taught in a manner that hampers the imagination of students so that they become fearful of making mistakes. This is why 'invented' spelling is acceptable in the early years. Our aim is to encourage students to become confident communicators who try to write in an interesting and informative way. They should not deliberately choose a simple word because they cannot spell a more difficult but more appropriate word.

Instruction about the process of writing from drafts to published product can show students how standard spelling can be arrived at. Teachers can point out that spelling errors can be edited in later drafts of the writing process, especially with computer tools that automatically check spelling. Accurate spelling is an important element of the final draft of a text.

Computer checking

Computer tools help students to improve their spelling. If the original work has been word-processed, errors picked up may be simply typographical (*hth/the*—computers tend to correct these automatically), but teachers should encourage students to take note of which spelling errors they make and why they might have made them. Explicit instruction is needed to point out the limitations of the spell-check facility, realising that this facility will not present them with an error-free text:

- how to choose from the list of spelling options in words
- why some misspelt words may not be picked up because they are homophones, e.g. *there/their, it's/its*
- words which do not appear in the computer's thesaurus, e.g. local place names and names of people
- the common American spelling variants, e.g. *centre/center*
- many spelling errors may not be located on a computer spell-check because they are grammatically the wrong word (though correctly spelt). For example, misspelt variants of a sentence would not be picked up: *They're* leaving! Put *their* suitcases over *there*.

Spelling 'rules' or generalisations

There are so many words in the English language that it is difficult for most people to spell them all correctly. There are, however, many systematic aspects of English spelling. By the end of the primary years of schooling, students should be able to

- spell frequently used words
- make an attempt at others they have not seen before
- use the dictionary to check spelling.

Focusing on the peculiarities of the English language may be fun, but there are many more regularities that have evolved to form conventional spelling. Spelling *is* systematic to a great extent despite the irregular forms that make English spelling unpredictable at times.

Sounds and letters often disagree

When the English tongue we speak
Why is 'break' not rhymed with 'freak'?
Will you tell me why it's true
We say 'sew' but likewise 'few'?
And the maker of the verse
Cannot cap his 'horse' with 'worse'?
'Beard' sounds not the same as 'heard';
'Cord' is different from 'word';
'Cow is 'cow' but 'low is 'low'
'Shoe' is never rhymed with 'foe';
Think of 'hose' and 'whose' and 'lose'
And think of 'goose' and yet of 'choose'
Think of 'comb' and 'tomb' and 'bomb'
'Doll' and 'roll' and 'home' and 'some';
And since 'pay' is rhymed with 'say',
Why not 'paid' with 'said', I pray?
We have 'blood' and 'food' and 'good',
Wherefore 'done' but 'gone' and 'lone'?
Is there any reason known?
And, in short, it seems to me
Sounds and letters disagree. (Quoted in
Williams 1977: 57)

These rules, put into a meaningful context, may help in teaching plural endings.

1. Add *s* to singular nouns: dog—dogs.
2. Words that end in *fe* or *lf* are made plural by changing them to a *v* and adding *es*: knife—knives, calf—calves.
3. If a word ends in *s x z ch sh* or *zz*, an *es* is added: bus—buses, witch—witches.
4. If the last two letters of a word are a vowel followed by a *y*, add an *s*: toy—toys.
5. If the last two letters of a word are a consonant followed by *y*, change the *y* to an *i* and add *es*: fairy—fairies, ferry—ferries.
6. Those words which do not add an *s* can be taught separately: fish, sheep, deer.
7. Others are still more irregular and change their vowel: tooth—teeth, mouse-mice, or add *-en*: ox—oxen, child—children.

Rhyming rule
I before E except after C
e.g. *ceiling, deceit, receive*

Teaching spelling and effective classroom practices

Spelling is best taught through the work that is carried on across the Key Learning Areas. Particular spelling lessons may be part of a Guided and Shared writing session, but for the most part spelling 'should be taught in the context of a talking, listening, reading or writing focus' (NSW Department of Education and Training 1998a: 7).

Much spelling instruction will occur as part of general literacy session, rather than as a more formal 'lesson'. Shared, Guided, and Independent language teaching strategies will provide many opportunities for the teacher to provide informal instruction (see Chapter 8). For example, in a Literacy Session focusing on 'Monsters', the following strategies could prove useful.

Shared Writing

The teacher and students suggest relevant words, phrases, and sentences that might describe monsters:

> *frightening, horrible*
> *the shocking appearance; a dreadful lurch*
> *The enormous ogre turned away.*

Words from topics studied, words from the curriculum, or high-frequency words can be written on cards. These cards are then given to students who have to sort them into particular sets. For example, they may sort them into verbs and make up sentences in which the words are appropriate.

Guided Writing

The class, with assistance from the teacher, might write sentences using some of the vocabulary presented on 'monsters'.

Write a dictation that uses words from the 'Monster' topic. Put the dictation on an overhead transparency with the key words highlighted. Discuss the correct version sentence by sentence so that students can easily see how the word is spelt. This activity can encourage editing and proofreading.

Independent Writing

Students can look up a dictionary and a thesaurus to find synonyms for words associated with *monsters*, e.g. *ghouls, scary, frightening, horror.*

 **Activity**

From the very beginning, students can be encouraged to keep their own personal word lists or dictionaries. They can record words, phrases, or sentences they have come across that are useful to them and that they want to reproduce accurately in their writing.

Students may also keep an additional list of word banks from their classroom activities.

With the help of students, teachers can compile lists that centre on a theme or a topic being discussed in class. This may help students to put words into context and remember them. Isolated words out of context do not have a 'hook' for students to peg their memory on.

'Look, say, cover, write, say, check'

This strategy works well for a wide range of students because it appeals to different senses. It may appear time-consuming but it is an effective strategy, especially in the early years. Naturally, as their ability increases and they apply the strategy almost automatically, students may choose to skip stages or say the word silently. Students are given explicit instructions to

1. look at a word carefully and observe its visual pattern
2. say the word aloud—a practice that helps to reinforce the memory of the structure of the word, especially if the word is pronounced in its syllables
3. cover—this gives time to ruminate about what the word looked like in print
4. write—a further reinforcement that mirrors the original word and reinforces the spelling pattern
5. say—by saying the word again, students may pick up whether it is accurately spelt
6. check—confirms accuracy of spelling.

 **Activity**

With instruction from the teacher, each student makes a personal 'Look, say, cover, write, say, check' folder that includes a section for writing down frequently used words, or words she finds difficult and another page for writing down spelling attempts. Encourage the use of this strategy for those students who will benefit from it.

Activity

1. Spelling can be made fun through games such as Sound and Word Bingo.
2. Children love games that play with letters and combinations of words—such as rhymes, word play, or crossword puzzles. In the early years, alliterative rhymes and tongue-twisters can help students recognise letters, e.g. 'Peter Piper picked a peck of pickled peppers'. Remember that students from a language background other than English may not easily understand some of these. Even better are sentences or rhymes students invent themselves.
3. *Homonyms* are words that are alike in some form. Technically, they are divided into *homophones*, words that sound the same but have different

meanings (such as *fare* and *fair*) and *homographs*, words that look the same when written but have different meanings, such as *minute* (unit of time) and *minute* (very small), *bow* (to bend over) and *bow* (the front of a boat).

Commonly confused pairs of homographs are:
bear, bear
by, buy
hear, here
pair, pear
piece, peace
their, there, they're
to, too, two
wear, where, we're
which, witch.

Give students practice in awareness of these words and using them in context so that they can understand the meaning.

Using the dictionary, the thesaurus, and word banks

Students in all grades should be encouraged to own a dictionary that is appropriate to their reading level. By Years 3 and 4 they should be using dictionaries whenever they do written work. The dictionary is not just a tool to check the accuracy of conventional spelling but can open up the world of words to students. A simple dictionary entry contains an enormous amount of information that may help students become aware of a word's meaning, how it is pronounced, with perhaps a phrase to illustrate what part of speech it is, whether it is used colloquially, and its etymology.

Students should be given many opportunities to familiarise themselves with the resources of dictionaries. In the early stages instruction should be given in how to locate words quickly and to practise alphabetical order. This may also be achieved through other resources such as telephone directories, indexes, street maps, or encyclopaedias.

Looking up a thesaurus can help students choose words that are most appropriate in context and that will communicate meaning more forcefully. Students can expand their vocabulary through a range of writing activities, complemented by specific examples (from an authentic text, if possible) that focus on expansion of word knowledge. For example, different words for *big* or *little* could be substituted in sentences, encouraging students to discuss why words such as *colossal* or *petite* might be more appropriate, interesting, or more specific in conveying meaning to the reader.

How to use this dictionary

The words defined (headwords) are in bold type. They are listed in alphabetical order.

Pronunciation is given when it is not obvious.

If a word is used as more than one part of speech, these are defined separately but no space is left between the entries.

Words are defined with Australian usage in mind.

Phrases are listed and defined under the part of speech to which they belong.

Unusual plurals are given.

Phrases (in italics) are given when useful to illustrate meanings by example.

Correct usage is indicated when doubt or error is common.

Parts of speech are printed in italics after the headword and before the definition.

[Latin, = white piece of stone etc. on which to write things]

albumen (*say* **al**-bew-min) *noun* white of egg. [from Latin *albus* = white]

alchemy (*say* **al**-kim-ee) *noun* an early form of chemistry, the chief aim of which was to turn ordinary metals into gold. **alchemist** *noun* [from Arabic *al-kimiya* = the art of changing metals]

alcheringa (*say* al-cher-**ring**-ga) *noun* the Dreamtime. [from Aranda (an Aboriginal language)]

alcohol *noun* **1** a colourless liquid made by fermenting sugar or starch. **2** an intoxicating drink containing this liquid (e.g. wine, beer, whisky). [from Arabic *al-kuhl*]

alcoholic *adjective* of alcohol; containing alcohol.
alcoholic *noun* a person who is seriously addicted to alcohol. **alcoholism** *noun*

alcove *noun* a section of a room etc. that is set back from the main part; a recess. [from Arabic *al-kubba* = the arch]

alder *noun* a kind of tree, often growing in marshy places.

alderman (*say* **awl**-der-man) *noun* (*plural* **aldermen**) a local government councillor in some Australian states and in England. [from Old English *aldor* = older, + *man*]

ale *noun* beer.

alert *adjective* watching for something; ready to act. **alertly** *adverb*, **alertness** *noun*
alert *noun* a warning or alarm.
on the alert on the look-out; watchful.
alert *verb* warn of danger etc.; make someone aware of something. [from Italian *all' erta!* = to the watch-tower!]

alga (*say* **al**-ga) *noun* (*plural* **algae**, *say* **al**-jee) a kind of plant that grows in water, with no true stems or leaves.

algebra (*say* **al**-jib-ra) *noun* mathematics in which letters and symbols are used to represent quantities. **algebraic** (*say* al-jib-**ray**-ik) *adjective* [from Arabic *al-jabr* = putting together broken parts]

alias (*say* **ay**-lee-as) *noun* (*plural* **aliases**) a false or different name.
alias *adverb* also named, *Robert Zimmerman, alias Bob Dylan.* [Latin, = at another time]

alibi (*say* **al**-ib-I) *noun* (*plural* **alibis**) evidence that a person accused of a crime was somewhere else when it was committed. USAGE It is incorrect to use this word as if it meant simply 'an excuse'. [Latin, = at another place]

alien (*say* **ay**-lee-en) *noun* a person who is

vi

Fig. 13.3   A page from the Oxford Dictionary

Using the computer

The computer provides an excellent resource for students to work independently on language skills. Some students enjoy working with commercial products that teach spelling. If a resource is useful for a particular student, then it is a successful learning strategy. Innovations exist such as reading pens which, when run over written text, can spell out a word letter by letter, break it into syllables, and provide a dictionary definition. Authenticity can still be found in computer-assisted learning and can facilitate the spelling acquisition process. Some of the interactive software is excellent for practising spelling, especially those that teach spelling through imaginative games. Talking books on the computer such as the stories from the Oxford Reading Tree allow students to highlight particular words and to hear the correct pronunciation at the same time.

SUMMARY

1. The writing skills of handwriting and spelling are important in conveying ideas clearly in texts, but they must be kept in perspective as the young writer may be easily discouraged.
2. Handwriting should not be taught in isolation from other language features.
3. Regular practice must be given in handwriting skills as well as touch-typing skills.
4. Multiple strategies should be taught for children to learn spelling.
5. There are various developmental stages in learning how to spell: the precommunicative, pre-phonetic, phonetic, transitional and correct spelling stages.
6. To spell correctly, students need a combination of phonological, visual, morphemic, and etymological knowledge.
7. Teaching activities for spelling should be varied and interesting, mostly relating to work done in the context of the curriculum: word webs, 'have a go' books, spelling lists, spelling 'rules' or generalisations, 'look, say, cover, write, say, check', using the dictionary, thesaurus, and word banks.
8. Computer spell checks as well as other aspects of computer technology should be used to aid better spelling.

Chapter 14

Writing Skills in the Classroom: Punctuation and Grammar

> **Focus**
>
> This chapter discusses punctuation and grammar within the writing process. Both are best taught through the students' own writings and reading. Familiarity with the basic features of punctuation allows students to write more expressively. The various elements of grammar (phonology, semantics, morphology, and syntax) will give students a framework for understanding how language works. Traditional grammar and functional grammar offer insights into the structure of language and can help students' ability to write.

PUNCTUATION

The importance of punctuation is often underestimated, yet a misplaced mark can significantly alter meaning. 'Let me be yours' is quite a different message from 'Let me be. Yours, … '. Punctuation allows the writer to show expression, to communicate rhythm, tone, and those paralinguistic features so easily conveyed in speech. Students are often inventive in their use of these features as they try to simulate the spoken word on the printed page or to convey a particular emotion. In the following sentence a student capitalised 'died' to emphasise the magnitude of the loss:

More than fifty-five thousand Turkish soldiers DIED in the Gallipoli campaign.

Once students learn how to use features such as brackets (parentheses), exclamation marks, and question marks, their writing can become more descriptive and meaningful as the punctuation marks mimic language features such as intonation and stress:

In written English, punctuation can be used to show information structure, although it cannot express it fully, and most punctuation practice is a kind of compromise between information structure (punctuation according to the intonation) and sentence structure (punctuating according to the grammar). (Halliday and Hasan 1976: 325)

Good punctuation allows a text to be read coherently without confusion. Ask students to read aloud from an unpunctuated text and see where they need to pause for breath. By this method some can quickly learn about sentence structure and how and why to write capital letters at the beginning of sentences and a full stop at the end. They can progress fairly easily to an understanding of how commas (similar to the pauses of speech) can divide clauses and how paragraphs can be set out so that a reader can follow the text more easily.

The first written texts did not possess punctuation marks. These were added later to help in reading aloud. The printing press further encouraged the standardisation of punctuation marks but punctuation is still a fairly idiosyncratic practice. Some authors punctuate heavily, others lightly. The modern trend is towards less punctuation if the meaning can still remain clear, but it is to some extent still a matter of personal preference.

Everyday literacy needs and graphic symbols

It is essential that students have an understanding of the diverse range in which information can be presented, for example, as symbols, figures, tables, graphs, pie charts, calendars, clocks, dockets, accounts, forms, maps, watches, timetables, TV guides, measurements, shapes, labels. It cannot be assumed that they will know how to interpret this kind of symbolic language; they will need explicit instruction and plenty of practice. Modern punctuation is more complex than might be imagined. It is more than the traditional and familiar punctuation marks because it also includes features such as various non-alphabetic marks:

@   # $ %   &   *

Spaces and indention can also be regarded as part of punctuation as students learn how meaning is conveyed by the way texts are organised into sentences and paragraphs. For more detailed explanations of punctuation, check grammar textbooks (Derewianka 1991, 1998; Winch and Blaxell 1999) and similar reference books.

Scope and sequence of teaching punctuation

Punctuation is best taught through children's own writings as they discover how meaning can be communicated more effectively and how punctuation signals the reading of a text. But the teacher may want to focus on particular features, e.g. Kindergarten students can be introduced to capital letters and full stops as they write sentences. As with most aspects of language, students may come across all the standard features of punctuation in a storybook they can read in Year 1. Nevertheless, it cannot be taken for granted that students will know how or why to use punctuation. Explicit instruction will be required.

The following sequence can be followed:

1. recognition of where there is a need for punctuation

2. explanation or discussion of which punctuation marks will assist in conveying meaning
3. applicable 'rules' of punctuation
4. punctuation of a student's text with a check to see which punctuation is more effective
5. further examples of punctuation in other contexts
6. practice in using features of punctuation to reinforce correct usage and/or to remedy incorrect usage.

These are some standard features of punctuation that need to be taught: capital, full stop, comma, semicolon, colon, hyphen, dash, brackets, exclamation and question marks, inverted commas, apostrophe, italics, indention in paragraphs.

The punctuation marks

Capital (capital letter)

This is an upper-case letter used as the first letter of the first word in a sentence, for proper nouns (e.g. Paul, Australia), and for the pronoun 'I'. Often capitals are used for personification when an abstract idea is represented as a person or creature

> *Old Time is still a-flying.*
> *Old Man River he just keeps rolling along.*

Abbreviations and trade names are usually given capitals, e.g. NSW or Cadbury's chocolate. Capitals may also be used for emphasis or to indicate loudness:

> *'Somers—S-O-M-E-R-S.' Harriet spelled it out.* (D. H. Lawrence, *Kangaroo*)

The stops

There are many 'stops' in the English language: the full stop, comma, semicolon, colon, dash and parentheses.

The **full stop** (.) is also called period or full point. 'Nobody will go to heaven for using *period*, nor to hell for using *full stop*' (Partridge 1953: 9). It is used to indicate the end of a sentence:

> *Chris and Paul flew to Australia from Canada.*

The **comma** (,) is one of the most frequent marks and indicates an interruption in continuity of ideas expressed, or grammatical structure:

> *As I said, the story of the fig is, at the deepest level, the same story as for every other living creature on this planet.* (Richard Dawkins, *Climbing Mount Improbable*)

The **semicolon** (;) is often used to separate a list of items or between connected or balanced ideas in a sentence:

Mr. Scully was going to die; he was leaving Ned perched on the top rung of a ladder built out of lies; the ladder was leaning against nothing. (Paula Fox, **One-Eyed Cat**, 1984)

The **colon** (:) marks a point in a sentence that often begins a listing of some kind:

Consider the following points when buying a toy for a child: its safety, its washability, and its appropriateness.

Dash

The dash functions similarly, but more strongly than, the bracket or the comma:

The athlete was running—faster than anyone had ever seen—into the stadium.
The dog was fierce—really fierce.

to highlight a word or phrase:

Leonardo da Vinci—the greatest painter of the Renaissance—is famous for his Mona Lisa.

to represent pauses in speech:

Three—um—three ice-creams.
I—I—I was afraid.

to indicate interruptions or omissions (e.g. expletives) in the text:

The man said, 'This is a f—ing hold-up, give me all the money' (Manly Daily, 11 December 1999: 1)

It can be printed as – or as—.

Hyphen

The hyphen (-) is used to join parts of a compound word:

The so-and-so looked daggers at me.
pro-environment, anti-nuclear, duty-free, non-English-speaking Australians

It is also used in some reference material to divide words to show syllabification:

Syd-ney

Brackets

Brackets (also called parentheses, which is the plural of *parenthesis*) contain an additional insertion in a sentence, as a comment or explanation, or as an afterthought. Brackets are also used around references such as dates.

A Devil's Advocate (Advocatus Diaboli) is a person who advocates an unpopular or opposing view.

Exclamation mark

The exclamation mark (!) is used after an exclamation, an outcry:

> *'Oweee!' shrieked the hen and it shot straight up into the air like a rocket.*
> (Roald Dahl, ***George's Marvellous Medicine***)

Question mark

The question mark (?) is used after an interrogative phrase or sentence:

> *'Why can't you be like the Happy Prince?' asked a sensible mother of her little boy who was crying for the moon.* (Oscar Wilde, ***The Happy Prince***)

Inverted commas

Inverted commas are also known as quotation marks, quotes or speech marks.

Double quotation marks are mainly used for direct speech, although dialogue is increasingly signalled by single quotation marks:

> *"Whatever happened to good manners?" his father said.*
> *Andrew jumped up to run after him. "Wait!"*
> *Mario pulled him back. "Let him go! We don't want him around."*
> *"He should come with us," Andrew replied. "If we find the Skymaze now, he should be with us."*
> *"Nah, he'll only mess things up even more. Come on, let's go. We've wasted enough time already."* (Gillian Rubenstein, ***Skymaze***)

> *'It's disgusterous!' the BFG gurgled. 'It's sickable! It's rotsome! It's maggotwise! Try it yourself, this foulsome snozzcumber!'*
> *'No, thank you,' Sophie said, backing away.* (Roald Dahl, ***The BFG***)

> *Vicki laughed. 'You are an ignoramus.'*
> *'Yeah, I just escaped from the zoo.'*
> *'Claaass!' Mrs Twaddle bellowed.*
> *'None of that here,' said someone.*
> *'Right! Who said that?'* (Tim Winton, ***Lockie Leonard, Human Torpedo***)

Single quotations marks are used for quoting from other text. For example,

Kay Cottee, after her solo voyage around the world, wrote 'the most bewildering and embarrassing outcome has been the number of awards and commendations bestowed on me since my return. I set out only to achieve a dream, a personal goal, not ever imagining that my country would respond in such a way'. (Cottee 1989: 202)

Apostrophe

The apostrophe (') is used to show

- where letters have been omitted, e.g. *couldn't = could not*; *it's = it is*; *she's = she is/she has*
- elisions

  o'clock = of or by the clock
  cont'd = continued

- possession

  the child's mother, horses' bridles

The *s's* is less commonly used now, e.g. *Mrs Jones' dog* instead of *Mrs Jones's dog*, possibly because the sibilant *s* sounds a little awkward. They are both acceptable alternatives.

The apostrophe seems to cause particular problems. It is normally omitted
- in place names and street signs: *Milsons Point, St Helens Park*
- in commonly shortened words: *plane* instead of *'plane* or *aeroplane*
- plurals of abbreviations or numerals, e.g. *MPs, PhDs, 1960s, sevens* (but *sixes*)
- plural nouns used adjectivally, e.g. *Secondary Boys School*
- with possessive pronouns such as *hers, theirs, its*.

The *'s* is such a bugbear that people often put it in where it is unnecessary. It is sometimes jokingly referred to as the feral apostrophe:

  Ripe Tomatoes For Sale √
  but not *Ripe Tomato'es For Sale or Ripe Tomatoes' For Sale* **x**

- Some try to avoid error or awkwardness by rewriting or rephrasing sentences without using the apostrophe 's'. For example, instead of *Mrs Chi's newsagency is open*,

  The newsagency belonging to Mrs Chi is open.

but this sounds formal and rather awkward.

Italics
In word-processed material, italic writing is equivalent to ordinary writing that is underlined (underlining and italics are not used together).
- Italics are mostly used for emphasis so that the reader recognises a word's relative importance in a sentence:

  'Oh, *could we*?' Sophie cried. 'Oh, *please!* I haven't eaten a thing since yesterday!' (Roald Dahl, ***The BFG***)

- Italics are also used to indicate foreign words (although some, e.g. 'status quo' and 'verbatim', are no longer italicised):

  sotto voce, raison d'être, in flagrante delicto

- Titles of books or newspapers are commonly written in italics rather than underlined or placed in inverted commas:

  Catch 22, *Catcher in the Rye*, *Such is Life*, *Things Fall Apart*
  The Age, *The Australian*, *The Sydney Morning Herald*

- Sometimes italics are used to transcribe verbatim speech instead of using quotation marks:

  The child said *Oh, it's not mine, it belongs to my brother.*

Indentation in paragraphs

Indentation (or indention) is the setting in of the text from the margin, often in the first line of a paragraph. Some writers prefer a block method where no indention is made and the new paragraph commences at the beginning of the next line. Verse and poetry is mostly indented so that it looks more appealing on the page. A quotation that needs to be given prominence is set out with the whole text indented, on one side or both:

> By establishing the order in which you wish to make the points of your exposition or your argument, to set forth the incidents of your narrative, the aspects of your description, you simultaneously and inevitably establish the division into paragraphs, and the natural, because the best— the best, because the entirely natural—order of those paragraphs. (Eric Partridge 1953: 168)

Punctuation should not be underestimated—it is part of the art of writing well.

 Activities

1. Ask students to write 'possessive case' verse, for example:

    My dog's fleas
    Your father's daughter
    The pen of my aunt
    La plume de ma tante
    The Secret Diary of Adrian Mole
    Australia's last hope

2. Punctuate the following so that it makes sense:

    *yes its true there is crime and violence in hawaii as there is everywhere else in the world only because hawaii was indeed a trouble free paradise for so many years people tend to ignore basic safety precautions (*from Frommer's *Hawaii on $50 a Day,* 1988–89 edn*)*

3. Plan a lesson to teach the use of the apostrophe with nouns in the possessive case to improve students' punctuation in a Year 5 class. Work out a simple rule that would help the students. Check a grammar handbook such as Gordon Winch and Gregory Blaxell, *Primary Grammar Handbook*, 2nd edn, 1999.

GRAMMAR

A definition of English grammar

Grammar can be defined as the systematic relationships that exist between elements of the English language such as the parts of speech, the formation and arrangement of words, and sentence structure, all of which indicate meaning and determine how we use our language. Rules and conventions about grammar change over time, so it is wise to recognise variations in usage.

Teaching grammar

The main argument in favour of the explicit teaching of grammar is that the more students learn about the nature of language the more efficiently they will be able to use it. A knowledge of grammatical concepts and terminology can help in the development of good literacy skills. However, grammar is best taught in an integrated way, not as arid lessons for which students see little purpose. The teacher's aim should be to teach grammar within the context of language experiences rather than as a series of isolated, decontextualised grammatical lessons. Teaching and learning the difference between *saw* and *seen* or between *write*, *wrote*, *writing*, and *written* should be done in context. The integrated nature of language means that specific grammatical activities at the level of word or sentence may seem irrelevant to students if they are not linked to meaningful usage.

In schools, instruction about grammatical structures and strategies to teach a particular structure can be made interesting and relevant if made part of the student's living language. Use real-life examples to explain what might be considered appropriate speech or writing in different contexts. A telephone-caller might say, 'Mick Doohan won the motorcycle championships five times. He done real good'. The message is conveyed clearly, if ungrammatically. Prescriptive or value judgments about language are *not* made by linguists, but teachers need to prepare their students for a society that often judges people on their perceived language ability. There is a 'linguistic consensus' in English-speaking communities that says *done* in the sentence above is not acceptable as 'standard English'; some dictionaries have usage notes that explain why one form of a word is acceptable and another not. A good speaker or writer will intuitively use 'correct' grammar without being able to explain it. Being able to *identify* grammatical features is not a necessary aspect of communication, but some knowledge of it can help to achieve the overall aim of acquiring literacy.

The usefulness of grammar is clearly stated in the NSW *English K–6 Syllabus* (NSW Board of Studies 1998: 9): 'grammar can be used as a tool to help students understand how sentences are structured so that they are meaningful, clear, and syntactically accurate. It also provides scope for exploring the grammatical patterns in texts to see how they build up the meaning'. Objections to teaching grammar because it is regarded as 'boring' and 'irrelevant' can be met by referring to these reasons and by lively teaching methods that do not make the study of grammar a tedious chore. A knowledge of grammar

1. *allows students to make judgments about appropriate usage of English.* Students will gain some understanding of why and how people speak and write differently in various contexts. Why and when should *I done it* or *I seen it* be corrected as *I have done it* and *I saw it*?

2. *improves literacy skills.* Explicit instruction in grammar should help students choose appropriate grammatical patterns that fit the purpose and structure of their texts. Writing with grammatical accuracy is achieved over time with plenty of practice, using examples from stretches of language and from extended discourse.

3. *enriches understanding of literature.* Students are able to see patterns of language more clearly. They may identify and enjoy metaphorical language and experimental structures.

4. *assists in learning foreign languages.* Anyone who has learnt another language realises that a knowledge of English grammar can help to explain the structure of other languages. In Mandarin the tenses are not indicated by inflections, so *Ta shi laoshi* could mean *He/she is a teacher* or *He/she was a teacher* depending on the context in which it is used.

5. *provides a metalanguage which allows students to talk about their reading and writing.* The terminology of grammar gives students a language to describe the language they use, hear, read, and write. While it is possible to speak and write 'grammatically' without being able to describe these features, an understanding of grammar gives students insight into how the language is constructed. Grammatical terminology provides a metalanguage to help understand how language operates in sentences, clauses, phrases, and words. It is important to show students how grammatical choices operate at the paragraph and text level. Understanding grammar is a means to an end.

Grammar includes a study of various elements:

- **semantics:** the study of the meanings of words and how they may change:

computer used to mean a person who made calculations
gay used to mean only happy, blithe
sandwich was named after the 4th Earl of Sandwich, who liked to eat meat in between slices of bread so that he didn't have to leave the gaming table to eat

- **morphology:** the patterns of word formation, which include inflections (word endings signifying grammatical meaning, or prefixes and suffixes) and the base or **root** (main body of the word carrying the meaning) derivation and the composition of words:

dresses, dressed, dressing, dressy, undress

In a word like 'inflexible', *flex* is the root of the word and means 'bend', so the word is built up from a negative prefix, the meaning-carrying root, and an adjectival suffix.

The teacher can integrate the morphology of words with vocabulary expansion and spelling instruction.

- **syntax:**   the patterns of formation of sentences and phrases from English words. For example, a common English sentence structure is:

The dog	*bit*	*the teacher.*
Subject	Verb	Object

It can also be written in the **passive** construction, where subject and object are reversed and the verb form changes, although the meaning does not:

The teacher	*was bitten*	*by the dog.*
Object	Verb	Subject

These grammatical features play a major role in creating discourses beyond the sentence level. For example, we say the words *I can run* in this order because we have an implicit knowledge of the grammatical rules governing syntax, the word order in English. Changing the word order to *Run, can I!* or *Can I run?* is also possible. The English speaker can tell which meaning is intended from various clues from the context and from the word order, punctuation, and/or intonation. In traditional poetry children may find a reversed sentence order that is a relic of older forms of the language:

Now came still evening on (John Milton)

Which grammar to teach?

Features of traditional grammar and functional grammar can complement one another, so the teacher is advised to draw on both. The terminology of 'traditional' grammar is widely known throughout the English-speaking world. The teaching of traditional grammar dropped away in the 1960s when the new grammars (Chomsky etc.) emerged in the universities, but it is again being taught in some schools. **Traditional grammar** is commonly regarded as the description of parts of speech and sentence structure. **Functional grammar**, however, provides a useful focus on how language functions in particular contexts, the importance of language choices, and the analysis of extended passages of text.

Traditional grammar

These are the eight basic parts of speech in traditional English grammar:

Noun	horse, car, day
Pronoun	she, he, it, they, I, we, you
Adjective	beautiful, small, red
Verb	run, laugh, eat
Adverb	swiftly, carefully, now
Preposition	over, into, under
Conjunction	and, but, because
Interjection or exclamation	oh! ugh!

Traditional grammar has some limitations in describing how language works, particularly beyond the sentence level. It describes written expression tolerably well but it is not so capable of describing other functional varieties of language, for example formal or informal speech, which are mapped in functional grammar.

A criticism of traditional grammar is that it is based on Latin and Greek. These are inflected languages where meaning is given to nouns, verbs, and adjectives by changing the word endings (inflections). For example, in Latin, *puer* means *child* and *pueribus* means *by*, *with*, or *from the children*. In English, however, meaning is mostly conveyed through a combination of word order and prepositions. Historically, the inflectional system of the original form of English, Anglo-Saxon, withered away, although some inflections survived.

Grammatical terminology can be daunting for students. The teacher must decide how much detail should be given at different stages of development and whether some is too specialised. The scope and sequence of teaching grammar can be presented in a formal program of instruction, linked to the writing of different genres. There will undoubtedly be much overlap between grammatical features in the genres. As Collerson (1997: Appendix A) advises, 'very few issues are purely grammatical' as most grammatical features have implications for broader aspects of meaning. When planning a language syllabus, grammatical features can be taught within the context of different text-types and the wider curriculum, for example when teaching how to write narratives.

Early Stage 1

Writing narratives is achieved by joint construction as students create a story from a Shared Reading session with the assistance of the teacher. At this stage they can write simple sentences; use the simple present and simple past and future tenses of verbs; develop a story through an orientation, basic descriptions, and conclusion; and use adjectives and adverbs.

Stage 1

Here emphasis can be placed on

- sentences and clauses using commas, capital letters, and full stops
- conjunctions to join sentences and to introduce logical relations, e.g. *because*, *although*
- pronouns used instead of nouns
- present and past tenses.

Here the teacher still plays a role in the construction of texts and may help with writing the final draft. At this stage the student has knowledge of commonly occurring words and can recognise letter–sound correspondences. Students may have keyboard skills and may type on the computer. Their writing will show more evidence of compound and complex sentences as well as pronoun references. They have more control of grammatical features and use tenses fairly accurately. There is increasing command of punctuation and the use of quoted speech. The students can edit their writing to some extent.

Stage 2

Here the following features can be emphasised:

- logical structure, e.g. using *first*, *second*
- use of modality, e.g. *could*, *must*, *should*
- the difference between first and third person narratives
- the use of dialogue and accompanying punctuation
- singular and plural

Students can write a narrative that contains an orientation, complication, a series of events, and a resolution. They have a fair degree of control over various grammatical features, especially capital letters, commas, and full stops within a sentence. Drafting and editing work is undertaken and the student recognises more difficult aspects of writing such as the organisation of the text and the need for more expressive language that will convey the narrative. At this stage they are capable of writing an individual narrative, perhaps based on a story they have listened to or read together. The student can write on a wide range of topics and can address different kinds of audiences.

Stage 3

Here the emphasis is on consolidating previous grammatical work and furthering knowledge of

- compound sentences
- adverbial phrases of manner, time, and place
- direct and indirect speech
- tense structure

- lexical cohesion (the cohesive effect achieved by, for example, reiteration of vocabulary in a text)

At this stage students write more confidently and provide more detail and coherence in texts. There is further evidence of elaboration of ideas with the appropriate grammatical structures to convey them. Students may experiment with different structures, building on the conventional narrative structure in a variety of ways. Different styles of writing and different formatting of texts may be explored. Joint constructions may still be used but students are capable of writing a narrative, for example, independently from the draft stages to a final edited version.

The primary school student will not need to know the terms *anaphora*, *cataphora*, or *exophora* although the concept of how words point backwards (anaphora), forwards (cataphora), or outside a text (exophora) are extremely important. Lexical cohesion establishes continuity in a text, for example by repeating words or synonyms of the word or by using **collocations**. Key words throughout a text remind the reader of what is significant and lead to a cohesive and meaningful text.

From their reading students will become familiar with many aspects of grammar but they will still need explicit instruction and considerable practice to make themselves adept at using the dizzying potential of the English language. Teachers can help children to become aware of the following features as they read many different types of texts. It is useful to help students to improve their writing by an explanation of, for example, number, person and gender.

Number: singular or plural (sing.—dog, pl.—dogs)

Person: 1st, 2nd, or 3rd (1st—I, we; 2nd—you; 3rd—he, she, it, they)

	Singular	*Plural*
1st person	I, me, mine	we, us, our
2nd person	you, yours	you, your
3rd person	he, him, his	they, them, theirs
	she, her, hers	
	it, it, its	

Gender: masculine, feminine, neuter

he, she, it

Other grammatical features to teach:

Phrases are words grouped together to form a meaningful unit. A phrase does not have a finite verb (see below):

holding a football

Clauses: A clause has a subject and a finite verb, and sometimes an object too:

She was holding a football.

It may be a principal (or main) clause, which can stand alone as a complete sentence, or a subordinate (or dependent) clause, which cannot:

When the game began she was holding the football.

It could also be two main clauses linked by a *coordinating conjunction*:

He liked football and he wanted to play, but his parents said no.

Sentences: A sentence contains a finite verb (i.e. a complete verb that can stand alone). A sentence begins with a capital letter and ends with a full stop, an exclamation point, or a question mark. Sentences are of four main types: simple, compound, complex, and combinations of these:

simple: consists of a main clause with a subject and predicate (the thing that is said about the subject, consisting of verb or verb + object):

She was holding a football.

compound: consists of two main clauses joined by a coordinating conjunction:

She was holding a football and she wouldn't let it go.

complex: consists of two or more clauses, at least one of which is a dependent clause:

She was holding a football, which was her birthday gift.

combination:

She was holding a football, which was her birthday gift, and she wouldn't let it go.

Direct speech and indirect or reported speech

Direct: 'Mirror, mirror on the wall, who is the fairest of them all?' she asked.
Indirect or reported speech: She asked the mirror on the wall who was the fairest of them all.

Possessive case: the *s* inflection:

Lewis Carroll's *Alice*

Personal pronouns:

his hers its mine ours their yours

Modality: the use of words expressing a writer or speaker's orientation towards possibility, probability, and certainty, such as *may, always, sometimes, usually*

Tense:

• tenses with the regular verb 'to start'

Cartman starts to behave strangely. (present tense)
Cartman started to behave strangely. (past tense)
Cartman will start to behave strangely. (future tense)

- tenses with the irregular verb 'to go'

We are going to the swimming pool. (present continuous tense)
We went to the swimming pool. (past tense)
We will be going to the swimming pool. (future continuous tense)

Voice:
- active voice

Mr Lee gave me a present.

- passive voice

A present was given to me by Mr Lee.

Functional grammar

Functional grammar, also known as 'systemic grammar', was developed by M. A. K. Halliday, Emeritus Professor of Linguistics at the University of Sydney (Halliday 1985a). In essence, functional grammar looks first at the general communication of a spoken or written text, giving greater attention to the importance of context (i.e. the context of culture and the context of situation). It focuses on how meaning is expressed and what forms of language express these meanings. It is clear that language is not an arbitrary set of words or structures since definite choices are made. This is different from traditional grammar, which first looks at specific items, emphasising the forms of words (morphology) and the forms of sentences (syntax). The focus of functional grammar is on the text as a whole, the extended discourse rather than the smaller unit of the sentence. Collerson expresses it well:

> A functional model of language treats language as a social phenomenon. It begins not with phonemes, words or sentences but with the social context, because this is the basis for the functions of language and their associated meanings. A functional grammar accounts for how these are realised in texts through the choice of grammatical structures and vocabulary. It also treats variation in language usage as an essential aspect of language and gives due recognition to the grammar of both spoken and written language. (1997: 25)

We can borrow terminology and useful concepts from functional grammar such as *field* (what is happening), *tenor* (who is taking part), and *mode* (the channel of communication). The field, tenor, and mode are features of the context of situation.
- **field:** the subject matter or field of a text relates to its content, who or what is involved. The field may be a shopping list, a recipe, a narrative, an explanation.
- **tenor:** the tenor of a situation determines the roles and relationships of the participants. Different language choices are made depending on factors such

as age, power, and status of the individuals involved. A person working in a Complaints Department is paid to be courteous to customers, and her language reflects this.

- **mode:**   spoken or written way of communicating.
- **cohesion:**   semantic relations in a text; **lexicogrammatical** relations.
- **text-type:**   general structure of the kind of text, e.g. correspondence, legal document, newspaper editorial.

In primary schools today we can use some of the terminology of traditional grammar and build on additional terminology and concepts such as those of functional grammar. Functional grammar can be seen as *enriching* traditional grammar, showing how to interpret the broad variety of discourses and registers used. It can throw light on how students use discourse in their speaking, reading, and writing.

It is not necessary to polarise the two grammars. Functional grammar can build on and enhance our understanding of traditional grammar. It extends the parameters of traditional grammar by allowing us to see how systematic language is in its structure, e.g. the hierarchical framework of sentences, clauses, phrases, words, and morphemes. As Halliday demonstrated through many examples, 'the key to a functional interpretation of grammatical structure is the principle that, in general, linguistic items are multifunctional' (1994: 30). He illustrates this in the clause *boys throw stones*, where *boys* is both 'actor' and 'subject'.

It is difficult to explain what functional grammar can offer without using its terminology that can more fully express the complexity of language. It is useful for understanding spoken language (notoriously difficult to analyse because it is so complex, since it is often spontaneous and interactional) and those 'texts' that are combinations of spoken and written, such as dramatic dialogue or written instructions. Both kinds of grammar can help to 'crack the code' of language. We can most usefully adopt a functional *approach* to language because it sees language fulfilling the needs of people for real purposes, emphasising the role of language in communicating meaning.

The functional approach in the classroom

Beverly Derewianka in *Exploring How Texts Work* (1991) demonstrates how the functional approach can be used in writing, analysing, and assessing texts:

> A functional model of language can be drawn upon during classroom activities based on a 'process' or a 'whole language' philosophy—wherever children are engaged in the construction of texts and opportunities are created for explicit discussion of these texts. Such opportunities might occur, for example, during the modelling of a text, or during a conferencing session. Sometimes these opportunities can be programmed, sometimes they may be spontaneous. They can occur at the whole class, small group, or individual level. (1991: 5)

Traditional and functional perspectives can be merged to some extent. Traditional terminology such as *verb* is used but an additional functional aspect is added to remind children of the different ways verbs are used, e.g. an action, saying, or thinking verb. In addition, where there are different types of nouns in traditional grammar (abstract, collective, common, and proper), further examples can be added to show how these words are actually used in texts, for example Derewianka (1998) refers to 'metaphorical nouns'.

New developments in language study

Even though the pendulum swings in recognising the importance of teaching grammar, teachers are wise to be receptive to the new insights that linguists provide into the nature of language. Developments in computer technology have opened up new areas of study of linguistic features, especially with the data collection of corpora consisting of wide expanses of written and spoken text that the computer can analyse with relative ease. To construct a corpus, language data are collected from a vast range of texts so that the corpus collection can be considered as a sample of how language is actually spoken and written. Whole sections of text may be included from newspapers, radio broadcasts, magazine articles, and conversations, and also from unpublished language such as informal letters, postcard, diaries, and printed forms. The analysis of these discourses and the compilation of dictionaries have benefited enormously from the application of computer techniques. Multi-model texts are increasingly common.

Grammar-checking facilities on the computer are becoming increasingly sophisticated, allowing checks for run-on sentences, subject–verb disagreements, redundancies, jargon, awkward phrases, and double negatives, as well as flagging style and readability considerations.

Teachers need to be Janus-faced in the sense that they can look backwards and borrow useful ideas from the past and yet look to the future to see what new ideas and concepts can make their teaching and learning more effective.

Implications for teaching grammar

The teaching of grammar should be linked with the reading and writing of real texts. In this way the features of the language, its structure, and its arrangement of words, can be taught in context. For example, verb tense can be taught with the help of tense forms that occur in narratives read by or to children, for example:

> *As he walked home, a priest suddenly appeared from nowhere.* (Junko Morimoto, **The Two Bullies**, 1997)

As children write their own narratives, correct grammatical structure is further reinforced and seen to be necessary for communication. In the primary school, experience with language use should be emphasised, rather than formal instruction in terminology. Instruction and practice can be given in

- manipulating sentence patterns
- practising different structures
- writing different text-types
- showing the differences between spoken and written English.

Most students come to school with a tacit knowledge of English and its language structure. They may not know grammatical terminology but this does not mean they cannot communicate in speech and writing.

 ## Activities

1. Syntax

Change the intonation and stress in sentences to give students an idea of how word order changes meaning:

What is she doing?
What *is she doing?*
*What **is** she doing?*
*What is **she** doing?*
*What is she **doing**?*

Encourage students to act out the different sentences.

2. Finding out about verbs

1. Read students a short poem, 'Me-Moving', by Gordon Winch:

I dart and dash,
I jig and jump,
I scamper, skate
and scramble.
I strut and stride
I slip and slide,
And frequently, I amble.

I leap and lurch,
I crawl and creep,
I rove and romp
and ramble.
I turn and trip,
I skid and skip,
And now and then—
I gambol!
(Winch 1989)

2. Ask the class what the person in the poem does. Note the concept of action words, i.e. verbs.

3. Discuss the meanings of the words and perform some of the actions.
4. Emphasise the fact that the chosen words are about actions (what the person does). They are all 'doing' action words, or, in grammatical terms, they are 'verbs'.
5. Find out about the various kinds of verbs and see how they are used in different texts.

Auxiliary and compound verbs

Auxiliary verbs help to form different tenses, e.g. be, do, have, shall/will

We will come to your party.

These are compound verbs or verb phrases:

We are coming to your party.

Transitive and intransitive verbs

Transitive verbs have an object:

The young girl opened her book.

Here the transitive verb is *opened* and the object is *book*. In intransitive verbs the meaning of the verb doesn't carry across to an object:

The young girl is singing.

Regular and irregular verbs

Regular verbs form their tenses in a conventional way, unlike irregular verbs, which do not follow the same rule. Historically, the difference comes from two different ways of forming the past tense and past participle: by adding -ed ('weak' verbs) or by changing the vowel ('strong' verbs). There are a few other especially irregular verbs like *be* and *go*, whose parts have a particular history.

	Singular	*Plural*	*Past participle*
Present	I smile	We smile	smiled
	You smile	You smile	
	He, she, it smiles	They smile	*Present participle*
Past	I smiled	We smiled	smiling
	You smiled	You smiled	
	He, she, it smiled	They smiled	
Future	I will smile	We will smile	
	You will smile	You will smile	
	He, she, it will smiles	They will smile	

There are several hundred irregular verbs. Here are a few examples:

Infinitive	Past tense	Past participle
be	was	been
choose	chose	(has/have, was/were) chosen
give	gave	given
go	went	gone
lie	lay	lain
run	ran	run
see	saw	seen
shrink	shrank	shrunk
sink	sank	sunk
speak	spoke	spoken
sting	stung	stung
stink	stank	stunk
take	took	taken
write	wrote	written

Participles, as the word suggests, are not complete verbs but just parts of them; they need another verb, *have* or *be*, to complete them. Participles are confusing enough to adults so will need careful explaining and demonstrating to children. You could tell them that the reason 'I seen him' is not acceptable (in standard English) is because 'seen' is a past participle so needs 'have' to complete it, whereas 'I saw him' is acceptable because 'saw' is a complete verb (past tense; see the list above). The theory is that a complete sentence needs a complete (or finite) verb.

3. Fun with adjectives

While individual exercises can consolidate understanding, try to use activities within an authentic context. They may be used to spark interest in a language issue (how to make your writing more interesting to a reader), or used later to reinforce a student's knowledge.

Simply, adjectives are used to describe nouns. They can go before the noun or after it:

a beautiful view
The view was beautiful.

Make adjectives from nouns—try out different sentences to see which is most effective in the context of a piece of writing:

the beauty of the scenery
the beautiful scenery

Extend meaning with adjectives:

a surfer
a skilful surfer
a skilful, strong surfer

Practise using different kinds of adjectives, which modify or limit a noun, in sentences:

> *one, two* (note that numbers are adjectives)
> *some, few, many*
> *this, that, those*
> *my, our, his, her, their*

Check understanding of the **comparative** (*er*) and **superlative** (*est*) forms of adjectives:

> *tiny, tinier, tiniest*
> *large, larger, largest*

Remember exceptions such as *good, better, best,* or *bad, worse, worst.*

Make writing more arresting by using more descriptive and/or specific words. Find synonyms for:

> *little, big, good*

Play with prefixes and suffixes to make additional adjectives and use them in sentences as part of a larger text:

> *kind, unkind*
> *dazzle, dazzling*

Use the student's own writing to indicate how adding or changing adjectives can help to make a text more evocative and informative.

4. In small groups, discuss what you would tell parents about the place of punctuation and grammar in your classroom. Suggest ways that parents might be able to help the students at home with language skills.

5. Discuss appropriate strategies or games for teaching aspects of spelling and grammar to students from language backgrounds other than English.

6. Explore ways of using different text-types to focus on grammatical concepts. For example, choose an Information Report and identify or highlight the following linguistic features:
    · use of general nouns
    · use of the timeless present tense ('Platypuses have webbed feet and duckbills')
    · use of technical terms
    · topic sentences and paragraphs to organise material.

7. Plan a series of lessons to give students practice in writing an *instructional* text. Discuss in what areas of life instructional texts are mostly needed. Why is clarity and accuracy so important? What can happen if the instructions are not clear or jumbled in some way? Clarify aspects of the text-type before you begin, such as the imperative mood with verbs; the precise language needed; the omission of articles; and so on. Provide different models of

authentic texts, e.g. how to cook using a simple recipe. Encourage creativity in texts.

SUMMARY

1. Punctuation is important because it adds significant meaning to writing.
2. Students need to know common graphic symbols used in everyday communication.
3. Punctuation is best taught through children's own writings and reading.
4. Children should be familiar with the following features of punctuation: capital letters, full stop, semicolon, colon, hyphen, dash, brackets, exclamation mark, question mark, quotation marks, apostrophe, italics, and indentation in paragraphs.
5. Grammar refers to the features of language (sounds, words, formation and arrangement of words) that determine how we use language.
6. A knowledge of grammar allows students to make judgments about appropriate usage of English; improves literacy skills; enriches understanding of literature; assists in learning foreign languages; and provides a metalanguage that allows students to talk about their reading and writing
7. A study of grammar involves various elements: phonology, semantics, morphology, and syntax.
8. Both traditional and functional grammar can offer insights into the structure of language. The basic parts of speech in traditional English grammar are noun, pronoun, adjective, verb, adverb, preposition, conjunction, and interjection. Functional grammar has important insights to offer into aspects such as cohesion, field, tenor, mode, and extended discourse.
9. Different grammatical features can be emphasised at different stages of students' understanding and development.
10. Activities for teaching grammar should be meaningful and designed to improve students' overall communicative ability.

Chapter 15
Assessment of Writing

Focus

There are many ways to assess writing, ranging from classroom assessment practices to national testing. This chapter focuses on the advantages of a language portfolio assessment, giving some practical advice on the planning and design of language portfolios within the context of assessing writing in the classroom.

Assessment practices are part of the teaching and learning cycle, allowing us to gauge the relative success of both student and teacher. Good assessment tells us what the abilities of the student are and his or her relative strengths and weaknesses. Armed with this information (gathered from data and observation), the teacher and student can address individual need.

Assessment is a general term to describe any activities used to judge a student's performance. It involves data collection, analysis, and the recording of information about a student's progress. A student's achievement is often measured against specific outcomes and indicators. Assessment can be **formative** (monitoring a student's progress), **summative** (gauging how learning objectives have been met), or **diagnostic** (examining specific areas of student need).

Evaluation is an appraisal process undertaken by a teacher that is designed to make judgments about the effectiveness and appropriateness of teaching practices and programs, and to identify any improvements needed. The teacher then implements ongoing practices and programming in order to help students realise their potential. Evaluation helps teachers judge the effectiveness of their teaching programs.

Validity and reliability are important and complementary aspects of assessment that determine how appropriate, meaningful, and useful are different assessment practices.

Validity refers to the degree to which accumulated evidence supports the inferences (or decisions) made from looking at the results. It involves the content of what is assessed, the ways in which students are assessed, and how they actually perform.

Reliability (necessary for validity) concerns how much the results of assessment involve errors of measurement or extraneous factors that affect the assessment practices. If a 'test' was repeated under similar conditions, would the results be the same?

National benchmarks in literacy

Attempts have been made at a national level in Australia to try to monitor and raise the literacy standards of children. At a meeting in March 1997, the Ministerial Council on Education, Employment, Training and Youth Affairs agreed on the goal 'that every child leaving primary school should be numerate, and be able to read, write and spell at an appropriate level' (Masters and Forster 1997b: 54). The measurement of student progress was considered as an essential element of a national plan, which set benchmarks in the form of prescribed minimum standards of student achievement at particular year levels. These benchmarks are being used for state and territory accountability and in the development of strategies for improving literacy and numeracy.

Assessment of writing

Generally the teacher wants to assess
- how a student handles different kinds of writing tasks
- familiarity with the content and structure of different genres or text-types
- a sense of the intended audience for writing
- ability to convey content and meaning through writing
- control over punctuation, spelling, and grammar
- the breadth of vocabulary used
- attitudes to writing
- a student's self-perception as a writer.

A knowledge of Bloom's *Taxonomy of Educational Objectives* (1956) can help teachers understand the complexity of the learning process and can encourage assessment of different degrees of difficulty, from 'simple' knowledge to more complex judgments. When applied to the writing process, teachers can assess different kinds of skills, not simply errors in syntax, vocabulary, and spelling but the general sense and coherence of what a student has written:
- knowledge (ability to remember or recall ideas, material)
- comprehension (ability to know, interpret, and use what is communicated)
- application (ability to use information in new situations)
- analysis (ability to break down information into its constituent parts; recognition of structure)
- synthesis (ability to put parts or elements together to form a whole)
- evaluation (ability to judge the value of ideas, to make judgments or to apply criteria).

Data collection

Data collection for assessment purposes may be gathered through informal observation of the student or through written or oral tests of ability. It is usually collected in a systematic way with the help of checklists, benchmarks, or some other indication that can form the basis of comparison. A student's progress can be compared with individual achievement over a period of time. Progress in writing can also be compared with other class members or with larger population groups (as with the Basic Skills Tests). Analysis of the data collected will allow teachers to set up various teaching strategies to help students. The results obtained will also point towards other needs, for example new resources that should be acquired, specialised staff development programs, or revision of the school's language programs. It is always a good idea to ask what the assessment is for. How can it be analysed to help the individual student and teacher?

Informal and formal assessment

The key to good assessment practices is perceptive observation by the teacher, by the parents, and by the students themselves. We need to be clear about why we need a particular assessment, what aspects are to be assessed, how the assessment is to be done, and for what purposes it will be used. Assessment that is integrated into the regular program of classroom work will feed back into the teaching and learning cycle.

The way information is recorded often reflects the purpose of the assessment. Anecdotal comments may be recorded in an A–Z book of children's names so that the teacher can remember information that would otherwise prove elusive. Other informal observation of children may be made on 'post it' notices as the teacher moves around the classroom. More formal recording is usually made through checklists that indicate what students can do, what they need to improve, and what they believe they cannot do. These can often be designed with the students and used as individual assessment grids.

Increasing recognition should be given to how the results of the assessment practices are conveyed. Are the results to be in language that the child can easily understand or should they be addressed to an adult audience, or both? For example, the Basic Skills test gives an individual student report that shows achievement over six bands in tabular form, listing the percentage of students across the state achieving in each skill band. Skills in reading, language, number, measurement, and space are itemised, indicating the skills tested in each band. These results are primarily intended for the use of teachers and parents.

It is sensible to include specific information about how to interpret the results of assessment, whether you are communicating with parents or students. For example, the Australian Schools English Competition (given to Year 6 students) outlines the types of questions and the individual's percentage mark gained compared with the state average for the student's year. Being placed in the 80th percentile from your school is quite different from being placed in the 60th percentile of students from the state and can cause confusion and upset unless it is clearly explained.

Australian Schools English Competition		
	Your mark	State average for your year
Vocabulary (13 questions)		
Language (14 questions)		
Punctuation		
Standard usage		
Everyday documents, diagrams,		
data (17 questions)		
Reading comprehension (16 questions)		
detail		
judgment (low-level)		
judgment (high-level)		

Basic Skills Tests

Basic Skills Tests are taken by students in Years 3 and 5 in New South Wales and South Australia. They test aspects of literacy and numeracy and provide information about where the student 'fits' on a skills band between 1 and 4, with Band 4 being in the higher range.

In the Year 3 test the student has to demonstrate ability in reading and language skills by

* reading a magazine and showing understanding of stories, tables, instructions, reports, and other kinds of writing
* identifying correct spelling, punctuation, and grammar.

Figure 15.1 shows the skills listed for the different skills bands.

Skills typical of students in each skill band

STUDENTS IN EACH SKILL BAND GENERALLY SHOWED THE SKILLS LISTED FOR THAT BAND AND THE LOWER BANDS.

	Reading	Language	Number	Measurement	Space
6	• Locate detailed numerical information from a complex description. • Connect information provided in separate parts of a text. • Identify the speaker of dialogue when it is not directly stated.	• Recognise the incorrect use of it's. • Recognise the correct spelling of 'surrounding' not 'surounding'. • Recognise the incorrect spelling 'enemie' for 'enemy'.	• Round off a decimal number to the nearest whole number (27.7 to 28). • Halve a four digit number selected from a table and identify values less than this. • Work out the number of five dollar notes needed to make up a given amount of money ($5 notes in $93).	• Use a scale drawing to work out the area of a shape in square kilometres. • Convert tonnes to kilograms (4.3 tonnes equals 4300kg). • Understand the concept: 'second half of this century' and find dates given in a table to solve a problem.	• Understand the concept of symmetry and identify the shape that has all lines of symmetry drawn. • Understand the mathematical term "net" and identify the nets of a cube.
5	• Sort relevant information about a process. • Infer meaning using clues given by the structure of a sentence. • Understand the format of chapters and headings and identify the title of a chapter.	• Recognise the correct use of 'quite', not 'quiet'. • Recognise the conjunction 'and' as correct, not 'but'. • Identify the incorrect use of the article 'the'. • Recognise the correct spelling of 'fields' not 'feilds'.	• Use information on a map and identify the lowest decimal number to one decimal place. • Add four amounts of money (45¢ + 50¢ + $1.20 + $1.05). • Extract information from a table and subtract two four-digit numbers involving decomposition/trading (1993 - 1977).	• Estimate the area of an irregular shape using the grid supplied. • Work out the perimeter of a shape shown on a scale drawing.	• Interpret information in a graph and match with a correct statement (8 out of 24 equals one third). • Use knowledge of compass directions to describe a path taken.
4	• Interpret a table to sequence information. • Make an inference from an explanation. • Identify the meaning of figurative language in a poem.	• Recognise that a country is a proper noun and must begin with a capital letter. • Choose the correct form of a verb to be consistent in tense and number. • Select the past tense 'took' to keep the tense consistent. • Choose the personal pronoun 'their', not 'there' or 'they're'.	• Extract information from a table and add two and three-digit numbers (170 + 70). • Use subtraction or a similar strategy to work out a problem involving two-digit numbers (36 - 17 =).	• Use information given in a table and convert metres to centimetres (1.5m to 150cm). • Know that a day is 24 hours and convert 12 hours to a fraction of a day (half). • Know how many days are in April and May and add them (30 + 31).	• Identify the cross section made by cutting into a solid shape. • Identify 2D parts needed to make a 3D shape (square pyramid). • Recognise a flip as a reflection of a shape over a line.
3	• Locate and compare specific information which is organised under sub-headings. • Use a labelled diagram to identify a specific feature. • Identify a text as a recipe. • Combine and relate technical information.	• Identify the subject of a sentence. • Select the preposition 'of' in a phrase that indicates possession – of Sydney Town. • Recognise that a verb must agree with its subject.	• Interpret a place value chart and write a number containing hundreds, tens and ones (369). • Use number facts to complete a number sentence involving multiplication (6 × ? = 72). • Recognise that division is the operation needed to solve a problem.	• Understand the relative term 'lightest', use a table and compare mass of three objects to find the lightest.	• Recognise a right angle. • Recognise a set of parallel lines. • Visualise and work out the number of blocks needed to fill a partially filled box. • Use information shown on a table to complete a column graph.
2	• Locate the time of an activity shown in a timetable. • Use a table to identify specific information. • Identify the actions of characters in a story. • Find specific information from the first section in a descriptive text.	• Recognise the correct use of the apostrophe in the negative verb 'wasn't'. • Identify the incorrect use of a preposition. • Select an adverb of degree. • Recognise the need for a capital letter to begin a sentence.	• Identify three single-digit numbers to equal 18 (4+5+9).	• Understand the concept of balancing objects of the same mass. • Understand that the level of water in a container rises when an object is dropped into the container. • Compare thermometers without a scale and identify change in temperature over time.	• Use a scale to compare frequencies in a column graph. • Use coordinates to show position on a grid.
1	• Identify specific detail in a text.	• Choose the correct spelling of the word 'special', not 'speshal' or 'specal'. • Select the correct conjunction to indicate time. • Recognise when to use 'for', not 'four' or 'fore'.		• Understand volume and select the container showing about half a litre.	

Fig. 15.1   Skills typical of students in each skill band

Writing assessment in the classroom

I WeT Tu
The limPies
aNb I: Sor
horses
              Tillie

Tillie, 5

Lambs jumped around friskily
tormenting their mothers for
nourishment. Cows lay lazily chewing
their cud among the buttercups.
A little foal galloped alongside
her mother on its spindly legs.
In another field a ploughman plodded along
behind his horses furrowing the field.
Butterflies fluttered from flower to flower ...
John, 12

These are two very different pieces of writing. It would be meaningless to assign one a mark of 1/10 and the other 9/10. What we can say with confidence is that the writers are at different stages in the writing process—on the one hand we have a beginner writer struggling to put meanings together with letters from the alphabet, while on the other hand we have a writer experimenting with literary devices such as alliteration and imagery—each finding the task challenging yet rewarding, each needing feedback and encouragement. Rather than saying X in the class is a better writer than Y, we should be saying that X is at a different stage along the writing continuum from Y. Teachers look for different *outcomes* that match different stages of ability in the student. Here are some sample outcomes of what a beginning writer might achieve:

Outcomes for Stage 1 in the NSW
English K–6 Syllabus 1998 include:

· Plans, reviews, and produces a small range of simple literary and factual texts for a variety of purposes on familiar topics for known readers.
· Produces texts using the basic grammatical features and punctuation conventions of the text-type.
· Uses knowledge of sight words and letter-sound correspondences and a variety of strategies to spell familiar words
· Produces texts using letters of consistent size and slope in NSW Foundation Style and using computer technology.

Board of Studies NSW 1998b: 106

Models of writing and assessment

Students learn about the conventions of writing from the models they see and practise. As they learn the structures and language features of a variety of text-types, assessment is made of how well they have mastered the conventions and, increasingly, how they modify the basic outlines to suit their own purposes and audiences. For example, the model for the Explanation text-type might be on the facts associated with 'What makes a kettle boil?' with accompanying demonstrations or illustrations. This might be written down quite simply with a heading (which might be a question) and a sequence of points or sentences about the phenomenon. The following language features are highlighted: the use of general nouns, action verbs, descriptive adjectives, use of time conjunctions, e.g.

What makes a kettle boil?

- water makes lots of bubbles when it boils
- the bubbles contain gassy water
- the water turns into a gas
- heating up the water makes it boil
- water can boil away into gas if it keeps boiling
- water boils when it reaches a high temperature.

Assessment of the writing may focus on the accuracy of the observations and the way the student has control of the relevant language features.

Language portfolios

Teachers who want to enhance their students' learning and understanding find inspiration in varied assessment practices. A systematic record of observations and judgments about a student's work collected in a 'portfolio' has many uses for the student, the teacher, and the parent. Portfolios are popular in the school context since they are a multidimensional form of assessment.

Definition of portfolio assessment

'A systematic collection of student work that is analysed to show progress over a period of time with regard to specific instructional goals.'

Language portfolios can include writing tasks, responses to reading, projects, and classroom assignments, as well as individual comments by the teacher and student. The rationale for using them lies in the educational advantages of closely linking classroom activities with assessment, involving the student more meaningfully in the learning process. 'One of the defining features of portfolio assessment is the involvement of students in selecting samples of their own work to show growth or learning over time' (O'Malley and Valdez Pierce 1996: 5).

Collections that chart performance and achievement in the language skills of speaking, reading, writing, and listening are particularly useful for the ESL student.

Advantages of portfolios

- variety in assessment procedures
- student involvement and responsibility
- suitability for the ESL student
- assessment factors
- accountability
- linking of assessment and classroom instruction or activities
- concrete evidence of students' achievement

Variety in assessment procedures

Portfolio assessment is a useful addition to a teacher's array of assessment strategies, complementing other kinds of assessment. A recently commissioned survey of upper primary classroom teachers by the Schools Council, National Board of Employment, Education and Training found that:

> Respondents reported learning attainments in a variety of ways including discussions with parents, informal feedback, written report against key criteria, profiles/portfolios and interviews with the students. Taken together with the responses to other questions in the survey, it was apparent that teachers wished to use a variety of methods to report on learning attainment—choosing the method which best suited the situation and would facilitate the growth and development of the individual student. (1995: 52)

Student involvement and responsibility

Portfolios can engage students in monitoring their own learning and can encourage them to be reflective about the learning process. A collection of evaluated work identifies strengths and weaknesses, helping students to realise their learning potential. A portfolio collection where students have worked collaboratively with teachers on setting criteria allows students to analyse their own development more easily and improve skills. Teachers and students can decide on the required and optional contents for a portfolio.

The ESL student

A particular advantage for ESL students is that the portfolio collection can gauge their ability more effectively than standardised tests, which are often measures of general knowledge and may be affected by cultural bias. The multidimensional nature of the portfolio allows a student's progress to be judged in a variety of ways and reveals improvement (or otherwise) made over a period of time.

Most assessment practices used in schools demand a high language involvement and an emphasis on written responses, so the ESL student is often at a disadvantage. By using the portfolio, students can be encouraged to respond in a variety of ways, for example ESL students can be encouraged to retell a text in their first language.

The *ESL Scales* (Curriculum Corporation 1994) provide profiles for reporting linguistic development that do not put the student from a non-English-speaking background at a disadvantage. The ACER (Australian Council for Educational Research) has validated the achievement levels within the language strands of reading, writing, listening, and speaking.

Assessment factors

Portfolios can provide concrete evidence of students' achievement and progress as they move from class to class or from one school to another. This is becoming increasingly important as population shifts occur for economic and social reasons. The assessment portfolio has a high degree of validity because it is a cumulative record of a student's progress. Multiple forms of assessment are commonly more reliable than isolated testing procedures.

Standardised tests such as the NSW Basic Skills Testing Program (primary school level) measure individual performance, but machine-scored tests have severe limitations. Most language tasks, especially in the area of creative writing, critical thinking, and problem-solving, cannot be adequately assessed by multiple-choice questions. As Masters points out, 'If we allow concerns for objectivity, reliability, and ease of processing to dominate assessment practices (as we often have), then we run the risk of sending distorted messages about the kinds of learning that we wish to encourage' (1991: 11). Objectivity and reliability are still crucial concerns of portfolio assessment.

Accountability

Reporting on student progress by reference to specific learning outcomes is increasingly necessary. If planned with systematic entries and evaluations, portfolios can provide accountability to the student, parent, teacher, and wider members of the community at various stages of the school year, or, indeed, over a period of years. 'Parents are likely to be most interested in knowing how students are performing in relation to teachers' expectations and in comparison with other students of the same age or grade' (Schools Council 1995: 54). Portfolios can provide an important record of students' learning and allow teachers and parents to discuss language ability in a more focused way since samples of work can be discussed. Involving other adults in children's learning can be a positive experience, especially when parents offer encouragement and assistance. When needed, items in the portfolio can be selected to show a tangible record of the work of a class, to help in professional development activities or to demonstrate the work of the school to the community.

Linking of assessment and classroom instruction or activities

By linking assessment with instruction, 'student performance is evaluated in relation to instructional goals, objectives, and classroom activities' (O'Malley and Valdez Pierce 1996: 35). The portfolio gives feedback to the teacher, who can then respond flexibly to the needs of different students. Teachers can identify a student's abilities and difficulties much more easily if systematic records are kept that incorporate the student's own view of learning development. Analysis of portfolios allows the teacher to see whether instructional objectives have been met and whether the teaching has been successful in assessing student performance relative to curricular objectives.

Planning and design of portfolios

Teachers can modify various kinds of portfolios for their own purposes:

- Working Portfolio: collection of day-to-day work;
- Documentary Portfolio: collection of work for assessment which documents the processes used to develop items;
- Show Portfolio: where a student's 'best' work is selected. (Masters and Forster 1996: 21)

Assessment in writing may be a section within a larger Language Assessment Portfolio. This is a combination of a student's perceived 'best' work as well as a record of progress that shows the *process* by which a student has worked towards a goal (e.g. through the inclusion of notes, rough drafts, and 'final' version of a text). Each item included is evaluated on criteria collaboratively identified by the student and the teacher. For example, a story-retelling activity might nominate performance tasks such as

- names main characters
- understands characters' motivations
- recalls plot sequence
- considers genre features
- evaluates major issues.

A writing checklist based on specific criteria is an excellent way of involving students and of providing a record of learning development. It is important to assess progress as part of the regular classroom activities so that instruction and assessment are closely interwoven. The design of the portfolio can be tailored to suit the needs of particular student groups or individual students, for example by providing an illustration or diagram that clarifies an item, and by ensuring that the instructions are clearly written and unambiguous. Evaluation items can be changed, when appropriate, to allow students to respond in their first language.

Organisation

Planning is necessary to forestall problems and to make sense of a portfolio collection. Clear instructions and guidelines are necessary so that students, teachers, and parents are aware of their roles and responsibilities. The following practical questions (and some possible solutions to them) should be considered by teachers before embarking on portfolio assessment:

1. Why do we need a 'portfolio' collection?
2. When do we find the time to make the evaluative comments?
3. How can we ensure that work is done by the individual?
4. Who 'owns' the portfolio?
5. Where is the portfolio to be stored?
6. What happens if students lose specific items or, indeed, the whole portfolio?

Similar difficulties arise in other contexts, and often there are systematic procedures and safeguards already in place to handle them. If the idea of an assessment portfolio is new to students, parents, or colleagues, you will need to convince them with educationally valid reasons that it is a worthwhile activity. Parents can be contacted by letter to inform them of the purpose of the portfolio, how the assessment criteria are designed to help the student, and ways in which they can contribute to the individual student's efforts.

A portfolio is a collaborative effort between the teacher and the student with a major role for the learner in deciding what will be included in the collection and how it will be evaluated. This kind of assessment is easier to implement and manage in learner-centred classrooms where the student is able to make some decisions about what is to be included in a portfolio and how the evidence of work will be assessed. Sufficient time must be allocated to plan, design, and respond to portfolio entries. Time can be saved by linking classroom-based activities and key learning areas of the curriculum to the assessment. Portfolios will appear burdensome and time-consuming if they are not seen as a regular part of classroom instruction.

Decisions must be made on how regularly the sample items are assessed and the results conveyed to students and parents. Convenient times for a formal reporting of results might be at the end of each school term, mid-year, and end of year. While students may keep their pieces of writing in a folder with accompanying editing checklists or comments by readers, the teacher may also keep additional records of observations about the student's writing behaviours and abilities.

Key features of a language portfolio

- samples of a student's work
- the evaluative criteria of the work done
- the opportunity for student self-assessment

Samples of a student's work

Decisions must be made about the appropriate number of entries to be collected in a portfolio. For example, there could be

- writing samples from classroom activities
- student choice of writing from different genres
- brief evaluation of books read
- oral interviews
- story or text retelling
- projects or exhibitions
- response to open-ended questions
- language activities from a range of curricular areas
- cloze exercises
- poetry

O'Malley and Valdez Pierce (1996: 129) suggest the following required and optional contents for a reading or writing portfolio:

Required	Optional
1. oral summary	1. list of books or stories read in class
2. story summary (writing or drawing)	2. list of books or stories read independently
3. writing sample (teacher choice)	3. reading list inventory
4. student choice of writing (any type)	4. literacy development checklist
5. student self-evaluation	5. content-sample (i.e. reading comprehension sample, project, report)
	6. student choice (any type)

Here is a sample of a diary entry from a language portfolio:

Dear Diary,

Yesterday Jacob and I went into Melbourne. Our parents dropped us off with our Aunty while they went and did Family History matters.

It was fun, we walked down the street a little and went into Time Zone and had our picture put on a sticker. We then went to a two dollar shop and had a look. We walked all the way to the end of the street and crossed the road and saw Flinders Street Station. We walked across a bridge and went past the Art Gallery and went down to the banks of the Yarra River. We walked a while down the river and got an ice cream and went back up to see some gymnasts out the front of the Art Gallery doing an act. We then caught a tram to St Kilda Beach and had KFC for lunch. I then rang my parents and we headed for Luna Park. We then met my parents at the front of Luna Park and left for my Uncle's house in the mountains and had a rest.

Daniel, Year 6

While the contents will vary according to the purposes of the portfolio (whether it is designed to showcase 'best' work or be a 'working' portfolio that reveals the process of mastering skills), it will still stand as an individual record of a student's progress towards learning goals. The cumulative entries allow comparisons that are often lost in other kinds of one-off assessment. Students can clearly see how their initial attempts at the beginning of a year improve over time and thus gain some insight into their learning styles. Cover sheets and summaries of portfolio items can give a quick indication of contents.

The charting of a student's progress is ongoing:

> There is no limit to the number of examples ('pointers') that could be assembled to enrich the description of a progress map, and there is no limit to the number of samples of student work that could be collected and used to better illustrate the nature of progress in an area of learning. (Masters and Forster 1996: 13)

There are various types of authentic assessment that teachers can incorporate into a portfolio of work, combined with observations of a student's learning development. Entries can be samples of students' writings in different genres that can be evaluated on criteria such as particular content or language features, with a rating scale that has been devised collaboratively.

Teaching programs that integrate the language skills of speaking, listening, reading, and writing provide authentic language tasks. Problem-solving activities can relate to meaningful, real-life situations. For example, a unit of work on anti-racism may include a debate about multiculturalism in the media, listening to different points of view, reading the speeches of politicians, and writing about their own views. The teacher (and students) can devise activities (e.g. a letter to a newspaper) that might be suitable for the assessment portfolio. The letter can be completed as a group exercise so that students can discuss the messages they want to convey.

Evaluative criteria in portfolios need to be clearly stated and entries should be regularly assessed to ensure that students are realising their learning potential. Formulation of useful criteria for assessment is essential, otherwise the material simply remains a collection. Teachers (and students) can identify particular aspects that need attention and that can be addressed in mini-lessons where input is given to the class as a whole or to small groups.

Writing comments are time-consuming, but the teacher can still make useful observations, perhaps on 'post it' notes that are filled in as he walks around the classroom and that can later be transferred to a student's portfolio. Writing descriptive comments does take longer than assigning a numerical mark. Be aware that subjectivity, prejudices, and gender stereotypes can affect judgment about student assessment and progress. Much of the observation of students can be done by means of checklists while students are actually engaged in the classroom activities.

Models of work at different levels of achievement are highly recommended so that students can see what is expected from them. Brainstorming ideas and providing contextual support for meaning will help all students to complete tasks satisfactorily. Students can become involved in constructing criteria based on their criticism of the 'benchmark' works. This can be done through group work and by the teacher eliciting appropriate criteria through a classroom discussion.

Progress maps

Portfolios can incorporate progress maps, which give a graphic display of a student's progress. The progress map (or developmental continuum) can give a broad perspective on a student's development from year to year over a long period, and show relative achievement of students of the same age or grade level. Progress maps provide a framework for monitoring student growth in an area of learning. Because this growth is monitored against a described continuum, a student's estimated locations on a progress map can be interpreted and reported descriptively in terms of the skills, knowledge, and understandings typically demonstrated by students at those locations (Masters and Forster 1996: 6).

Forms and checklists

Writing strategies checklist

Student   *Date*

Writing approaches   *Comments*

      Works through edited drafts to finished product
      Uses mechanics of writing to aid meaning

Ability to write in different genres

- accuracy of content
- attention to logical organisation
- recognition of audience's needs
- uses correct grammar
- spells accurately
- uses resources to improve work, e.g. dictionary
- self-edits or asks peer

Student self-assessment

Self-assessment is an essential feature of the portfolio (Tierney et al. 1991). The following might be included to help students learn standards for good writing:
- checklist of strategies used for reading a particular text
- self-assessment checklist of learning goals.

Portfolios encourage students to see learning as a process and to become more directly involved in their own learning. For example, a student might select a piece of work for the portfolio because it showed an improvement on an earlier piece, indicating a learning growth. Students will be more actively engaged in self and peer assessment if the teacher encourages these activities within the classroom. Some students may not have come from a school background that is learner-centred where they are encouraged in self-assessment.

The portfolio can help students in setting their own educational goals and developing new interests. Students can become involved in observing how standards work: whether an entry meets a standard in an exemplary fashion or whether there is much room for improvement. Once the portfolio has sufficient entries and the student has assessed the work according to the agreed criteria, there is a record of what the student can actually do and a judgment of relative strengths and weaknesses.

If students are given the opportunity to assess models of work in a non-threatening environment they learn to judge relative strengths and weaknesses and are more ready to apply the criteria to their own work. Benchmark models can be collected from previous years to show to new classes. Clemmons and associates (1993) suggest having a partner who can review an item and judge whether it meets criteria and how a particular piece can be improved. Students need practice in setting realistic goals and in judging what their partner did well or could improve.

Here is a sample of a checklist for self or peer-assessment that could be modified for assessing particular features of writing in relation to different genres:

Writing Assessment

Name   *Date*

Title of text

Genre

Writing Strategies

Purpose and organisation   *Yes*   *No*

1. I stated my purpose clearly with a main idea
2. I organised my thoughts in a logical way
3. I did some research or background reading
4. My work has a beginning, middle, and end
5. I tried to make my writing interesting to the reader

Use of words or sentences

6. I chose words that helped make my point
7. I wrote complete sentences
8. I used correct grammar with subject–verb agreement
9. I used verb tense correctly

Mechanics or format

10. I spelt words correctly, using a dictionary when necessary
11. I used punctuation correctly
12. I word-processed the text and/or wrote legibly

Editing

13. I edited my text with a checklist and/or by reading it aloud
14. I gained feedback from others to help edit my work
15. I paid attention to specific features of the writing genre (different language features could be added here)

(Adapted from O'Malley and Valdez Pierce 1996: 157)

Portfolios can complement other kinds of assessments and need not necessarily supplant existing practices. Major advantages of the portfolio assessment are the involvement of students in setting goals for their own learning and the encouragement of reflection about the process of learning. The focus on individual student growth is readily seen in a portfolio collection rather than the pass/fail information provided by some tests. The collaborative planning and design of a portfolio encourages student self-evaluation, helps to monitor progress, and links classroom instruction more closely with assessment. The work of O'Malley and Valdez Pierce (1996) provides practical examples of strategies for expanding the range of assessment practices and gives useful checklists of evaluative criteria. As many classroom teachers have discovered, the portfolio can bring about significant changes in teaching, learning, and assessment practices.

A caveat: remember that portfolios are part of a balance of evaluation practices. To find out what students can do, use varied methods and multiple sources of information. Data drawn from a range of assessment practices will reflect more accurately an individual student's abilities.

SUMMARY

1 Assessment practices gauge student performance and progress. Validity and reliability are fundamental considerations in assessment.
2 Assessment of writing involves familiarity with the content and structure of different genres as well as control over language features.
3 Both informal and formal assessment are needed.
4 Portfolios contain samples of a student's work, evaluative criteria of the work done, and opportunity for student self-assessment.

5 Portfolios enhance student responsibility as independent learners by engaging them in monitoring their own learning through the selection of entries, the identification of criteria for assessment, and self and peer assessment.

6 Language portfolios provide variety in assessment procedures.

7 Portfolios have particular relevance for assessing the language abilities of students from diverse language backgrounds.

8 Assessment should be linked with classroom instruction or activities.

Tasks

Discussion

1. Discuss some of the principles of classroom assessment in relation to students' writing skills.
   - what is considered 'correct' English?
   - why should assessment be integral to classroom activities?
   - why should assessment strategies be varied and cover a wide range of features?
   - why is it important to assess aspects such as strategies, motivation, and effort as well as other skills of writing?

2. What are the benefits of a student's self and peer-assessment of the writing process? Can you think of any problems and how these might be addressed by the classroom teacher? Design a self-assessment sheet for a particular grade level and for a particular text-type.

3. Design an editing checklist suitable for senior students' (Year 6) writing.

Activities

1. Construct a cloze test with a class to show them how it is done. Explain different kinds of cloze exercises. Ask pairs of students to create their own, eliminating every seventh word. Exchange with other pairs and see if the appropriate words are selected. As a whole class, discuss why the choices were made.

Cloze exercise: non-fiction text
Suitability: Upper Primary

Dinosaur is the name of a kind of reptile that lived millions of years ago. The word 'dinosaur' comes from two Greek words meaning terrible lizard. Dinosaurs were not lizards. But the size of some dinosaurs was terrifying. The biggest ones were the largest animals ever to live on land. They weighed more than 10 times as much as a full-grown elephant. Only a few kinds of whales grow to be larger than these dinosaurs. (*World Book Encyclopedia*)

Exercise

Predict and insert words which make sense:

Dinosaur is the name of a ---- of reptile that lived millions of ---- ago. The word dinosaur comes from ---- Greek words meaning terrible lizard. Dinosaurs ---- not lizards. But the size of ---- dinosaurs was terrifying. The biggest ones ---- the largest animals ever to live -- land. They weighed more than 10 ---- as much as a full-grown elephant. ---- a few kinds of whales grow -- be larger than these dinosaurs.

2. Read the first poem by C. J. Dennis to the class and provide students with a copy. Brainstorm some of the criteria that make a good poem. Encourage students to write their own poem and, in a subsequent session, ask them to apply the same criteria to their own poem.

The Looking Glass

When I look in the looking-glass
I'm always sure to see—
No matter how I dodge about—
Me, looking out at me.

I often wonder as I look,
And those strange features spy,
If I, in there, think I'm as plain
As I, out there, think I.

C. J. Dennis

Example of student response:

The Looking Glass

When I look in the looking-glass,
I'm always sure to see,
A thermometer of all my thoughts,
Happy or angry.

The most infuriating thing,
Of all, I really think,
Your reflection, that stupid thing,
Will always think as you think.

by A.C.

Part III *Children's Literature*

Rosemary Ross Johnston

This part provides a critical study of the theory and application of children's literature in the primary classroom. It builds on Parts I and II by presenting creative ways of using children's literature to foster literate practices, in reading, writing, speaking, and listening. It strongly endorses children's literature as literature, and as part of an artistic continuum in which children should be encouraged to participate and share. It also argues that children need 'courteous' exposure to texts and ideas beyond their immediate capacities.

Tasks for tertiary students and practical activities for the classroom are interspersed throughout the text. Specific books have been used but only as exemplars; children's literature is a rich and diverse resource and teachers can adapt these tasks and books to suit their particular teaching situations.

Chapters 16, 17, and 18 introduce children's literature within a context of critical literacy and link the 'pure' study of children's literature with its application in the classroom. Chapter 19 discusses the impact of the new technologies and explores concepts of the 'new literacies'.

Chapters 20, 21, and 22 relate children's literature theory to pedagogical practice, using theory as conceptual base, creative idea, and teaching structure. The significance of intertextuality is discussed and related to the idea of 'prior knowledge' as an important factor in children's literacy learning. Children's literature is explored as a locus of literate practices involving listening, speaking, reading, and writing.

Chapter 23 provides a brief sociohistorical overview of folktales and fairytales and outlines their cultural influence. Chapter 24 discusses the special relationship between the words and pictures of picturebooks and notes the particular contribution these books can make even for older children. Chapters 25 and 26 consider the resources that children's literature provides in the multicultural classroom, as a forum for the discussion of social issues, and for exploring history and fantasy. Chapter 27 considers some responses to children's literature, linking literature with popular song.

The emphasis in Part III is that theory informs the practice of reflective teaching. There is more information in this part, as in the preceding ones, than a practising teacher may need. Much of this 'bonus' material is boxed for easy reference. However, teachers, perhaps more than any other profession, must model principles of lifelong learning. As educators, we need continuously to challenge and to be challenged into developing our own ideas about theory and practice.

An important premise of this is that literature is a mosaic of multiple literacies—reading, writing, speaking, listening. We need to be aware of the capacity of literature to contribute to all aspects of children's lives, to their knowledge of the world, to their play, and to their hopes and dreams.

Chapter 16
Language into Literature

Focus

This chapter looks at the power of language and considers literature as applied language. It considers the significance of literature in the development of 'knowing readers', 'knowing writers', 'knowing speakers', and 'knowing listeners'. It discusses the idea of cultural literacy.

'Children's literature is a creative art. It is of course conceived creatively but it is just as importantly received by an audience which is itself in a constant state of flux and re-creation.'

Language and being

Language articulates what it is *to be*. The ancient Hebrews represent one of many racial groups who believed that words produced reality.

The relationship between language and being is complex, and is addressed as much by philosophers as by linguists. This is reflected in folktales and fairytales in which the power of the name is of great significance; it is also reflected in the cultural customs of many countries.

Some ideas to contemplate and explore

· Ludwig Wittgenstein (1889–1951), Austrian philosopher: 'The boundaries of language are the boundaries of "life-world"'.
· Martin Heidegger (1889–1976), German philosopher: 'I am what I say'.
· Jean-Paul Sartre (1905–80), French author and philosopher: 'Language is a form of life'.
· Michel Foucault (1926–84), French philosopher: 'Language is a structure of power'.

· Noam Chomsky (1928–), US linguist: 'Language grows in the mind-brain of the child'.

Note the power of the name in, for example, some Aboriginal cultures: after a person dies, their name must not be mentioned because doing so may interfere with their journey to the next world.

Language creates. It is powerful and transforming, an infinity of arrangements, relationships, and networks of meaning. An observer at the launching of Apollo 17 in 1975 remarked how the wonder of that moment changed people's behaviour, made them act differently, made them more aware of each other. The wonder of language similarly transforms, opening up what one writer has called 'windows on other worlds' (Wallace 1988: 163), but more importantly, opening up *self* to a world of *others*, and others to a world of self.

Literature as applied language

Literature is applied language. It is language in action, working parts working, a model of what Gee (1997: 5) calls many 'language-ings'. It has enormous variety. It is a multisensory experience: we see, we hear, we touch the book and turn the pages, we say the words; we imagine, we enter in; our 'life-world' and the imaginative world of the text merge seamlessly if only for a moment. This does not imply that we allow ourselves to be mindlessly manipulated, or that we have to 'identify' with particular characters; we need to learn to resist such positioning and teach our students to do so. But a creative negotiation between ourselves and the words of the text takes place and, as we read, some form of a merged world is uniquely ours. Literature is a kind of virtual reality.

The place of literature in the classroom

Children's literature is the practice of all aspects of literacy. It relates not only to reading and writing, but also, just as significantly, to speaking and listening. Literature is *literacy given form*:

> Literacy involves the integration of speaking, listening and critical thinking with reading and writing. Effective literacy is intrinsically purposeful, flexible and dynamic and continues to develop throughout the individual's lifetime. (*Australian Language and Literacy Policy* 1991: 9).

The place of literature in our classrooms (primary, secondary, tertiary) needs to be confirmed, affirmed, and redefined, not only for what it reveals about language and how it develops literacy but also for what it reveals about self and about others. Noam Chomsky claims that it is likely that literature will always give a far deeper insight into 'the full human person' than any model of scientific enquiry could ever hope to do.

Literature does not, however, belong only in the English class. Nor is literature in the classroom designed purely for endless analysis of its parts, or repetitive questions on each chapter or act or verse. When we admire and respect something, finding out how it works can be an edifying and exciting exercise. But before pulling something apart, an appreciation is required of what it actually looks like whole, otherwise something of its essential form may be lost, or the original wholeness may not be recognised or appreciated.

Children's literature—including its unique offspring, the picturebook—is a fundamental and integral part of this process. For the pictures in picturebooks are not just a prop to language; they are a part of it. This will be discussed more fully in Chapter 24, but it is important to note from the outset that the propinquity of words and pictures in picturebooks creates something more than simply the sum of the words and pictures. In fact it constitutes a 'third space' (to borrow from cognitive science), which generates properties that can be found in neither of the 'input spaces'(Turner 1996: 57–8; Johnston 1998b: 35). The pictures of picturebooks do not simply illustrate the language, they inflate it; they add something different, stimulating an inner imaginative process that is in itself another type of 'language-ing'.

Literature and the development of 'knowing readers'

Young people in secondary school who are required to do close textual analysis of complex literary texts need a picture—and love—for what these texts look like whole. They don't need to see themselves in the text, but they do need to have a glimpse of what it will be like when they approach a text with fresh and knowing eyes, revisit it with a more knowledgeable appreciation, stand beside it alone, and share it in company. By the time they complete their primary school education children should be **knowing readers**—readers who not only have all the skills they need to read, but who also read with knowledge and expectation of how texts work, of how great the reading experience is, of its infinite capacity for variousness, of its personal rewards and continuing challenges, and of the deep sense of satisfaction that comes from persevering with texts that at first seem too difficult.

So they need a memory bank of reading that includes large numbers of children's books to which they have been introduced in primary school, preschool, and the home. It is this 'repertoire' (Nodelman 1996: 141) that will give them a clear understanding of what a book is and what it does, of its codes and conventions, narrative patterns and thematic structures, its word-pictures of narrative time and place. The mood, confusions, jealousy, and passion of Emily Brontë's *Wuthering Heights*, and an understanding of the representation of these in narrative, are more readily perceived in the context of a panorama of reading that has included diverse articulations of similar ideas in picturebooks such as *The Wolf* (Barbalet and Tanner 1994) and perhaps *The Werewolf Knight* (Wagner and Roennfeldt 1995), and that has seen jealousy, possessiveness and fear at work in

John Brown, Rose and the Midnight Cat (Wagner and Brooks 1977). An apparently simple wordless picturebook such as Istvan Banyai's ***Zoom*** (1995), in a continual challenge to reader complacency, prepares young children for thematic ideas about expectations and judgments that may in fact be proved incorrect, and about perspectives and ideas that may later help them to understand better the position of the various voices in Brontë's masterpiece. The complexities of Shakespeare's plays need to be read not as isolated fragments for intensive study that suddenly appear in the latter years of secondary school, but rather as part of a continuum of artistic, literary texts that includes hundreds and hundreds of children's books, humorous, sad, realistic, fantastic. In this way, books as diverse as ***Leaves for Mr Walter*** (Brian and Cox 1998), ***The Selfish Giant*** (Wilde 1979), ***Playing Beatie Bow*** (Park 1985), and Gleeson's ***Skating on Sand*** (1994) series will have foregrounded later encounters with themes of foolishness and blindness (as in *King Lear*) and of the complexities of family relationships (as in *Hamlet* and *Macbeth*).

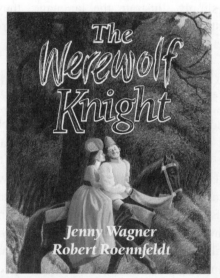

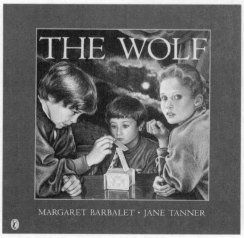

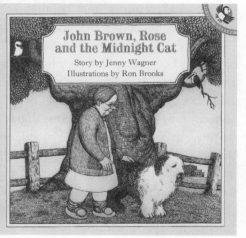

Children's books are an extremely significant part, a vital part, of a lifelong participation and engagement in literature. They may look simple but they help to prepare an intellectual, aesthetic receptivity for abstract ideas and complex concepts. For example, let's follow through the notion of themes noted above and consider the idea of 'outsiderness'—marginality, inclusiveness versus exclusiveness, otherness. Books can help children develop innate awarenesses of what it means to be an outsider, of how it feels to be on the margins, and of how such positioning is constructed within narrative. Consider the illustration below by Greg Rogers of the street boy and the skinny kitten looking through the window at the fat cat in Hathorn's text **Way Home** (1994), and then read Thomas Hardy's depiction of Tess of the D'Urbervilles as an outsider: 'She was not an existence, an experience, a structure of sensations, to anyone but herself. To all humankind, Tess was only a passing thought' (*Tess of the D'Urbervilles* Chapter 14).

From the same two texts, there is something of the verbal picture of Tess and Sorrow, the young outcast mother holding the outcast baby, in the darkly shadowed visual picture of the homeless boy holding the kitten in the folds of his jacket (see Johnston 1997). Taro Yashima's *Crow Boy* (1983) tells another story of marginality, classroom outsiderness, and difference.

Children's literature is part of an artistic continuum and it functions as a creative, enjoyable, and stimulating introduction to the great world of art and ideas, opening up that world at multiple, user-friendly points of entry. Readers are exposed, sometimes without realising it, to a mass of complex themes that, like icebergs, may show only as tiny tips. But these tips are indicators of great depths and they act as subtle and implicit guides in the development of knowing readers. Exposure to pictures of outsiderness (or *outside-ness)* in books such as **Way Home** prepares the way for deeper understandings of ideas relating to the social environment, or to prejudice, injustice, and exploitation—ideas that may later be encountered in such diverse texts as Alexander Solzhenitsyn's *One Day in the Life of Ivan Denisovich*, or Mark Twain's *Huckleberry Finn*, or the music of Bob Dylan, or the contemporary novels of Toni Morrison.

Literature as the practice of all aspects of literacy— reading, writing, speaking, listening

Mikhail Mikhailovitch Bakhtin (1895–1975) was a Russian literary theorist. Some of his work is complex, but he is worth browsing for his insights into how texts work. Think about this, for example:

> Each large and creative verbal whole is a very complex and multifaceted system of relations. With a creative attitude towards language, there are no voiceless words that belong to no one. Each word contains voices that are sometimes infinitely distant, unnamed, almost impersonal ... almost undetectable, and voices sounding nearby and simultaneously. (1981)

Consider this in the light of the classic opening lines of the fairytale, which will be discussed more fully in Chapter 23. The words 'Once upon a time ...' contain, if we think about it, the 'voices' of many different fairytale texts that we have read both as children and as adults, the voices of parents and teachers from our past who may have read them to us or to others in our presence, our own voice as we have read or said those words to others, voices from other media—film, radio, television—that we have heard, perhaps the voices of small children who are saying or reading the words to others. Some of these voices are so far away in time or place that we are hardly aware of them; some may be recent and close by.

Words such as 'Once upon a time ...' trigger layers of voices—read, written, spoken, heard. They access layers of different relationships, of different times and places, and of accumulated 'meaning' that go far beyond themselves.

Bakhtin is not saying that we actually 'hear' the voices—it is an inner, deeply innate experience—but he is alerting us to the richness and diversity of words and the richness and diversity of literature. There are layers and layers of speakers and listeners, readers and writers. Bakhtin's words highlight the fact that *literature is a mosaic of all aspects of literacy—reading, writing, speaking, listening.*

Children's books as mini-worlds

Literature is more than a collection of texts making up a past; it is more than *cultural memory* and more than *pantheon*. Literature, and particularly children's literature, is of the moment; its focus is inherently present. Even historical books, locating action in an obvious past, are reproduced within a sense of the ideas and ideologies of the present out of which they are written (see Chapter 26).

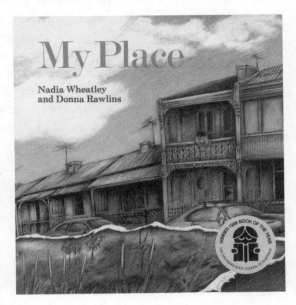

An obvious example of this is *My Place*, by Nadia Wheatley and Donna Rawlins (1987). This book clearly reconstructs a series of historical moments from the perspectives of its present—Australia on the edge of the 1988 Bicentennial.

Each book is a mini-world, a microcosm of the culture that is its context. Culture is not just what things are—clothes and houses and food, for example; it is also *attitudes*: attitudes to children, to people from other races, to the roles of parents, to the shapes of families, to what little girls are and what little boys are, to grandparents, to the environment. Children's literature, with its late 20th-century proliferation of picturebooks, represents an up-to-date, of-the-moment, highly contemporary sociocultural document. In words and pictures it shows by implication and by explication not only what life looks like, but also local and cultural ideas and attitudes about what it *should* look like and, particularly, what it should look like to children.

Children's literature and cultural literacy

Children's literature is a powerful resource in opening up ideas and discussions about culture and cultural perspectives, that is, about the two prongs of **cultural**

literacy: *knowledge of the world*, and *the knowledge, understanding, and appreciation of diverse ways of being*. Knowledge of the world is sometimes referred to as *cultural schemata* and relates to all the bits of knowledge that we piece together in order to make sense of language and the social structures within which we live. Deep understandings of our own world should lead to respect for the world of others, which of course is a world we all share. Cultural literacy is an appreciation of this otherness, but 'otherness' is an inherently subjective and loaded concept, while the idea of 'diverse ways of being' puts us all on more equal ground. This knowledge, understanding, and appreciation of diverse ways of being doesn't mean simply including pictures of people from different races as part of a background group, or talking about different foods, clothes, and houses. *It means becoming aware with integrity of the enclosures of our own thinking. It means being open to and experimenting with different ways of doing things, different sorts of formats, different ideas about beginnings and endings, different ideas even about what language should be, and different ideas about literacy.* Cultural literacy has particular relevance to second-language learners (see Chapter 25).

Real cultural literacy gives space for these diverse ways of being, and appreciates without question the fact that 'many worlds are possible' (Bruner 1986: 149). Ian Abdullah's two books, **As I Grew Older** (1993) and **Tucker** (1994), tell of one such world, and they do so in the writer's own authentic voice, allowing readers to view his expressive style of pictures and engage in what may be a different experience of the telling of story, and a cyclical rather than linear narrative frame.

Task 1

Read *As I Grew Older* and **Tucker** by Ian Abdullah. Note the double text— Abdullah's original and the standardised English version of it.

· Why do you think the publisher decided to add a standardised version?
· Do you think this is helpful? Why or why not?
· How would you introduce this text into your classroom?
· How would you introduce it if there were Aboriginal children in your class? Would this make a difference? Should it?
· Discuss the power of the words 'Now it is hard to find good spots along the River Murray'(*Tucker*, fifth opening). Thinking back to Bakhtin's ideas about words (page 292), what voices can you hear behind these words? What cultural ideas can you hear?

Theory into practice: examples of classroom activities

The following Activity not only expands children's awareness of the traditions and experiences of diverse cultures, but also enhances awareness of their own culture and of the significance of each family being able and free to create different traditions within their own mini-cultures. Making the published book (i.e. the book produced by the class) available to other classes extends these ideas into the wider school community.

Implicit to this task are outcomes relating to cultural literacy and to the acceptance and understanding of difference. In a postmodern world of few absolutes, educators at both the primary and secondary level must seek to evolve and develop pedagogical practices that are culturally inclusive. The complex relationships between literature and language and between literature and literacy present a wide range of opportunities to develop such understandings, understandings which are of increasing significance in a multicultural, technological, and increasingly global society.

Activity 1

Many of these activities will be modelled on the 'Tell Me' approach of Aidan Chambers. Teachers initiate discussion through a 'tell me' invitation rather than the common 'why?' question. This approach stresses speaking and listening, anticipating, in Chambers' words, 'conversational dialogue rather than an interrogation' (1993: 49).

Years 3–4
Read *Tucker* by Ian Abullah (1994).
1. Divide the class into small groups.
2. Ask the children to 'tell you' about food traditions in their family. You may want to talk about celebrations such as Christmas or Easter, or birthday traditions, or picnics, or shopping expeditions, or going out for dinner.
3. Ask children to try to find some tradition that is a little different from the others in their group. Ask them to tell how this began in their family (if they know) or why they think it may have begun.
4. Each child writes a few sentences to describe that tradition. They also illustrate it as meaningfully as they can.
5. Compile these into a class book that can be called *Tucker*, or whatever other name the class likes.
6. Set this book up on a table in the classroom and invite members of other classes to come and read it at suitable times.

Years 5–6
This task can be adapted for Years 5–6 by expanding the written task into a longer composition, and by setting the children a research assignment to explore other texts depicting the traditions of different cultures. Both the research and writing component of this task could be computer-based.

Years K–2

This task can also be adapted for Years K–2. Begin discussions by asking the class to tell about favourite foods—write them on the board. Note how everyone has different favourites. Discuss how people are different, even in the same family. Discuss some of the foods their parents like that they don't. Emphasise the difference.

Read the book to the class. Ask them to tell about food traditions—special cakes and special foods for festivals such as Christmas and birthdays. What special birthday cake do they ask for? Tell them your favourite cake. Some children may mention festivals such as Hanukkah or Ramadan.

Also read **Let's Eat!** by Ana Zamorano and Julie Vivas (1996).

Let's Eat!

Written by **Ana Zamorano**

Illustrated by **Julie Vivas**

So we have to eat without my brother.
"Ay, qué pena!" sighs Mamá.

Writing, speaking, and listening

As the preceding activity demonstrates, it is clear that as well as developing knowing *readers*, literature also helps to create

- knowing writers, by giving children access to a huge variety of purposeful models
- knowing speakers, both because of the exposure to the speaking of others beyond their immediate world (i.e. in literary texts) and because of the classroom speaking that takes place in response to literature
- knowing listeners, listening with both 'inner' and 'outer' ears, not in a physical sense but in a personal one. Listening is more than hearing. It is integral to the development of oral skills but it does not produce sound, as speaking does, nor a physical product, as writing does. Listening, like literacy in all its forms, is complex, perhaps more private than public. Literature gives opportunities for motivated listening.

Activity 2

Years K–2

Let the children sit comfortably. Tell them you are going to read them a story and that you want them to *listen carefully*. Ask them to draw a picture of each animal they hear you mention. If appropriate, they could write the name of the animal. You are also going to play some soft music, and will pause between 'scenes'.

Read ***Time for Bed***, by Mem Fox and Jane Dyer (1993). Play some music, then turn the tape down a little and read the first lines:

> *It's time for bed, little mouse, little mouse,*
> *Darkness is falling all over the house.*

Pause, with music gently turned up. This is an individual activity. Then continue. When finished, ask the children to tell you about the animals and write their names on the board. You may like children to choose their favourite picture and write their own story about it.

Pass the book around the class so children can link what they have heard and the mind-pictures they formed with the actual text.

Years 3–4

As above, but read **My Many Coloured Days** by Dr Seuss (1998). Play a suitable tape, and ask the children to sketch the colour and main thought of each scene:

> On Bright Red Days
> how good it feels
> to be a horse
> and kick my heels!

The first two openings are more abstract—inform the class that you will reread those at the end so that they can represent what they hear in a more informed way (when they have knowledge about the rest of the text). Circulate the book at the end.

Years 5–6

Introduce children to the idea of the *literary factual text*—books that convey 'real' information about a particular topic but that do so in a literary way, perhaps in story or in creative pictures or both. The increasing number of literary factual texts being published provides a rich classroom resource.

Read **Chameleons are Cool** by Martin Jenkins and Sue Shields (1997). Choose suitable music and proceed as above. Ask children to note down as many facts as they can while you read. Pause at each page turn:

> Some lizards eat bananas—chameleons don't
> Some lizards walk upside down on the ceiling—chameleons can't.
> There's even a lizard that glides from tree to tree—
> A chameleon certainly won't do that!

You could also use books such as **I Know How We Fight Germs**, by Kate Rowan and Katherine McEwen (1988) and **A Street Through Time: A 12,000 Year Journey Along the Same Street**, illustrated by Steve Noon and written by Dr Anne Millard (1998).

The connectedness of reading and writing

Literature, like language, is dynamic; it is significant and life-changing. And for the purposes of teaching children literacy, it is crucial to see in literature the intrinsic connectedness of the processes and practices of author (writing) and reader (reading). Literature in the classroom is an *experience* and may include everything and anything that is a part of *this reading and this writing and this moment*. It also includes the *listening* and the *speaking* of this moment. This is a realistic and helpful notion of literature for us as teachers:

- it draws attention to literature as part of the literate practices of reading and writing, speaking and listening
- it opens up windows of opportunity for discussion and exploration into a range of diverse areas
- it gives children the flexibility to relate literature more authentically to their world.

SUMMARY

1. Language is powerful and articulates who and what we are.
2. Literature is applied language.
3. Children's literature is a mosaic of all aspects of literacy: reading, writing, speaking, listening.
4. Children need to be encouraged to become knowing readers.
5. Having access to as many books as possible, from as young an age as possible, will help children become knowing readers.
6. Cultural literacy has two significant aspects: knowledge of the world and the knowledge, understanding, and appreciation of diverse ways of being.
7. Knowledge of the world is sometimes called cultural schemata and relates to all the many pieces of knowledge that are used in order to make sense of language and the social structures within which we live.
8. The knowledge, understanding, and appreciation of diverse ways of being refers to more than the recognition of otherness; it means being aware of the integrity of many possible worlds, many different ways of doing things, and many different ways of thinking.
9. Literature also helps children to become knowing writers, knowing speakers, and knowing listeners.
10. Literature in the classroom is an *experience* and may include everything and anything that is a part of *this reading and this writing and this moment*.
11. Children's literature is a vital part of a lifelong participation and engagement in literature.

Chapter 17
What is Children's Literature?

Focus

This chapter discusses ideas and definitions of children's literature, noting that such definitions include societal attitudes about children (the 'construct' of the child). It notes that children's literature is both a field of academic study and a professional field, and that its texts reflect sociocultural ideologies. It emphasises that children's literature is part of a literature continuum, and that children need to be exposed to a variety of texts across that continuum, some of which should be beyond their immediate needs.

Children's literature is now firmly established as a field of rigorous academic investigation and study at both undergraduate and postgraduate level in many countries. That courses in children's literature appear in different faculties in different universities—education, arts and humanities, social sciences, sociology, nursing—is an indicator of the many-faceted significance of this subject. Teachers, publishers, editors, writers and illustrators, librarians, psychologists, and sociologists comprise many of its students.

Professional organisations such as the *International Research Society for Children's Literature* and the *Children's Literature Association* provide forums for scholars from all over the world to share their expertise and research interests. Journals address, from a variety of perspectives, practical and theoretical approaches to historical and contemporary issues and ideas in the world of children's books.

Children's Literature Journals

Bookbird	*The Lion and the Unicorn*
Canadian Children's Literature	*Magpies*
Children's Literature in Education	*Orana*
CHLA Quarterly	*Papers*
CREArTA (an interdisciplinary arts focus)	*Signal*
Literature Base	*Reading Time*

Children's literature is usually defined as *literature for children* or, less commonly, as *literature of children*. Leaving aside the question of what constitutes 'literature', the preposition showing the relationship between *literature* and *children* is revealing. If this literature is *for* children it tends to open up obvious questions about positions of power, and about cultural and narrative ideologies and judgments: who makes the decision about the type of literature that is designed *for* children, and so on. The literature *of* children implies more agency on the part of the child, not as producer necessarily but as *owner*. The dilemma of children's literature is not only that so many people who are not children are involved in its processes, but that everyone has once had the experience of being a child, and therefore is a stakeholder—and an expert!

Ideas of 'childhood' and 'the child'

Childhood itself is a very subjective concept. It may be a state of remembered innocence or selfishness, holiness or unholiness. Childhood, where children live, is a space that each of us has inhabited, and that each of us now remembers in a particular way. Different cultures have different ideas about children and their relationships to society. Childhood is therefore a common but highly contested space, often loaded with nostalgia.

The concept of *the child* is similarly a contested construct. Children in stories have been diversely represented over time as small adults, as angels, and as little devils. Michael Benton, writing on the representations of the child in painting and literature in the period 1700–1900, describes six images in three oppositional pairs of images: the polite/impolite child, the innocent/sinful child, the authentic/sanitised child. His seventh representation is that of the holy child, usually with the Virgin Mary, which he describes as 'that superordinate icon which influences all writers and painters in western culture'. Benton notes that each age reinvents the child in its own image, and concludes: 'The image of childhood, in all its manifestations, was generally a construction by adults of the child they wanted to see' (1996: 57, 58–9).

Task 2

It is important that teachers and all those working with children have an understanding of these ideas about the sociocultural construction of 'the child'.

1. Read Benton's paper in the international journal *Children's Literature in Education* 27(1) 1996 and critically annotate it as part of a bibliography.
2. Choose a particular period of approximately 50 years. Referring to at least five literary works containing child characters (poems, plays, books, and children's books), describe the image of the child that seems to emerge. Discuss possible reasons for this.

Activity 3

The above task, designed for trainee teachers, can also be adapted for upper primary school children. Compiling an annotated bibliography is a *literate practice* (see Morley-Warner 2000). Helping children to understand constructions and representations of childhood assists critical literacy (see Chapter 18). This could also be adapted to a *media task*:

Years 5–6

1. Choose five advertisements from television or magazines that feature children.
2. In small groups, ask the children to tell each other about the features of the child—Clean? Dirty? Attractive? Good clothes? Shabby clothes? Naughty? Good? Lots of friends? Lonely? Siblings? Parents? House? Bedroom? Tidy? Untidy? Toys?
3. Make a group list. Discuss the reasons that the advertiser has chosen to depict the child in this way.
4. Each group reports back to the class.
5. The class compiles a list of representations of different images (in words or pictures) of the child and posts examples.

Towards a definition of children's literature

The term *literature* has become controversial in a postmodern world, but for our purposes, literature is a body of writing—fictional and factual—that includes novels, poetry, drama, biographies and autobiographies, and essays; it may also include other writings in fields such as philosophy, history, and science (think of the books of Stephen Hawking and Paul Davies). Literature is usually read in a written form, but can be performed, and in an age of new technologies may be printed or broadcast electronically. This is just a new version of the old *oral literatures* that are so much a part of world culture.

Literature is the expression of the human need to communicate, as readers and/or writers, as speakers and/or listeners. It is story shared. The best of literature probably tells our deepest stories, and addresses our deepest human concerns, in a way that is not only artistically or aesthetically satisfying, but also engages both senses and intellect.

Children's literature is literature that is usually written by adults, *for* children and *to* children. Thus it can become a complex revelation of what societies are concerned about and how they see themselves. The history of children's literature clearly reveals pedagogical concerns that in themselves reflect:

- confidence in the receptivity of the young
- confidence in the power of story.

Books for children were traditionally designed to 'teach' and 'socialise' and 'acculturate', in earlier times about religious and moral matters, and in later times about general education. Children's books of our time continue the tradition: many seek to teach (and implicitly or explicitly advocate particular stances) about the social issues that dominate contemporary political and social agendas, notably the environment, indigenous cultures, multiculturalism, the changing shape of families, and gender and gender roles.

However, children's literature is more than pedagogy and advocacy. It invites children into corporate story, and into participation in the ongoing search—which continues to confront and perplex adults—about what it is to be human. It offers the opportunity to dip into those 'deepest stories' of living—stories about change, frailty, failure, success, loss, growth, mortality and ideas of immortality, and the gamut of human emotions associated with these.

Children's literature is an artistically mediated form of communication—a conversation—that a society has with its young. It is shaped by the concerns of the many stakeholders that are part of the 'world that creates the text' (Bakhtin 1981:253): authors and illustrators, editors and publishers, educators and critics, as well as parents and children.

Children's literature texts are characteristically forms of prose narrative, although they may also include poetry, drama, and factual writings. They have adapted the basic structure of the novel to meet the needs of their readers, and use plot, characterisation, and motivation. The protagonist is generally a child, or a stand-in child, which may be an animal or toy. Picturebooks are a unique adaptation of the novel form: very short, and using visual as well as verbal text for the carriage of story (see Chapter 24).

Children's literature as *literature*

Children's literature is not something 'less than' literature—it is *part of a literature continuum*. It *is* literature, no matter who is reading it. This needs to be reiterated and become an assumption underpinning the way we treat books in the classroom. Young children reading Sendak, or the Brothers Grimm, or one of the Ahlberg texts, or a Margaret Wild or Allan Baillie picturebook, are reading literature, according to their physical and intellectual capacities.

This idea of a continuum, however, means that children need a diet that is not wholly made up of 'children's books'. Continual opportunities must be made for all children to be exposed to a wide range of texts from that literature continuum.

Exposure beyond immediate needs

Sometimes, as educators, we tend to overestimate level of difficulty and underestimate the abilities of the child. Doonan notes Jerome Bruner's remarks that 'any subject could be taught to any child in an intellectually honest form at any stage of her development: it was simply a matter of finding a "courteous translation"' (1993: 49). We need to develop a similar philosophy and set about finding ways of introducing our students, courteously, to all sorts of material from across the literature continuum. This also fits in with the idea, first articulated in the context of literacy by Don Holdaway, of continually exposing children to books beyond their immediate needs—and, I would add, capacities (1979: 40).

This is where Shared Reading (see Chapter 8) is so important. Even after children can read for themselves, teachers need to continue to read with them, but to read books that are challenging, and that children may never pick up to read for themselves. *Children need to be read to and read with, even when they are competent, independent readers.*

When reading aloud to children, be bold and adventurous in the choice of texts and in your expectations of children's interactions with them. Interrogate by practice conventional ideas about the difficulty of certain texts. For example, the rhythms and rhymes of ***Each Peach Pear Plum*** by the Ahlbergs (1978) are not so very different from Ariel's Song in Shakespeare's *The Tempest*:

Each peach pear plum
I spy Tom Thumb.
Tom Thumb in the cupboard
I spy Mother Hubbard.
Mother Hubbard down the cellar
I spy Cinderella.

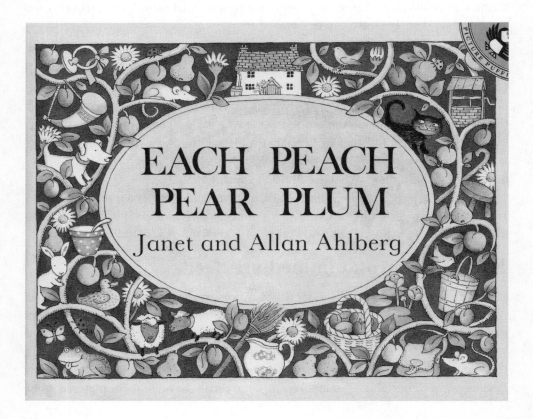

Where the bee sucks, there suck I:
In a cowslip's bell I lie:
There I couch when owls do cry.
On the bat's back I do fly
After summer merrily.
Merrily, merrily shall I live now
Under the blossoms that hang on the bough.

Nor are they very different from Robert Frost's evocative lines from 'Stopping By Woods on a Snowy Evening'.

The woods are lovely, dark and deep,
And I have promises to keep.
And miles to go before I sleep,
And miles to go before I sleep.

Allusions to the characters of nursery song and story are often no 'easier' or readily 'known' than allusions to characters and things in poems and stories that we would categorise as 'literature'. These nursery characters, many of them arguably increasingly less appropriate to 21st-century children who are being encouraged to consider themselves as members of an international community, become a part of childhood knowledge achronologically (out of order, so to speak) just as the language of the Shakespeare and the Frost poem do. In fact in *Each Peach Pear Plum* the words 'cellar', 'ditch', and 'den' are problematical in the sense that they are unlikely to be part of the average Australian small child's language. They may well be as far removed from that child's experience as the 'cowslip' of Ariel's song, and Frost's 'woods' (Australians know about the bush and the forest but 'woods' is not a term in common use).

Read such poetry to children, without worrying too much about explaining what it 'means'. In pedagogical practice, we have placed a lot of store on 'meaning' (a highly contested word in a postmodern world). But literature—like music, art, dance—is more than meaning (see Johnston 1997). The Formalists saw the essence of poetry as not what it means but what it sounds like, its euphony: its language and rhythm and cadence (Eichenbaum 1998). The Symbolists stressed the importance of symbol and image. The point is that literature is a deep experience that we respond to in many different ways and at many different levels.

> Symbolism refers to a late-19th movement in French poetry that privileged symbolic over actual meanings. There was a similar movement in French art. It is interesting to read children's books, especially picturebooks, with these ideas in mind.

Exposure to different ways of seeing the world

It is clear that books 'mean' different things to different people. This is precisely the reason children need to be exposed to a wide and diverse range of books from the whole continuum, including as a matter of course non-Western literature. It is also part of the development of cultural literacy.

Activity 4

A wonderful book for opening up discussions about different ways of seeing the world and different ways of using language is **A Caribbean Dozen**, a collection of Caribbean poetry edited by John Agard and Grace Nicholls (1994). Another is the Australian text **Do Not Go Around the Edges**, by Daisy Utemorrah and Pat Torres (1990).

Years K–2

1. Bring a mirror to class. Ask the children to look at themselves in the mirror. Then ask them to think about how they know that it is a reflection of themselves. Discuss at an appropriate level the idea of identity—of how clothes, hair colour, and language are part of their reflection. Does that tell the whole story about who they are? Ask them to tell you what other things make them who they are.

2. Read 'Who's Dat Girl?' from *A Caribbean Dozen*. Discuss how the language sounds different. What does that tell about who we are? Explain any difficult words—perhaps have some props.

3. Ask children to draw a picture of themselves, showing all the things that make up who they are (family, where they live, where they used to live, how they feel about things).

4. Put pictures up in the classroom.

Years 3–4

As above, but instead of the picture, ask the children to write a poem about seeing themselves in the mirror. Explain how *poetry* gives freedom from grammatical structure, allows the expression of personality in all sorts of different ways, and encourages variety of language. Give an example of a structure if your class needs it:

> *I looked in the mirror*
> *And saw ...*
> *... hair,*
> *... eyes*
> *...*
> *But there was more ...*
> *...*
> *...*
> *Yes, that is me!*

(Note that this is an excellent model for encouraging creative writing in ESL and EFL classrooms. Children who are learning another language relish the freedom that writing poetry can give, and also enjoy telling their own story in different ways. Offer them opportunities to illustrate their work, or to bring you in some of their own music, or books in their own language. See also Chapter 25.)

Years 5–6

1. Begin with as much of the above as you would like.
2. Then read *Do Not Go Around the Edges* with the class. Read in a comfortable situation if you can, and have children as close as possible to the book.
3. Point out that this is a triple text. It contains:
   · an autobiography (life story)
   · a poetic response to Daisy's life story
   · a picture, showing another sort of response.
4. Discuss with the class the simplicity of the autobiographical sentences. Tell them that autobiography is interesting to write because we are all experts about our own lives. (If you have not covered this earlier, discuss the differences between autobiography and biography.)
5. Ask the class to listen carefully to what they think the poems are saying about how Daisy feels now. Discuss the idea of listening with an inner ear (hearing beyond the words). Ask them to tell you what feelings and thoughts and emotions the words of the poems express that the sentences of autobiography don't.
6. In roundtable groups, or as a class, ask the children to discuss what the pictures express and what they add to the text.
7. Begin an Autobiography Project, modelled on this book, but encourage creativity. The class will produce a written autobiographical text and a poetic response to it. Discuss structure: how many pages do you want, how do you want them to present their work? Encourage visuals as well—some children may like to make a montage, or paint, or include a photograph as a basis for further artistic expression.

   Play some background music as the children work. Ask the children to bring in any tapes suitable for use in this way.

Extension Activities, Year 6

Read the first chapters of **Deadly Unna**, by Phillip Gwynne (1999). (This is classified as a 'Young Adult' book; check that you are comfortable with the subject matter and language.) Read in an informal context (take the class out to the playground, or have them sit on mats on the floor, or in a circle, or read in the library). Focus on the enjoyment and challenge of a shared story. This book will open up many opportunities for discussion and enquiry, for example:

1. 'It's like they're playing another game, with completely different rules' (p. 5). Do you think these words describe more than a football game?

2. Talk about the use of the first person. What effect does it have? (the reader hears an authentic adolescent voice, understands the narrator's point of view, may feel closer to the action, may be limited to the narrator's perspectives).

Teachers' reading

When appropriate, books on related themes will be suggested for teachers' enjoyment. *Angela's Ashes* by Frank McCourt (1996) tells the story of the author's early life in Ireland.

Literature and *jouissance*

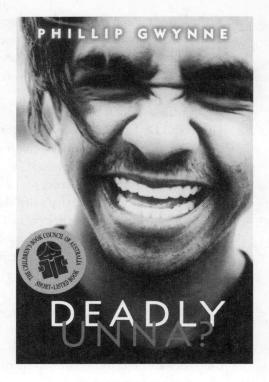

As will be discussed in Chapter 24, the language of children's books, and especially picturebooks, has much in common with poetry. Poetry is interior and exterior pictures—both the pictures that we see in front of us and the pictures-in-words and pictures-in-sounds that are a part of imagery. Poetry and literature are creative response as much as they are intellectual apprehension.

We need to remind ourselves of this. Just as we need to keep in mind the philosophical premise that as teachers we must continue to expose children to texts beyond their immediate capacities, so we must also continue to challenge ourselves. The theoretician Roland Barthes talks about the *jouissance*, the joy of the text, the pleasure of the text. In his discussions of 'the pleasure of the text' he makes the point that it is in persevering with texts that are difficult to understand that mere *plaisir* becomes *jouissance*, a term that is connected to orgasmic ecstasy! (1976).

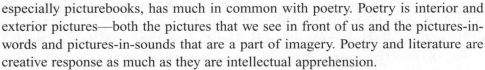

Roland Barthes (1915–80) was a French literary critic who was particularly interested in semiotics, the science of signs and symbols. In *Mythologies* (1957) he looked at signs in everyday life, including in toys, advertisements, and wrestling. In *The Pleasure of the Text* (1970) he analyses literary text from a **structuralist** perspective that was to become increasingly unorthodox.

The structuralists were inspired by the work of the Swiss linguist **Ferdinand de Saussure**. They believed that texts should be analysed in terms of their structures and systems of relations.

As adults, we are 'guests at the table of children's literature' (Hollindale 1997: 29). But the table is a long one, and it is groaning with the richnesses of its fare. Nor are the plates always arranged in carefully separated categories—suitable for children, suitable for adults. Just as children's books can 'replenish the completeness of a strenuous adult mind' (Hollindale 1997: 36), so texts from the wider corpus of literature can help to develop a taste for all sorts of different flavours and textures, can if fact nourish the fledgling growth that will become that adult mind.

Beyond teaching

A cautionary note, however. The literature-based curriculum has been a boon to classroom teachers but this does not imply that books are simply a tool or resource for teaching practice. Children's books—highly visual, highly energetic, highly contemporary—are wonderful resources, and while these chapters will demonstrate many ways of using books for teaching purposes, they are also much, much more. It is important for teachers to keep reminding themselves of this and to reflect on the ways they use books in the classroom.

In this technological age, books are still 'wonder books'. It has become unfashionable and even suspect (as if one is ignorant of literary theory) to talk about books purely in terms of life enhancement, but we need to restore into the academy the simple acknowledgment of the fact that books give pleasure and they enhance lives. They wouldn't exist if they didn't.

Literature and ideology

However, it is also important to note and to help students understand the fact that literature reflects cultural ideologies. It not only contains *themes* that are ideologically constructed—that is, that emerge out of the writer's assumptions and beliefs about the world he or she inhabits, or out of that specific society's implicit beliefs about itself that spill over into the background world of the text, sometimes without the writer's even knowing—but it also constructs its *narrative* in ways that are influenced by ideology. John Stephens argues a theory of narrative that among other things sees narrative structure as an 'ideologically powerful component of texts' (1992: 6). The decisions made by the author as to what is included and how it is represented can encourage and coerce readers into responding in particular ways. That is, every text is culturally and ideologically encoded in both what it says and how it says it. In Barthes' words, 'No text is innocent'. Even so, and indeed because of this, texts are living artefacts, anthropological and archaeological remains of the *past*—of what it was to *be* in that past and of what its culture *thought* it was to be—and sociological documents of the *present*.

If we look at any one of a number of Shirley Hughes' books, for example, we see a background picture that may be quite separate from the actual story of the book.

This is a picture, seen through Hughes' eyes, of life in a particular slice of 20th-century England: what the houses look like, what people wear, what they do, what activities are happening, what food is on the table, what the children are doing, how the children relate to their parents and the parents to their children and so on. We see what Hughes wants us to see; that is part of what I mean about narrative structure (and illustrations) being an ideological choice. She does not choose to depict a mugging or a bag-snatching incident for example—but then, such things may not commonly occur in the suburbs that she draws anyway. And even that choice becomes significant when we consider the text as an artefact made for the edification of the construct that our society has made of *the child.*

However, it goes further than the intentions of the writer and/or illustrator. In composing the shapes and pictures of their texts, every writer and illustrator unconsciously reflects ideas and attitudes that are a part of the society and culture in which they live and out of which they are writing. When Mary Grant Bruce wrote the *Billabong* books in the first half of the 20th century, she did not mean to be racist or classist but she unconsciously reflected the prevailing implicit cultural and national ideologies of her time. Thus the book becomes ideologically dated, a representation of much more than the author ever intended. It is interesting that it is in fact the ideology that has dated such books as Billabong, Biggles, and Enid Blyton's works—and that this is what has had to be expunged in the 'sanitised', republished versions.

Survival of the book

Books are objects, but their essence is not in their physical form. The value of books is in the mysterious alchemy of words and narratives that somehow rises up to meet readers, privately and personally, as they engage with those black marks of print on the page. Whatever shape or form 'books' may take in the future, I am sure that *the book*—what it is within itself—will survive. In fact part of why it may survive is the very permanence of its current hard copy form, as opposed to the ephemerality of Web-based material, and the propensity of children (and adults for that matter) to want to read and reread favourites. The Web is an exciting and growing resource, but unless there are developments in the future that we cannot even imagine, it won't wipe out the book, although it may alter its look and format. However, even if an electronic pocket book is developed that contains every book ever written available at the touch of a button, this would just be a different way of accessing 'books'. It may in fact add to their popularity and open up increasing opportunities to participate in a worldwide club of readers and readership.

Literature as map

The latter part of the 20th century saw a growing contemporary interest in autobiography—'what writing is not?' asked Sneja Gunew (1985: 107). As mentioned earlier, children's literature describes and reflects spaces that in some way are a part of a common story—the inhabitating of childhood by children. Its numerous texts constitute a type of map, an inner geography that some recognise at one point and some at another. A map gives us clues to who and where we are and helps us to claim our unique place and significance. The Canadian writer Aritha Van Herk, discovering a book written about Edmonton, remembers:

> Someone had dared to write about a place I knew, about me. I finally had a map ... I now live somewhere, in a place created by Alice Monroe and Audrey Thomas, by Marian Engel and Matt Cohen, by Margaret Atwood and George Bowering ... I have a map. (Olinder 1984: 71)

Such maps are of course highly subjective, and points of interest to some will be meaningless to others. Joy Hooton, in a critical study of autobiographies of childhood by Australian women, and discussing the significance of national identity as part of personal identity, writes:

> The most striking aspect of the autobiographies studied here is that there are many different Australias. Not only is 'national' inappropriate as a descriptive term, but even 'regional' is too prescriptive, for, as George Seddon has commented, 'there is no such thing as an Australian environment,' but rather 'a great variety of different places' ... Place depends on 'the logic of the perceiver's state of mind' and certainly one of the most liberating features of women's autobiography is the diversity of their subjective Australias. (1990: 341–2)

Children's literature is a map of childhood, and childhood is a diverse and subjective space. Children's literature reflects this diversity and offers children the opportunity to create their own maps and to traverse it in their own way. John Williamson's picturebook *Christmas in Australia* (and the accompanying CD)

(1998) is a subjective representation of Christmas in just such a subjective Australia as Hooton describes, but there are bits that some of us may be able to relate to, *if we want.*

 Task 3

1. Look through as many Australian picturebooks as you can.
2. List and briefly describe the different 'subjective Australias' that you find represented:

The bush	*The suburbs*
The city	*The country*
Schools	*Play places*
The beach	*Holiday places*
The house	*Family and people*

3. Note that what is part of the depiction of the everyday (background rather than foreground) is likely to be most revealing.
4. Think about and discuss the notion of your own 'subjective Australia'.

This task could be adapted to apply to the picturebooks of any country.

 Activity 5

Years K–2

1. Make an overhead of one of the maps from **My Place** (choose a suitable opening).
2. Talk about the idea of maps. Ask children to discuss features about their home and neighbourhood.
3. Introduce ideas of the school as a place, a *my place*. Ask the class to draw a map of the school, labelling as they are able.
4. Ask the children to tell you about their maps. Note that everyone sees the same place in a slightly different way, and that certain features are more important to some than to the others (the gate you come in by or leave by, for example).
5. If the class level is appropriate, you may like to draw a large composite map of the school. Divide into sections and give each group a section, then join the sections. Put up the map in class.

Years 3–4

1. Talk about the idea of books giving a map.
2. Look at *My Place*. Note the importance of the map. (It gives obvious coherence to the text and is part of the narrative structure.)
3. Ask the children to draw a map of their own place, with labels and notes, after the one in *My Place*.
4. Publish the maps around the classroom.

Years 5–6

As above, but add:

1. Encourage children to draw a map of all the spaces they inhabit: school, home, sport, family, friends, neighbourhood. Discuss.

2. Discuss ideas of ownership and of the land. You may want to relate this to other areas of the curriculum.

3. Discuss ideas of belonging to two lands: perhaps a country of birth and a new country (Australia). Share stories of different cultural backgrounds. Make a world map showing the represented countries.

4. Ask children to read John Marsden's ***Tomorrow When the War Began*** (1994) (read the first few chapters in class). What ideas about land and ownership are debated within this book?

Extension Activity, Year 6

Read ***All in the Blue Unclouded Weather*** by Robin Klein (1991). This is in part autobiographical. What picture of an Australian country town is seen in this book? When do you think this story is set? Teachers may like to read the class Tennyson's poem 'The Lady of Shalott' (the title of the book comes from a line in this poem).

Why do you think the author chose this title? 'I love that poem', Vivienne said. 'Specially that line that goes "All in the blue unclouded weather". It's like summer here in Wilgawa'. (Klein 1991: 57)

Ask the class to write a creative piece—poem or story—with this title.

Choose an episode in the book (each chapter tends to be an episode in a series of memories) and turn it into a playscript for either a stage or radio play (see Chapter 8, the Literacy Session). Choose appropriate accompanying music. Perform the play.

Teachers' reading

Dresses of Red and Gold is the sequel to *All in the Blue Unclouded Weather*. These books are not straight autobiographies; they are rememberings of memories given narrative shape: 'rememories'. *A Space for Delight* by Colleen Klein (1988) is a well-written and engrossing story about a woman looking back over her map of a subjective Australia.

It is important to note that recognising maps and ideas about a subjective Australia does not imply that we have to see ourselves in the text. Awareness of this freedom and of this choice is part of critical literacy (see Chapter 18). Children

don't have to identify (although some will) with the main character, or any other character for that matter. It is enough that they are for a moment viewing (observing) another equally valid way to *be*, which is being shaped in language.

Authors and texts

Children need the skills to enable them to resist being manipulated into a particular reader position. Sometimes understandings of the author's background helps to achieve this. Although such ideas have been unpopular in literary criticism, there is no doubt that *children* are interested in authors: books seem to become more meaningful for them when they talk with their creators and discover, for example, that the Henry of **Henry's Bed** is a real-life boy, the son of the writer and illustrator (Perversi and Brooks 1997). We need to remind ourselves that literature is of both *reading* and *writing*. The author does not have to be 'dead' nor does the critically astute reader have to be without agency.

The Death of the Author

Michel Foucault and Roland Barthes, in announcing the 'death of the author', were signalling the idea of the post-structuralists that the author was not the centre and principal organiser of the meaning of the text.

Post-structuralism is a theory of literature that seeks to interrogate any idea of absolute 'meanings' or 'truth' within a text, claiming that all underlying assumptions, ideas, and concepts in a literary text are open to valid questioning. In a nutshell, the post-structuralists believe that no text can mean what it seems to say, and that there are gaps and inconsistencies in all texts.

Reader response theory has grown out of post-structuralist thought. It proposes the idea that these gaps allow readers of the text to negotiate and create their own meanings.

Children's literature and its relationships to other genres: the *Bildungsroman*

Children's literature is a literature of growing. It commonly describes important aspects of development—the first day at school, the birth of a sibling, a significant adventure, the death of a grandparent, an epiphanal moment. It can be meaningfully related to the *Bildungsroman*, the novel of development, of growing up. Everything in the *Bildungsroman*, according to Paul Ricoeur, 'seems to turn on the self-awakening of the central character' (1985: 9–10).

The **Bildungsroman** is a German term for the 'education novel', the novel of adolescence, of growing up, of development. It usually deals with emotional and psychological development. The original *Bildungsroman* is generally recognised as *Wilhelm Meister's Apprenticeship* (1795–96), by Johann Wolfgang von Goethe (1749–1832).

A Portrait of the Artist as a Young Man (1916) by the Irish writer James Joyce (1882–1941) is a well-known example of a 20th-century *Bildungsroman*.

The plural of *Bildungsroman* is *Bildungsromane*.

Children's books are commonly perceived as focusing on action rather than on character development, and so may superficially seem unrelated to the genre of the *Bildungsroman* as described above by Ricoeur. However, let's consider **Each Peach Pear Plum** again.

This book is written in the first person, through the perspective and focalisation of the small child's seeing eye. (Note that **focalisation** is a technical term that alerts us to the fact that the writer has chosen to describe or depict an event from a particular viewing point, looking through particular eyes or listening with particular ears. Whose eyes we see through and whose ears we hear with in a text will tend to influence how we react as readers. See pp. 355–6.)

The child in the story looks around its world, probably its narrative world—the world of its books, itself an interesting depiction of the significance of books in a child's life. The conclusion is a triumph—everyone is now in the picture, in their place in the child's world. A moment of growing, of becoming more conscious of self in a world of others, has taken place. And doesn't the same thing happen to John Brown in **John Brown, Rose and the Midnight Cat**?

A children's literature canon

Questions about definitions of children's literature open up debates about *canons*, that is, what some would define as an exclusive list that the 'Establishment' has set in place as a hierarchy of 'literary worth'. Power structures are based within some sort of ideological framework that influences decisions about acceptability and non-acceptability, in-ness and out-ness, inclusion and marginality. Ideas of a canon have become very unpopular, first because of the subjective nature of those assumptions, and second because of the groups such a hierarchy has actually excluded (groups pertaining to gender, race, and class). It is interesting to consider so-called 'classics' such as *Robinson Crusoe* (a book originally written as an adult book) and *The Wind in the Willows* in the light of questions about the position they assign to women, to ideas of 'lower classes' (for example, the stoats and the weasels in *The Wind in the Willows*), and to ideas of Empire.

However, part of the richness of children's literature is that, while certainly there are some books with 'classic' canonical status (although whether these books are actually read much by children is another matter) there are just so many diverse texts, with so many different visual and written images of the world in which we live, that they present not an exclusive picture but an increasingly inclusive one. A book such as ***My Place***, by Nadia Wheatley and Donna Rawlins, not only makes a powerful implicit plea for indigenous land rights, but gives, decade by decade, every child character—girl or boy, Aboriginal or Greek or Irish or German or English or American—their own space, their own time and, most importantly, their own voice: 'My name's Johanna and this is my place'. 'My name's Bridie and this is my place'.

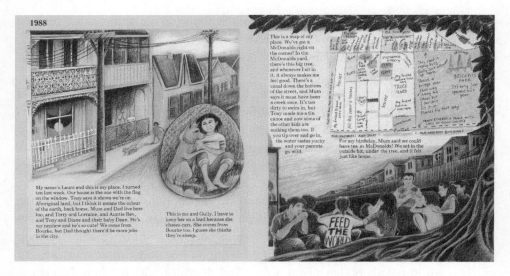

As Smith notes, 'literature' has grown to include any reading material (1991: 516). Boundaries between 'high' and 'low' culture texts across society have become increasingly slippery. It is also important to note that the WWW itself is a print-based medium—words are *written* and words are *read*. The Web in fact helps us to shake off any ideas of a fixed set of rules; it helps us to think in an egalitarian hypertext and challenges us to continually relocate our centre. In a diverse, technological postmodern world of many cultures, ideas of literature are expansive and exciting. Poetry, playground rhymes, drama, skipping songs, how-to-do books, books about surfing and sport, alphabet and concept books, wordless picturebooks, even comic books and magazines are all part of the collective literature of a print-based, print-rich society.

This is not to say that all literature is equal. The real test of worth is probably *longevity* and *impact*: how long and how deeply does this piece of writing stay with us? How many times can we return to it, finding something a little more, a little different, each time? How complex is the map of being that it gives us? How strong was the jolt of recognition—perhaps of self, perhaps of others, perhaps of circumstance, perhaps of predicament? How much of it do we carry to readings of other books? How much of it, if any, do we write into our own lives?

Task 4

What books that were important to you in your childhood would you include in a canon? Why? Share ideas with others. Do you all agree? Why or why not? What does this show about any notion of a canon?

Read *Edward's First Day at School* by Rosemary Wells (1996).

· What does this story reveal about ideologies of family structure?
· What picture of the preschool and teacher does it convey?
· What attitudes to child development does it represent?
· What attitudes to the rights of the individual does it represent?
· Relate this book to 20th-century constructs of the child.
· Relate this story to the *Bildungsroman*.
· Select other picturebooks that reveal aspects of growth and development as the frame of their narrative.

 Activity 6

Years 5–6

1. Ask the children, as a class, to discuss ways of growing—physical, mental, emotional, being able to do something you couldn't before, learning new things about people, understanding things in a different way, learning new things about yourself. Find as many stories as you can that describe an aspect of growing. In small groups, sort them into categories: learning to do something you couldn't do before, adjusting to a new situation, moving to a new place, overcoming some difficulty, changing attitudes about something.

2. Read *Cherry Pie* by Gretel Killeen, Francesca Partridge, and Franck Dubuc (1998). In what way does the person telling the story grow? Discuss in small groups and report to class.

3. Read *Leaves for Mr Walter* by Janeen Brian and David Cox (1998). Who does the growing in this story? Does more than one person grow? In what way?

4. Who are the champions in *Champions* by Jonathan Harlen and Emma Quay (1998)? What message does this book give to us?

5. Set up a class table of growing books. Perhaps you could place other growing things on it as well—seeds, sprouts, an artwork someone is working on over a longer period than usual.

6. In groups of about six, choose a favourite piece of music and compose a dance or growing tableau. Write out your growing themes on a poster or an overhead. Set aside practice and performance times.

Years 3–4

1. Read *John Brown, Rose and the Midnight Cat*. What sort of growing takes place in this book? Who do you think grows? Why?

2. Write a poem about a time of growing.

Years K–2

1. Read any of the *Edward* books by Rosemary Wells. Discuss ideas of being ready and growing. Draw a picture and write a sentence about a time when you grew.

2. Tell the class a story about something you have seen grow.

Teachers' reading

Read *Deadly Unna* (see Activity 4), even if you do not think it suitable for your class. Think about the sorts of growing and self-awakenings that are a part of this story. You may also like to re-read Mark Twain's *Huckleberry Finn*, Sally Morgan's *My Place*, and Harper Lee's *To Kill A Mockingbird* as stories of self-awakening.

The Russian-born linguist, Roman Jacobson, wrote: 'The object of literary study is not literature but "literariness", that is, what makes a given work a literary work' (Rivkin and Ryan 1998:8).

Jacobson (1896–1982) was born and educated in Moscow. In 1920 he left Moscow for Prague, where he produced a structural theory of language sounds. After being forced to leave Czechoslovakia in 1939, he went to Scandinavia and later emigrated to the US. He was influenced by Russian formalism, a school in literary theory that defines literature in terms of the formal structures of the text only. (See also page 410.)

SUMMARY

1 Children's literature is a field of rigorous academic study and is of interest to people from a wide range of disciplines, including educators.

2 Children's literature is literature for children, but 'children' and its related concept 'childhood' are cultural constructs and depend on prevailing attitudes in society.

3 Children's literature is *literature* and is part of a literature continuum. It is an artistically mediated communication that a society has with its young.

4 Children, and adults, should be continually exposed to literature beyond their immediate needs and capacities.

5 We must not underestimate the abilities of children, nor overstate the difficulties of the text: as educators, we should always try to give children a 'courteous translation'. This means that we must develop ways of teaching that encourage children into literacy by making difficult tasks and difficult texts accessible.

6   Literature is more than 'meaning'. We need to allow the flexibility for children to enjoy texts in a range of ways, and understand that they do not always have to articulate the experience of a text. What is important is that they have the experience, provided courteously.

7   Although children's literature is a powerful teaching resource, it is much more than this.

8   Children's literature gives pleasure to its readers.

9   Children's literature is a carrier of ideologies in its themes and in its narrative structures.

10 Children's literature provides a diverse assortment of maps of being.

11 Children's literature frequently addresses in different ways themes of growth and growing and can be related in this way to the *Bildungsroman*.

12 Any idea of a canon has become a contested notion, but the diversity of children's books, and the sheer number of books published in the latter part of the 20th century, continues to work towards inclusivity.

13 The real test of lasting worth is probably longevity and impact: how long and how deeply does this piece of writing stay with us? How much of it do we carry to other readings of other books? How much of it, if any, do we write into our own lives?

Chapter 18

Children's Literature and Critical Literacy

Focus

This chapter investigates the three aspects of critical literacy: reading with a knowledge of the workings of a language; reading with an awareness of what and how the text is making you feel; and reading with the ability to discern the ideas and attitudes and assumptions behind the text. The theoretical distinction between 'story' and the process of 'the telling of the story' (discourse) encourages awareness of the writer's craft and helps in the development of critical literacy.

Critical literacy
- reading with a knowledge of language and how it works
- reading with an awareness of where the text positions a reader
- reading with a perception of the ideas and values and attitudes that constitute the implicit framework of the text and out of which texts are generated.

Critical literacy as a life-skill

Children need critical literacy not simply to analyse texts but as a life-skill. They need to be able to understand the power of the text and to determine *where* the language is positioning them as readers or as listeners; *how* it is making them feel; *what* it is making them feel, what it is trying to make them *do* and *why*. This is part of being a *knowing reader*.

This conceptualisation of critical literacy includes **visual literacy**—reading and understanding the signs of an increasingly visual society—and **cultural literacy**—knowledge of the world, and knowledge of diverse ways of being (see Chapter 16). Books, and in particular picturebooks, provide arenas for the development of both these aspects of critical literacy, or both these critical literacies.

For example, the language of ***The Fisherman and the Theefyspray*** (Jennings and Tanner 1994) serves to encourage the reader into sympathy for the little fish,

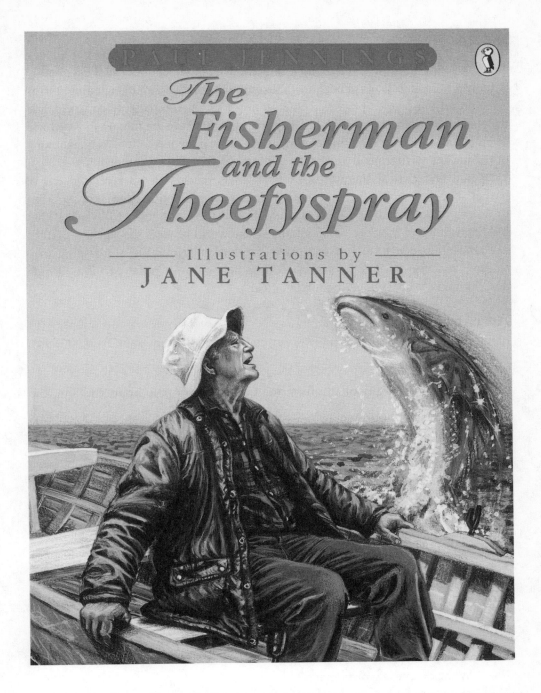

who is 'deep' in 'cold shadow', in a 'lonely lair'. The unusual syntax and slightly heroic feel of 'There was not one other like her now' is compounded by the alliterative description of the other fish:

> *Starfish swarmed. Garfish gathered.*
> *There were twos. And threes.*
> *And thousands.*

The illustrations in the text operate as a system of signs. An obvious example is the several pictures with the shadow of the boat above the mother and her hungry baby: these signify (are signs of) an imminent danger, which the reader can readily perceive. More subtle is the beautiful illustration on the last double opening: this is a picture of two worlds portrayed as a section—on the top the surface world, and the fisherman going home with his empty basket, but beneath him a vibrant world of colour and life. We read this picture as the artist intended us to—as a testimony of the marine environment and of the generous spirit of the fisherman.

Visual and critical literacy skills help us as readers to interpret the empty basket, a key symbol in this text (note its inclusion on the title page), not as a sign of failure or defeat but as a sign of triumph. It is the emptiness of the basket that has contributed to the continuing vitality of the world beneath the surface. 'Truth' and 'meaning' depend on perspectives—the basket, symbol of the fishing trip, 'means' success, or lack of success, depending on your point of view. Which description is 'true' is equally problematical.

Activity 7

Read *The Fisherman and the Theefyspray* by Paul Jennings and Jane Tanner (1994).

Years K–2

- Find all the signs of the fisherman in the story (the boat, the line, the basket).
- What is the underwater world like? Ask children to think of as many words as they can to describe it (bright, colourful, full of life, active, etc.).
- *Tell me:* would you have put the theefyspray back?
- Draw a picture and write a sentence telling a story about saving something.

Years 3–4

Organise the class into small groups. Ask them to discuss the following, sharing the recording of their responses:

- Tell the story in one sentence.
- Why didn't Jennings tell the story as simply as that?
- What words make you feel sorry for the theefyspray?
- What sort of words are most of these? (adjectives) What work do these words do? (describe)
- What do these words mean?

... a pain grew and flowered,
deep inside her.

- Why do you think Jennings chose the word 'flowered'? What other words could he have used? Have you ever heard that word used in relation to pain before? What does it make the reader feel?

Years 5–6

Add the following:

· *Alliteration* is the name for when several words near each other start with the same letter, thus giving a similar sound, e.g. 'shrill shriek'. Find as many examples as you can.

· *Assonance* is the name for when several words near to each other have the same vowel sound but don't actually rhyme, e.g. 'deep', 'theefyspray', 'green'. Can you find any other examples of assonance?

· The class reports its findings. Discuss the poetic nature of the language and the idea that the language of poetry tries to make you see ordinary things in a new way.

· Individual task: write a short poem about something you have seen today or know you will see today. Try to describe it in such a way as to make your readers see the thing in a new way. The class may like to use the computer to help them set out text in innovative ways. (Show some examples of poems that do this.)

· If you were told that the fisherman was very poor and had a hungry family at home waiting for him to provide food for them, would you see the story in a different light? Discuss.

 # Task 5

1. Critical literacy alerts us to the assumptions and attitudes often hiding in places where we don't expect them. Read **Robinson Crusoe** (Daniel Defoe), **The Wind in the Willows** (Kenneth Grahame), and **Charlie and the Chocolate Factory** (Roald Dahl).

2. Comment on these texts and any others you consider appropriate in terms of the following ideas about an Imperialist worldview:
   · cultural assumptions that indigenous people need to be 'civilised'
   · cultural assumptions that the wilderness needs to be tamed and frontiers of civilisation extended
   · the historical context of patriotic conquest
   · the importance of power and empire
   · class structure.

3. Then read some or all of the following: **Window**, **Island in My Garden**, **Paddock**, **The Story of Rosy Dock**, **The Hidden Forest**, **As I Grew Older**, **Enora and the Black Crane**, **The Burnt Stick**.

4. Discuss these texts in relation to a 21st-century environmental world-view:
   · cultural assumptions that the wilderness must be protected against the creep of civilisation
   · the significance of the natural environment in sustainable futures
   · equal rights of indigenous peoples to maintain their culture.

Teachers' reading

The Testament, by John Grisham (1999) is an example of an international bestseller that has a strong environmental theme underlying its story.

How texts work

We have already noted that in some ways a literary text is an artefact—something created by the author, turned into book form by editors and publishers, and recreated by the reader. If we consider it in a scientific way, and cut a section (i.e. the representation of a solid object as it looks when cut by an intersecting plane, so that you can see what's inside it), we would see that the text consists of a number of different levels:

- the level of story
- the level of the telling of the story
- the level of themes and significance (understory).

The level of story

There is obviously a level of story. The **story** is what is narrated. It is what you see at a glance. It emerges out of the events that take place, the actions its characters engage in, and the time and the place of the setting.

The irony of story, however, is that although it is what is seen at a glance, it is not actually what appears in the black marks of writing on the surface of the page. For example, the story of *Theefyspray* could be told in one sentence:

> *The last theefyspray had a baby who was hungry and was caught by a fisherman who put it back in the water because he had seen the mother's beautiful colours.*

Or the story of *Where the Wild Things Are* (Sendak 1963) could be something like this:

> *A little boy was naughty and was sent to his room but he had a fantastic (probably imaginary) adventure with some wild animals and when he came back his hot supper was waiting for him.*

The telling of the story (the telling of the text)

Neither Jennings nor Sendak have chosen to tell their stories with these words. So 'story' is a curiously insufficient term and only a superficial way of describing what happens in a text. It does not adequately describe the process of *the telling of the story*, a process that we need to understand if we are to be critically literate.

This *telling of the story* refers to all those choices that the author has made about the words used:

- the arrangement of the words (*syntax*)
- the meanings of the words (*semantics*)
- the sound and look of the words (*graphophonics*).

It refers to what is actually on the page, the order in which events and characters appear, the mode or register of the narrative, and the point of view and focalisation of events, characters, and setting. For example, Jennings describes the birth of the baby fish with the words 'a pain grew and flowered deep inside her'. The unusual use of 'flowered' in relation to 'pain' jolts readers with what Shklovsky calls the 'roughened' language of poetry (see page 410).

So, in our scientific sectioning of the text there is a paradox—what we see at a glance, the story, is not what actually appears on the surface, although readers usually think it is.

Discourse

This distinction between the story and the telling of the story, the *process of the telling* if you like, is given different names by different theorists (see e.g. Martin 1986: 107–08) but one of the most common terms, and that used by, among others, Gerard Genette (1980), Seymour Chatman (1978), Perry Nodelman (1992: 61–3), and John Stephens (1992: 17–18) is *discourse*.

Discourse is a term with various applications but it commonly refers to the process of narrating, how story is told on the surface of the text. **Narrative** includes both the *story* (what is narrated) and the discourse (how it is narrated).

Readers make, create, negotiate, construct, interpret story from how they read the discourse. Discourse is the language of the text, the actual words on the surface of the page. Story appears to fly free from the page, but in reality of course it is very much dependent on it.

Underneath the discourse is a whole **understory** of what the discourse hints at. This is the rich pool of resources that have been the reservoir out of which the author has made his or her selections in the telling of the story. Each word on the surface—the discourse—still smells and tastes of where it has come from and where it has been, and it is this smell and this taste that helps to give narrative its significance and to express its themes.

Understory

The simple term *understory* relates to the under layer of themes and significance. It helps to explain narrative and thematic cohesion, as well as the points of connection to other texts. Narrative cohesion refers to how the elements of story (characters, actions and events, time and place) are stuck together and ordered in such a way as to make some sort of whole. Thematic cohesion is like an undercurrent, pulling together words, concepts, and pictures into a coherent and significant idea or theme that goes beyond story.

If we look at Patricia Mullins' *V is for Vanishing* (1993), particularly at the powerful opening 'Xx eXtinct,' the discourse—what actually appears on the page—is a very simple statement (not technically accurate anyway: 'extinct' begins with *e* not *x*) and some short scientific labels. This is a book without a conventional 'narrative'—no traditional verbal linkages—but ordered in a

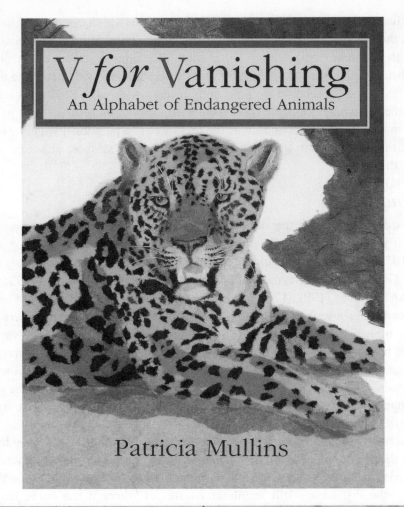

recognisable generic structure, the alphabet book. However, narrative and theme emerge loud and clear and reach beyond the brevity of its discourse (scientific labels). The *story*, told through the poignancy of its illustrations, is about animals and how the animals it names are becoming extinct; the *theme* is about a world environment under threat. The powerful advocacies of this book (its themes and significance) come from the taste, smell, and feel of the layers and layers of visual and verbal understory that still cling to what appears on the surface, that flavour that surface, and that provide textual and intertextual connections, contrast, and cohesion. Contemporary cultural ideas about the sanctity of the environment (cultural ideologies and societal agendas) are a significant part of that understory.

Activity 8

Year 3–4

1. Read as a class **Way Home**, by Libby Hathorn and Greg Rogers (1994). If you can, darken the classroom.
2. Make an overhead of the thirteenth opening. After you have finished the story, turn this overhead on and let the class reflect on it for a few minutes.
3. Discuss the idea of visual perspective or point of view:
   - from what other perspectives could the artist have drawn this picture?
   - why has he chosen this perspective?
   - where are we looking from?
4. Now look at the words on this page. You might like to introduce children to the idea of *the telling of the story*.
   - whose eyes are we seeing through?
   - what is the advantage of direct speech as part of the telling of a text?
   - what is the effect of the three lines in third person? (You may need to explain these terms to your class. If so, reinforce them as often as possible in subsequent discussions.)
   - what ideas and attitudes in our society does a story like this show (concern about homeless children, the division between rich and poor, waste of resources, etc.)?

Years 5–6

Add the following:
5. Look at the pictures again. What signs in the pictures are about society?
6. Some of the above tasks can be open class discussion, or you may prefer it to be done in small groups. Divide the class into small groups now, if you have not already done so. Ask each group to think about how the story of this page could be told by a different person with a different point of view. Encourage them to give the person a name and explain their reasons for thinking the way they do. Each group writes a short script of what their person says. Then each group presents their script to the class, with one person in the group briefly explaining who the person is, another setting the

scene, another presenting the script, and another describing how point of view changes how you see things.

7. Give the class time to reflect and to take some notes.
(This type of exercise can be adapted using many books.)

Teachers' reading

Highways to a War by Christopher Koch is an Australian story, rich in description and perspectives, about a news photographer in Vietnam.

SUMMARY

1 Critical literacy is reading with a knowledge of language and how it works.

2 Critical literacy is reading with an awareness of where the text positions a reader.

3 Critical literacy is reading with a perception of the ideas and values and attitudes that constitute the implicit framework of the text and out of which texts are generated.

4 Critical literacy is a necessary life-skill.

5 Critical literacy includes visual literacy and cultural literacy.

6 Visual literacy is reading and understanding the signs of an increasingly visual society. (For more on visual literacy, see Chapter 24.)

7 Exploring and discussing how texts work help us to enhance all literacy skills, particularly critical literacy.

8 Texts consist of story (what happens) and discourse (the telling of the story).

9 Understory is a helpful term for the deep layers of theme and significance in texts. It includes the resources out of which textual and intertextual connections (see Chapter 20, page 357) are made and which help to give cohesion.

10 Cultural ideas, assumptions, and attitudes are a part of understory; awareness, knowledge, and understanding of these ideas, assumptions, and attitudes represent the development of critical literacy.

Chapter 19
Children's Literature, Technology, and the New Literacies

Focus

This chapter focuses on the impact of technology on literature and on the development of the new literacies. It notes how technology has changed literacy habits and has extended traditional notions of literacy. It stresses the significance of the literacy of the imagination as the core of all literacies, and the significance of literature in imaginative growth.

Books first appeared as clay tablets in about 2500 BC (Kilgour 1998). Although there were some huge tablets (6 square metres) for important reference 'books' such as the Middle Assyrian Code of Laws, most early Mesopotamian tablets were usually approximately 7.6 centimetres square (sometimes oblong) pads of clay that fitted comfortably in the hand. 'A book consisted of several such tablets, kept perhaps in a leather pouch or box, so that a reader could pick up tablet after tablet in a predetermined order' (Manguel 1997: 125).

Then, about 500 years later, came the new technology of the papyrus scroll. The look changed and the book was to remain in this form for over 2000 years.

In AD 150 another new technology changed the look of the book. The codex—a sheaf of bound papers—was unsuitable for the old materials of clay and papyrus and so the new materials of parchment and vellum took over. Because it was convenient, this parchment codex became the common form of the book. It also changed the organisation of texts.

The scroll had possessed a limited surface—and, as Manguel notes, we are aware of this today, '*having returned to this ancient book-form on our computer screens, which reveal only a portion of text at a time as we 'scroll' upwards or downwards*'. On the other hand, the codex allowed the reader to flip to other pages, and 'thereby retain *the sense of the whole*—a sense compounded by the fact that the entire text was usually held in the reader's hands throughout the reading' (Manguel 1997: 126–7; my emphasis).

The appearance of paper in Europe (during the Crusades) and the invention of the printing press in the middle of the 15th century, revolutionised the crafting of books and made them increasingly accessible in the form that we know them today.

Many believe that the book is destined to disappear. In a paper entitled 'Electronic Text: Literacy medium of the future', Anderson-Inman notes the following seven advantages of digitised text:

- it is modifiable (easily edited, updated, and altered by both author and user)
- is programmable (adaptable to needs of individual user)
- it is linkable (user can set up non-linear links)
- it is searchable (by word or phrase)
- it is collapsible (can be hidden from view)
- it is collaborative (multiple users can work at different workstations from the same text at the same time) (1998: 678–82).

Those who believe that the book will survive, perhaps in new forms, could well argue that the present format of books presents similar options: books come out in new editions, they can be turned into film, they can be marked and adapted, they give references, they have indexes and glossaries, text can easily be hidden from view, and multiple copies of books mean that multiple users can work at different workstations from the same text at the same time.

These ideas present a basis for discussion and for the following exercise for students.

Task 6

Discussion

This is an exercise in reading an example of the literature (that is, the academic research and discussion) about children's literature. Reading such literature is a way of consciously keeping aware of current ideas and practices. Teachers in training will want to develop their own literacy skills in reading journal articles, as many of them contain research discussions that can inform teaching practice. Reading academic literature also enhances our practice as educators by exposing us to ideas that may be beyond our immediate reach, but that, with effort, become accessible and often exciting.

The following paper, 'The Literacy of the Imagination' (Johnston 2000), was published in the journal *Bookbind*. It sums up many of the ideas about children's literature discussed in this book. It also discusses the influences of technology and contemporary ideas about multiple literacies.

Critically read this paper.

· List and describe in one or two sentences the new literacies mentioned here. Add any others you consider appropriate.

· Briefly note the main thought of each paragraph.

· What are the three main arguments?

· Write an abstract (no more than 250 words) describing this paper.
· Write a considered response, describing your own position. Engage with the arguments of this paper. (1000 words)

The Literacy of the Imagination

'Literacy', writes Margaret Meek, 'has two beginnings: one, in the world, the other, in each person who learns to read and write' (1991: 13).

Literacy—reading and writing—is important because we are social beings in a world of others. That this is also a world of ever-increasing technologies complicates conceptions of literacy and demands of us a rethinking of the links between literacy and literature. Is the world of children's books soon to become obsolete?

The 'world' at the beginning of the new millennium is an interesting place. The 20th century began in an explosion of modernism—jarring, confrontational, exciting. It ends in a melt of postmodernism—in the collapse of canons, traditions, orders, universals, 'truths', and 'meanings'. Postmodernism has cleaned out the cupboards of the centuries, but it has left us strangely empty and vulnerable. Its essentially self-reflexive nature has helped to create the 20th-century construct of an individual-centred universe. However, in opposition to this and irrespective of the individual, technology continues inexorably to reshape the topography of the universe, both reskilling and deskilling its inhabitants.

Literacy is a plurality of complex skills. As Meek's comments imply, prescriptive language symbols are processed not only communally by sociohistorical consensus but also privately by the individual. Words on the page both hark back to the old and push towards the new. Bakhtin refers to the concept of *napravlennost*, the impulse that 'reaches out beyond' what he calls the 'naked corpse of the word' (1981: 292). When Max leaves the wild things and comes back 'into the night of his very own room where he found his supper waiting for him' (Sendak 1992), 'supper' and 'very own room' connote much more than a meal or a place of habitation, but just what precisely they connote will depend to some degree on the individual reader. Similarly, when Alice and her father 'had another cookie' at the end of Nodelman's picturebook *Alice Falls Apart* (1996), they are doing more than assuaging hunger; the impulses that reach out beyond these words are also likely to be recognised differently by different readers. Literacy is of the world, and it is also of us, of the individual worlds that each of us inhabits.

Traditional concepts of literacy are expanded in this age of *new* and *multiple* literacies. Such literacies include obvious technological literacies—for example, being *computer-literate*, reading and writing with

CD-ROM and desktop publishers, using faxes and email and the Internet as part of literate, communicative, goal-seeking activity. There are new 'languages'—words that have moved out of 'jargon' into popular arenas (often because of *media literacy*), and new understandings of culture and of how culture defines social practice (*cultural literacy*). In a more complex way, and directly related to postmodernism, educators are challenged by provocative and eclectic understandings of what literacy is and of what it should be—to an Aboriginal or migrant child, for example, and how much, or how little, such children should be pressured to conform to traditional notions of literacy standards.

It is important to note that although understandings of what literacy is may have altered the way its *practices*, especially its educational practices, are being constructed, its *processes*, challenged as they may be, remain at the heart of these other literacies. The new literacies of course have their genesis in the old literacy and they depend on it for making meaning. Understandings of what a second language is, or responses to an indigenous appropriation of a colonial language, must connect at some point with notions of the process of literacy as learning to read and write. The simplicity (and the complexity) of this 'essence' of literacy must not be overlooked (or downgraded) amid fashionable ideological perceptions of literacy as a socially constructed tool that sets in place societal agendas. The discussion of such perceptions, however, encourages enhanced educational practices, and is the foundation of *critical literacy*—of being what I have elsewhere called 'knowing readers', readers who perceive the implicit and explicit ideas, values, and attitudes that constitute the architecture of words and out of which texts are constructed.

Technology has changed our literacy habits. The Internet and the ready communication of emails and faxes have resurrected communicative writing practices as part of everyday life—creating their own discourses and giving contemporary shape to the quick note, the postcard, and the Victorian letter. I write to more people as part of my everyday activity than I have done for years. Education packages such as TOPCLASS structure synchronous and asynchronous 'chat-times' within their programs; these are currently *written* chat that is interactive and contextualised. They provide great opportunities for teachers to encourage reading and writing in new ways and in meaningful contexts.

The new literacies, however, not only involve new skills, defined by social experience, but also involve new, metaphorical ways of reading the world. Thus *visual literacy* becomes more than the critical ability to read signs and images and pictures; it also becomes part of the ability to map subjects and objects, and centres and margins, as part of the process of recognising the ideologies of perspectives, focalisation, shape, and form. It lends itself to allegories of cognitive mapping and to different modalities, such as positionality and movement. Part of the vocabulary of the new literacies has been conceived at least initially out of metaphor, out of a way of thinking that imaginatively links aspects of dissimilars because of one process or one quality which they share and at which point they connect (*rapport*). I am writing this chapter using a *mouse*—although I hope that the computer I am using is free of *bugs*.

Metaphor (and metonymy) are inherently imaginative processes. As Ricoeur and Proust have noted, metaphor both specifies and liberates (Ricoeur 1985: 198); it hones in on and pins down a specific innovative meaningfulness even as it sets previous meanings free. Reading itself is an imaginative process—linking signifiers to signifieds, decoding, analysing, making meaning, enjoying vicarious experiences through black marks on a page.

signified

signifier

Source: Applegate and Huxley (2000), *Rain Dance*

Ferdinand de Saussure (1857–1913) introduced the terms 'signifier' and 'signified' into linguistics.

Signifier: the word (speech sounds or written marks) used to describe the thing, e.g. 'dog', '*chien*'.

Signified: the concept of the actual thing being described, e.g. the four-legged animal that barks.

Saussure believed that language is a system of signs, and that each sign is composed of these two parts. The relationship between the two parts is arbitrary, as the fact that different languages have different signifiers for the same signifieds indicates. Saussure's ideas emphasise the autonomy of language.

It is the *literacy of the imagination* that lies at the heart of the process and practice of literacy in all its forms—reading, writing, speaking, listening. The essence of imagination is the ability to visualise, to make pictures in the mind. The word 'imagine' derives from the Old French '*imaginer*', to make images, which in turn comes from the Latin '*imaginari*' meaning 'to picture to oneself'. Picturing to oneself not only stretches the muscles of the mind, it is also the imaginative process through which we understand otherness, the coherence of the other; as Peter Dickinson points out, it is imagination that is the core of our humanity: 'All morality, all that is in us that we regard as good and worthwhile, from the highest religious impulse to the smile at a child skipping across a bit of wasteland, derives from the imagination' (1986: 45).

Dickinson defines imagination as 'the leap of the mind that places one perception alongside another and sees that somehow they fit … the sudden flash of thought … the imaginative leap' (1986: 43, 51). He notes that this leap of the mind not only enables us to recognise the validity of otherness, but also can take us, for a moment at least, into that other's place. Of course, as Bakhtin states, 'aesthetic activity proper actually begins at the point when we return into ourselves and to our place outside the other person' (1986: xiii).

This pattern—away from the safety of home, into the wild place (the place of the 'other') then back home with fresh and enlarged world-understandings and maturity—represents what has been a fundamental narrative pattern in children's literature, although, as Nikolajeva (1996b) and others have pointed out, the pattern no longer necessarily includes the resolution associated with a closed ending. It is important to note, however, that both happy endings and closed endings have been imposed by Western ideas; the fact that children's literature texts are no longer bound by such expectations reflects what Sell (1996) refers to as 'cultural mediation'. Nonetheless, they do offer endless opportunities for the imaginative leap that promotes enhanced understandings of human behaviour and of the human condition.

Heidegger expresses a similar idea in his concept of 'the leap of thought' that encapsulates the search for knowledge and truth. (This relates to the 'leap of faith' of religious philosophers such as Kierkegaard.)

Children's literature opens up infinite possibilities for the leap of the question 'why?' and for that further imaginative leap that is in part its answer. Literature does not just expose, in context, the graphophonic, semantic, syntactical, and orthographic relationships in which language operates, the theoretical and practical knowledge of which gives a child what we call literacy. It does not just demonstrate to young people how language works, how it can be used to set up reader positions, how it can denote and connote otherness, how it reflects and transmits ideologies, and how it attributes power. Literature, in giving us 'images to think with' (Chambers 1985: 3) and in allowing us to 'converse with more voices than we hear from the speakers around us' (Wallace 1988: 143), nurtures and is nurtured by imagination. Concepts of rightness and wrongness are always going to be socially constructed, but literature offers possibilities and options to enter into imaginative dialogues that test these notions and experiment with them. It offers endless opportunities to take that imaginative leap into a knowledge, however fleeting, of the validity of otherness; this knowledge activates moral positioning—concepts of rightness and wrongness that represent an immanent response to shared humanity.

Television, video games, and the Internet can complement and supplement imaginative processes, but they don't of themselves provide sufficient opportunities for personal input, for interior programming, for the development of that ability of 'picturing to oneself'. And we need to explore other possibilities for the type of narratives they tell and the characters they create. We can play with the Internet and become completely engrossed in it, but whether or not we are being imaginatively creative or passively receptive is problematical. We can't play with television or film—although we may be able to retell their stories and play with the commercial products that emerge out of their ideological narratives (Luke 1996: 179). There is a physical permanence and convenience about books that should not be discounted. Media texts are fleeting, even with instant rewind and replay; despite all their technology, they are more limiting about where they can be accessed.

Television and video games present children with a world of images that are ready-made. I have written earlier (Johnston 1995: 8) that programs such as *Sesame Street* fire images like bullets with the overt aim of teaching children to know their alphabet and to 'read', that is, to become literate. It all happens so quickly that children have little opportunity to visualise or to put into place their own internal pictures or images of narrative, of character, of place. The barrage of visual images to which children are subjected don't so much preclude them from that experience of picturing to oneself as make such an effort unnecessary. Why should they bother? The pictures are already there for them, with sophisticated special effects and amazing stunts that ironically, in being 'beyond imagination', cramp and inhibit the imaginative potential and capacity for the imaginative *doingness* of the child.

This is not to criticise *Sesame Street*, but it makes a convenient and valid example. Children who watch television a lot and read only a little (if at all) don't have much practice in picturing to themselves. They don't have much practice in transcribing text into their own interior images. Media texts construct a reality that the child imaginatively engages with, but not at the deepest level of making mind-pictures; moreover, these texts also construct a version of reality that children may not question. Children's images of Cinderella and Snow White and Pocahontas are now not drawn by their own imagination, or even by the illustrators of a number of books; a common picture for all has been drawn and imposed by Disney.

The immediacy of moving text has certainly expanded worldview and given children a visual topography that makes the world appear more accessible. But while television and video games teach and entertain, they do not sufficiently challenge active imaginative input. It can be argued that their extravaganza of images stimulates the imagination. It can also be argued that there is a strong imaginary component in video games. In answer to the first argument, I agree that images are *stimulated*, but they are not *created*. I drove home from the latest James Bond movie acutely conscious of a mental traffic jam of images of fast-moving cars that were not my own. In answer to the second argument, video games present their own images; imagination is required only to pretend they are real. It is my observation that video games are not so much played to imagine as for the fun of the game itself.

Books do things that the other texts can't, at the moment anyway, and it is the responsibility of educators to continue as their advocates while at the same time taking our own leap of faith into the new technological literacies. Peter Hollindale has noted that in an age of multiple literacies, literature has become 'something that you do things with … You reply to it, you rewrite it, you convert it for yourself into a message for another medium' (1995: 251). In other words, the new technologies take books into new areas.

In human terms, it is the imagination that makes connections between memory and experience, between present and future, and between past and future. Imagination is not just a learned response, like the salivation of Pavlov's dogs, although such learned responses may be a part of it. Imagination can rewrite memory, can construct patterns. Imagination is a sort of super hypertext. Memory may access particular moments, but it is imagination that sets up linkages, that overlays an individual experience or event with metaphor and significance. As in the act of reading, the experience of one moment thus accesses a hundred moments that have gone before, and anticipates a hundred others that are yet to come. The child goes to bed on Christmas Eve stirred by the experiences of other Christmas Eves and by the anticipation of the morning. The experience of the moment is given added lustre, perspective, and texture: 'This ideal morning filled my mind full of a permanent reality, identical with all similar mornings, and infected me with … cheerfulness', writes Genette (1980).

The notion of imaginative passivity versus imaginative activity is significant. Consider these opening lines of *The Violin Maker's Gift* by

Donn Kushner, a book that won the CLA Book of the Year for Children (1980).

> *Babette, the toll-keeper's wife, paced the corners of her look-out*
> *tower, scanning the forest below with a long brass telescope.*
> *   'Matthias!' she cried. 'The warriors are coming!'*
> *   No answer came.*
> *   Babette gasped and thrust the glass to her eye again. Past a steep*
> *ravine, on the hillside where a road just showed itself now and again*
> *between low, twisted pines, a curious object appeared ...*

The eye reads the signs, the brain decodes into words, the words release a tumble of the mysterious imaginative processes that create an interior picture of *mindscape*, not just *landscape*. If this were a film, the image would be there for the taking, in Technicolor; Babette would have a face, the tower a particular architecture, the forest a particular shape and form, and while the imagination may have been stimulated, it would not have been involved in its core business of 'making pictures for oneself'.

Paradoxically, picturebooks are particularly significant in this discussion. Although they present images, the images are discontinuous, moments of *thisness* (see Johnston 1998a). The narrative agendas of picturebooks are not set wholly within the verbal text nor wholly within the visual text: narrative thrust occurs in the unique spaces across, between, and beyond both. Film presents a synchronised 'reality' where image matches sound; in picturebooks the matches (and mismatches) of visual and verbal text have to be made by the reader. Picturebook images may have all the impact of a stage set, but they also allow literature's privileged access to the interior worlds of the characters. Further, picturebooks anticipate and extend worldview, promote intellectual activity rather than passive viewing, and stimulate the creative pulling together of links as an act of making meaning. They leave gaps for readers to fill in their own images, to read and write their own story. These gaps breed literate behaviour and grow the imagination. .

A picturebook is a mini-world. Picturebooks uniquely accommodate the child's viewing eye and demonstrate to it a range of autonomous worldviews. This helps to grow cultural schemata and knowledge of the 'real world'. Literacy is a social activity, and reading worlds are socially constructed. As Freire (1987) writes: 'Reading the world precedes reading the word, and the subsequent reading of the word cannot dispense with continually reading the world'. Conceptualising Bakhtin's 'impulse that reaches out beyond' (which encompasses ideas of what he calls social dialects, world views, and individual artistic works) helps to define the delicate relationships and balances of these three interrelated notions: the significance of reader response, the significance of the literary decisions of the author (including how the text is crafted), and the significance of social world, both of author and reader. Janet and Allan Ahlberg's books for small children are successful not only because of the way they are crafted (text and illustrations) but also because of the way they cleverly represent anticipation and extension of *knowledge of the world* and, most significantly, *overtly focus on the child's worldview*. It is the child's viewing eye reading an expanding world that is at the centre of both *Each Peach Pear Plum* (1978) and *Peepo* (1981). In the former it is an 'I Spy' game:

> *Each Peach Pear Plum*
> *I spy Tom Thumb*

In *Peepo* a small cutout, a porthole both limiting and focusing attention, opening up and indicating a route (resembling a portal of the new media), deliberately represents what the child views and 'reads' as world knowledge, and how worldview and knowledge expand into context on turning the page. This is a literary representation of a highly reflexive process; the act of reading expands worldview, which expands the act of reading, which expands worldview. Response depends on context, worldview, and knowledge: the adult reader, seeing beyond the text, may glimpse beneath the gentle illustrations of this book a rich understory of war, of impending departure and the possibility of loss and grief, similar to that expressed by the young war poet, Wilfred Owen:

> *What candles may be held to speed them all?*
> *Not in the hands of boys, but in their eyes*
> *Shall shine the holy glimmers of goodbyes.*

All texts, including those of the media, reflect social practice and cultural assumptions; the Internet is arguably Western and non-negotiable in its implicit and explicit cultural orientation. On the other hand, children's literature theorists describe texts as 'sites of multiple meaning', places where, in the words of Bull, 'contesting literacies and literatures exist' (1995: 267). Such culturally 'contesting' conventions—of story, narrative structure, narrative time, and narrative place—promote imaginative and intellectual activity. Exposure to a rich landscape of sites of multiple meaning encourages a literate imagination to raise the threshold of tolerance and receptivity to difference. Books 'multiply possible worlds and in so doing enlarge private worlds' (Kushner 1996: 1). In the terms of the new literacies, they combine the best of RAM and the best of ROM into an interior and intensely private program that randomly accesses memory and transforms 'read only' memory into imaginative understandings that can be recalled, that can be saved, but that can endlessly be rewritten into layers and layers of new significances and meanings.

So, while we should not overstate the case, we must not downplay it. Children's literature has a unique role in encouraging imaginative literacy, not least because it is likely to be the first sustained art-form that children will encounter (television is not a sustained art-form, although film is). Waugh has written that the aesthetic is the 'only space of individual freedom' (1997: 22). Space, verbal and visual, gives shape to picture books. In fact their use of spaces, real and symbolic, could lead children's literature beyond postmodernism into hyperspace, new mindscapes, mini-worlds of infinite space. Technology has helped us to contemplate the infinite and to consider such things as virtual reality and virtual space. The illustrations of Gary Crew and Shaun Tan's recent picturebook, *Memorial* (1999), are a wonderful example—this book about three generations of an Australian family and their experiences at war constitutes cultural and personal spaces of remembering and forgetting, of past and present, of history and geography. While interrogating contemporary society, it leaves spaces (gaps) for different readings, it speaks in many voices (**heteroglossia**), it evokes the imagination and provokes the imaginative leap, it is intertextual (related to other spaces) and dialogic.

Meek (1991: 182) writes that literature 'is its own kind of deep play'. It is this deep play that both emerges from and grows the literacy of the imagination. In turn, imaginative literacy fosters the practices and processes of other literacies and nurtures understandings of the other. It also reinterprets postmodernism into creative spaces. Far from becoming obsolete, children's literature may play a vital social role in reconceptualising postmodern voids into a new and dynamic spatialism—liberating, inspiring, and vigorous.

SUMMARY

1   The history of the book demonstrates the changes in its shape and form that have taken place over the centuries.
2   It is possible that the book may again change form (even radically), but it will survive.
3   In an age of new technologies, literacy has become a plurality of complex skills.
4   Visual literacy is more than the critical ability to read signs and images. It is also part of the ability to map subjects and objects, centres and margins, as part of the process of recognising the ideologies of perspectives, focalisations, shape, and form. (See also p. 406.)
5   In an age of multiple literacies, literature becomes something that you 'do things with'.
6   Imagination and the imaginative process lie at the heart of the practice and process of literacy in all its forms.

Chapter 20
Theory Informing Practice

> **Focus**
> This chapter seeks to demonstrate the relevance of theory to teaching practice. It notes that theory can be used as conceptual base, as creative idea, and as teaching structure, and that the traditional tensions between theorists and practitioners can be productive and stimulating. It introduces the theoretical concepts of *life-world*, the *everyday*, books as *comprehensive grasps of the world*, *the chronotope*, *place* and *subjective space*, *the implied reader*, *subjectivity*, *focalisation* and *agency*, and *intertextuality*. It also builds on the idea of teaching as a 'courteous translation'.

Tensions—a vital sign

Children's literature has been and still is to a degree fraught with tensions between, on the one side, the academics, who concentrate on theory and complex textual analysis, and on the other side, the practitioners in the field—teachers, other educators, librarians, writers, and illustrators—who have a more practical focus.

The truth is that, like most tensions, this is a very healthy one. Too much pull in any one direction will result in collapse and slackness. It has been the burgeoning of children's literature criticism and the development of a *children's literature poetics* (a formal and systematic literary study of its nature, form, and aesthetics) that have led to the growing status of children's literature as a subject of rigorous study in tertiary institutions. This would not have happened were it not for the contributions of such theorists as Perry Nodelman in Canada, John Stephens in Australia, Jean Perrot in France, Jack Zipes in the United States, Maria Nikolajeva in Sweden, and Peter Hollindale, Peter Hunt, Aidan Chambers, and Margaret Meek in the United Kingdom. It is the richness and complexity of their writing that has both staked a place for the study of children's literature within the academy, and provided the tool for that study. Other writers in the field, who tend to concentrate on the broad overview and on practical applications rather than on the specialised intensive theoretical study of particular texts, are enlarged by the presence of the theorists; the theorists are kept in line by the practitioners. Each can help, to paraphrase a now infamous political statement, to keep the other side 'honest'.

An Australian political leader of a minority party once said that the aim of the party was to 'keep the bastards [of the major parties] honest'.

Theory as template

A template is 'a pattern, gauge, or mould of a thin piece of wood or metal, used in shaping a piece of work'. Figuratively, it can mean 'any model on which something is formed or based'. It has more technical applications: 'a horizontal piece under a girder, beam, or any other long supporting piece to distribute downward thrust', 'a piece for supporting joists or rafters, as over a doorway or window', 'a wedge supporting the keel of a ship under construction' (*World Book Dictionary*).

All of these definitions are significant when we consider theory—both critical theory (i.e. theory about the narrative, shape, and expression of literary ideas) and pedagogical theory (i.e. theory about the actual practice of teaching).

Theory is often considered as abstract, remote from the real world, but the reality is that everything that we do is based on some sort of theory. Nowhere is this more true than when we are operating in a relationship of *teacher* with others who are *learners*.

Using theory to develop 'courteous translations'

The expression 'template' is used here in its fullest sense, and certainly not in a narrow sense of uniformity or conformity. Teaching is a dynamic activity that is characterised by and stimulated by the individuality of both teachers and students. But we have much to learn from those who have gone before, and from those who have sought to discover more about *what* is taught and *how* and *why* it is taught.

Theory, both literary and pedagogical, gives a pattern on which we can shape our teaching; it can provide useful models; it can help us distribute 'downward thrust'—that is, to prepare and teach something in such a way that it becomes do-able, not too heavy for the growing learner to bear.

This is another way of thinking about Bruner's concept of the 'courteous translation'—presenting complex ideas (because they push us into thinking more deeply) but translating them with thoughtfulness and consideration. If we think of this definition in relation to the shipbuilding industry, the template of theory can help to support the whole growing construction of a classroom of learners.

The concept of 'life-world'

Philosophers talk about the idea of 'life-world'—the world in which we see ourselves as living. Life-world is fluid, changing; it is what we perceive. The life-world of children, and adults as well, is in a continuous state of what Montaigne called *becoming*. It is never complete; it is always growing, shifting, transforming.

Jürgen Habermas, a European philosopher, argues that life-world is 'the horizon-forming context of processes of reaching understanding' (1981: 135). This is an important idea for teachers—what are the contextual horizons of the children in our classrooms? Come to that, what are our own horizons (background knowledges against which we come to understandings of the world; the boundaries within which we think)?

Our task as teachers is to push out horizons, to push out boundaries, to open up possibilities of new facets and new dimensions in the child's process of becoming. Books provide wonderful resources for doing this.

Consider the picturebook *Henry's Bed*, by Margaret Perversi and Ron Brooks (1997). Understandings are enhanced when we think about this text in the light of the theory of 'life-world' as a state of *becomingness*, and as an 'horizon-forming context'.

They are also enhanced if we consider this book in relation to the ideas of the Russian theorist Vygotsky, who believed that

- all learning is dialogic, like a conversation;
- there is 'social speech' (speaking with others) and 'inner speech' (speaking within self)
- there is 'talk-thinking' (talking what you think to others) and 'thought-thinking' (talking within self).

> **Lev Semionovich Vygotsky** (1896–1934) was a Russian psychologist who was interested in the symbolic processes of language.

Henry's Bed tells the story of a little boy called Henry who is or has been (depending on your reading) scared to go to bed alone. Those words, however, are never actually said; readers pick them up in the interaction between words and pictures and in the way that interaction implies inner and outer voices, talk-thinking and thought-thinking.

> *Henry is going to sleep in his own bed tonight.*
> *Oh yes!*

Whose voice is this? It could be the parent's voice, or the parents' voices. It could be the narrator's voice. It could be two voices, a speaker and a respondent ('Oh yes!')—parent and parent, or parent and Henry, or narrator and parent, or Henry and parent. Or, as one of my students said, it could be Henry's voice, claiming growth and independence. And it could be, as another student said, a deeply ironic conversation.

Whoever's voice it is, it is clear that underneath the speaking (or behind it or above it) runs a whole dialogue of other voices and preceding conversations: the conversation recorded in this text has happened before. Reading between the lines, listening to the talk-thinking and the thought-thinking, helps us to hear the 'inner speech' of both Henry and his parents.

So, even by just touching on the ideas of Vygotsky, and remembering Bakhtin's ideas about voices behind words (Chapter 16, page 292), we suddenly have a new way of seeing this book and a new way of talking about it. And that gives an added dimension to our teaching (and to our own reading). Not that we are going to teach children about Vygotsky, any more than we teach them about Piaget. But we can use these enhanced theoretical understandings of teaching and language to inform what we actually do in the classroom, in our daily practices. And we use them because as teachers we want to push out horizons, to extend the limits and limitations of 'life-world', to open up new ideas and new imaginings.

Children's literature theory helps us to teach children literature, and promotes creative ways of encouraging children into literate practices. Knowing more about golf and how the various types of clubs work helps a player choose the best club to play the stroke. Fans who follow the lives of movie stars or are interested in the art of the cinema appreciate films more because of what they know goes on behind the scenes. *Tea with Mussolini* has an added texture when we know that it is based on the story of the director's life.

Building up knowledge of theory helps us as teachers to perceive more about children's books and therefore enriches our teaching. It pushes and provokes us to find and describe seams and layers of meaning that enlarge our own thinking.

This is important because the best children's books have many layers. In *Henry's Bed*, for example, there is
- a layer of simple narrative (telling the story)
- a layer of parent frustration (the story behind the monologue or dialogue)
- a layer of childhood fears (implicit as what Vygotsky calls 'inner speech')
- a layer of independence and growth.

When the layers are pulled back further we find a rich seam expressing the human fear of change and loneliness; peel them back again, and there, beneath everything, is a gentle context that helps to put it all into perspective—the world of nature where everyone has a special place. We could even peel it back again and find a deep layer representing the cycle of life—day following night, season following season, even arguably death following birth.

So, in the simple narrative of this picturebook, *Henry's Bed*, we can recognise:

> Dialogic conversation: Narrating voice
>   Responding voices
>   Implicit voices
>   Inner voices

Task 7 Integration of theory and practice

Theory is about understanding— it 'stands under' what we do. It gives us the language and understanding to explain what is happening in texts and gives us the tools and understanding to teach critical literacy.

Considering Vygotsky's ideas about texts, construct the boxes of dialogue in *Henry's Bed*, addressing the following questions. You may like to use Chambers' 'Tell Me' approach (page 295).
· What voices are heard in this text?
· How do you know? Or, why do you think so?
· What do you hear the inner voice of Henry saying?
· What do you hear the inner voice of the narrator saying?

Activity 9

Years K–2

Pretend to be Henry. Tell me: what is he saying and doing?

Years 3–4

1. Whose voices do you hear in this book? Is it one voice or many?
2. Write a short play using the voices of Henry and his parent about what happens at Henry's bedtime. Act out the play with your partner.

Years 5–6

1. In two columns, write down the monologue or dialogue of the text. Why do you think the author has not included inverted commas?
2. What are some of the ways in which we can make sense of this text? With your partner, read it in as many different ways as you can.

Teachers' reading

Teachers will enjoy listening for the different voices in *Snow Falling on Cedars* by David Guterson, and *Beloved* by Toni Morrison.

Children's literature texts open up and reveal mini-worlds, microcosms of larger cultures glimpsed around the edges. These worlds are a part of the fictive life-world of the fictive child, but they can also become a part of the 'life-world' of the child reader. Children's literature, then, is not only part of life-world but can help constitute it.

Children's books covertly and overtly, implicitly and explicitly, reflect a great deal about the world in which they are written. They are responded to out of the world in which they are read. In reading, children bring with them a parcel of ideas and realities and responses that constitute their own life-world. They encounter in the text

*   the fictive world of the text (the world of the book);
*   the fictive world that the text 'projects beyond itself' (Ricoeur 1985: 100) and allows readers to glimpse on the horizon of the text: the world implied beyond the text;
*   the world of the author (customs, values and attitudes, ideologies and agendas, beliefs and disbeliefs, innocences, and knowledges);
*   their own life-world as it intersects in whatever way (e.g. identification, resistance, rejection) with the text.

Task 8

Read ***Where's Mum?*** by Libby Gleeson and Craig Smith (1992).

*   What is the fictive world of the text?
*   What is the fictive world the text projects beyond itself?
*   What can you guess about the world of the author?

· What can you guess about the world of the illustrator?
(Note that your guesses may or may not be correct.)

Note that fictive life-world will always be culturally encoded, and will similarly be decoded according to sociocultural context. A telling example of this is again *Robinson Crusoe* (see also Chapter 18). When Defoe wrote this text in 1719, it reflected, implicitly and explicitly, the ideas of his life-world. It was a time of Empire, of colonisation, of the desire to 'civilise' native peoples. When Crusoe names the native who has saved his life according to the day on which he found him, and teaches him 'to say Master, and then let him know that was to be my name', he is expressing the ideals and cultural assumptions of his time. When we read these words today, however, we read them within the cultural values of our own life world, and they jar us with their autocratic imperialism.

The Wind in the Willows is another example. It has been criticised for its treatment of women, although I don't completely agree with this criticism: the women who are there have quite a deal of agency. More interesting is the uprising in the last chapters against Toad of Toad Hall. Again, when this was written in 1908 it reflected the social attitudes of its time. When we read it today, from the point of view of our own social attitudes, we are aware of feeling that Toad was a pretty awful landlord, that Badger was very class-conscious, and that the stoats and the weasels had a strong case.

Depiction of the everyday

Because children's books represent children's life-worlds, which tend to be everyday worlds, they reveal a great deal more about that world than perhaps the writer or illustrator intended. Reading a picturebook text, we *see* a host of background material without really *noticing* it. Illustrators include clothes, furnishings, food on the table, kitchens, bedclothes, gardens, transport, school rooms, shops, houses, streets, transport, suburbs, and cities. They also include depictions of how children and adults relate to each other, how children and teachers relate, what happens at breakfast times and what happens in school rooms. Kate Walker and David Cox in **Our Excursion** (1994) reveal as much about everyday life in an Australian city of the 1990s as they do about what happens on a school excursion (despite the fact that both depictions are of course stylised, exaggerated, and represented humorously).

It is obvious that the experiences and the purposes of author and illustrator will inevitably influence their depiction of what this everyday world looks like. But literature in general and picturebooks in particular (because of the amount of visual detail used to depict these 'seen but unnoticed' aspects of everyday life) may unwittingly disclose more deeply rooted societal ideologies, attitudes, and cultural assumptions.

Edward's First Day at School by Rosemary Wells (1996) is a late 20th-century moral tale. Both text and illustrations overtly depict an everyday world where fathers and mothers play an equal role in caring for children (the father dresses Edward, the mother feeds him his porridge, 'together they put him in the car'); where parents are supportive (both parents at school having discussions with the teacher); where children are allowed to be different ('not everyone is ready …'), and where teachers are wise.

More covertly, however, it encodes an ideological shift in societal notions of power. The 20th-century construct of the individual-centred universe is at the heart of this text. There are only two double-page illustrations: the first is of Edward being driven by his parents to playschool and the second is of him being driven away from it. The first shows the car against an unpeopled backdrop of houses, and only the top half of Edward's face. The second shows the car decisively turned away from the group at the school gate and pointing in the opposite direction. The car here is more whole and therefore stronger—it is drawn three-quarters on rather than side on (as in the earlier picture). In the *thisness* of this moment, Edward is also more whole, his eyes are less apprehensive, and we see part of his mouth, which looks satisfied if not triumphant. The thrust of this second picture is a celebratory *going away from* the cluster at the gate that represents society. The individual, who doesn't 'want' to paint, or slide, or conform, withdraws from the 'everybody' who cheerfully support his right to do so (Johnston 1998a).

Children's books as 'comprehensive grasps' of the world

The French philosopher Merleau-Ponty, in discussing what it is to *be*, uses the phrase 'the world contracted into a comprehensive grasp' (1986: 408). Each child's book does just that—it contracts 'world' (the large macrocosm) into part of every-day 'life-world' (microcosm). Books fit world, or versions of it, to a child's grasp.

This is not to say that all books are of the everyday—they are not. Many are fantasy. Part of the charm of children's literature, however, is how fantasy accompanies the everyday. Fantastic imaginary worlds can help to shape and make sense of the 'real' and become part of the contraction into a comprehensive grasp, as in Sendak's **Outside Over There** (1981), and there are many books that remind us that the world of fantasy is concomitant to the everyday world anyway; **Where the Wild Things Are** (1963), **Drac and the Gremlin** (Baillie and Tanner 1988), and **Come Away from the Water, Shirley** (Burningham 1977) are obvious examples.

Activity 10

Years K–2

1. Read *Come Away from the Water Shirley* to the class. Perhaps you could set the scene by having a beach ball and a picture of a pirate ship. Ask the children how these two things could be connected.
2. Bring the children up close so they can see the pictures. Don't talk about the pictures until after you have read the book.

3. Discuss with the class what the pictures represent. Are they a different world? Or are they pictures in Shirley's mind?
4. Ensure that children understand the unique capacity humans have for imagining.

Years 3–4

Add the following, as appropriate:
1. What are the points of connection between the two worlds? In groups, make a list of these connectors.
2. Discuss: how do the worlds affect each other? Do they change anything? If so, how? Write a story about a time when you imagined something different from what was actually happening.

Years 5–6

Choose as much as you would like to do from the above, but add:
1. In roundtable groups, write a script for what happens in the pictures.
2. Devise creative ways of acting out the two worlds of story. Children may choose to do parallel stories, or consecutive stories. They may want to run the stories together as one.
3. Groups present their play to the class.
4. Discuss the way in which imagination can be used to transform situations.

Teachers' reading

Girls in your classes may enjoy you reading L. M. Montgomery's *Anne of Green Gables* with them as an example of using imagination in everyday life. Years 1–4 (and you) will enjoy the imaginative and humorous adventure of Anne Fine's *Bill's New Frock* (1990). Other good stories include Libby Gleeson's *Eleanor, Elizabeth* (1984) and *I am Susannah* (1987) and Katherine Paterson's *Bridge to Terabithia* (1977). You may all enjoy reading the cartoon stories of *Calvin and Hobbes*.

The chronotope

Life-world doesn't just happen in a place, it happens in a particular place at a particular time. The **chronotope**, a term introduced into literature by Bakhtin (see page 292), refers to the relationship between people and events on the one hand, and time and space on the other. In Bakhtin's words, it is 'the organising centre for the fundamental narrative events of the novel' (1981: 250). The chronotope shifts critical discussion beyond traditional ideas of 'setting' and 'place' and 'location' in three main ways:
- It expands understandings of the centrality of time and place in the organisation of narrative.
- It reformulates the notion of objective *place* into subjective *space*, that is, place and time perceived, experienced, or described from a particular point of view, or from multiple points of view.

- It explicitly recognises that the representation of such perceptions, being subjective, are ideological and value-laden, reflecting personal and sociocultural ideas, attitudes, and experiences.

The chronotope is a more expansive way of describing and understanding genre and text-type, and gives a critical language to identify its features (e.g. see Nikolajeva's discussion of a fantasy chronotope [1996a: 122f.]). Some texts, like *My Place* (Wheatley and Rawlins 1988) overtly use their chronotope as a structural principle.

It is important to note that the chronotope does not necessarily present time and space in 'equal' quantities; they may be combined with many differing emphases. J. K. Rowling has chosen to organise her Harry Potter books with the *space* element (representations of suburbs, attitudes, and language of an ironically stereotypical English social class) clearly defined from the first few lines but with the *time* element vague:

> *Mr and Mrs Dursley, of number four, Privet Drive, were proud to say that they were perfectly normal, thank you very much. They were the last people you'd expect to be involved in anything strange or mysterious, because they just didn't hold with such nonsense.* (1997: 7)

Developing the concept of a *visual chronotope* expands on Bakhtin's ideas to refer to the representation of time-space in picture book illustration. It describes the visual depiction of the relationship of people and events, to time and space. This is a particularly helpful way of considering the interaction between verbal and visual text in picturebooks. Visual markers used to illustrate the relationship of people and events to time and space are easily identified and clearly reflect ideological choices and cultural attitudes. For example, a fishing basket represents the *space* of a fisherman; an empty basket may represent a specific *time* of failure, but in *The Fisherman and the Theefyspray*, as we have seen (page 322) it represents a specific *time* of success and a particular social attitude to the environment. *Verbal* chronotopes may match *visual* chronotopes and express a similar organisation of time and space in a text, but they may also be quite different, as in Burningham's *Come Away from the Water Shirley*, and Baillie and Tanner's *Drac and the Gremlin*. The last illustration of Jeannie Baker's *Where the Forest Meets the Sea* projects a visual dimension of *future* into the *present* moment of verbal text, creating a chronotopical emphasis on what a different *time* may bring to the *spaces* of a threatened environment.

Clocks represent time in a close, specific sense, and the natural cycle of the day represents time in a more general, distanced sense. We could argue that representations of time-spaces in urban life tend to be hectic and hassled (think of Gleeson and Smith's *Where's Mum?)*, whereas those of rural life tend to be rhythmic and gentle (think of Wagner and Brooks' *John Brown, Rose and the Midnight Cat*, which uses both a clock and the natural cycle of the day as time markers).

The chronotope is a particularly useful term for discussing children's literature because it emphasises the connectedness of time and place. At its simplest, place is, as Bal implies, 'location' (1985: 43). It is the 'somewhere' where events happen, the fictive physical situation in which the characters move. Place as location also implies a situatedness in time and a situatedness in a culture. Reflecting on the chronotopes—visual and verbal—opens up another way for understanding the complexity of picturebooks.

Activity 11

Years 3–4
1. Discuss the idea of time-place (a bite of place and time together).
    How many time-places can you find in *My Place?*(1988)
    How many time-places can you find in *Peepo?* (1981)
2. How is the idea of time-place used as part of story in these books? (In *My Place* it gives the frame of the story and ties in with the history of Australia. In *Peepo* it shows the cycle of the day.)

Activity 12

Years 5–6
    This activity would follow well from the previous one on the imagination.
1. Depending on and as appropriate for your class, talk about the idea of time (*when* things happen) and place (*where* they happen). Note how time and place come together as space for story.
2. Build on earlier discussions about the imagination.
3. Read *Let the Celebrations Begin*, by Margaret Wild and Julie Vivas (1991). Set it in historical context, explaining that this is a story of a particular time-place.
4. Discuss the ways in which the women and children in the concentration camp used their imaginations.
5. Do you think this book makes a very terrible time in human history too trivial? (Your class may like to know that in the United States and Europe, publishers refused to give the book its Australian title, and called it *A Time for Toys*.) Or do you think it shows something strong about the human spirit?

Teachers' reading
The Diary of Anne Frank; *Born on the Fourth of July* by Ron Kovic. The movie *Forrest Gump* plays with the ideas of time-spaces, inserting pictures of Forrest in old news footage.

An advanced class may like to extend time-place into time-space and discuss time-space in terms of being a *gift*. The women give their clothing so that the children can have toys, and the time-space for play, but they do so as a sacrifice; they have so little to give.

In a very different circumstance, but in a similar way, the mother in **Drac and the Gremlin** (Baillie and Tanner 1988) plays along with her children's game and so gives them time and space to imagine. You may like to compare this with David McKee's **Not Now Bernard** (1980).

Educators may like to introduce philosophical ideas about gifts and giving here. Jacques Derrida, a contemporary French philosopher, says that the essence of a gift is the *madness of its giving* (1991).

If you have discussed the concept of *otherness* with your class, you may also like to talk about gifts as the *affirmation of the other*. That is, gifts say how much the person we give them to is valued. You could also discuss how books such as **Guess How Much I Love You** (McBratney 1994) give other sorts of gifts.

This could be developed into a philosophical inquiry.

Place and identity

Perceptions of place also tend to function, to adapt an idea of John Shotter, as 'extensions of ourselves' (1993: 21). Shotter later points out the 'complex relation between people's identities and their "hook-up" to their surroundings' (1993: 35).

This is particularly true of the world of children and therefore particularly significant in terms of children's literature. Think of *Anne of Green Gables,* for example. Place—often a secret place, as in **The Secret Garden**, or **Bridge to Terebithia**—becomes a part of growth and psychological development. Children identify with their place—**My Place** (Wheatley and Rawlins 1987) is the most obvious of countless examples. The place may be a house, a neighbourhood, a room, a special hiding place, even a bed. **Ginger** (Voake 1997) is a story about place, and about a cat not wanting to share its place with the new kitten. **Leaves for Mr Walter** (Brian and Cox 1998) is a story about place. So is **John Brown, Rose and the Midnight Cat** (Wagner and Brooks 1977). So also is **The Fisherman and the Theefyspray** (Jennings and Tanner 1994), and **Window** (Baker 1992). **You and Me, Murrawee** (Hashmi and Marshall 1998) is a story of intersecting chronotopes—two little girls who live 200 years apart share a common space.

Place as subjective space

We have already noted that 'place' is a more concrete and passive term; 'space' is active and abstract, and opens up more readily to metaphor. Space is place perceived—made subjective, part of the inner as well as the outer world. Think about the common contemporary expression, 'having my own space'. **Do Not Go**

Around the Edges (Utemorrah and Torres 1990) is about place, but it is much more accurately described as being about space—*perceptions* of place, perceptions of belonging and belongingness. Space is a much richer term, and a much more accurate one for discussing the 'place' of children's books. It is less geographically bounded: think of the differences between *cyberplace* and *cyberspace*.

Many of the spaces in children's books are the spaces of the mind—again, think of *Come Away from the Water, Shirley* and *Drac and the Gremlin*. **The Great Bear** (Gleeson and Greder 1999) is about space—its chronotope is that of a folktale, a sort of nowhere/everywhere space, nowhere/everywhere time. In this book, space opens up into cosmic space. Yolan and Baker's **All Those Secrets of the World** (1991) thematically plays with ideas about subjective time and space, while setting the story within a clear chronotope—the United States during World War II. A recent film that (controversially) represents intensely subjective space within a horrific historical chronotope (a Jewish experience in Italy during World War II) is the 1999 Oscar winner, **Life is Beautiful**.

Activity 13

Years 3–4

1. Organise the class into small groups. Look at the first opening of **You and Me, Murrawee**.
   · *Tell me:* What can you tell about the place of the story? Each group should list its clues.
   · What can you tell about the characters in the story?
   · What do you guess about the time of the story? (Stress that right and wrong does not matter—we are still looking for clues.)
   Then:
2. Let the children get comfortable but keep them in their groups. Read them the story. If they all have a copy on their roundtables, let one person turn the pages as you read.
3. Make a list of all the things that are the same for both girls—note how many times the word 'same' is used.
4. Make a list of the things that are different.
5. Choose a scribe at each roundtable. Each group will write two or three sentences explaining the last opening. Give plenty of time for discussion.

Years 5–6

Add the following:

6. Share sentences and ideas as a class. Talk about the idea of time and space coming together. If the class level is appropriate, discuss different concepts of time—time machines, Aboriginal concepts of cyclical rather than linear time, films like *Back to the Future*. Take a few weeks to read *Playing Beatie Bow* by Ruth Park (1980), which is a mixture of historical novel and time-shift fantasy.

7. Individual writing task. Write a story about time-space. It can be science fiction, or fantasy, or realistic, or about imaginary meeting places in the mind.

Teachers' reading

An Imaginary Life by David Malouf.

Task 9

Discuss: Children's literature is of
· the now-time of the writer
· the now-time of the reader,
· the now of the time that it seeks to represent.
Look through a selection of picturebooks. Find examples where the above differ. What effect does this have?

The implied reader

In children's literature, ideas of life-world, time, and space all relate to the fact that children's books are written for children or, in Wall's (1991: 9) words, *to* children. Children's literature is not here defined in terms of its borders, or in relation to or opposition to, the corpus of 'adult' literature (see, e.g. Saxby 1997: 18–22, Stoodt et al. 1996: 4–5) because the philosophical conceptualisation in which Part III is grounded is that it is a part of an artistic continuum.

So, children's literature writers compose their texts with an implicit understanding that the person reading it will be a child. This child for whom the text is written is called the **implied reader**.

> The 'implied reader' is a term coined by **Wolfgang Iser** (1926–) and used by literary theorists to describe the reader implied by the text. There will always be a tension between the real reader—real child, adult, critic, teacher, parent—and the position of reader set up within the narrative structure by the author.
>
> **Umberto Eco** (1932–) uses the term 'model reader' to describe the reader inferred by the text.

Sometimes texts have a 'narratee', someone within the text to whom the story is being told. *Winnie the Pooh* is a good example of this—the story is being told to Christopher Robin, who is the narratee.

Texts make it clear who their implied reader is, in children's books usually by the level of language. The implied reader relates back to ideas about the construct of the child and of childhood, because authors will either consciously or unconsciously write for the child their culture has constructed.

Task 10

1. Choose three picturebooks. Consider the implied reader of each, giving your reasons.
2. Choose one picturebook.
   - Make a list of all the things that you learn about the world of the text: the fictive world.
   - What are some of the things you learn 'accidentally'?
3. Consider what you have to know before you can fully understand this book: for example, in **Where's Mum?** you would have to know what a kindergarten is. This helps us to determine the person the author has seen as implied reader of the text.

 Activity 14

Years 5–6 (could be modified for middle primary)

Arrange the children in small groups (no more than four). Give out, or allow children to choose, a number of picturebooks.

1. Look at one book. Ask children to brainstorm a list of all the things that readers of this book must know and be able to do if they are to understand it. Model a number of examples such as **Edward's First Day at School** (Wells 1996):
   - They must understand how books work—turning the pages, beginning at the front (in Western culture), knowing what a title page is, reading the left side before the right side of an opening.
   - They must be able to read.
   - They must know what a school is.
   - They must know what a teacher does.
2. Ask children to describe the picture that the text gives of the reader of the book. You do not need to use the term 'implied reader', although you may choose to do so. What you are doing is showing children that the writer has constructed a story for a particular reader with a particular sort of cultural knowledge and knowledge about the world. You are helping children to grow into understandings of *critical literacy*, using your knowledge of theory to encourage them to have enhanced perceptions of how texts are constructed and what they do.
3. Ask children in groups to make a list of all the background things that happen in the book. What sort of world do they show?

Narrative patterns: the quest

Children's literature articulates a culture of growing. The archetypal story of all literature is the story of the quest, of the odyssey, of the voyage out and the coming back in, with equilibrium usually restored, and with growth—physical, emotional, spiritual—having taken place. Quests can be external—like Peter Rabbit venturing into Mr McGregor's garden for example—or they can be internal, like *You and Me, Murrawee*, which among other things is a quest for identity, for understanding of others, for reconciling shared space, and perhaps for a sense of nationality.

Children's literature and the developing sense of self as a site of consciousness and meaning

At the heart of the quest is the search for a sense of self. Small children live in a world that is essentially solipsistic—centred on 'me'. Children's books tell stories about others but they also help to articulate a developing sense of self in relation to others. As well as this, they allow opportunities to test other selves and other ways of being.

Subjectivity

The sense of self as a 'site of consciousness and meaning' (Webster 1990: 80) is called *subjectivity* in literary theory.
· This site of consciousness is distinct and separate from the surrounding life-world.
· It is formed in relationship to the others in that life-world (i.e. in intersubjective relationships).
· It is constructed out of what Bakhtin calls 'dialogic' encounters with those others.
  Bakhtin's term is specific but it is being used here in the general sense of a dialogue, a conversation, or intersubjective expression of relationship between a self and an other, or others.

Literature gives privileged access to what its characters are feeling and thinking and how they define themselves as different from others. The literary representation of **subjectivity**—the sense of identity and individual being—in literature is a powerful dynamic. In children's literature the representation of subjectivity is part of deep structure. *Edward's First Day at School* is all about Edward and his life-world; *Where the Wild Things Are* is about Max and his inner and outer life-worlds.

As noted earlier, the subjectivity of the child reader, his sense of identity and sense of self, are in a continual state of becoming. Awareness of individual identity is formed in dialogic relationships with others, with cultural ideologies and with cultural atitudes. These relationships and interactions include what is read, what is talked about, what is watched on television, what happens around the family dinner table.

Subjectivity is a psychoanalytical term that draws attention to the significance of the sense of self, of being an 'I' who is separate and individual from all the other 'I's in the world. As teachers, we have the opportunity to encourage children to read books offering a diversity of other, fictional subjectivities.

Task 11

1. Consider the multifaceted representation of Daisy's subjectivity in **Do Not Go Around the Edges**.
2. What are some of her dialogic relationships? (Think about the people of her world, and about her relationship with the land.)
3. There are many voices in this text (Bakhtin referred to this as *heteroglossia*). Some are clearly heard, others are implicit (Daisy's parents, the officials who carry out government policy). What voices do you hear? List and discuss.

Teachers' reading

Read the first chapter of *David Copperfield* (1849–50), by Charles Dickens and then read the early chapters of *The Catcher in the Rye* (1951) by J. D. Salinger. Think about the different implied readers and the different representations of subjectivity.

Focalisation and agency

Focalisation pertains to the way we see things and the way we hear things. The author chooses to write from the perspectives and ideas of a particular character, or sometimes from the more removed position of omniscient (all-knowing) narrator. The illustrator shows us how things appear from a particular angle.

One illustration from William Mayne's **Mousewing** shows how the owl saw the little mice; another shows how the mice saw the mighty wings of the owl as it swooped down on them. The illustrator's choices *instruct* viewers how to see these images. The cover positions the viewer *below* the mouse; this reflects its significance as protagonist, firstly by enlarging physical size, and secondly by letting us see more or less what it is seeing.

Understanding focalisation is a part of critical literacy because it helps us to to be aware of where the verbal text is positioning its reader. This gives readers *agency*; that is, the knowledge and power to accept, resist, or reject such positioning. The key questions to ask about focalisation are:

- Whose eyes are we seeing with?
- Whose ears are we hearing with?

The theoretical concept of focalisation alerts us to the significance of point of view and perspective. Perspectives relate to frameworks of seeing. Point of view has come to mean attitudes and opinions but it can also mean literally the point from which something is seen or viewed. Where we stand, of course, is likely to influence what and how we see.

Focalisation gives us a tool to interpret literary narrative in an objective way.

All Those Secrets of the World (Yolan and Baker 1991) is overtly about literal perspective: 'When you are far away, everything is smaller' (see Chapter 25, page 416). But it is the implicit focalisation that is much more revealing. This text purports to be the focalisation of a child: 'I was four when my father went off to war'. The scene of her father's departure is overtly seen through her eyes: 'But everyone had a good time, except Mama, who cried all the way home ...'

However, covertly, this is a retrospective, a real-life adult focalisation of a significant time and a significant learning experience of childhood. The dedications in the peritext (the writing around the actual pages of story— explanations, publishers' blurbs, etc.) make it clear that 'Janie' is Jane, the writer. We are really not seeing through little Janie's eyes; we are seeing through the eyes of the grown woman, who is nostalgic, sad, and knowing. It is precisely this focalisation, and the clever illustrations that capture the chronotope (time-space) of this remembered childhood so well, that give this book its charm. The focalisation of the illustrations—what we see—is always from a grown perspective; the grown-up is looking back at the child and the child-time. The only moment when we look in any way through the child's eyes is the mirror scene. The rest of the time we view at a distance—and of course it is just this sense of a distance that situates the text in its clearly delineated time-space.

Activity 15

Read ***The Great Bear*** by Libby Gleeson and Armin Greder (1999).

Years 3–4

1. Organise into small roundtable groups.
2. Ask children to discuss: 'Whose eyes are we seeing with?' in relation to the illustrations. Does this change? If so, when?
3. Why do you think it changes? What do you think the illustrator is trying to do?
4. Describe how the illustrator has drawn the people's faces. Why?

Years 5–6

Add the following:

5. Now look at the words of the text. We see with the eyes of a narrator, but in the last opening with verbal text we see with the eyes of the bear. What effect does this have?

6. Choose something that you feel strongly about. Write a short composition looking through the eyes of the person or thing which is being treated badly. (You may prefer to write a short play, or a poem.)

The written component of this activity could be a computer task. Ask children to experiment with using different fonts and text to represent different perspectives.

It is interesting to note the differing focalisations in *The Great Bear*, where the illustrations are strongly evocative of well-known paintings by famous artists. The faces in the crowd (focalised by the bear) remind us of the works of the Flemish painter Pieter Bruegel; the opening illustrations of distant landscapes evoke van Gogh's *Black Crows over Wheat Field*. (This particular association becomes more complex when we note that it was to these wheat fields, in Auvers near Paris, where on 27 July 1890 van Gogh took a borrowed revolver and shot himself, dying two days later.) Teachers may like to show these pictures to their class and ask students to comment on similarities and differences. What effect does knowledge of these artistic relationships have on our reading of the book?

This leads very well into a discussion of intertextuality.

Intertextuality

Intertextuality refers to intercourse between texts. The traditional meaning of 'intercourse' is interaction—but the common sexual implication that most of you will read there is not unhelpful.

Intertextual relationships, overt or covert, are intimate relationships that reach across, between, and beyond texts. Anthony Browne's **Voices in the Park** overtly reaches *across* to his earlier text, **A Walk in the Park**, setting up connections that influence our reading of the later text. Angela Barrett and Josephine Poole's **Beware, Beware** reaches overtly into the mixed spaces between fairytales and cautionary tales, and covertly into the spaces between fairytales and adolescent 'wild side' literature. Shaun Tan's illustration of the tree in **Memorial** reaches *beyond* this book into the art world, to the famous lithograph 'The Cry', by the Norwegian artist Edward Munch. It also taps into, as part of textual understory, Munch's view of human beings as tormented, isolated, without agency.

When one text simply refers to another text, or even talks about it, it is making *allusions* or *references* to that text—which as we have seen does not have to be a literary text but can be, for example, a media text or a painting. This is not necessarily intertextuality, any more than saying someone's name necessarily means a close relationship. In a reference and allusion, the text being referred or alluded to remains more or less untouched, and all the meaning clearly stays in the text being read.

Intertextuality goes further than this. It touches. It excites and provokes. It gives new significance to reader relationships with the old text and old significances to reader relationships with the new text. These relationships make a sort of collided meaning that impacts on both. For instance, Perrault's **Cinderella** assumes a greater significance when we note the countless intertextual encounters it has had (particularly in feminist retellings); it gathers to a new meaning that is beyond that of its original and beyond the bare bones of the new retelling.

Intertextuality is also significant to educators for how it interacts with learning theory. Learning theorists know that *prior knowledge*—knowing something beforehand about what is going to be taught—contributes significantly to the success of the subsequent teaching or learning experience. Intertextuality depends on and accesses prior knowledge. There is a sense of delight in recognition—a delight that encourages receptivity. Intertextuality is a narrative structure that feeds on this delight of recognition. This is not to say that it always simply corroborates prior knowledge; rather, it uses prior knowledge as a springboard to a new idea or application—extending, interrogating, or even resisting the old.

In another way, then, principles of intertextuality intersect with learning theory. Intertextuality provokes reinterpretations; it engages with ideas of altered understandings—what Saljo described as comprehending the world by reinterpreting existing knowledge (1979). Feminist retellings of fairytales have changed our understandings of the representation of gender roles and gender-specific behaviours and caused us to reinterpret and question the fairytale as cultural paradigm.

Another example of intertextuality can be seen in Pat Torres' **Jalygur, Aussie Animal Rhymes** (1988). Consider this short poem, 'Gumbun, The Mangrove Man':

> *Gumbun, Gumbun,*
> *Look out, look out,*
> *It's the Gumbun man,*
> *Run, run as fast as you can.*

The well-known refrain of the nursery story *The Gingerbread Man* is an obvious intertext, and Torres has told me that she deliberately sought a familiar pattern so that it would make the rhyme more accessible to non-Aboriginal children. This is a powerful intertext for another reason, however. It interacts with other aspects of the gingerbread man story—his cheekiness, his cockiness, and his ultimate disaster—and inflates the Gumbun with something of the same meaning. In other words, Gumbun looks scary but it's a fun scariness—don't worry too much, he won't get you. Not only that, but when children then revisit the Gingerbread Man story, they will see a little bit of Gumbun the Mangrove Man there as well.

Intertextuality can pertain to story and narrative patterns, to events and incidents, to character and character relationships. It can consist of a single deep connection at one point of a text or of a string of *motifs* and *leitmotifs* that configure the whole text.

> **Motif:** repeated image or images in a text. Imagine a gold thread running through a jumper, only showing in parts here and there but clearly visible in certain places and contributing to the overall design.
> **Leitmotif:** a strongly recurring motif (originally used of Wagner's operas).

There are many, many texts that are wholly constructed around intertextual relationships: ***The Frog Prince Continued*** (Scieska and Johnson 1991) (you'll never read *The Frog Prince* again in the same way!), ***The Stinky Cheese Man and Other Fairly Stupid Tales*** (Scieska and Smith 1992), ***Yours Truly Goldilocks*** (Ada and Tryon 1998), ***Where's Mum?*** (Gleeson and Smith 1992), ***Each Peach Pear Plum*** (Ahlberg 1978), and so on. However, it is a more subtle text already mentioned that reveals very clearly what I now want to consider.

Beware, Beware (Hill and Barrett 1993) is an intense, intriguing picturebook. It begins with a kitchen scene that contains all the familiar elements of cosiness and security: a warm kitchen with a bright fire, spicy smells, and the sound of a kettle singing on the hearth. All of these things are comfortable symbols of home and belonging: kitchen, warmth, cooking, kettle, fire. The illustrations at first are equally comfortable. It is the human figures that are disconcerting, and that continue to disconcert; they are very separate from each other (except on the cover). However, it is the intertextuality that is of great interest here: the child venturing out by herself despite warnings (Peter Rabbit, etc.), being lost, at first without fear and then with an ever increasing sense of terror as the text crowds with intertextual associations of fairytales and stories about all the bad things that can happen in woods:

> *Trolls Goblins*
> *Elves Sprites*
> *Mysterious lights*
> *Fingers beckon*
> *Eyes stare*

The list continues. Placing these together has a cumulative effect that strengthens each of the individual intertexts and makes the 'woods' subsequently more potent. So the 'meaning' has moved from within each separate intertext to somewhere between, across, and beyond them all. Separate stories are linked and accumulate narrative and thematic significance.

Activity 16

Read *Where's Mum?* by Libby Gleeson and Craig Smith (1992).

Years K–2

1. Discuss all the other fairy stories that are a part of the story of this book.
2. Draw pictures of all the characters.

Years 3–4

1. Organise the class into roundtable groups.
2. Ask each group to make a list of the fairytales and nursery rhymes that become a part of this story. Note how students fill this story with characters.
3. Each group chooses one intertext. Give the students a short time to prepare a creative telling of that rhyme or fairytale to the rest of the class. They can get costumes from the prop box if you like, and act it out. They may like to mime or sing or dance.
4. Performance time.

Years 5–6

5. Writing task: Make up a short story where you meet some characters from books. Perhaps these could at some point be read to the class and a big poster could be made up of all the intertexts that have been used.
6. Or, as a class, construct a story outline on the board. Organise the class into writing groups, and divide the story into parts. Each group is to write their part of the story, using a well-known intertext of their choice as a model. For example, the intertext could be *Rosie's Walk*; their story could be *Bluey's Run*, or *Blackie's Stroll*.
7. Introduce the idea and text-type of *parody* (a humorous, sometimes ridiculous, imitation of something well known).
   Note: You may like to call these other books 'understories' in this context. The idea relates well to what was earlier called the understory of a text.

> The Time-Warner film *Pleasantville* provides an example that teachers may enjoy. This is an ironic depiction of the contrast between the 1950s world of the perfect but unreal family of black and white sit-coms and the 1990s *fin de siecle* (end of the century) world of broken families, sexual realities, and coloured television. At one point, the 1950s female teenager gives the 1990s male teenager an apple. This immediately (but in a very confused way) sets up the story of Eve in the garden of Eden as a deliberate intertext.

SUMMARY

1 Theory and practice operate in a creative and stimulating tension.
2 A knowledge of theory helps teachers' understandings and enriches teaching practices.
3 Teachers, however, must find ways of teaching using 'courteous translations'—challenging children but doing so in a way that is appropriate to class and context.
4 Children's literature articulates life-worlds and helps grow them.
5 Each work of art constructs a version of the world contracted into a comprehensive grasp; that is, it presents the complexity and immensity of the world in such a way as to allow the child to make sense of it.
6 The notion of the chronotope, time-space, helps us to perceive the way texts are organised. A visual chronotope is the representation of time-space in picturebook illustration.
7 The implied reader is the reader envisaged by the author when writing the text.
8 Subjectivity is a psychoanalytical term referring to the developing knowledge and awareness of a sense of self.
9 Diverse representations of literary subjectivity are an integral part of children's process of becomingness.
10 Focalisation gives us a useful tool to interpret literary narrative and encourages us to ask:
   - Whose eyes are we seeing with?
   - Whose ears are we hearing with?
11 A knowledge of focalisation gives readers agency; that is, power to accept, resist, or reject what the author/illustrator is positioning them to see or think.
12 Intertextuality refers to intimate relationships between texts. Intertextuality is more than reference and allusion; it is a relationship that is part of story and structure and that pertains to thematic significance. It provokes rereadings of the old text (the intertext) as much as new readings of the new text.

Chapter 21

Children's Literature as a Locus of Literate Practices

> **Focus**
>
> Children's literature is a locus of literate practices, offering reading experiences, engagement with writing experiences, talking and listening experiences. It presents a multitude of sites for giving children the opportunity to encounter, demonstrate and practise all literacy skills in meaningful ways and in meaningful contexts.

Speaking and listening

Books are a dynamic and energising part of the process of literacy—not only the literacy of reading and writing but also the literacies of speaking and listening. As noted earlier (Chapter 16, page 297) literacy involves the integration of speaking, listening, and critical thinking with reading and writing. Children's literature helps us as educators to give children the opportunity to listen, to hear voices other than their own and those of their own world. It opens up a multitude of possibilities for speaking—for speaking about those other worlds and with other voices, and speaking of their own worlds and with their own voices. The common community perceptions of literacy as reading and writing need to be extended: children must also be equipped as effective speakers and effective listeners. Literature provides a locus for the activation of these speaking and listening skills, giving them purpose and direction.

Children's literature is one of the places where children encounter in a non-threatening way a diversity of possible perspectives on philosophical issues, worldviews, social ideas, and cultural practices. *Being literate* connects children to this diversity and connects them to *outer* worlds—to community and to society. It also, however, connects children to their *inner* worlds, to a sense of their history (the linear, vertical idea of identity: who they have been, where they have come from) and to a sense of their geography (the horizontal view of identity: where they are, the horizons and landscape of their world). We speak to the outer world and we listen in our inner world.

Books articulate the processes of literacy as a multitude of close encounters. In representing the ideas, thoughts, and feelings of others, and in telling *their* story, it gives shape—words and pictures—to one's *own* story, to personal ideas, thoughts, and feelings.

The life cycle of the process of literacy

Literacy is for life, and the ongoing development of the multiple literacies is part of lifelong learning.

As we have seen, children's literature represents language in context. Books help us to understand how language works. As children come to appreciate the processes of language, they will grow into a more mature appreciation of the written word. We all tend to like what we understand—an interest in a particular sport encourages us to follow a particular team or a particular player, to learn more about the rules and the game; our preliminary interest thereby grows into a knowledgeable one that is intensely satisfying and that promotes further and more detailed interest and investigation.

Books help us to understand language better; understanding language better helps us to further appreciate books. This is part of the life cycle of the process of literacy. We listen, we speak, we read, we write. It is not a consecutive cycle but an endlessly changing and interacting one.

Free-range reading

Children should be encouraged to be free-range readers. The important thing for educators to note is that, at whatever level children are currently reading, they need continuous and stimulating exposure beyond it, with lots of handholds and support for the next jump. (This is true for us all, no matter how old we are.) This is where the shared reading experience, whether it be parent and child or teacher and class, is invaluable.

As educators, we need consciously to present to children a range of texts that is as wide and diverse, as simple and as complex, as culturally similar and as culturally different, as we can possibly find.

> Even when children are good independent readers, they *need to be read to*, and they especially need to be read the books that they may not choose to pick up and read for themselves.

Literature and oracy

It is also important that we resist giving children endless written tasks about texts. You will notice that most of the tasks included in these chapters involve oral discussion—lots of group work, with children being able freely to share their spoken responses, formally and informally, around a table. Children learn from each other, and guided discussion promotes many literate oracy behaviours: it improves vocabulary, offers opportunities for more sophisticated sentence constructions and syntax, and lets children hear the sounds of words as their peers say them.

It is rarely helpful to read books and then ask for tedious written responses about story or character or whatever as a standard teaching strategy. Never underestimate the significance of getting children to talk and to listen to each other in a structured way. Aidan Chambers in his wonderful little book *Tell Me* (see Activity 1), which provides many valuable suggestions for promoting classroom discussion, writes:

> Talking well about books is a high-value activity in itself. But talking well about books is also the best rehearsal there is for talking well about other things. So in helping children to talk about their reading, we help them to be articulate about the rest of their lives. (1993: 10)

Literature also offers children the freedom to speak out about issues and ideas that may not emerge in normal conversation. It opens up fields of discussion in the classroom in a non-contrived and non-threatening way. As Jerome Bruner notes:

> I have tried to make the case that the function of literature as art is to open us to dilemmas, to the hypothetical, to the range of possible worlds that a text can refer to … to render the world less fixed, less banal, more susceptible to recreation. (1986: 159)

This can of course connect to other disciplines. Children's literature does not just belong in the English syllabus and in the teaching of English. It relates significantly to history, geography, the sciences, sociology, visual arts, drama, and dance.

Children's literature and philosophy

You may be interested in reading *Sophie's World* by Jostein Gaarder (1995). This gives a very interesting introduction to the study of philosophy.

Literature of course has a strong relationship to philosophy. Current critical writing in the field of children's literature is much concerned with ideology, defined by Stephens as 'a system of beliefs by which we make sense of the world' (1992: 8). Ideology is clearly related to philosophy, which pertains to ways of understanding the world, to the study of the truth or principles of knowledge, general principles of the universe, systems for guiding life, principles of conduct, religious belief, and traditions.

Philosophy takes all knowledge for its province. The word 'philosophy' comes from the Greek *philo*, meaning 'love' and *sophos*, meaning 'of wisdom'— philosophy literally means the love of wisdom. In simple terms philosophy has a dual purpose: first to give each person a sense of a unified picture of the universe, a theoretical basis on which to base the practice of living; and second as a practical tool to promote critical (and arguably theoretical) thinking. It involves thinking deeply about the direction of life's activity, about views of knowledge and reason and spiritual belief, and about the relationship between the individual and the community.

Sophie's World is an interesting text, although complex, which overtly introduces older children to the study of philosophy and to the idea of philosophical enquiry. But every book contains a worldview that can be discussed and debated. *Leaves for Mr Walter* (Brian and Cox 1998), for example, can be used to stimulate discussions and ideas about more than just being a good neighbour. *The Great Bear* (Gleeson and Greder 1999) can obviously stimulate discussions about issues of performing animals, but it also can be interrogated for what it says and portrays about human nature (and mobs). Anthony Browne's *Zoo* (1992) not only can open up ideas about animals in captivity but can also provoke discussions about point of view, about families, and about representations of the roles of women. *The Story of Rosy Dock* (Baker 1995) can be read as much more than a story about the introduction of a weed into the desert.

Using children's literature for language lessons

Reading books with children, often and in a fun way, provides a wonderful opportunity for children to see language in action. Books also provide a great resource for more formal learning about the structures of language and a locus for learning about these structures in meaningful contexts.

Activity 17

Read *Rosie's Walk* by Pat Hutchins (1968)

> We can use simple books in sophisticated classrooms if we use them creatively. (The converse of this is also true—we can use sophisticated texts with very young children if we translate them 'courteously' by using them creatively.) The following are some examples using *Rosie's Walk*—adjust the ideas to suit your particular class and its particular needs. *Rosie's Walk,* as well as being a wonderful little story, also shows the variety of the prepositional phrase and so is a useful instruction in grammar.

1. Children can write their own Rosie story, making up a character of their own and taking them on a similar prepositional path.

   Homer Simpson went for a walk
   > *Over ...*
   > *Up ...*
   > *In ...*
   > *Through ...*

Round ...
Under ...
And .. .

2. Children can demonstrate the qualities of prepositions, with little labels on the two things that the prepositions relate.

The cow jumped OVER the moon
Rosie walked UNDER the bridge

Books show an abundance of varieties of sentence and paragraph constructions, and grammar in action. Again, I believe in plenty of discussions and small-group roundtables to discuss language and grammar. Endless writing and copying out of examples is non-productive and can help take away the pleasure of the text.

3. *Living sentences*: Ask children to make labels of the parts of speech, at a level appropriate for the class. For example, as a follow-up to the exercise on prepositions, have children make labels (writing) for relevant *prepositions* and *nouns*. Children choose a label and wear it. The nouns all stand in a circle. The prepositions have to find the two nouns that they link in the story and stand together. You could add the *verbs* to this game, and *articles*, so children can construct living sentences. You could also do this as a competitive team game—if you have lots of space and can cope with the fun of this sort of grammar lesson.

4. Extend this by making a pool of different parts of speech in each corner of the room (children wearing labels) and have teams write a story by choosing words, putting them together, and making living sentences. Swap teams so that everyone has a chance to be a word and everyone has a chance to make sentences.

5. Perform *Rosie's Walk* as Readers' Theatre: that is, dramatic reading from the text, with lots of vocal energy but a minimum of props and movement. Have Rosie tell the story (change to first person) and then have the fox tell the story. Discuss: are there differences? Why?

6. Set up a television interview. Ask children to work in groups of four, interviewing Rosie and then interviewing the fox. How many different versions of the story does your newscast relate?

 ## Activity 18

Read ***Owl Babies*** by M. Waddell and P. Benson (1992).

Writing tasks about literature should be creative, rather than endless questions about story and character.

1. After reading *Owl Babies*, ask children to write their own story, real or imagined, about when they thought they were alone somewhere. You might

like to read some poems about being alone (such as the relevant verses from Coleridge's 'The Rime of the Ancient Mariner'—*Alone, alone, all all alone/Alone on a wide wide sea*).

2. Point out some constructions you would like them to include; perhaps, in this case, it could be *direct speech*, with *questions* and *exclamations*. Talk over the examples in the text:

   > *'Where's Mummy?' asked Sarah.*
   > *'Oh my goodness!' said Percy.*
   > *'I want my mummy!' said Bill.*

   As part of this story exercise, children learn what these sentence constructions are and how they are punctuated; they also learn the difference between direct and indirect speech. (Indirect speech: 'Bill said he wanted his mummy'.)

3. Initiate discussions about how direct speech in books lets us hear what the characters are thinking and feeling. Find some examples in other books containing direct speech.

4. How does the direct speech in *Owl Babies* reveal character differences? How do the characters of Sarah, Percy, and Bill differ? How are they the same? This book works well as Readers' Theatre for Years 3–4 (and possibly 1–2).

Activity 19

Read *Tidy Titch* by Pat Hutchins (1991).

1. Appropriate to their level, children could find and discuss examples of *contractions* and the *use of the apostrophe* in *Tidy Titch*:

> 'I think I'll throw that old space suit out,' said Peter, 'and that cowboy outfit. They're much too small for me!'
> 'They're not too small for me!' said Titch. 'I'll have them!'
>
> ...
>
> 'My room is still untidy,' said Mary. 'I think I'll get rid of this broken pram and these old games. I've played with them hundreds of times!'
> 'I haven't,' said Titch.
> 'I'll have them!'

2. Discussion ideas:
   · Why does direct speech contain so many examples of contractions?
   · What happens in more formal writing? Why?
   · Teach *it's* as an example of the abbreviation of *it is*.

3. Also discuss (Years 3–4) what this story shows about its culture (children have their own rooms, they have many toys, tidiness is good, useless things contribute to untidiness, things can be discarded when they are broken, children have the freedom to decide what they are going to do with their own things).

Years 5–6

Read Tohby Riddle's ***The Tip at the End of the Street*** (Riddle 1996). Compare (note what's similar) and contrast (show what's different) these two stories (particularly the similar and different ideas about things that are discarded).

Activity 20

Read *Voices in the Park* by Anthony Browne (1999).

Years 5–6

1. Read the text to the class. If possible, read Browne's earlier text ***A Walk in the Park*** as an introduction.
2. Divide the class into groups of four, to represent the four voices. Let the children read the text in groups, in their 'voices'. Then swap roles and read in at least one different voice.
3. Come back together as a class. Discuss:
   · How did you feel in the character's role?
   · Did your feelings change when you swapped roles? How?
   · Which character do you most have sympathy with? Why do you think this is?
4. Collaborative class project: Turn the book into a movie. Discuss and allocate roles and timelines:
   · Scriptwriters: write a script.
   · Producers: consider how and where it will be produced. Make a schedule. Decide budget.
   · Cinematographers: decide shots, background, etc. Write and illustrate schedule.
   · Actors: learn parts.
   · Directors: rehearse with actors and cinematographers.
   · Designers: make costumes and props.
   · Music: write introduction and background (encourage original songs).
   · If you have access to a video, make the movie. If not, act it out as if it is being shot.

   (There are many other books which would lend themselves to this type of activity. Anthony Browne's ***Zoo*** or ***Piggybook***, for example, could prove very interesting as dramatisation.)

Activity 21

Read *Ginger* by Charlotte Voake (1997).

Years 3–4

1. Discuss as a class what the story is about. Can anyone relate this story to anything in his or her life?
2. This story has longer sentences than some picturebooks. After spending time enjoying the story, focus on the first opening.

> *Ginger was a lucky cat.*
> *He lived with a little girl*
> *who made him delicious meals*
> *and gave him a beautiful basket,*
> *where he would curl up ...*
> *and close his eyes.*

3. Explore this sentence to the level appropriate to the class. You may want to label the clauses or you may choose to simply highlight the *finite verbs* as a clue to where the clauses are ('was', 'lived with', 'made', 'gave', 'would curl up', 'close'). You may want to discuss, for example:
   · *adjectival clauses* ('who made him delicious meals')
   · *coordinate clauses* ('and gave him a beautiful basket', 'and close his eyes')
   · *the coordinate conjunction* ('and')
   · *adverbial clauses* ('where he would curl up').

Years 5–6

Add the following:

4. Ask children to write their own sentence following as much of the pattern as you consider appropriate for their level. You could give them part of the sentence, for example:

> *Kenny was a happy kookaburra. (Or just give them the word 'happy' and let them make up the rest.)*
> *He ....*
> *who ....*
> *and ....*
> *where ....*
> *and ....*

5. When the children have composed their sentences, let them share them and peers correct around their roundtable. Get everyone to do a finite verb check of the clauses.
6. Share sentences with the rest of the class. Encourage children to suggest any corrections.

In all of these examples of literature as a locus of literate practices, the most important role for the teacher is that of enthuser and motivator. Demonstrate daily your own enjoyment of language, your own love of reading, and your own love of books. Tell your class about the books you are currently reading.

SUMMARY

1   Children's literature provides unlimited opportunities for both teaching about and practising all literacy skills, including speaking and listening.
2   It helps children give shape to their own stories.
3   It presents language in a variety of authentic contexts.
4   Books help understandings of language; understanding language better means enjoying books more. This is part of the life cycle of literacy.
5   Children should be allowed to choose books freely.
6   However, teachers must continue to share challenging books with children, and make opportunities to read such books (books that children would not choose for themselves) with them and to them. This is part of the exposure beyond immediate needs that is so significant in the development of knowing readers.
7   Literature gives diverse opportunities for discussion, sometimes about difficult issues.
8   Literature connects with other disciplines.
9   Literature connects with philosophy and ideas about worldview.
10 Literature is a great language and grammar resource but teachers need to be creative in using it for these purposes.
11 The most important literate practice that teachers can pass on to their students is a lifelong love of language and books.

Chapter 22
The Classroom as a Community of Learners

> **Focus**
> This chapter considers the classroom as a teaching and learning space and notes that children will remember their school experience all their lives. It discusses some ideas for assessment and for a number of classroom activities, including a unit of work on sustainability.

A classroom is both a physical space and a mental space. Children will carry the memory of these spaces with them all their life. Their attitudes, not just towards literacy but also towards learning, towards discipline and self-discipline, towards challenge and difficulty, and towards *self* and *others*, will be shaped to a considerable extent by what happens in their classrooms.

As educators, we must try to make both spaces rich, vibrant, and supportive. This is our working environment as well. The two most important gifts we can give the children we teach are an *excitement about learning* that will last them all their lives, and an *excitement about who they are and what they can do*.

Literacy is a welcome into the world. We want to make the welcome memorable, continuous, and sustainable. We want our classrooms to be spaces that celebrate learning and that celebrate, from Kindergarten until the last day of school, social and scholarly community.

The word 'celebrate' comes from the Latin *celeber*, meaning 'honoured' and also 'frequented'. 'Frequented' means, according to the *Concise Oxford Dictionary*, 'gone often or habitually to'. Educators want their students to develop *habits* of literacy, *habits* of social and scholarly community.

Literature uses language to tell the stories of communities distant in both time and place. Filling the classroom spaces with story helps to create an environment where habits of literacy and literate practices can grow, be sustained, and endure.

Ideas to enhance the classroom as a physical space

As much as resources allow, fill the classroom with verbal and visual story. Children's compositions and artwork make the most beautiful decorations of all—but keep them changing.

1. Set up a Book Corner (comfortable spaces to read, books to choose from, good light).

2. Make a Book Worm (or draw one). Share it around the class. Perhaps the person with the Book Worm can choose a book for shared reading or discussion. Perhaps the Book Worm could be a badge of some description and the person wearing it for that week is responsible for organising the Book Corner for that week. Stress that this is not just a tidying task but one to stimulate reading of particular books.

3. Be creative and think about how you can relate books and activities in unusual ways. (The Sustainability Unit later in this chapter is an example.)

4. Have a display of *different genres*: fairytales, folktales, myths, legends, adventure stories, historical fiction, family stories, fantasy, poetry, drama, cookbooks, travel books, factual texts, manuals, newspaper editorials, advertisements. Organise the class into groups looking after one category and get them to make labels and give a brief presentation.

5. You could relate this to text-types: *literary text categories:* narrative, poetic, dramatic; *factual text categories:* recounts, procedures, information reports, expositions, and general communications. Each group could present as many and as varied a sample of a particular text category as possible.

6. Introduce class to the *Literary Factual Text* (see Activity 2, page 298). Find as many different examples as you can. Discuss with the class: how is this different from other factual texts?

7. Set up an Autobiography Table (see Activity 4, pages 306–7).

8. Set up an interdisciplinary display on a particular theme, e.g. 'water': books, science, poems, art, advertisements for saving water, editorials, water catchment areas for your region, and so on.

9. Many of the classroom activities in this book have talked about *roundtables*: children sitting around a table as a collaborative teaching and learning group. Extend the idea of the roundtable into a Reading Circle. Children could choose different groups and be part of a circle that shares books, reads to each other, and plans activities for the rest of the class based on books. For example, one circle may be interested in science fiction, another in boats, and another in stories about animals. Each Reading Circle could present a short segment to the class in any way the students choose.

10. Set up a History of Books table, and plan activities around it. Make some clay tablets. Make some scrolls (have some papyrus grass as a feature). Find examples of parchment and vellum (or something that explains what they

are). Talk about ancient Chinese paper and ask children to research how paper came to Europe during the Crusades (relate to Robin Hood). Do a computer research assignment on the invention of the printing press. Relate these ideas to the new technologies. See Chapter 19.

11. Have a Fiesta of Reading and invite parents to participate. Ask parents to bring or, if they can't come, send with their child a favourite book from their own childhood. If they have a different cultural background, and if appropriate, ask them to read the book at least in part in their own language. If the child speaks the language, give the child the opportunity to read to the class in the family heritage language. Open up discussions and other stories about family heritage and customs. See Classroom Activity 1, page 295.

12. Link this to a Family History project. Introduce children to family trees. If possible, use a software program such as *Generations* (Sierra) in the class-room. Use as many different research tools as possible: oral history (talking to older relatives), photograph albums, old letters, and scrapbooks, books, lists (e.g. the First Fleet), television programs, other memorabilia (books with names and dates written inside, books given as school and Sunday school prizes, etc.).

13. Extend the Fiesta of Reading activity into a community program and ask local celebrities and community officers (mayors, business proprietors, club members, etc.) to come to share their favourite books with your class.

14. Run your own Book Week. Elect judges, or institute voting procedures. Discuss categories and criteria (introduce this idea to the class if you have not previously done so). Nominate, shortlist, and select winners. Perhaps write a letter to the winning authors and illustrators—they may be happy to visit your school to receive their awards.

15. Create Web pages linking to authors, children's literature organisations, and journals. Create a pool of ideas for links.

16. Create a class library of Web books (i.e. write the stories on the Web pages, illustrate them with graphics, set up a classification system and add as links). Discuss in a class forum this new form of the book in relation to the history of the book. What is similar? What is different? What are the problems? What are the advantages? (See Chapter 19, pages 329–39.)

17. Set up times for synchronous and asynchronous electronic chat times (using programs such as TOPCLASS). Set relationships in place with other schools, other classes (use your colleagues as contacts). Work on collaborative projects on the Internet.

Assessment

Much assessment in the area of children's literature will take place either informally as observation or as part of the assessment of reading and writing (see Chapters 7 and 15).

The whole thrust of Part III, however, is that theory informs practice. Teachers will want to confirm this for themselves and to reflect on what worked best for them in any particular situation, what didn't work so well and why, and what could be improved and how. They will also want to use their professional knowledge to adapt, modify, change or extend any activities they introduce into the classrooms, whether in children's literature or anything else.

Observation therefore is extremely important. When children are reading, the teacher needs to watch what is happening. It is tempting to use this time to catch up on marking and the thousand other things that are part of a teacher's busy day, but this wastes an opportunity to *observe the literate behaviours of children in informal contexts*.

It is helpful to *structure observations*:

- Do the children procrastinate or go directly to a reading activity?
- Do they read the book or simply flip through a number of books?
- What general type of book do you notice that they choose?
- What general level of books do you notice that they choose?
- Do they commit themselves to the literature activities?
- Can you determine why or why not?
- Which of the activities do they commit to and appear to enjoy?
- Can you creatively develop more activities in this area relating to books?
- If they lack confidence as readers or writers, can you find activities that they feel more confident in and use these as a way to build up their reading and writing skills?
- If they are children from language backgrounds other than English, how can you use books and literature activities to help them find their place in the class community?

It is likely that evidence of achievement in children's literature activities will be reflected in reading and writing assessment. However, children can build up their own reading portfolio and work as roundtable groups towards extending their reading as widely as possible. Many of the activities suggested in this section could also be peer-reviewed: as teachers know, peer reviews reveal almost as much about the reviewer as they do about the person being reviewed.

There are many opportunities in children's literature activities for formal assessment, but too much emphasis on such practices is not likely to be beneficial to the long-term future of the child as a reader (this is not to say that you can't do a little formal assessment when it is obviously appropriate). Rather, use children's literature as the opportunity for observing the child

- speak and listen
- read and write in different ways
- develop communication skills
- negotiate cultural differences
- lead discussion

- promote discussion
- initiate discussion
- engage imaginatively in a class or individual project
- work collaboratively in a team
- respond intelligently
- respond intuitively
- respond creatively
- respond emotionally
- respond spiritually.

The following are examples of activities designed to stimulate further creative ideas by teachers.

Activity 22

Read *Each Peach Pear Plum* by Janet and Allen Ahlberg (1989).

Introduce this text to the class. Discuss these key concepts:

- Sounds and rhyme
- Rhythm
- Game: 'I spy'
- The idea of the child's 'seeing eye'
- Reader interaction: invitation to enter the text:

> In this book
> With your little eye
> Take a look
> And play 'I spy'.

Note how the magic happens and the 'you' becomes 'I' in the text.

- Intertextuality: what are the intertexts and how do they contribute to the book?
- Ideology: what cultural assumptions and attitudes lie behind this text? (Think about ideas about babies and how they are treated. Think about the sort of world that is depicted. Whose world is this? Whose world isn't it?)

Years K–2	Years 3–4	Years 5–6
Story	Ideas of character	Structure of narrative; unity
Draw a character	Write another 'chapter'	Conclusion or *finale*. What does a *finale* represent? Visual versus verbal emphasis. Draw a diagram of the plot. How to write a story: set the scene. Genre.
Rhyme	Other rhyming games	Assonance: 'each peach'. Alliteration: peach, pear, plum.

Nursery rhyme characters	Other nursery rhyme characters	Who is a little different and why (Robin Hood, folk-tale, and oral legend)? What other folk-tale characters could you include (e.g. King Arthur)?
	What symbols represent what characters?	What would you draw to symbolise them and why? Discussion of symbols. Illustrations or links. What inferences (e.g. pail)?
Play 'I spy'	Play 'I spy' with letters	Make up an 'I spy' game. How do the pictures expand the text?

To think about
- Describe the implied reader of this book.
- What assumptions does this book make about the child's life-world?
- What attitudes does it convey?
- Who may find this book difficult? Why? (This could become part of a discussion on cultural literacy.)

Suggestions
1. Make a list of favourite books for children to put up in class.
2. Institute a Book of the Week.
3. Have a Fairytale Collection: ask everyone to bring in any versions they have at home. Compare the versions—illustrations and text.
4. Make up a class fairytale play. It can incorporate as many fairytale characters as you like. It can be as humorous as you like. To stimulate creative ideas, read a number of retellings such as those mentioned in the last chapter. You could also refer to the movie *Ever After*. Divide the class into groups to write different scenes, after an initial plan has been made.
5. If you haven't got a prop box in your classroom, start accumulating one. Ask for suitable old clothes from home. Old curtains make good cloaks. Make a few crowns if need be.
6. Rehearse the play and perform it at lunchtime for the other classes. You may be able to charge 20c entry and put the money towards another class book.
7. Video the performance if possible.

Activities for other curriculum areas
- Drama: Mime the story; construct a series of tableaux.
- Music: Characters march on and sing the nursery rhymes; use body percussion.
- Dance: Play *Peter and the Wolf*; choreograph different parts of the music.

Activity 23

Read *Memorial* by Gary Crew and Shaun Tan (1999).

Key concepts for discussion

- place
- space
- sociocultural history
- geography
- Australian history
- the environment
- inclusivity
- subjectivity

Focalisation:

- Whose eyes do we see through?
- Whose voices do we hear?

Years 5–6

1. Read *Memorial* in class.
2. Discuss as many of the following concepts as are appropriate for the level of your class:

Place	Australia (but also other places experienced, e.g. France, Vietnam)
Space	Historical spaces The town space The memorial space Family space Spaces of memory
Sociocultural history	Australia from World War I until the present
Geography	An Australian country town Geography of the battlefield
Australian history	Involvement in wars Progress Interest in the environment
The environment	Progress Effect of fumes on the tree Attitudes towards trees
Inclusivity	The voices of four generations The mind-spaces of different speakers
Subjectivity	Different subjects from different generations

3. Ask children to research in groups any aspect of the above, e.g. Australia in the wars, country towns, battles of World War I, Anzac Day, changing attitudes to the environment, memorials, fashions of the interwar period.
4. If your town has a memorial you may be able to visit it as a class. What words appear on it? What pictures or sculptures? What do the words indicate is being remembered? Ask children what they think is being remembered.
5. Show the class photographs of the US Vietnam Memorial in Washington. This is a reflective memorial—it reflects the faces of those looking at it. Discuss the ideas behind building a memorial in this way.
6. Ask children to research their own family history. Have a Memorial Day and ask them to bring relevant photographs, old letters, etc. to school. Stress how precious these are. Also stress that memorials do not glorify war; in fact this book is doing the opposite: showing the terrible impact that war has on everyday lives.

Activity 24

Exemplar of unit: **Exploring sustainability through children's literature and the creative arts**

(This unit is designed for upper primary school classes but could be adapted to suit the needs of younger children at the teacher's discretion.)

Background for the teacher: theoretical idea of sustainability

Sustainability is:

- an economic and social practice which actively seeks to ensure that the demands of the marketplace do not threaten, deplete, or destroy the natural environment
- a universal imperative in a global society
- a philosophy that conceives of human well-being thriving in just and equitable societies where citizen rights and citizen responsibilities operate in a creative tension
- the use, conservation, and renewing of energy, including human energy.

> Sustainability is using, without *using up*.

This relates sustainability to community, to inner as well as to outer environments, to the heritage and evolution of culture, and to the human spirit. Human beings are more than a body that needs to be sustained and the world is more than a geographical and ecological landscape that provides physical sustenance for those who inhabit it. Sustainability is, in Ellyard's words, 'human thrival' (1997). Discussions about sustainability or thrival must take into account all aspects of human well-being. Sustainability is a practice for survival.

Rationale for using the creative arts

1. Using the creative arts to teach and stimulate awareness of sustainability issues is part of a long tradition. In fact the world's greatest environmentalists, those who have most celebrated the environment and who have most argued for it to be preserved—long before the terms *environmentalism* or *Green* were ever thought of—have been the poets and the artists. They have always known that humans and their environment are linked—by songline, by dreaming, by the need to represent an ecology of connectedness in visual forms, in aural forms, and in kinaesthetic forms. They have always noted human interdependence as inhabitants of a shared planet.

2. The creative arts promote sustainable futures by nourishing spirit, the deepest, most intimate, and arguably the most threatened part of human beings. Individual life is a tenuous, fragile environment, briefly inhabited. Humans are connected to each other and to their environment in a worldwide web of everyday actions and commonplace happenings. The creative arts allow us to explore and test and represent that connection.

3. Approaching issues of sustainability with an arts focus stimulates wide-ranging dialogues about the inner and outer habitats of a world of diverse people, all of whom are continually threatened by the processes of time and change. It promotes non-threatening discussions about cultures and multicultures, and allows representations of a variety of cultural perspectives.

4. This unit is designed within a transdisciplinary perspective of sustainability. It will leave openings to make overt connections with history and geography, science and environmental science, as well as with arts-related fields. Mathematical activities can also be based on sustainability issues.

5. Using children's literature within a context of creative arts promotes positive outcomes:
   - the opportunity for and development of the capacity to make individual responses within a corporate experience
   - the development of complex thinking processes that can involve the whole body (and that help to physically sustain both the body and the mind)
   - the capacity to articulate being
   - interpersonal and intrapersonal communication skills
   - inner role-plays and the development of the literacy of the imagination
   - an increased capacity and confidence for creative problem-solving
   - visual literacy and increased cultural literacy.

1. Literature introduction

Read as many children's literature texts pertaining to sustainability and the environment as you can find:

> *Window* by Jeannie Baker (1992)
> *Where the Forest Meets the Sea* by Jeannie Baker (1987)
> *The Story of Rosy Dock* by Jeannie Baker (1995)
> *The Hidden Forest,* by Jeannie Baker (2000)
> *The Wonder Thing* by Libby Hathorn and Peter Gouldthorpe (1995)
> *The Paddock* by Lilith Norman (1992)
> *Islands in My Garden* by Jim Howes and Roland Harvey (1998)
> *V is for Vanishing* by Patricia Mullins (1993)
> *The Fisherman and the Theefyspray* by Paul Jennings and Jane Tanner (1994)
> *Memorial* by Gary Crew and Shaun Tan (1999)

2. Classroom Activities (Upper Primary)

2.i Library task

Theme: Find as many definitions of the verb 'to sustain' as you can:
- keep up, keep going, keep in existence, maintain, prolong, aid, assist
- supply with necessities or nourishment, supply with food and provisions
- hold up, support, keep from falling or sinking, prop
- bear, endure, support the spirits or vitality or resolution of, encourage, withstand, stand

- suffer, experience
- allow, admit, favour
- agree with, confirm, corroborate, sanction, affirm the validity of.

Derivations: French from Latin *sustinere*, to hold up: *sub* (under) + *tenere* (to hold).

2.ii Writing

After sharing and noting library definitions of the verb 'to sustain', discuss the specific meanings that the noun 'sustainability' has acquired at the beginning of the 21st century. This is a great opportunity to show children that language is living and dynamic: that meanings and usages change.

Class task: Brainstorm as many ideas about sustainability as you can. Research both in the library and on the Internet. Write a class definition of 'sustainability'. Publish it in a prominent place in the classroom.

Individual writing task: Write about sustainability in the context of the classroom. What measures can be put in place to further sustainability practices? Remember to discuss sustainability in terms of human energy as well.

Publish these as part of a class newsletter to the rest of the school, to encourage discussion throughout the school. Invite responses from other classes. Include the best of these in a class newsletter to parents. For the purposes of the newsletter, elect an editor, an editorial team, illustrators, and distributors. Perhaps the class could also write a letter to the Principal, requesting that these letters are distributed at P&C and P&F meetings.

2.iii Reading and research

Theme: Developing a concept of world heritage arts in the classroom.

Rationale: Think about the word ecology in relation to the arts. 'Ecology' refers to the relationship between organisms and their environment. The arts express an ecological relationship of human beings and their environment; they have done so for thousands of years in cultures all over the world.

At the Wet Tropics World Heritage Area in Cairns, the Education building contains a plaque that reads:

'This Wet Tropics World Heritage Area was created in 1988. It is one of only a handful of sites in the world that meet all four of the natural heritage criteria.'

This area has several functions:
- it represents *eight major stages* of the world's history
- it contains areas of exceptional natural beauty and aesthetic importance
- it represents *significant ecological and biological processes* in the evolution and development of plants and animals
- it contains *significant natural habitats* for conservation of biological diversity, particularly rare and threatened species.

Task

Apply these criteria of the Wet Tropics World Heritage to a concept of a **World Heritage of the Arts**. (Children will need to understand that 'the arts' includes literature, drama, visual arts, drama, and dance.)

· The arts—in story, poetry and song cycle, in rock art, anecdotal sculptures, and traditional dance—represent the major stages of the experience of humankind in the world's history.

· They contain areas of exceptional beauty and aesthetic importance.

· They represent significant engagement with, and responses to, the processes of living, of being alive in a particular place at a particular time.

· They contain significant 'habitats' in which are conserved the verbal, visual, and movement stories of a world of diverse people, many of whom are already extinct, and all of whom are continually threatened by the processes of time and change.

2.iv Reading

In groups, read one of the picturebooks on the list, or any picturebook with a related theme.

• What message about sustainable futures does this book give to its readers?
• What are the things that must be changed?
• Does the book give us any ideas about how these practices can be changed?
• Is there anything that we can do as part of our everyday life to help towards making these changes?

2.v Literature as a continuum

1. Explore the work of the poets and writers and artists who are a part of the World Heritage of the Arts. Relate the picturebook and its message to other messages about sustainability and the environment within the broader continuum of literature.

> 'No man is an island, entire of itself. Every man is a piece of the continent, a part of the main; if a clod be washed away by the sea, Europe is the less, as well as if a promontory were ... Any man's death diminishes me, because I am involved in mankind.' John Donne (1572–1631)

2. Writers and poets of all ages (e.g. the Romantic poets of western tradition) have seen their work in many cases as a sacred trust. They have actively fought for the preservation of the environment. In 1879, Gerard Manley Hopkins mourned the felling of a group of trees—'not spared, not one'—and grieved that people who came after would never know the beauty that once existed:

Binsey Poplars
Felled 1879

Gerard Manley Hopkins (1844–89)

My aspens dear, whose airy cages quelled,
Quelled or quenched in leaves the leaping sun,
All felled, felled, are all felled;
    Of a fresh and following folded rank
        Not spared, not one
        That dandled a sandalled
     Shadow that swam or sank
On meadow and river and wind-wandering weed-winding bank.

   O if we but knew what we do
     When we delve or hew—
Hack and rack the growing green!
    Since country is so tender
To touch, her being so slender,
That, like this sleek and seeing ball
But a prick will make no eye at all,
Where we, even where we mean
      To mend her we end her,
    When we hew or delve:
After-comers cannot guess the beauty been.
   Ten or twelve, only ten or twelve
    Strokes of havoc unselve
     The sweet especial scene,
   Rural scene, a rural scene,
   Sweet especial rural scene.

3. John Donne's words remind us about how our world and the people in it are
all connected. Think about the characteristics of living systems:

- they have diverse roles within a unity (for example, the unity of a tree—like a
Binsey poplar tree—has both soft leaves and a hard wooden trunk)
- they have permeable boundaries within the structure
- they have energy flow
- there is a *synergy* of the whole, i.e. their energies combine to create a strength
that neither leaves nor trunk possesses on its own.

An ecology of humankind sees everything as connected.

Indigenous cultures have always celebrated spirit within cultural practice: a
spirit that must be encouraged and kept going if that person is to endure, to bear

up, to sustain, and to be sustained. The arts work towards sustainable futures by voicing or representing experiences real or imagined in such a way as to give meaning to individual life.

2.vi Play-building exercise

1. Create a class play about sustainability. Encourage children to think of as many different aspects of sustainability as they can. Go back to the definitions at the beginning of the unit and make sure all aspects are covered. They can act, dance, mime, or sing. Encourage the use of poetry.
2. Elect a script director, director, stage manager, and choreographer.
3. Work towards a lunchtime performance for the rest of the school.

2.vii Poetry

1. Encourage children to find poems about the environment or about the human spirit.
2. Read these aloud, and tell them that it does not really matter if they don't understand every line. Concentrate on the sound and feel of the poems.
3. Some children may like to write their own poems. Some may want to paint an artistic response to issues of sustainability. Publish poems in the classroom and hang an exhibition of the paintings.

Some examples of poems from the literature continuum follow. There are countless others.

The tide in the river
The tide in the river
The tide in the river runs deep
I saw a shiver pass over the river
As the tide turned in its sleep.

By Eleanor Farjeon

The woods are lovely, dark and deep,
But I have promises to keep,
And miles to go before I sleep
And miles to go before I sleep.

By Robert Frost

'Tiger! Tiger! burning bright
In the forests of the night,
What immortal hand or eye
Could frame thy fearful symmetry?'

By William Blake

Summer is y-comen in,
  Loud sing, cuckoo!
Groweth seed and bloweth meed
  And spring'th the woode now—
    Sing cuckoo!
Ewe bleateth after lamb,
  Low'th after calf cow;
Bullock starteth, buck farteth.
  Merry sing, cuckoo!

Anonymous

Clown's Song from *Twelfth Night*

  O Mistris mine where are you roaming?
  O stay and heare, your true love's coming,
  That can sing both high and low.
  Trip no further pretty sweeting.
  Journeys end in lovers meeting,
  Every wise man's sonne doth know.

  What is love, tis not hereafter,
  Present mirth and present laughter:
  What's to come is still unsure.
  In delay there lies no plentie,
  Then come kiss me sweet and twenty:
  Youth's a stuffe will not endure.

By William Shakespeare

  maggie and milly and molly and may
  went down to the beach(to play one day)

  and maggie discovered a shell that sang
  so sweetly she couldn't remember her troubles,and

  milly befriended a stranded star
  whose rays five languid fingers were;

  and molly was chased by a horrible thing
  which raced sideways while blowing bubbles:and

  may came home with a smooth round stone
  as small as a world and as large as alone.

  For whatever we lose(like a you or a me)
  it's always ourselves we find in the sea

by e. e. cummings

(Note that although these tasks have been designed for Upper Primary, the creative teacher can adapt them for the use of younger children as well. Again, this unit has been written on the philosophical premise that children respond positively to guided exposure to concepts and tasks that challenge their existing skills.)

Summary

1   The classroom is a physical and mental space that shapes attitudes that children may carry with them for life.
2   Classroom spaces must be rich, vibrant, and supportive.
3   The most significant gifts teachers can give children are an excitement about learning and about who they are and what they can do.
4   Literacy constitutes a welcome into the world.
5   Teachers need to observe the literate behaviours of children in informal contexts.
6   Children's literature and the literature continuum can offer creative ways of exploring contemporary issues.

Chapter 23
Fairytales: A Pervasive Paradigm

Focus

This chapter considers the fairytale as it has emerged from its historical contexts. It touches on its network of associations with oral and folkloric literature and discusses the way it influences and continues to influence popular culture, noting the significance of this for teaching.

'Human life is always shaped and this shaping is always ritualistic (even if only aesthetically so). The artistic image can always rely on this ritualism.' (M. M. Bakhtin)

Fairytales as the province of children

Children's literature usually begins with fairytales. Note that it is not the intention of these chapters to discuss the history of children's literature; for those interested in this area there are a number of excellent texts (e.g. Hunt 1995; Saxby 1997; Saxby has written a number of books on the history of Australian children's literature).

Fairytales, however, have not historically been the province of children, and nor do they, in the history of our times, remain as the province of children. The influence of fairytales has reached deep into our culture, not only into literature but into films, advertising, and the language of everyday life. They have become pervasive cultural paradigms, artistic images that remain with us as we grow, and that many critics have observed affect in diverse ways how boys and girls think about their life options.

Jack Zipes, a prominent scholar of folktales and fairytales, notes that 'the fairytale is myth' and goes on to explain: 'That is, the classical fairytale has undergone a process of mythicization' (1994: 5). 'It is the fairytale as myth that has extraordinary power in our daily lives, and its guises are manifold, its transformations astonishing' (1994: 16). Zipes is referring here to the classical tradition of ancient myths, that is, to mystical stories of sacred origin. Traditional fairytales do indeed have a 'mythic' quality in this sense, but they have also increasingly been criticised as 'myth' in that derogatory contemporary sense of being 'untrue' or separated from reality. Sacred myths were concerned with the activities of the gods, whose territory was removed from that of mortals in the ordinary world. However, the rituals of secularised myth (divorced from the sacred) are theoretically accessible to all. Zipes points out in his spirited defence of the mythic fairytales of classical tradition that modern writers of these mythic fairytales (not as appropriated and commodified by Disney) can keep alive 'alternatives for a better future' (1994: 161).

It was indeed upon such hopes that fairytales historically gained popular currency.

Children's literature and oral traditions

Fairytales emerged as one strand of the folktale (magic tale or *Zaubermärchen*) tradition (Zipes 1994: 11). Folktales were an integral part of communal story, a strong oral tradition that celebrated pasts and defined futures. In some cultures, this story was illustrated in pictures, in rock art or body paint, or in anecdotal sculpture.

Oral storytelling is a linguistic form of communication that involves a speaker and listeners together at the same time. Folktales were commonly part of social rituals and special functions and the same stories were repeated over and over again, in community. It is interesting for our purposes to note that the general features of the story told by the tale-teller did not vary greatly in content, but the actual telling of the story (words chosen and so on) did change quite radically with each retelling, depending on context and listeners.

That the form of the story changes according to audience points out the significance of the *implied reader* (see Chapter 20, page 352), or in this case, implied listener. Storytellers adjust their tale to suit the moment—the listeners, the time available, the cultural time-space. Writers do the same thing, although they obviously cannot be quite so flexible and quite so variable. They write for the implied reader.

Remember the distinctions between

· *story:* the events, characters and setting of the narrative
· *discourse:* the telling of the tale, the words chosen, the shape of the chapters, the order of the telling, the way it is told (see Chapter 18).

Oral storytellers may change the *discourse*—the way the tale is told, the order of the events, the voice (register) they tell it in—but they will only minimally change the *story*.

This helps understandings of the differences between *discourse* and *story*.

Characteristics of the oral tradition

Stories told orally tend to be repetitive, with recognisable language structures, and narrative structures clearly signalling beginning and endings:

* *Once upon a time:* the story is starting, get ready to listen, and it's a 'no place, no time, any place, any time' story.
* *They all lived happily ever after:* the end of the story, all the threads of events have been pulled together into a perfect conclusion.

The '*playground stories*' of the Jennings type (e.g. Jennings' *Uncovered*, 1995) are arguably a type of 20th-century folk story, telling tales about playground lore and attempting to capture in the permanence of print the ephemeral linguistic fashions of the particular school community. In these texts

* stories are told and retold
* jokes are slightly changed to suit a particular audience
* books are usually written in a very conversational, slangy way that is geared to its audience and understood by its community.

Archetypes

Folktales are the archetypes of our storytelling traditions. An *archetype* is an original model after which other similar things are patterned, a prototype. Carl Jung defined the archetype as an inherited idea in the individual unconscious that he argued derived from the collective experience of being human. Northrop Frye believed that all literature comes from the archetypes of folktales.

Folktales

The roots of folktales, then, are in oral tales: 'tale' means 'speech', 'talk' in Anglo-Saxon. They are a part of the history of cultures all over the world but have in contemporary times become the province of retellers, collectors, interpreters, and illustrators. Their purpose was often cautionary. Common themes of folktales were greed, jealousy, love, and the need for security.

Folktales were not elitist—they belonged to the community and were stories 'of the folk'—the people. They are set in an indefinite time but usually in a specific area: the 'folk' share space and a particular region; they also share identity and history. Folktales reinforced local cultural values and operated to acculturate children into communal traditions and beliefs. They often featured magical transformations. Their structures are repetitive, utilising rhyme and rhythm (think of 'Chicken Licken', 'Henny Penny', 'Run run, run as fast as you can …'). Their narrative conventions, like those of fairytales, allow for unremarkable (i.e. everyone in the story accepts it as normal) communication between animals and humans, often as equals, as, for example, in *Goldilocks and the Three Bears*.

There are three types of folktale:

- **Myths** tell about gods and supernatural beings. Myths are often etiological, that is, they explain human origins, natural events, and geography.
- In **legends** the main characters are often based on actual historical figures (or composites that become one figure). Legends develop their own rhetoric and their own charisma, and the stories often develop with the telling. Thus King Arthur becomes the epitome of chivalry and chivalrous behaviour, and Robin Hood becomes a hero who looks after the poor.
- **Fables** are folktales that often use animals to explicate what a specific culture understands as a particular 'truth' about some aspect of human behaviour. They are short and snappy, and are frequently tagged at the end with a clear moral statement. The most famous examples are the fables of Aesop, which were orally transmitted from about the 6th century BC and were later translated into Latin by Phaedrus (3rd century AD) and Avianus (4th century AD). Many scholars believe that Aesop himself is a legendary character who probably never existed.

Fairytales

'A real fairytale, a fairytale in its true function, is a tale within a circle of listeners.' Karel Capek (Warner 1994: 17)

As we have noted, most fairytales emerged out of the oral traditions of folk literature. At their simplest, fairytales are folktales with fairies. Fairies, however, were not always the pretty little creatures in frilly skirts we see in modern books; they were originally trickster figures. *The Faerie Queene*, by the English poet Edmund Spenser (*c*.1552–99), established a new tradition of fairies, and this was continued in the fairy world of Titania and Oberon in *A Midsummer Night's Dream*, by William Shakespeare (1564–1616). However, the figure of Puck in this play relates back to earlier figures: Puck is a trickster with a range of human emotions (like Ariel in *The Tempest*). A similarly interesting representation of a fairy with 'human' emotions is Tinker Bell (in J.M. Barrie's play *Peter Pan*), who is jealous, petulant and annoyed when she does not get her own way. Other fairy folk include sprites, goblins, elves, and brownies. Australian writers have sought with varying success to create Australian fairies—among the most interesting (and controversial) has been the attempt by Patricia Wrightson to create fairy characters based on indigenous traditions and culture.

Fairytales appear to be 'universal'—for example, more than a thousand versions of Cinderella have appeared in cultures all over the world, and the earliest extant (still in existence) version emerges from 9th-century China.

Literary fairytales

When a fairytale has no oral tradition and is created by an author, it is called a literary fairytale. The most famous writers of literary fairytales are Hans Christian Andersen and Oscar Wilde. Note that literary fairytales tend to explore particular aspects (often from a moral standpoint) of the human condition. Note also that this is not necessarily a standard definition; sometimes the classical fairytales are referred to as 'literary' (as of course they are). But the classical fairytales have clearly emerged out of a folkloric past; the literary fairytales as defined here have been created by their writers within a classical genre.

The birth of the fairytale in literature

In 1697, at the court of Louis IV of France, one of the courtiers, Charles Perrault, put together the collection of fairy stories that would begin a tradition: *Histoires, ou contes du temps passé, avec des Moralitez* (Histories, or stories of times past, with moral lessons). These soon became known by the inscription in the frontispiece of the first edition, *Contes de ma mère L'Oye* (*Mother Goose Tales*). The stories included Cinderella or The Little Glass Slipper, Red Riding Hood, Puss in Boots, Sleeping Beauty (which Perrault had written and published in 1696), Bluebeard, and Tom Thumb. The stories had a short verse-moral at the end, which of course highlights again, in the context of history, their cultural significance and explicit expectation of influence. However, these stories were written, not for children, but for the French court; Perrault's concern was with 'demonstrating how French folklore could be adapted to the tastes of French high culture and used as a new genre of art within the French civilising process' (Zipes 1994: 17).

Earlier, in 1550, in Italy, Giovan Francesco Straparola had published a book of fairytales, and in 1634–36 Giambattista Basile published fairytale collections that included versions of Cinderella and Beauty and the Beast.

Later, in Germany in 1812, the Brothers Grimm, German philologists, students of language and lovers of words (Wilhelm produced the first German dictionary), compiled the first edition of their fairytales. They wrote the tales in idiomatic German, the language of the folk, but this was to become the model for literary German and start a fairytale tradition.

The publication of fairytales in England began much later, with the collections of Andrew Lang. Lang drew on English literary traditions in editing *The Blue Fairy Book* in 1889. This collection included Beauty and the Beast and Jack and the Beanstalk.

The influence of Perrault

Perrault was to have arguably the greatest influence on perceptions of the fairytale until the advent of the 20th-century cinematic reteller, Walt Disney. He wrote in the courtly French of his day and this quickly became the language flavour of the genre. He addressed his tales to the ladies at court. Illustrators have perpetuated this French fairytale chronotope (time-space, see Chapter 20, pages 347–9): pictorial depictions of the world of fairytale were often stylised images of the French court of Louis XIV—beautiful women with pompadour hairstyles, dainty heeled slippers, and elaborate gowns; men in the court dress of the time; the carriages and architecture and social customs of the period.

We have already discussed the significance of sociocultural time-spaces in literature. Perrault wrote out of the history of his times, his historical context, and this context influenced the way the tales were told. The late 17th century (beyond the French court) was a time of mass poverty, widespread malnutrition, and the everyday presence of death. Child marriages were common, and there were large numbers of widows and orphans, and of widowers looking for mothers for their dead wife's children. So the presence of stepmothers and mothers-in-law (*belle-mère*) was a social reality. There were no state structures to care for those who could not care for themselves.

Characteristics of the fairytale

When we consider the characteristics of the fairytale within the context of the prevailing social conditions of Perrault's time, and indeed against those of later periods of history, it is not difficult to guess why this archetypal pattern of story has enjoyed such lasting popularity across the world.

Think about the ideas (and hope) inherent in the following common features of fairytales:

- the triumph of those with least agency—the youngest and the smallest (an atttractive prospect to everyone younger and smaller)
- the defeat of large or threatening figures such as giants, ogres, and witches (i.e. of any frightening figures in your life)
- going out into the world to successfully make your fortune (very attractive to most people, especially those for whom this would be a nigh impossibility)
- enduring a time of trial or suffering before a happy conclusion (giving hope in tough times)
- the wicked stepmother/good true mother opposition offering contrasting responses to maternal figures (assuaging guilt about conflicting feelings)
- the resolution of conflict between an older woman and her 'daughter', with the younger one winning (again, very attractive to the younger and less-enfranchised woman)
- the transformation of the 'beast' or 'frog' bridegroom into a handsome prince (a very pleasant thought if you are married to someone much older and unattractive; it also has a clear sexual connotation)
- the attainment of wealth and power, often by supernatural means (again, an attractive prospect).

It is clear that stories incorporating these features present a very enticing escape package for people with little agency, that is, historically, for women and children.

Sanitising fairytales

Modern readers are usually shocked when they read a translation of Grimm's original Cinderella, where the mother urges the two sisters to cut off parts of their feet so that they will fit the slipper, and where birds pick out the sisters' eyes to punish them for what they had done (Zipes 1987). Grimm's tales met with criticism about their cruelty and harshness even in their own time and a number of 'sanitising' changes were made for the second edition. In the original 1812 version, for example, the 'stepmother' was Snow White's real mother. When the tales were republished in 1819, this was changed to the stepmother version that is common today. In 1812, Hansel and Gretel's real mother and father sent them away; in 1819 their mother became a stepmother and the father more sympathetic. It is interesting here to consider later retellings, for example Anthony Browne's 1981 *Hansel and Gretel* (where the witch and the stepmother are illustrated as being the same person) and Fiona French's *Snow White in New York* (1986).

Interpretations of fairytales

Fairytales are now commonly seen as children's stories, but they continue as part of the ideas and language of everyday life. The English archbishop conducting the wedding of the Prince and Princess of Wales in 1981 referred to the fairytale quality of the wedding (a sadly ironic comment in the light of future events). Films such as *Pretty Woman* (starring Richard Gere and Julia Roberts) have obvious connections to fairytales as well as, in this case, to the myth of Pygmalion and Galatea; *Erin Brockovich* is another type of retelling.

Interest in the interpretations of fairytales began seriously with Bruno Bettelheim, a psychologist born in Vienna in 1903 who worked in the United States from 1929. Bettelheim brought a Freudian psychoanalytical perspective in his text, *The Uses of Enchantment: the Meaning and Importance of Fairytales* (1976). One of Bettelheim's assertions was that fairytales offer a release valve; for example, they deflect children's mixed responses and ambivalences to the mother who both loves and disciplines them. Any mother then is two persons, and young children split the image so they can be angry with the 'false mother' without guilt and thus release their anger towards their own 'real' mother.

Jack Zipes, a scholar and professor of German, in *Breaking the Magic Spell* (1979) and a host of other publications, interprets fairytales from historical-social perspectives. Zipes pointed out that Perrault's fairytales reflected historical social reality; for example, the conflict of what today we call blended families, whereby older men with motherless children remarried younger women who then had their own children.

Marina Warner also argues the significance of historical and social perspectives in her very readable account of fairytales, *From the Beast to the Blonde* (1994). Warner takes issue with Bettelheim, and re-examines the conditions of the time. She notes that in France the word for stepmother is the same as the word for mother-in-law (*belle-mère*) and that the fairytale stereotype of wicked women may be more about mothers-in-law than stepmothers. She points out that in the custom of Perrault's time, arranged marriages between boys and girls as young as ten were common. The promised brides then lived in the homes of their husbands-to-be, and were of course ruled by their future mothers-in-law. Warner believes that Bettelheim's view is dangerous because it perpetuates and reinforces society's prejudices against women.

Deconstructing the Hero, by Margery Hourihan (1997), is a very helpful and stimulating feminist account of the construct of the hero in fairytales and literature. And Clarissa Pinkola Estès' *Women who Run with the Wolves* (1992) is a powerful Jungian analysis of fairytales and folktales concerned with discovering Wild Woman—the source of psychological/spiritual power in women that enables them to 'grow' their souls or psyches.

The complexity of fairytales

Fairytales happen in one world, 'where, within the frames of the genre, everything is possible: animals talk, wishes come true by magic, fairies give or withhold blessings, pumpkins turn into coaches, people can fly, etc. All of these supernatural elements are taken for granted, and never does the protagonist wonder at them' (Nikolajeva 1988).

The irony is that these stories that have become the classics of children's literature are far from being simple and innocent stories. They can be explosive records of the worst of human behaviour and emphasise, among other things:

- sibling rivalry—for example, the Ugly Sisters and Cinderella
- rivalry between women who all want to marry the Prince
- ambivalent attitudes towards mothers represented in images of the stepmother, the dead real mother, and the good fairy godmother
- women's dependence on finding a husband
- the idea of true worth and beauty being hidden beneath rags and surface grime (but note that the goodness still shines through—and has to be discovered, usually by a prince).

These characteristics highlight other problems inherent in the fairytale paradigm:

- the implication that goodness is useless without beauty (which is always visible when cleaned up and given fine clothes)
- the representation of goodness as meek and submissive obedience; Cinderella, for example, must not break out and go beyond the boundaries set for her: she must obey the rules and be home by midnight.

Implicit values

Fairytales are characterised by the dream that humans of the 21st century recognise as easily as those of earlier centuries did—the tempting, comforting, tantalising dream of upward social mobility.

This dream of course reinforces the significance of hierarchical structures in society: the importance of position, of becoming one of the nobility, of 'marrying money'. We have only to read the social pages of our newspapers to realise that this dream is alive and well. The implicit context of fairytales is not a pretty picture; it is a society of gross inequalities, of gross poverty, and of often equally gross treatment of the weak and helpless. In Perrault's times, wealth was recognised by its trappings (signs): coach, livery, clothes; all of these were essential for those who wanted to appear (and thus implicitly *be*) 'noble'.

Fairytales also clearly perpetuate stereotypical sex roles. Women's tasks are domestic chores; their concern is their appearance and their claims to physical beauty are of paramount concern (one wonders if much has changed when looking though women's magazines of the new millennium). Their pleasures are social rather than intellectual. Their ultimate achievement is marriage. They have little or no power of their own; their destinies are held in the hands of men—father, king, prince. The implicit ideology of fairytales is that this is the natural structure of society and that this is the proper role of women.

However, despite these all too obvious problems, fairytales have redeeming features:

- they immerse children in language, sometimes (depending on the retelling) the language of the classical tradition
- they represent and so help understandings of the human condition
- they are a fundamental part of cultural literacy
- they can be used by teachers to encourage children into critical literacy
- they lend themselves to many humorous and skewed retellings which can make children aware of the stereotypes they contain and help them to resist easy positioning
- and, yes, they do contain that element of magic that Zipes talks about, and as such, read against parodies and revisions and feminist retellings, can still captivate and, in Zipes' words, 'compel us to rethink the meaning of utopia and freedom in reality and in the realm of the fairytale as well' (1994: 161).

Characteristics of contemporary retellings of fairytales

As the early chapters of this Part noted, cultural ideologies influence texts both explicitly and implicitly. Retellings of fairytales in our own times reflect modern concerns. Feminist literature has helped us to rethink roles and behaviours and to resist cultural encoding that denies women freedom of choice. Thus a film such as *Ever After* (starring Drew Barrymore) features a resourceful princess who is not only quite capable of looking after herself but also saves the prince. There are many wonderful children's books that open up possibilities and potentials in retellings within the fairytale tradition. Some that come to mind are Munsch and Marchenko's ***The Paper Bag Princess*** (1980), Babette Cole's ***Princess Smartypants*** (1986) and ***Prince Cinders*** (1987), and Martin Waddell and Patrick Benson's ***The Touch Princess*** (1986). (See Chapter 20, page 359 for some other humorous retellings of fairytales.)

A more subtle change in contemporary readings of fairytales is in our conceptions of 'the Beast'. The idea of the beast has always had sexual implications; what young girl in the time of Perrault or even in later centuries would not like to believe and hope that beneath the apparent beastliness of a beastly husband there was a prince (or anything)? A 'beast'—wild and untamed— was an apt metaphor for bad behaviour and crassness. However, we live in a different era, an era that no longer believes that everything should be 'civilised', and that has different attitudes towards beasts, and their taming. Anthony Browne's **Zoo** is an example of a new way of thinking about animals and animal rights. The world of the third millennium seeks to conserve its wilderness and its native species. So 'beasts' are no longer such an apt metaphor, and in contemporary retellings of the fairytale beasts are not the awful things that they once were; they have become more appealing—sometimes more appealing than the handsome foppish prince. The beast in Disney's film *Beauty and the Beast* was frightening perhaps, but I would argue was explicitly represented as inherently appealing, even before his transformation.

It is also interesting to note that in Grimm's original fairytale, Cinderella's ugly sisters weren't ugly, just cranky and unpleasant. They became ugly in the retellings of a society that equated ugliness of spirit with physical ugliness. However, again in the film *Ever After*, the 'ugly sisters' reverted to Grimm's original—they were unpleasant but not unattractive.

Fairytales as 'culture's sentences' and as 'socialising'

Commenting on the fairytale, Ellen Cronan Rose notes Bettelheim's comments that fairytales 'depict in imaginary and symbolic form the essential steps in growing up and achieving an independent existence' and that they 'represent in imaginative form' the 'process' of human development (1983: 209). Rose makes the point that this allows us to discuss them as tales of *Bildung*, narratives of growth and development, quoting Sandra M. Gilbert and Susan Gubar's comments that fairytales 'state and enforce culture's sentences with greater accuracy than more sophisticated literary texts because they reduce a complicated process of socialisation to its essential paradigm'. (Rose 1983: 209)

Notwithstanding the fact that Bettelheim is no longer considered so authoritative (especially when gender is the issue), this reiterates the potential powers (and dangers) of the simple fairy story. The phrase 'culture's sentences' does not merely refer to an articulation or representation of cultural customs; it also indicates that these are edicts, judgments, sentences that impose a certain rule of behaviour and response. A short fairytale, say Gilbert and Gubar, can sum up everything a society thinks about what's important.

Most teachers are now alert to these issues; part of critically literate practice is to recognise this and to lead children into awareness of it. There is, however, another significance that the history of fairytales highlights, and one that we can take on board as part of our teaching philosophy. Zipes make the point that when the printing press revolutionised folklore, and put it into print, it became necessarily elitist (1994). Its language changed, its audience changed, and it became the province of the educated ruling classes. In other words, it was no longer 'of the folk'.

As teachers, every time we help children into reading, every time we make something accessible that was previously inaccessible, every time we share a book in community and tell stories together, and listen to each others' stories, and every time we help children develop the skills to enable them to enter a place from which they had previously been excluded, we are helping to address such issues and to restore such equity.

 ## Task 12

Woman is Sleeping Beauty, Cinderella, Snow White, she who receives and submits. In song and story the young man is seen departing adventurously in search of a woman; he slays the dragon, he battles the giants; she is locked in a tower, a palace, a garden, a cave, she is chained to a rock, a captive, sound asleep; she waits. (Simone de Beauvoir)

1. Explore these ideas and give examples from fairytales. Find and discuss books which actively work to change this paradigm. How do they do it? Why? In what ways is this significant for us as teachers?
2. Consider the influence of Walt Disney on the fairytale.
3. Consider the words of Ellen Cronan Rose (above). Think through the positives and negatives of what she is saying.
4. Start your own collection of versions and retellings that you can use in the classroom to help your students into critical literacy.

 ## Activity 25

(Adapt as appropriate to any level.)

Fairytales are a part of our cultural *understory*—a reservoir of rich resources that have influenced not only books but also films, advertising, and other media.

1. Make a class list of as many books that you can find that are related to the fairytale.
2. Make a class list of as many films as you can think of that are related to the fairytale.
3. Set up a fairytale table with as many versions of one particular fairytale as you can find.

Teacher reading

Read *Eucalyptus* by Murray Bail (1998) as a fairytale. Think about the role of the daughter and the role of her would-be suitor within this paradigm. Think about analogies with the enchanted forest surrounding the home of the beautiful princess. *Eucalptus* is a complex text with a dream-like, mythic quality that is a surreal depiction of the Australian landscape.

SUMMARY

1   Fairytales emerge from a rich historical folkloric context.
2   Originally, they were not particularly written for children.
3   The patterns of their stories were and are attractive to those with little power.
4   Classical fairytales need to be carefully reconsidered as they are intensely and powerfully culturally pervasive.
5   Fairytales can stimulate us to think about roles and gender issues, and about how books and films construct these in certain ways.
6   They can also remind us about the human need to dream of more equitable futures.
7   And, they can provoke us as teachers to renew our efforts and inflame our philosophy to work towards helping *all* children into literacy and literate behaviours.

Chapter 24
Picturebooks: The Third Space

Focus

This chapter discusses the visual and verbal art of picturebooks and the unique qualities of the internal conversation between them. It discusses visual literacy and visual processing. It also focuses on using picturebooks to help children into understandings of poetry.

The explosion of large numbers of picturebooks in the marketplace was a 20th-century phenomenon (see Saxby 1997: 184–204). Originally such books were designed for very young children who could not yet operate as competent independent readers. Pictures, it was considered, helped children to 'read' by placing *signifier* (name) and *signified* (the thing) in close visual proximity to each other, after the style of alphabet or vocabulary books (see Chapter 19, page 333). These pictures give children clues and cues about the story and the characters, as well as helping to make the texts more attractive and aesthetically appealing.

The pictures of picturebooks, then, emerge from a pedagogical tradition of teaching children literacy on the one hand, and the publishing tradition of the random use of illustrations in fiction texts on the other. Some of these books 'with illustrations' were infuriating to the careful reader as it was quite clear that the illustrator often had not read the book, and there was frequently significant discrepancy between words and pictures. Sometimes it was only the line of text beneath the picture (caption) that gave the reader any idea of what incident in the book it was meant to represent.

In contrast, any discrepancy between the words and pictures of a modern picturebook is meant to be there. What's more, it is likely to be part of what Doonan calls the picturebook's 'narrative thrust' (1993: 39).

For example, let's look at Anthony Browne's ***Zoo*** (1992). This text presents readers with the focalisation of the young boy narrator, but as we progress through the story there is an increasing sense of unease and discrepancy between what he says and what the pictures 'say':

'We went into the elephant house which was really smelly. The elephant just stood in the corner stuffing its face.'

'Then we had to go and see the polar bear. It looked really stupid, just walking up and down, up and down.'

The pictures accompanying these pieces of text in both cases accurately represent the bones of the words: the elephant *is* standing in its house eating; the polar bear *is* walking, presumably up and down. However, just as the boy focaliser's language choices ('just stood' 'stuffing its face', 'really stupid', 'just walking up and down') extend meaning by conveying a particular attitude, so the pictures, while they in no way contradict what he is saying as literally true, interrogate his perspectives and work towards a moral contradiction of them.

If we apply the linguistic idea of **register** to the pictures as well as to the words, it is clear that there is a deliberate mismatch of registers. The words are in one register—the colloquial language of a boy uninterested in the social situation of a family outing—and the pictures are in another, quite different register—the visual language of a deeply concerned animal-lover whose intention is to use this literary context as a protest against keeping animals in zoos.

This concept of register in relation to the pictures of picturebooks is helpful. Register pertains to the significance of the social situation in which words are uttered—who we're speaking to and where we are may not always determine what we say but it certainly influences how we say it. It draws attention to the importance of situation in how we seek to achieve our communicative purposes. Browne's visual language speaks in a noble register that is the antithesis of the slangy conversation of his young narrator. This visual language is the serious and emotive language of advocacy.

The elephant stands within a space configured with sharp and heavy horizontal lines on a hard floor littered with a few pieces of either food or faeces, the only light coming from a horizontally barred ceiling, and a small door, man-size (not elephant-size, another representation of human power and animal helplessness), apparently the only way out. On this third opening, pictures and words are entering into a conversation of differing ideologies—a dialogic conflict—with each other. By the time of the polar bear (the eighth opening), the different registers used in the depiction of the bear, in its artificial and horizonless cave, are opening up textual spaces of meaning beyond either the verbal or pictorial text.

It is the way that the pictures work *against* the verbal text that tells the story of *Zoo*; the pictures would lose a major part of their argument without the words that conflate them. 'Argument' is a good word: this text argues Browne's worldview about the confining of animals in zoos for the indiscriminate and uninterested pleasure of families such as this. By the tenth opening, when the orang-utan crouches in a corner, the pictures have become such a powerful 'voice' that the narrator's perspective of 'miserable thing' rings with an awful irony.

The text opens up to further dialogic relationships when we recognise the distinct similarity between the mother and the orang-utan—it could almost be the back of her head that we see huddled in the cage.

Writers and illustrators working together

Anthony Browne is one of many children's writers who illustrate their own books, but there are also many writers who write only and illustrators who illustrate only. It is interesting to note that not so very long ago the name of the illustrator might not have appeared on the book cover; when it did it was usually much smaller and less significantly placed than that of the writer.

That this is no longer the case is an indication of increasing understandings of the literary form and structure (poetics) of this genre. Illustrators are co-producers of picturebooks and share the telling of their story. It alerts us to the fact that the pictures are not just ornaments or frills or visual embroidery but part of the narrative process.

Sometimes authors and illustrators work independently of each other. While this may or may not be desirable, it appears to be a publishing reality. This opens up provocative questions as to individual artistic conceptualisations of 'meaning'. A study of one book noted that the illustrations were carried out with very little input from the writer (Winch 1999); the anecdotes of other writers reveal that this is not an unfamiliar scenario.

Verbal and visual languages of picturebooks

We have earlier discussed Bakhtin's conceptualisation of the novel as containing many voices—i.e. heteroglossia (see Chapter 19, page 339, and Chapter 20, page 355). While he is not referring to picturebooks, it is interesting to consider his ideas about the verbal art of the novel in relation to what we could call the 'double languages' (verbal and visual) of the picturebook genre:

> All languages of heteroglossia, whatever the principle underlying them and making each unique, are specific points of view on the world, forms for conceptualising the world in words, specific world views, each characterised by its own objects, meanings and values. As such they may be juxtaposed to one another, mutually supplement one another, contradict one another and be interrelated dialogicly. (1981: 291–2)

Zoo is clearly a heteroglossic text: its words and pictures work together to transmit many 'voices'—that of the boy focaliser, the father, the mother, Browne's philosophical position, societal ideas about zoos, and, of course, the animals.

The pictures of picturebooks in tandem with the verbal text represent a unique many-voiced language that is increasingly, deeply, intertextual, in its words and in its pictures. This intertextuality represents a conversation not only between this and other verbal texts, but also between these and other illustrations (see the earlier discussion on *Memorial* and *The Great Bear*, Chapters 19, 20, pages 339 and 357–8).

As Nikolajeva (1996a: 153–4) points out, intertextuality is about 'codes' and conversations between works of art or between works of art and cultural codes and practices. Anthony Browne's **Piggybook** (1986) is powerful not only because of the internal conversation between its words and pictures, and its argumentative intertextual relationship to all those books where mother does the household chores and wears an apron, but also because it contains a provocative intertextual dialogue with patriarchal and feminist discourses. This enlarges its obvious semiotic codes—the car is a 'sign' traditionally associated with masculinity, the multiplying pigs are signs not just of animals but of certain associated behaviours; the flying pigs play with the well-known idiom expressing impossibility, 'Pigs might fly'.

The internal conversation of picturebooks

At the heart of the picturebook is the dialogic conversation it has within itself, between the art of its words and the art of its pictures—the interaction it sets up in the spaces between and beyond its words and its pictures. This conversation constructs its worldview, and works in a synergistic tension extending or interrogating meaning by juxtapositions, by mutual supplementation, by contradiction, and by dialogic interrelationship. Remember that Bakhtin interprets 'dialogic' as the many voices behind and inherent in language; it is the internal and external voices we hear beyond the actual words, sentences, and pictures, which help us as readers and beholders to make meaning.

Pat Hutchins' simple little tale **Rosie's Walk** (1968) provides a great example of how words and pictures work together to create something that is across, between, and beyond each of them. This is an interdisciplinary space that is neither completely words nor completely pictures. It is a unique *third space*, which has as part of its deep structure *intratextuality*—a sort of within-the-text intertextuality. Like intertextuality, which also reaches across, between, and beyond, intratextuality sets up points of interconnectedness that are fragile and often characterised by heterogeneity.

For example, there is no overt connection in the words of *Rosie's Walk* with the fox who stalks her. Whether or not she is aware of its presence is a matter to debate with child readers: what is interesting in this discussion is the points of intratextual connection between the words and the pictures and the pattern that emerges from these. In terms of structure, there are obvious links to the classic narrative structure of the journey away from home and back again, a structure that children will increasingly recognise. The causal link is of course Rosie—*Rosie's Walk* is a type of **picaresque** picturebook, with either Rosie or the fox as rogue-hero. It is a story whose order and sequence of events follow the progress of its main character through a number of adventures in different places. The visual story connects, in a signifier–signified relationship, with the name of the place through which Rosie walks (across the yard, around the pond, past the mill, through the fence, etc.). This is a homogeneous, stable connection. The connection becomes more hetero-geneous when what was safe for Rosie becomes a place of disaster for the fox; irony extends and amplifies the narrative way beyond the words by what is depicted as happening to the fox in Rosie's wake. Not only that, but also the pictures then infuse the words with other images about foxes getting their come-uppance—Brer Fox is an obvious example.

Counterpoint

Phillip Pullman writes: 'The complexity of interplay between picture-meaning and text-meaning … and what that interplay allows is the greatest storytelling discovery of the twentieth century: namely, counterpoint' (1989: 160–86). This is a helpful analogy: **counterpoint** is a musical term that refers to the musical technique of combining two or more melodic lines in such a way that they establish a harmonic relationship while retaining their linear individuality. But I am not sure that the pictures and verbal text of picturebooks, after they have been read, can maintain their 'linear individuality'. Pictures are read in non-linear ways; children read pictures in all sorts of movements, with their eyes moving apparently randomly around the page, free from the reading of text from left to right. And although the first time we read a book we may read in a linear way, any subsequent reading is influenced by the intratextual reading that has already occurred. The second time we read *Rosie's Walk*, the pictures and meanings we made from the first reading are part of our reading repertoire. We can never recapture the innocence of a first reading.

The pleasures of predictability

Not that children want to anyway. Research continually indicates the significance of *prediction* in reading success (see Chapter 20); part of predictive skill is being able to anticipate a familiar text or genre. This probably explains the popularity of series books, from the *Famous Five* to *Sweet Valley High* and *Goosebumps* and the *Animorphs*. It is also significant to note that children are very highly focused close readers, as any parent or teacher who tries to skip bits of a favourite story knows. There is certainly a great pleasure in meeting the familiar; nonetheless, the particular pleasure of the picturebook and of children's literature in general is in the act of revisiting the familiar but discovering something new in the process. Margaret Meek writes that a page in a picturebook is to be 'contemplated, narrated, explicated by the viewer. It holds the story until there is a telling.' Readers have to learn 'which of the pictorial events carries the line of the story … The essential lesson of *Rosie's Walk* depends on there being no mention of the fox, but the reader knows there would be no story without him. Nowhere but in the readers' interaction with the text can this be learned' (1988).

Picturebooks have developed their own conventions: covers and title pages that reflect a significant moment; endpapers that usually reflect or symbolise thematic intent or cultural location; the convention of an illustration at every opening; sometimes decorations of words and opening initials that evoke the illustrated manuscript of past times; sometimes an afterword of explanation (usually serious and often didactic); sometimes a tiny picture on the back page representing the return to equilibrium or the new status quo.

Task 13

Take a number of copies of the text, and an overhead print-out (on one page) of the text of **The Fisherman and the Theefyspray** (Jennings and Tanner 1994):

· read the verbal text from the overhead
· retell the story
· note any narrative gaps
· now look at the illustrations only
· note how the pictures help to tell the story
· now consider the whole text
· how do the pictures fill in the gaps? What do they add?

Activity 26

Read **Where's Mum?** by Libby Gleeson and Craig Smith (1992).

Years K–2

1. Read the story to the class.
2. Ask children to draw pictures of all the fairytale characters.
3. Ask children to write their own fairytale.

Years 3–4

1. Read the verbal text to the class without showing them the pictures.
2. Then, in roundtable groups, read the text again, this time also reading the pictures.
3. Carefully examine the pictures in relation to the words. What do the pictures tell us that the words don't (the messiness of the house, the hassled dad)?
4. Check out the pictures for little connecting signs: eg. dad holding an egg as they talk about Humpty Dumpty.
5. 'Tell me': what is the surprise at the end of the story?

Years 5–6

As above, but add:

6. In your group, write or script what else Mum told her family.

The language of pictures

'A picture is worth a thousand words'—so the old saying goes. This statement may be challenged, but nevertheless we can see that the unique status of picturebooks is that they are *literature*—books—whose story is told in two different types of texts or 'language-ings' (that is, words and pictures). Pictures as noted above are non-linear—and the idea of 'reading the pictures' fits in very well with an increasingly electronic age in which features such as hypertext challenge previous reading hierarchies and stimulate non-linear print cultures. Icons are visual symbols and in contemporary culture stand for everyday actions and processes as well as for representations of the abstract and/or sacred. The current debate in educational circles about *visual processing* and *visual literacy* reflects the growing awareness of the different types of texts that children today engage with, and the significance of this in the reading (meaning-making) process.

Reading is a visual and cognitive process, and how print is arranged on a page makes a difference to how it is read. *Visual processing* may appear to categorise the small print on a product as less important than the large print featuring the product name—*visual literacy* helps us to recognise that the smallest print may contain the most important information (of course, this also represents knowledge of the ways of advertisers, which is a part of cultural and critical literacy).

Conventional ideas of illustration have obviously tacitly played with ideas of visual processing—in alphabet books for example, the child sees an apple, sees an 'Aa' and puts the two together. This is a type of *word–picture assimilation*. Picturebooks however have on the whole moved beyond such ideas—not to multiculturalism but to a sort of **multitextualism**, an awareness of the richness of textual difference. Words and pictures do not have to assimilate (blend together like the *Aa* and the picture of the apple); they can do different things and can interrogate and problematise as well as support (think of ***Zoo***). This is a particularly significant attribute for children growing up in an age of multiple texts and multiple literacies.

An indication of the impact of the visual in the reading process is the current experimentation with all sorts of different representations of the verbal text in picturebooks. Words run up and around pages which may have to be tilted to be read, they hide in different parts of the page, they appear randomly and in different fonts and sizes—think of Maya Angelou's ***My Painted House, My Friendly Chicken and Me*** (1994). The growing use of the term 'viewer' or 'beholder' in discussing the implied 'reader' of picturebooks reflects a challenge to (or an enlargement of) traditional notions of literacy.

Visual literacy

The particular strength of picturebooks is that their pictures as well as their words are designed to convey messages that 'mean'. We live in a world where pictures 'mean'—a world of images, symbols and logos—a semiotic world of signs. Teaching children about how the pictures in picturebooks work, with and against the text, helps them to develop visual literacy, an increasingly important literacy in a world of diverse textual communications. Visual literacy is more than the ability to decode images (to work out what images mean). It is the ability to analyse the *power of the image* and the *how* of its meaning in its particular context. (See also p. 339.)

In defence of the pictures

Increased understandings of visual processing and visual literacy, and of the theory of the dialogic relationship between the words and the pictures of picturebooks, helps us to understand how important such books are in the reading history of children. But picturebooks have their critics. Protheroe writes: 'Using pictures and visual aids to subserve language learning is a very suspect activity and may not only adversely affect children's linguistic ability but permanently stunt their intellectual growth' (1992: 10).

A diet of the bland illustrations of some school reader series books may certainly be suspect, but as we have seen, the picturebooks of today are on the whole anything but bland. They are increasingly subtle and abstract. Protheroe's advocacy of the significance of the imagination for children is something with which I wholly concur, and, with a proviso, I also concur with her conclusion: 'Right from the beginning [children] need stories without pictures'.

Yes, they do. This is part of the shared reading process—for educators to read books without pictures, *as well as* books with pictures; to read difficult and challenging texts, while at the same time reading texts that are simple and relatively accessible. But to blame picturebooks for the promotion of illiteracy seems to me to ignore the contribution of this genre to children's literature and to fail to engage with the sophisticated processes through which picturebooks actually work.

There are a number of codes and conventions in picturebooks that we learn to accept very quickly:

- pictures are two-dimensional but they represent a three-dimensional world
- not everything can be included so some things have to be left out
- the picture is a highly limited and focused space
- sometimes there are backgrounds, sometimes there are parts of backgrounds and sometimes there is a lot of white unfilled space
- there are particular conventions for showing movement, and sometimes for indicating speech and thought (often comic book conventions are used)
- sometimes there are frames around pictures and sometimes pictures spill off the page.

Pictures can be discussed in terms of shape, proportion, colour, light and shade, space, focalisation, materials (collage, woodcuts, watercolours, oils, and pencils), use of black lines, shadows, and composition.

There are an increasing number of books and papers specialising in picturebook art. One of the first and most helpful is Perry Nodelman's *Words About Pictures*

(1988). Other useful references include Jane Doonan's *Looking at Pictures in Picture Books* (1993) and *CREArTA* (International Journal of the Centre for Research and Education in the Arts), 1(1) 2000).

The visual chronotope

In Chapter 20 we noted Bakhtin's idea of the chronotope—the relationships of *people and events* to *time and space* in novels. We proposed the extension of this idea into the concept of a visual chronotope, that is, the *visual* depiction of the relationships of *people and events* to *time and space* in the pictures of picture books.

Teachers may not want to use this theoretical metalanguage in the classroom, but their own understanding of such ideas may inspire new ways of approaching picturebooks and stimulate creative classroom discussion and enquiry.

For example, *A is for Aunty* by Elaine Russell (2000) takes the traditional form of the alphabet book but is in fact deeply autobiographical; Russell uses the

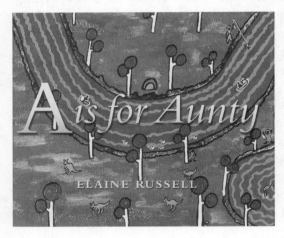

sequential letters of the alphabet to give narrative shape to her memories of an indigenous childhood. In the words of the text, people and events are related to time and space through the normal chronology of the narrator's lifetime: 'The mission where I lived as a child was like a small suburb outside the main town, in the bush near a river.'

Each letter of the alphabet stimulates a memory of the past:

I is for Inspection Day. The manager's wife visited each house on the mission to make sure our homes were clean and tidy—which they were!

L
is for Lagoon

A lagoon is a great big pond way out in the bush. Wild ducks, swans, cranes and other animals gather there, mainly in the mornings or late in the evenings, to drink the water. We Aboriginal people would say this is the animals' Meeting Place, where they can rest and get together.

M
is for Mission

The mission where I lived as a child was like a small suburb outside the main town, in the bush near a river. The government built the houses — all in rows — for the Aboriginal families to live in.
There was a school, a church and a dance hall. The manager and his family lived in their own house on the mission.

So the past that is clearly expressed in words is the remembered past of an older person looking back, the past of an individual lifetime, but this does not fully explain the impact of the book. However, if we bring the concept of a visual chronotope into play, and consider how the people and events are drawn in relation to time and space in the *pictures* of the text, it is clear that the visual chronotope of this story reaches into a past that is beyond that of an individual lifetime. The past expressed in the illustrations is unbound by the restrictions of a normal lifespan; it is a dense cultural past/present that could be called a type of Dreaming chronotope. The pictures construct multiple references—to totemic figures, to the circles of sites, camps, waterholes, campfires. The roads present an imagery of paths and movement, while the river that dominates most of the illustrations reminds us of Water Dreamings, and/or of a snake or Rainbow serpent—of a type of genesis, life-giving and connecting.

In prose (without its pictures), this is a 20th-century story told in a warm but matter-of-fact way; it is a charming story of random memories, with a deep but not bitter subtext implicating sociocultural attitudes, practices and policies in relation to indigenous people. In pictures (without its prose), this is a story that in depicting a 'modern' Australia reaches back into an Australia before white settlement. In the form of a picturebook, with both prose and pictures carrying narrative and coming together in story, the visual chronotope amplifies the verbal chronotope to something beyond an individual experience. This does not devalue that individual life experience; it enriches it. The relationship of people to the time-spaces of the illustrations is different from the relationship of people to the time-spaces of the verbal narrative, and the effect of this difference is to transpose *A is for Aunty* into a different cultural dimension.

Picturebooks and poetry

Poetry is spare, euphonic (pleasant-sounding) language that operates very much like data compression: one word can hold and then release a tumble of information. A poet has only a short space (even in long poems) to convey his or her thoughts, and so must work towards making every word count.

Picturebook text has many similarities to poetry. It too tends to be very spare, very succinct, as Nodelman points out, and very powerful. Simple words, cohabiting with their illustrations, unleash a whole host of ideas, thoughts, feelings, meanings; they call out to other words from the understory and bring them up to play. Picturebook and poetic text depend on the semiotic (see page 308) and semantic process of signs and symbols; the words of their discourses are much fewer than the words of their stories.

Picturebooks, like poetry, sound best read aloud—they have an acoustic function, an articulatory function, and a semantic function. Read for example, the words of *The Fisherman and the Theefyspray*—savour the saying of them; do the same with William Mayne's beautiful little story *Mousewing* (1987). Listen to them as other people read. Think about how the words mean, and how they make you react the way that you do. In this way, picturebooks (and any books read aloud with a group) relate to the discussion of folklore in the previous chapter: they offer a corporate, community experience of shared story.

This is an experience that we need to give children. Let them read aloud, not as part of oral reading—as a task—but because reading aloud is fun. Even reluctant readers feel confident when reading what looks like a short and simple text. After the reading, call attention to the words, and how the writer has put them to work. Ask children to listen to the story with pencils in their hands and jot down any words that come into their minds as they are listening (do this on a second reading of a text). Prove to them how words contain other words inside them (like those little sets of Russian dolls) and around them. Share in the activity and let the class see how much you too enjoy language.

> Russian **formalism**, a literary theory that emerged in the early part of the 20th century, claimed that the essence of literary language was **defamiliarisation**. That is, words are used and put together in such a way as to sound unfamiliar, different, sometimes startling. This has the effect of making readers perceive a familiar thing or consider a familiar process in a new way. Poets have to make ordinary things sound strange so that we focus on *seeing* them as if for the first time, rather than just knowing them from lots of other places. The formalist Shklovsky writes, 'The language of poetry is, then, a difficult, roughened, impeded language' (Rivkin and Ryan 1998: 21).

Picturebook language is also sometimes 'roughened' in this way (see box above)—words that are quite normal and everyday and that usually glide smoothly into sentences without our even noticing them suddenly seem to stand out, surprisingly rough around the edges, not able to fit in so easily without our stopping for a microsecond (or longer), thinking about them and giving them a bit of an intellectual push. They catch and snag on each other. Then we suddenly see that this fits into place in a whole new way and we see something fresh, with 'growing eyes'.

Look at the text of *Theefyspray:*

> *Deep in the still cold shadows the last*
> *Theefyspray looked out of her lonely lair.*

'Lair' feels rough and incongruous for a fish, but when we stop and think about it as a den or a hiding place, it adds to the sense we already have of something wild and beautiful under threat. The unusual word order, the alliteration, and the almost unconscious assonance of 'deep' and 'theefyspray' also help to roughen up the language, preventing our reading superficially. Jennings wants us to hear (and touch and feel) every word:

> *There was not one other like her now.*
> *Not in the heavens. Or the hills.*
> *Or the deeps of the hushed green sea.*

The *story* of these lines is that 'there was no other theefyspray'. But the *discourse* reaches again down to the understory and picks up strangely inappropriate words for a fish: 'Not in the heavens. Or the hills'. Nowhere in the whole wide world, or even outside it—and the alliterative 'heavens' and 'hills' release data about 'aloneness' which some people may find almost biblical.

There are many picturebooks that are poetic in their discourse. Consider any of Sendak's texts:

> *[Max] sailed off through night and day*
> *and in and out of weeks*
> *and almost a year*
> *to where the wild things are. (1963)*

> *If Ida backwards in the rain*
> *would only turn around again*
> *and catch those goblins with a tune*
> *she'd spoil their kidnap honeymoon! (1993)*

We can savour the language of almost anything from the Ahlbergs. And what about this from **You and Me, Murrawee**?

> *We walk this same brown earth—*
> *You and me, Murrawee.*

Poetry and picturebooks share a linguistic freedom—sentences can be incomplete or ungrammatical, words can be left out; it is the sound and saying and the sense that matter:

> *The boy called Shane strokes the scared fur.*
> *He talks and talks until growls slide into silence …*
> *Over the bins and garbage bags, past a row of seamed-up houses.*
> *'Yeah—you're with me now, Cat. You'n me, Cat.*
> *And we're going way away home. (**Way Home**, Hathorn and Rogers*
> *1994).*

Most children enjoy the sounds of picturebooks. They also enjoy poetry— rhythm and rhyme and the feel and taste of words. That's why they chant rhymes in the playground, and while skipping, and on the bus, and in their games. We as teachers kill poetry when we focus on 'meaning' all the time—as edifying as that can be a little later in our development. We sometimes forget that the sounds and rhythm of words are part of their meaning and a fundamental element of the poetic experience.

Beware Beware (Hill and Barrett 1993) is a miniature *Bildungsroman*—a story about growing, about the call of the world and the call of the wild, maybe about ambivalence and the desire to 'walk on the wild side' (Doonan 1998). Its language is intensely intertextual, as discussed earlier (see Chapter 20, page 359); it is also intensely poetic:

Setting sun
Rose red
Light falls
Across the snow

This book lends itself to being spoken and acted out. Experiment with different voice combinations. Is this a monologue—a conversation with inner voices? Or is it a conversation—a cautionary one—between the little girl and her mother? And what about when she gets into the woods—are the voices she hears from inside or outside herself? Ask children to think of different ways to mime the story.

You can use picturebooks like this one as a stepping-stone to poems across the literature continuum. For example, for me, these lines evoke Tennyson's 'Blow Bugle Blow', especially the second stanza:

O hark, O hear! How thin and clear
  And thinner, clearer, farther going!
O sweet and far from hill and scar
  The horns of Elfland faintly blowing.
Blow, let us hear the purple glens replying:
Blow, bugle: answer, echoes, dying, dying, dying.

Read this, and any other poem that the story may evoke to you, to the class, but don't stress its meaning—any more than you stress the meaning of **Beware, Beware** (I am not sure exactly what the picturebook means). Sometimes we need to grow into meaning. That's part of the pleasure of literature. And sometimes meaning is beyond words anyway.

Ask the class to pick out the words that may seem related—to show them how words connect with each other, sometimes without our realising it. Doing this sets up a link between picturebooks and poetry and exposes children to the wider literature continuum, helping to build up their own capacity for understory.

You could also explore other picturebooks for connections to *Beware, Beware*. Fairytales are obvious intertexts for the adventure in the woods—perhaps the 'Rose red' plays with images from *Snow White*. Josephine Poole's retelling of this fairytale has a much longer text than *Beware, Beware*, but the poetic type of language is still there:

One day the queen sat by the window, stitching pearls into cloth of gold. It was winter, and very cold, and presently it began to snow.

  She opened the window to listen for the sound of the king's hunting horn. But as she leant out, she pricked herself with her needle, so that a drop of blood fell onto the snow. When she saw it, she wished in her heart, 'Oh, that I had a child as red as blood, as white as snow, and as black as the wood of an ebony tree!' (Poole and Barrett 1991)

Matt Ottley's **Mrs Millie's Painting** (1998) represents part of its text as a rhythmic wave that is an interesting pictorial representation of what poetry does and what it looks like:

They arrived home at dusk, as the air was filled with fireflies.

Children may like to try to write their own poetry in wavy lines, or in some other way that visually represents the sense of rhythm they are trying to create. This could be a very interesting computer task. They may also like to do a painting—perhaps to try to paint a neighbourhood, as Mrs Millie does.

There are many, many wonderful poetry books for children, but the language of picturebooks is, very often, a poetic language. Understanding and becoming familiar with that language, and constructing more and more links to its understory, not only gives children confidence and enhances literacy skills but also gives them pleasure.

SUMMARY

1   The words and pictures of picturebooks function together in a unique way to tell a story.

2   If we think of the pictures in picturebooks as another kind of 'language-ing', we can talk about them in terms of the linguistic idea of register: how we speak, the words we choose, and the way we say them depends on who we are with, what we are saying, and where we are.

3   In some books the pictures are in a different register from the words.

4   Visual and verbal text are dialogic (talk to each other) and heteroglossic (contain many voices).

5   Across, between and beyond the pictures and words of picturebooks is a third space, where words and pictures meet, 'dialogue', and bounce off each other.

6   Visual literacy is more than the ability to decode images (to work out what images mean). It is the ability to recognise and analyse the *power of the image* and the *how* of its meaning in its particular context.

7   The idea of a visual chronotope (see Chapter 20) helps us to understand and describe how picturebooks work.

8   The language of picturebooks can help children to grow into understandings of poetry.

9   Picturebook language, like poetry, has an acoustic function as well as a semantic one.

10   Picturebooks in the classroom offer a corporate, community experience of shared story.

Chapter 25
A Locus for World Community

Focus

Literature expresses awareness of self and otherness. In the classroom it can open up and stimulate a sense of world community by offering multiple intercultural meeting places. This chapter explores the particular contribution that literature makes as such multiple representations of diverse cultures, and outlines ways that it can be used in classrooms to benefit ESL students and students from language backgrounds other than English.

At a time when educators are striving to impart a sense of value and values to children (a difficult task in a world that seeks to be inclusive), literature serves a significant function in learning about what we could broadly call *citizenship*. This does not just mean being a citizen of a particular country but rather being a citizen of a sustainable world. The importance of some sort of conceptualisation of world citizenship is an essential component of a global society. As Radim Palous writes in *The Changing University?*:

> The drama of our times is the exodus from particularity and the advent of universal community. Mankind must relinquish individual and social games on separate playing fields. The second half of the twentieth century is an entrance onto the scene, where people take part in the common performance of the drama, 'the world'. Leaving egoistic cells and prisons and entering worldwide openness can be called education (from the Latin *educa[re]*, 'to take out, to bring out, to lead out'). (1995: 176)

Globalisation, if it is to mean anything at all beyond consumerism and commodification, should imply not only physical connectedness but also a philosophical connectedness that transcends ideologies and politics. Classrooms and stories in the classroom can provide rich spaces for connection in this way.

This is because story is a connector, and all cultures have stories that can fill our schools and our lives with richness and diversity. These stories provide non-threatening opportunities for encountering difference and for creatively engaging with our own difference and differences. Each book that is read in class can become a stimulus for provoking, discussing, and challenging ideas about self and others, about ways of life that are both familiar and unfamiliar, and about customs that may at first seem strange.

For this reason we must not confine literature to the English class—it needs to play a part in all classes. Story gives opportunities for that imaginative leap that crosses discipline and cultural boundaries. Wise teachers can use story (and by story is meant books and plays and poems and texts about cultures and songs and picture-stories) to express community and a sense of 'home-ness'—especially when children may be suffering from a sense of *unheimlichkeit* (a German word meaning 'not-at-homeness').

Literature also can open our eyes to social problems and injustice in very powerful ways. Teachers need to remind children about the power of books to act as the social conscience of a culture. We have already noted how Anthony Browne uses **Zoo** to try to highlight his ideas about animals in cages. This is an important issue, but literature has engaged with, for example, the much greater issue of people in the cage of slavery. Don't just read stories, *tell* stories—that is part of a teacher's 'telling' role. Tell the story of, for example, **Uncle Tom's Cabin**, by Harriet Beecher Stowe. Stowe (1811–96) was an American woman who had worked as a teacher and who wrote this book in serial form after her brother asked her to 'write something that would make this whole nation feel what an accursed thing slavery is' (Carpenter and Prichard 1984: 500). Even read them a little of the text. It is dated and the language may be difficult, but it is part of a history of literary advocacy that we need to celebrate. Writing one's cultural story enables others to enter in and begin to understand.

There is an ever-increasing number of texts that not only tell stories of indigenous cultures but that also emerge authentically from them. **Do Not Go Around The Edges**, by Daisy Utemorrah and Pat Torres (1990), is a trifurcated text—an autobiographical narrative, a poetic response, and an illustration—which presents a life story through the media of history and art. It tells of the importance of place, and describes a sense of dislocation and yearning, and the quest for ideas of 'home' and identity.

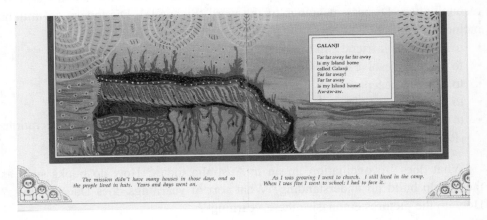

GALANJI

Far far away far far away
is my Island home
called Galanji
Far far away!
Far far away
is my Island home!
Aw-aw-aw.

The mission didn't have many houses in those days, and so the people lived in huts. Years and days went on.

As I was growing I went to church. I still lived in the camp. When I was five I went to school; I had to face it.

Far far away far far away
Is my island home
Called Galanji
Far far away!
Far far away
Is my Island home!
Aw-aw-aw.

This text provides a wonderful beginning for talking about Aboriginal literature. Discuss the difficult issue of appropriation—taking over stories, without acknowledging ownership. (Compare it to Western concepts of breaking copyright.)

Aboriginal culture is full of stories that were told in pictures, on rock and cave walls. Read some Dreaming legends, and remind the children that there are different ways of looking at the world (and different ways of telling stories). The stories about the Dreaming are stories about the beginnings of things—how the birds got their colours, how the moon got in the sky, and so on. But the whole concept of the Dreaming is that it is continuous, not finished; it is still going on. This is part of a different perspective of time—cyclical, rather than linear, as in Western culture. Beginnings and endings aren't so fixed. Unity happens by repetition rather than by a close relationship between what happens at the opening and closing of a story. Also discuss different ideas of perspectives. In Aboriginal art, the perspective is aerial—we look down on the picture from above. This clarifies some of the circular patterns and animal tracks that work in a different way from Western notions of perspective, which traditionally changes the size of what is being painted in relation to the position of the viewer. We could argue that this is a very individual-centred idea of the universe—big trees become small because of where I happen to be standing (after all, they are not really small). This opens wonderful areas of discussion and 'telling me' times.

Introduce the children to Magabala Books, and encourage them to check inside for the acknowledgment of ownership of the story by tribal elders. Read with the class some of Daisy Utemorrah's poetry and discuss it in relation to issues of reconciliation. Discuss meanings of the word 'reconcile'. Dictionary definitions include:

- to re-establish friendship between
- to settle or resolve a dispute
- to bring to acceptance or aquiescence
- to make compatible or consistent
- to purify a consecrated place in a special ceremony after an act of desecration.
(Readers' Digest Universal Dictionary, 1988)

What does 'reconciliation' mean in Australia today? How do books such as these help build up understanding? What sort of yearnings does Daisy express? How do the pictures emphasise these yearnings?

Our dream and our past is buried under the ground.
When the sun rises and begins another day
all is empty, ground and hill shake on us,
overwhelmed with people everywhere.
The dream the past—where does it stand now?
The burun burun whirrs in the night time
And the owl calling!
And the dingo howling!
The moon shines on the water, all is ended—
and the dreamtime gone.

This book can inspire children to write their own story and create both a poetic and an artistic response to it. Because the line of autobiographical narrative is so simple (sometimes only one sentence) it is a particularly encouraging creative writing model for ESL children. Remind children that they are the experts in their own story.

Note that writing a poetic response frees children from the restraints of normal sentence construction and the conventions of grammatical structure (see Chapter 24). Give some examples of writing poetry, being creative in your setting out. Encourage children into writing fragments of lines, glimpses of ideas:

Narrative:

On my first day at the new school I had lunch under the big tree in the playground.

Poetry:

> *Eating my lunch, under the big tree ...*
> *Green marks on my legs,*
> *Grass prickles*
> *Hot sun,*
> *I eat my lunch and it tastes ...*
> *like home.*

Giving ESL children the opportunity to draw an illustration for what they have written gives them the opportunity to display a skill that is not hampered by lack of language, and that therefore encourages self-confidence and self-esteem in the classroom. Much research has indicated the significance of these qualities in developing literate behaviours (see Johnston 1995).

Activity 27
(See Activity 4, Chapter 17)

Years 3–4

1. Write and illustrate an important moment in your life. You will write a few sentences telling what happened, and a poem about how you felt about

what happened. Then create a picture, which also tells something more about what you felt then, or what you feel about it now.

2. This task could also be expanded for advanced upper primary children to talk about time perspectives, historical perspectives, and cultural perspectives.

Years 5–6

3. Write and illustrate the story of your life, using *Do Not Go Around the Edges* as your model.

Teachers' reading

My Place by Sally Morgan; *Wandering Girl* by Glenys Ward

Literature in the ESL classroom

Reading books draws people together in a non-threatening way. All the second-language research indicates that 'children's literature can provide a vast language resource for teachers to draw on' (Catholic Education Office 1990).

Literature provides both the micro-context of situation and the macro-context of culture. It gives the 'knowledge of the world' (cultural schemata) that so many ESL children need in order to understand their new environment (see also Chapter 17). Reading is a sociocultural activity and its difficulty is increased without a working knowledge of cultural customs and practices.

Teachers can use literature in child-friendly ways. Start with trying to find common ground.

1. Try to find as many collections of folktales and fairytales as you can from a variety of cultures. Search at fetes and second-hand bookshops. When I was teaching in an ESL/EFL class, I had a wonderful book of folktales, now out of print, from all over the world. The great thing about this book was that it had all the tales in their original languages, as well as in an English translation. This meant that children could find their own story, recognise it and perhaps show me, and the class, some key words, which we could then put up around the room. This is not a language exercise—although it expands the thinking of the rest of the class about other languages, and can consolidate knowledge about parts of speech (nouns, for example). It is first and foremost an exercise to make ESL children feel more comfortable by bringing some of their past into the present. It is one small way of providing a 'courteous translation'. It also tends to make children more receptive to the second language.

2. When reading folktales and fairytales from different cultures look for similarities
   - between characters
   - between events
   - between themes.

Some of these stories tell about the beginnings of things. They tend to focus on a common world and aspects of a shared human experience.

3. Fill the classroom with as many books set in different cultures as you can find. To supplement school library books, encourage the children to go to their local library and borrow one book set in a different country—and have a special day (or week) set aside for a special class event something like 'The World as a Global Village'.

4. Further explore similarities:
   - story: same basic story, different setting
   - setting: same country, different story
   - character(s): same type of character, in different stories and places
   - theme: different story, characters and setting, but exploring the same underlying truths.

5. Pick up an idea that seems to emerge and expand it into creative activities. For example, the Japanese character Issunboshi (Little One-Inch) can be compared with Tom Thumb. Let children create their own miniature character and write a description and perhaps one adventure. Tell the class that they can use only one page so they must make every word count, as it does in picturebooks. Do a draft, and then peer-edit. Publish around the room.

6. The more cultures you have represented in your classroom, the more resources you have. Borrow books in other languages to show all the class: this not only enriches the experience of the ESL children whose language it is, but also enriches the experience of everyone in the class. Note difference in writing scripts when appropriate. Consistently build up the idea, through reading and discussion, that we are all citizens in a shared world.

Activity 28
Read *At the Crossroads* by Rachel Isadora (1991).

Years K–2
1. Encourage prediction of country and story from the title and cover. Look at the signs: the glimpse of the shantytown, the book, the smiling faces, the huge blue sky.
2. Read the story. Then read the story again, encouraging children to join in the refrain and use body percussion.

Years 3–4
1. Discuss what crossroads are and what they represent: more than one way to go.
2. Read the story.
3. Who is speaking? Whose eyes are we looking through? What is the grammatical name for this (first person plural)?

4. The sky is a very significant part of the illustrations and helps to tell part of the story. How? (It is the horizon of the children's world, and it shows the passing of time—morning, sunset, evening, sunrise the next morning.)

5. Look at the linguistic features of this simple text: make a word bank of the verbs (*shout, sing, rush, play, beat*). Note how they are all verbs of excitement and energy, and how this adds to the sense of anticipation.

6. Act out the story as a drama. Make the musical instruments: the guitar, drum, and shaker. Use body percussion. Use a chorus for the refrain: 'Our fathers are coming'.

Years 5–6

As above, but add the following as appropriate:

1. Discuss with the class how compressed but full of meaning the language is:

> *Warm nights blow.*
> *The crossroads are very dark.*

2. Ask them to write those two lines in another way to convey the same feeling.
3. Introduce the idea of crossroads as a metaphor.
4. Later, you could read with the children the Robert Frost poem 'The Road Less Travelled'.
5. Write a story about anticipation

Extension reading for Year 6

Read Nancy Farmer's '21st century adventure story' and fantasy of the future, *The Ear, The Eye, and The Arm*, set in Zimbabwe. This is a very original and interesting text for older readers, with a richly drawn African setting and a strong environmental theme.

Activity 29

Read *My Painted House, My Friendly Chicken, and Me* by Maya Angelou (1994).

Years K–2

1. Discuss the difference between the children's town life and home life.
2. Tell me: which do you think they preferred?
3. Write a story sentence about your pet, real or imaginary.

Years 3–4

1. Read the story. Tell the children that Maya Angelou is also an actress, and that she appeared in the film *How to Make an American Quilt* (they won't have seen the film but it gives them another point of reference).
2. Discuss the contrasts between the children's town life and home life. Which do you think they prefer?
3. Discuss the different sizes and style of script.

4. Discuss the use of the first person singular. How does this make you feel?
5. If appropriate, add a variation of the work for Years 5–6.

Years 5–6

1. Discuss the idea of conventions of print and story. Why does this book play with these conventions? What effect does it have?
2. Ask children to write a short story about themselves, a thing, and an animal with a particular characteristic (described as an adjective): 'My Bike, My Curious Beetle, and Me'. They can use different style and size scripts if they choose, but these must be orderly, as Maya Angelou's are. Encourage them to use computer text and consider the type of illustrations they would use.

SUMMARY

1   Literature offers multiple representations of diverse ways of being.

2   It has a particular contribution to make in classrooms with ESL/EFL learners.

3   Classrooms can be spaces for connection.

4   Children should understand that literature can act as social conscience and has a history of advocacy.

5   Teachers need to be tellers of stories as well as readers of stories.

6   Children's books by Aboriginal writers and illustrators provide a wonderful resource for learning about Aboriginal culture and for learning about Aboriginal perspectives and ideas.

7   Teachers should try to find common ground with EFL/ESL children and select books such as folktales and fairytales (where stories may be similar even if the language is different); books with similar characters, themes, or events; books in different languages (to let children show you—and perhaps the class—how well they can read in their own language); books with the same stories but different settings, or about the same country but with a different story, or about similar characters in different settings.

8   The more cultures represented in your classroom, the more resources you have as teacher.

9   Work towards the idea, through reading and writing and talking and listening, that we are all citizens of a shared world.

Chapter 26

A Forum: Social Issues, History, Fantasy

> ### Focus
> This chapter discusses the significance of children's literature in providing a forum that gives classroom opportunities for dealing with social and cultural issues. It notes that books that explore aspects of social problems, history, and fantasy are related by the desire, often profound, to confront issues and dilemmas of the human condition. It also notes the importance of teacher sensitivity to socioeconomic and gender issues as they are represented in their classrooms.

Literature is a meeting place. Its physical structures are flexible, dynamic, and often highly experimental. Books can be all shapes and sizes; they can be made of soft or hard materials (even cloth and thick board); they can turn various ways; their words can be upside down, around the page and across the page, as in *Fox*, by Margaret Wild and Ron Brooks (2000); they can be part of the illustrations; text can be different sizes; scripts can be different; there can be no words; there can be lots of words; there can be an orderly arrangement of pictures; there can be pictures scattered anywhere and everywhere.

The subject matter is equally varied. There are children's books about all aspects of life, from birth to death, from illness to divorce, from cultural difference to physical and intellectual difference and disability, from sibling rivalry to learning to live with next-door neighbours. There are picturebooks that open doors into abstract questions about the meaning of life and the consequences of the smallest action—think about Roger Vaughan Carr and Ann James' *The Butterfly* (1996), for example. There are controversial books for young adults about homosexuality, and about the social problems of incest and suicide.

Because literature contains narrative gaps, it opens up prolific and densely personal spaces across which the reader is required to construct bridges. Is Max's rumpus in *Where the Wild Things Are* a dream, a fantasy, a science fiction adventure, or is it 'real'—and what is real anyway? Where exactly is John Burningham's *Cloudland* (1996)—and is it a fantasy, a dream or a near-death experience? What happens in *The Great Bear* (1999)—does it live, does it die? And what is 'living' and what is 'death', especially in relation to cosmic space?

Such questions illustrate how problematical it is to try to categorise children's texts as either 'real' or 'fantasy'.

In the classroom, these gaps provide authentic opportunities for talk, for listening, and for sharing and testing ideas. Children's literature thus becomes a forum, a place where issues and problems can be held up to diverse points of view and discussed openly with peers. It gives connection to diverse people, diverse families, and a diverse world, as we have seen in the preceding chapter; it also gives connection to a thinking community. These books and discussion times don't have to be serious; a book such as Jacqueline Wilson's *The Suitcase Kid* (1992) describes the dilemma of a ten-year-old when her parents break up, but it does so with humour and compassion. Gleeson's *Skating on Sand* series gives another picture of family relationships, especially the latest *Hannah and the Tomorrow Room* (1999), where Hannah has to give up her room to her ailing grandfather. The picturebook *Hello Baby* describes another family choosing to join in the celebration of a home birth (1999).

Social issues, history, and fantasy may seem an unlikely combination, but they interlink in many ways, and they can all be part of this forum. Historical books, that is, books written in the present about a past, usually try, from contemporary perspectives, to impose some sense and meaning on that past. Stephen Muecke writes:

> The power of history, I would suggest, is not just in its secular making-sense. Rather, its effective magic is its ability to recast our conception of the present: 'every image of the past that is not recognised by the present as one of its own concerns threatens to disappear irrevocably,' says Walter Benjamin in his thesis on the philosophy of history. (1999: 29)

For example, *My Place* (1997) is an historical unfolding of the story of Australia, but its narrative structure is unified on the principle of the social and moral issue of Aboriginal land rights. It also uses the diversity of immigration as a method of unravelling past decades and making sense of Australia's multicultural present.

Tucker (Abdullah 1994) is a retrospective of childhood, but is also a sociological document, a case study, of what it was like growing up in that particular place at that particular time.

Similarly, fantasy may be concerned with an exploration of the social problems of a 'real' world transposed to an imaginary world, within clear parameters set by the text, and set free from any restraining present-day realities. Because it tends to address the profound nature of the essential human dilemma—good versus evil, right versus wrong—fantasy is closely related to folklore, and to the construction of alternative worlds. *Outside Over There* (Sendak 1981) constructs an alternative world. So does *Cloudland*. Tolkien's *Lord of the Rings* (1954–55) and the *Narnia* books of C. S. Lewis (1950–56) are obvious examples of alternative worlds constructed out of an understory of folklore. There are many variations. *You and*

Me, Murrawee (Hashmi and Marshall 1998) is a type of historical-fantasy time shift, a past operating simultaneously with a present; it is a dual chronotope but its whole premise emerges from a sociological concern.

In a discussion of science fiction (a specific type of fantasy premised on future worlds moulded out of scientific achievements), Sollat notes that it consists of 'thought models in which elements of reality are separated from their actual contents and represented as estranged in a fictional future' (1997).

Fantasy itself need not of course be of the future—it can be very much of the present. Clearly, children's literature is, by convention, 'fantastic' anyway. There are talking animals, interactions between humans and animals, imaginary worlds, magic thresholds, fairies, magic wishes, and drawing and saying magic.

The public debate about what social issues are suitable for children to read about and what are not is always going to be controversial, but it is a productive argument to have. First, it shows that the community is acknowledging the significance of the books read by its children. Second, it demonstrates community desires to do the best by its young. Third, it raises the level of community awareness about difficult issues and brings them to the surface, where they may not be solved but where some of the problems that have contributed to this particular issue may be addressed.

For example, street kids are a dark subject in the world of Peter Rabbit, but they constitute a real and troubling issue. However, the concepts of 'reality', 'social realism', and 'realistic' pose a number of problems. Are the depictions of some of these issues 'realistic', or are they romantically contrived anyway? Hartnett's *Wilful Blue* (1994) deals with a young man's suicide, but does so in a highly fanciful way. *Sleeping Dogs* (Hartnett 1995) is powerfully written, but the language at times is so mystical that it has the surreal feel of a dream (or more accurately, nightmare). Neither of these texts are appropriate for primary school children, but teachers need to have read them, and other books like them, so that they can formulate with intellectual integrity their own position.

But what about, for example, *Way Home* (Hathorn and Rogers 1994)? How realistic is the picture of the 'real' kid in this text? It seems to me that the greatest community debates emerge when there is an unresolved or 'unhappy' ending, but in a sense this is the most realistic part of some of these texts. Life doesn't always have happy endings. But nor do 'unhappy' endings need to be without hope.

It is important that we as educators expose children to a diversity of texts—from a diversity of points of view, and discuss openly any issues that arise out of them. Television and video have made this a generation of children from whom very little is hidden. The skewed and contorted images, purporting to be 'realistic' of life, that appear on television sets every night need to be balanced by other images, ideas, and ways of being, some of which are part of contemporary children's literature. These may not always be 'happy' but they do need to present other possibilities of thinking and doing, and of developing or challenging worldview.

Teachers need to be sensitive to the demographics of their classrooms and choose a range of books that are authentic for this particular group of young people. Mix talking about books with talking about films. Watch Disney's *Pocahontas* and set it in its historical context. Discuss it in contemporary terms as a clash of cultures. Listen to what the children in your class are talking about and the movies they have seen, and try to find books that link up in some way. Use the Internet to find contemporary material and encourage children to conduct their own searches whenever possible. Always remember that your task as teacher is to open new horizons, not just stick to old ones.

Teachers also need to be aware that boys and girls usually have different tastes in books. There is currently great debate about literacy standards in general and boys' relatively poorer standards in particular. While this must not be overstated, it is an area of legitimate concern. John Marsden, Morris Gleitzman, Paul Jennings, and John Larkin are all writing books—some fantastic, some science fiction, some dealing with social issues—that many boys seem to enjoy. The **Tomorrow** series by John Marsden is enormously popular with boys as well as girls and has been re-released for adults (1993–99). It explores ideas about fear, war and relationships with the land. **Only the Heart** by Brian Caswell and David Phu An Chiem (1997) is a complex novel for older readers; it is historical (about the Vietnam War) but also deals with the social issues of Vietnamese immigration and Cabramatta gangs. Other books for older readers are Matt Zurbo's **Idiot Pride** (1997) and Judith Clarke's **The Lost Day** (1997), which are written in a teenage idiom, very pronounced in the case of the Zurbo book. These last three books all contain sophisticated themes. However, Allan Baillie's **Secrets of Walden Rising** (1997), also a book for older readers, is one that may interest upper primary school children and could be used in the classroom. This is a well-written story about growing up, but it is set in a wonderful past-present context that is almost an allegory of the story of Australia.

Discussion of community perspectives on Aboriginal issues is fraught with political difficulties, but James Maloney, in his award-winning trilogy, **Dougy**, **Gracey** and **Angela**, uses the art of narrative to throw open the differing points of view, and provoke an open discussion of all the issues. Advanced upper primary students should be encouraged to read these books; they are an honest depiction of attitudes that many Australians will recognise.

Another book to recommend for older readers is **Johnny, My Friend** (1985) by the Swedish writer Peter Pohl. This book is set in Stockholm and tells the story of a growing up, and a growing into a realisation that it is not a perfect world. Beverley Naidoo's **No Turning Back** (1995) is set in Johannesburg and tells the story of a 12-year-old boy escaping from a violent home. It is based on the real experiences of young black South Africans living on the streets.

The Sterkarm Handshake by Susan Price (1998) tells a gripping and thoughtful story about the planned exploitation of the 16th century by the developers of the 21st century, and explores a new type of imperialism and environmental degradation.

Some of these books are classified as Young Adult (YA) fiction. This category is commonly defined by the age of its readership—sometimes 12–18, sometimes older. The most defining feature of YA novels, however, is not necessarily that they portray a person in a marginal situation (Nikolajeva 2000: 205)—although they often do. YA fiction does not just portray; rather, it allows the protagonist to describe events and convey perceptions, feelings and emotions from a highly subjective point of view which is constructed by the author (and accepted by the author's culture) as an ideology of adolescence.

I want to return to the idea of hope. Many of these novels for older readers deal with difficult issues and there are others that are particularly bleak. While it is true that children must grow into an awareness of social problems, it is also true that any books we present to young people should be characterised by an *ethics of hope*. An ethics of hope does not mean that everything is always presented as perfect, or perfectly happy. Far from it. It does imply, however, moral as well as artistic integrity, and the presentation of many different possibilities of being. It recognises that children have futures and that a 'future' implies options. It represents the realities of agency in personal response (even in circumstances beyond personal control). It is also concerned to present images that are characterised by principles of positive potential and openness to freedom and creativity.

Always read any book before you either recommend it or present it in class, and consider its suitability for your particular classroom context.

SUMMARY

1   Literature provides a non-threatening, authentic forum (meeting and discussion place) where a range of issues can be contemplated.

2   Social issues relate to history and fantasy because these two genres are often concerned with the exploration of social problems, and the struggle between right and wrong.

3   History often tries to make sense of the present by making sense of the past.

4   Fantasy explores the profound human dilemma of good versus evil.

5   The distinctions in children's literature between fantasy and 'real' are often problematic.

6   Teachers need to be aware of the reading tastes of the girls and the boys in their classes, but not limited by them; and they should also be aware of the range of literature that children can be encouraged to read as they come to leave primary school.

7   Teachers should always be sensitive to the needs of their particular class and school situation.

Chapter 27
Responses to Children's Literature

Focus

This chapter is a summary chapter and focuses on children's literature and the spaces that it gives for individual and corporate response within the classroom. It provides a number of models:
· texts as examples of reader response
· texts as mirrors
· texts as minicultures
· texts as popular culture

As a conclusion, it considers children's literature in terms of theatre.

Texts as reader response

Mrs Prochazka	We're going to read a story about the Depression
Mai Ling (thinks)	It sounds sad—perhaps like a war—
Junko (thinks)	I wonder if there was a depression in Japan.
Naomi (thinks)	The depression wasn't as bad as the holocaust.
Ben (thinks)	My family were all still out in the country then.
Wesley (thinks)	I wish I were in the pool right now!
Mrs Prochazka	Can anyone tell me something about the Depression?
Sally	I remember my grandparents talking about it—they didn't have any money and couldn't get married for a long time—about five years I think, because my grandfather didn't have a job.
Mai Ling (thinks)	I wonder what jobs my ancestors did at that time.
Junko (thinks)	They probably did—it was all over the world I think.
Naomi (thinks)	Nothing could ever be as bad as that.
Ben (thinks)	Probably wasn't so bad in the country.
Wesley (thinks)	I wish I were in the pool right now!
Mrs Prochakza	Let's read the story.

Task 15

Note how first-person dialogue such as this—even when it is inner speech rather than outer speech, as most of the above is—allows and promotes:

· the expression of subjective point of view, letting the reader focalise through each of the characters
· inclusivity rather than exclusivity.

This passage reminds us that all children bring their own life-world not just to the reading of any text, but into the classroom.

Consider the different backgrounds and cultures represented in this scenario. What implications does this have for teaching?

Texts as mirrors: feeling rejection, isolation, feeling 'out of it', feeling different

Activity 30

Years 5–6

Read the following excerpts from texts. Where do they position the reader? What choices of reading do we have? (We can identify, we can empathise, we can look on.) How are these excerpts different? How are they similar? What do you think were the authors' purposes in writing these texts?

Mr Riggs hoists a rolled-up wall-map onto the hook above the blackboard and lets it flap down over the date, 30 October 1932, chalked in blue.

'Who can tell me about The Granites?' he asks, tapping the red centre of Australia with his cane.

Straight away, kids put up their hands. 'Sir, sir, me sir, please sir.'

I don't say anything. I look away.

Mr Riggs lost an eye in the war, and his other eye fills me with dread. I do my best to avoid it.

Too late.

'Paul,' he says. 'How nice of you to be awake for a change. What can you tell me about The Granites?'

'Please sir,' I say, 'granite is a hard rock.'

They laugh. They always do. I arrive some mornings and find the whole school aware of things that I've missed.

Gary Disher, *The Bamboo Flute* 1991: 12–13

Who's dat wide-eyed likkle girl
Staring out at me?
Wid her hair in beads an' braids
An' skin like ebony?

    ...

Who dat girl? Who dat girl?
Pretty as poetry?
Who dat girl in the lookin' glass?
Yuh mean that girl is me?

Valerie Bloom, in Agard and Nicholls, *A Caribbean Dozen* 1994

Dad was playing his music again.
   Opera.
   Who else's dad would be caught dead playing that kind of stuff? ...
   As I opened the front door, there was a quiet point in the music.
His voice drifted out to me.
   'Lisdalia! Non essere tardi'.
   Don't be late.
   'I won't be'. As usual I replied in English. My language.
   I shut the door gently behind me.

Brian Caswell, *Lisdalia* 1994

Texts as mini-cultures: school and playground experience

Activity 31

Years 5–6

How do the following excerpts from texts represent the school experience? Do you think they were written by children? Why, or why not? Do you think they were written *for* children? Why, or why not? Write a story about some aspect of your school experience. Your writing may take the form of narrative; it may be poetic, it may be an **acrostic** or **limerick**, it can be a recount (retelling something that happened), information report, or media release; it may be a popular song. Set out your writing in the way you consider most appropriate. Use the computer if possible.

I dreamt last night of times gone by
   Of overflowing days and far high sky
   Of rainbow colours bright like tinted cellophane
I dreamt last night I was a child again ...

Me (6):   The worst part is going through the gate (don't be late)
          there's a whole lot of playground (sticky when it's hot)
          and a whole lot of people and they push and they shout
          and my room's far away and my shirt's pulled out
          the worst part is going through the gate (now I'm late).

From *Life-Times* by Rosemary Darling

By the morning recess we all had writer's cramp and mental exhaustion, but Miss Belmont looked quite calm and relaxed as she sailed into the staffroom for coffee. I'd never cared to associate with the riff-raff in the playground at Barringa East Primary. I went into the office and asked Miss Orlando, the school secretary, if I could lie down during recess because I had a headache. On my medical card in the office it said I was prone to nervous headaches, rhinitis, sinusitis, bee-sting allergy, rheumatism; suspected hypersensitivity to wattle pollen, horsehair, dust mite, clover and Clag glue; tested for diabetes, arthritis, gallstones and hiatus hernia; and that I didn't have to put my head under water when we went swimming because of a punctured eardrum. Mum didn't write any of that information on the sheet they'd sent home for parents to fill in; I'd supplied it to Mrs Orlando over the six years I'd been going to Barringa East Primary.

Robin Klein, *Hating Alison Ashley* 1984

Texts as popular culture

'It seems to me you lived your life like a candle in the wind ...'

Elton John

Children's literature is involved with story and feelings, with ideas and concerns, with imagery and metaphor, with the imagination. So, very often, are popular songs. We respond to these because we have an innate sense of poetic expression, rhythm, and rhyme, and because we can understand or empathise with the stories they tell.

Encourage children to bring popular songs into the classroom, and then, with them, discuss the language—simile, metaphor, abstract ideas, and concerns. Make a collection of lyrics on a noticeboard in the classroom, and vary it frequently. Children are highly motivated to look at the words of popular songs. If we can set up meaningful links to books and to poetry, poetry and books can become part of the understory of popular culture.

These models can be adapted in many ways. For example, in 'Texts as mirrors' I have focused on the idea of rejection and difference, but teachers could just as easily choose to discuss ideas of 'change' or 'excitement' or 'happiness'.

 ## Activity 32

Years 5–6

Play the song to the class.

Telegraph Road *(Dire Straits)*
A long time ago came a man on a track

Walking thirty miles with a sack on his back
And he put down his load where he thought it was best
And he made a home in the wilderness.
He built a cabin and a winter store
And he ploughed up the ground by the cold lake shore
And the other travellers came riding down the track
And they never went further and they never went back
Then came the churches then came the schools
Then came the lawyers then came the rules
Then came the trains and the trucks with their loads
And the dirty old track was the telegraph road
Then came the mines—then came the ore
Then there was the hard times and then there was a war
Telegraph sang a song about the world outside
Telegraph road got so deep and wide
Like a rolling river

And my radio says tonight it's gonna freeze
People driving home from the factories
There's six lanes of traffic
Three lanes moving slow ...
I used to go to work but they shut it down
I've got a right to go to work but there's no work to be found
Yes and they say we're gonna have to pay what's owed
We're gonna have to reap from some seed that's been sowed
And the birds up on the wires and the telegraph poles
They can always run away from the rain and the cold
You can hear them singing out their telegraph code
All the way down the telegraph road
You know I'd sooner forget but I remember those nights
When life was just a bet on a race between the lights
You had your head on my shoulder and your hand on my hair
Now you act a little colder like you don't seem to care
But believe in me baby and I'll take you away
From out of this darkness and into the day
From these rivers of headlights these rivers of rain
From the anger that lives on the streets with these names
'Cos I've run every red light on memory lane
I've seen desperation explode into flames
And I don't want to see it again ...
From all of these signs saying sorry but we're closed
All the way down the Telegraph Road.

Responses
1. How many pictures are there in this song?
2. How many voices do you hear?
3. How many people are there in the story?
4. How many stories are there in this song?
    *   the story of progress
    *   the story of civilisation versus the untamed world
    *   the story of growing up
    *   the history of our times
    *   history of own growth
    *   history of a country's growth
    *   history of the world

Compare with *Window*, by Jeannie Baker.
1. Write the story of the text from the little boy's point of view
2. Write it from the mother's point of view
3. How have ideas about the 'wild place' changed?
4. Compare with 'The night sky' by Sally Morgan (*The Flying Emu and Other Australian Stories*)
5. Tell the story in a comic strip form. Write a text to the pictures.
6. In groups, think of some of your favourite songs. Make a draft list of the songs and what they are about. When you have a collection of songs, go to the library and see if you can find any books relating in some way to the themes of your songs. Compile a roundtable list of the song, the theme and the book.

Conclusion: children's literature as theatre

In conclusion, it is useful to consider children's literature as theatre. Perry Nodelman notes that the production process of each book represents a collaboration of different people with different skills (1988: 81). There are many ways in which we can think of both the texts of children's literature, and children's involvement with them, as theatre, as an interactive event, with a cast and a stage, with props and costumes.

Theoretically, children's books have a great deal in common with theatrical conventions. First, much of what happens between words and pictures in a text and between the words and the pictures and the reader, is *dramatic irony*: the audience (readers) knowing something that the characters on the stage (and on the page) don't (think of *Rosie's Walk*). This not only adds to the effect of the dramatic moment, but also draws young readers in, giving them a sense of superiority, offering opportunities for them to predict, to enjoy being 'in the know'. Interactive moments in children's theatre are based on this very principle: 'Where is it?' or 'Where did he go?' asks the befuddled stage character to an audience who know exactly (and will say) where it is and where he has gone.

Second, directors seek to construct stage pictures, using lighting and sets and costumes to create images that communicate to the audience. In a play these pictures are linked by the movement of the actors; in a picturebook, the reader turns the pages (think of how this works in, for example, *The Great Bear*, *Hello Baby*, and *Beware, Beware*).

Third, a number of the elements of theatrical genre can be seen in picturebooks. Many stories are domestic theatre—stories about particular moments in the everyday life of a child. Pictures are moments of *thisness*—expressions of the particularity of that moment—and the theatre is a representation of *thisness*, that is, of particular moments in a continuum (perhaps a blur) of moments. Walter Benjamin refers to 'the strict, frame-like, enclosed nature of each moment' in a 'whole state of living flux' (1966: 3). The particularity of these moments can be represented in all sorts of ways, from the 'real' to the surreal. For example, the dramatist August Strindberg was an expressionist, seeking to express dramatic action as being inside the mind of a person dreaming, shifting time and space as it shifts in dreams. Many contemporary picturebooks are expressionistic—consider again Gleeson and Greder's *The Great Bear* (1999), and Crew and Woolman's *The Watertower* (1994), and Crew and Rogers' *Lucy's Bay* (1992), but also consider *Come Away from the Water, Shirley* (Burningham 1977) and *Drac and the Gremlin* (Baillie and Tanner 1988) and, for that matter, *Alice in Wonderland*. On the other hand, in some children's books, particularly of the *Dr Seuss* type, there is a strong element of farce and slapstick. One of my students pointed out that *Rosie's Walk* is pure pantomime, complete with villain and, in her words, 'hapless (or is she?) female,' and with each picture setting up for the disaster (and fun) of the next (Sinclair 1999).

Why mention this as part of a conclusion?

I want to do more than draw parallels (interesting as they are) between literature and theatrical genres. The whole underpinning philosophy of Part III is that theory informs practice. As educators, we need to understand that, *in practice*, children's literature *in the classroom* is a type of theatre, the theatre of the classroom. Every time we read a book with children it is a *viewing*, as theatre is: a viewing of the text, of the imaginary experience that is the invitation of the text, and of each other's participation in that experience. Like theatre, it is a corporate experience of being involved in shared story. The word *theatre* derives from the Greek word *theatron*, meaning *a place for viewing* or a *place for seeing*. I like the idea of *the classroom as a place for seeing*. Children's literature accesses the opportunity to see beyond who we are and where we are.

A reading event is a metafictional *mise-en-scene*, a sliding between a present 'real' setting and an imagined 'un-real' setting. As classroom story (a teacher reading a book to a particular class in a particular place at a particular time) slides into the story of the book, the actual book itself takes on a number of roles. Its physical page boundaries act like a proscenium arch, framing the scene, showing us where to look. Every turn of the picturebook page is a shift in scene; the teacher's hand turning the page is a *stagehand*. Readers are part of the *stage crew* in this reading event, getting things ready and making links between what is seen and what is unseen and filling in the gaps by running around in the backstage spaces of imagination. In the way teachers hold up picturebooks to show the pictures as they read, the book functions as much more than just a prop: sometimes it's like a puppet (something that is given voice by the person controlling its movements), sometimes it's like a narrator or chorus (making the links between the audience/viewers/readers and the action and characters of the story), sometimes it acts as an interruption to the story it tells (jolting us back to its pages). Sometimes we lose sight of it altogether and it disappears from view, like the threshold of a doorway that we have already passed through.

In practical ways, children's literature clearly lends itself very readily to drama. Every reading with a class is a dramatic performance. Children are part of the performance: they can be encouraged to play with texts and turn them into scripts, or create their own mime, Readers' Theatre, dramatic dance, tableau, radio play, television script, poem, song, artwork, or comic strip. These creative responses activate the multiple intelligences identified by Howard Gardner (1983): verbal-linguistic, logical-mathematical, natural, bodily-kinaesthetic, visual-spatial, musical-rhythmic, interpersonal, and intrapersonal. The process also stimulates real and authentic language in all its forms—speaking and listening to it, reading and writing it.

But most of all, children's literature in a generous classroom becomes a catalyst for learning about life and its unities and diversities, not only for developing and expanding traditional concepts of literacy but also for developing sophisticated skills in critical literacy, for accumulating cultural and visual literacies; in other words, for building up layers of individual understory.

The well-known drama teacher Dorothy Heathcote, who sees language and communication at the core of the education system, developed and worked with a concept that she called 'the mantle of the expert'. As part of the learning process both she and her students assume the role of experts, and set about role-playing and subsequently developing expertise: focusing on what the knowledge they need to acquire might be, considering its value, and learning how.

Heathcote's teaching philosophy gives to students the space to grow and to teachers the grace to let them. They see the world with growing eyes. Teacher and students become experts together, learning collaboratively.

The way we use literature in the classroom can give similar space and grace. Reading together, writing together in a range of print and electronic media, talking together about texts with an increasing knowledge and understanding, listening and making creative responses, philosophically inquiring, and arguing sometimes, gives all of us the scope and potential to grow into experts, to communicate better, and to push beyond current capacities and skills. We can perform, try on roles, engage with language not our own, and engage with new ways of using language.

In this way, literacy becomes, appropriately in a postmodern age of new technologies, multi-active, multipurpose, and multidimensional.

Afterword

e, the authors of this book, have been careful to keep to the brief
that we have given ourselves in the Preface and Introduction. The
key points do not need repeating in detail, but it is important to
emphasise a few of them.

Literacy: Reading, Writing, and Children's Literature covers the spectrum of
the theory and practice of the teaching of literacy in a modern and fast-changing
world; it addresses the findings of current research while facing the practicalities
of teaching children to become literate in primary school classrooms around
Australia.

Although the vital importance of learning to read and write in English, our
universal common language, has been stressed, the book has recognised the
contribution of other languages and other cultures to our national life. We have
stressed again and again that literacy operates and develops in a sociocultural
perspective and that every literacy act is specific to and dependent on the situation
in which it occurs.

The complexity of literacy and literacy learning is also recognised and the
concept of different forms of literacy such as social literacy, critical literacy, and
computer literacy has been addressed. Coupled with this, the authors have been
careful to write in the context of the changing face of literacy, realising that young
readers of the future will require a very different set of literacy skills to operate
effectively in a more demanding and more complex environment.

Looking to the future

It is important, therefore, to consider briefly what future generations may require
to be able to function effectively. What literacy skills and knowledge will be

needed for effective participation in the society of the 21st century? How will information be accessed and decisions made about which information to select? How much will online services be used? Will the prominence of book-based literacies decline? How will we ensure equity of access to effective literacy for all in a rapidly changing world?

Whatever the impact of technology on future learning may be, it seems clear that literacy will continue to rely on the encoding and decoding of text and images in both book-based and technological forms. There will need to be increased emphasis on the ability to be selective and critical in what we access and use. Effective literacy will rely much more on our ability to be a literate thinker.

As Trevor Cairney has pointed out in his Foreword to this book, reading programs of the past, which focused entirely on the acquisition of a set of reading skills, 'had a very narrow view of all we now recognise as literacy'. They failed to make effective use of connected texts to teach children how to *think* about what they were reading. They failed to show children how to make decisions about the text, its purpose, its author's reasons for writing it, and its use to the reader. Such programs produced ineffective readers because they failed to produce understanding of the way texts work in our society to carry and transmit meanings.

Similarly, programs that taught children only the subskills of writing, such as spelling, punctuation, grammar, and handwriting failed to teach them how to apply these skills to structure real texts for real purposes. This resulted in writers who lacked the ability to employ effective writing to convey meaning.

The real challenge for tomorrow's teachers of literacy will be to teach children how to read and write critically.

The issue of equity is a crucial one for the future of our society. Not all students benefit equally from the experiences that schools now offer them. How can we meet the literacy needs of all students? What is it about the structure of schools or the experiences they provide that fail some students? Why do girls, as a group, do better at literacy learning than boys? Why do many students from socioeconomically disadvantaged communities do less well at literacy than their more economically advantaged peers? Why do some schools fail to meet the literacy-learning needs of students from indigenous backgrounds? How can schools capitalise more effectively on the linguistic resources brought to school by students from language backgrounds other than English?

The way culture and literacy practices are interwoven (Heath 1983) leaves us with a dilemma: either to aim at social change in schools by introducing new practices and new relationships with students and their families or, on the other hand, to socialise students into the literacy practices that will enable them to succeed.

There is a middle road:

While some might question this road, I believe it can be travelled.

What I am suggesting is that we must continue to seek reform of schools and society, breaking down the privileging of a limited range of literacies, and attempting to recognise multiple literacies. As part of this process, however, we have a responsibility to introduce children to the literacy practices that do offer the greatest potential for educational success, employment, and personal empowerment. (Cairney 1995: 16)

Governments throughout Australia are addressing these and other key questions related to the teaching and learning of literacy. At the federal, state, and territory levels, considerable resources are being spent to improve the learning of literacy for all groups of students within the community. Programs are being put in place that address the literacy-learning needs of students from a range of groups and with a range of needs. Detailed information that supports the operation of these programs is being gathered and evaluated.

An increasing number of schools throughout Australia are finding solutions to the problems that exist, while heralding future change. Many schools serving economically disadvantaged communities, Aboriginal and Torres Strait Islander communities, and non-English-speaking background communities are now achieving literacy results equal to those of the Australian community as a whole.

In many of these schools we find similar sets of features, which include the following:

- The whole school community has a strong desire to improve students' literacy learning.
- Literacy is a school priority and improvement in literacy is tackled through a planned whole-school approach.
- The principal provides strong leadership and support for the implementation of a focused school literacy plan.
- All teachers work to improve their knowledge of literacy learning and their skills as literacy teachers by engaging in regular professional development.
- Parents are involved in the literacy learning of their children and contribute actively to the school's programs.
- Teachers and parents have high expectations of all students and work to make these expectations a reality.
- All students are carefully monitored using a range of assessment practices, and individual students receive extra support when needed.

We can learn a great deal from what these schools are achieving and apply their successful practices to literacy education across the board in the future. The practices outlined in this book are typical of such development.

In conclusion, it is important to underline the fact that we live in an increasingly globalised world whose differences and distances are being rapidly and dramatically reduced. Such a world is a challenge to us all. It is a particular challenge to teachers of literacy, with their clear mandate to prepare children to take their place in it.

⌐Appendix

Key Australian Literacy Contacts

The following select list of literacy contacts contains addresses, telephone numbers, fax numbers, and web sites of professional organisations, government departments, and other bodies concerned with literacy in Australia. For instance, the Australian Literacy Educators' Association supports teaching practice in literacy across all age levels and curriculum areas. It holds annual conferences, local conferences and publishes a variety of literacy material. The Primary English Teaching Association focuses on English teaching in its many forms at the primary school level. It also holds conferences and has a large list of publications. The various states and territories of Australia produce their own curricula while the Commonwealth Department of Education, Training and Youth Affairs deals with literacy matters at a national level.

Australian Council of TESOL Association (ACTA)
25 Kimmax Street
Sunnybank Qld 4109
Tel: 07 3345 9391
Fax: 07 3345 8382
http://www.acta.edu.au/

Australian Literacy Educators' Association (ALEA)
PO Box 3203
Norwood SA 5067
Tel: 08 8332 2845
Fax: 08 8333 0394
email: aleamail@nexus.edu.au

Australian School Library Association (Inc.) (ASLA)

PO Box 450
Belconnen ACT 2616
Tel: 02 6231 1870
Fax: 02 6231 2092
asladaw@atrax.net.au
www.w3c2.com.au/asla/

Australian Teachers of Media (ATOM)

Locked Bag 9
Collins Street East
Melbourne Vic. 8003
Tel: 03 9651 1310
Fax: 03 9651 1311

Australian Association for the Teaching of English (AATE Inc.)

PO Box 3203
Norwood SA 5067
Tel: 08 8332 2845
Fax: 08 8332 0394
email: aatemail@nexus.edu.au

Australia Library and Information Services Association (ALIA)

PO Box E441
Kingston ACT 2604
Tel: 02 6285 1877
Fax: 02 6282 2249
email: enquiry@alia.org.au

Children's Book Council of Australia (CBCA)

PO Box 48
Hughes ACT 2605
Tel: 02 6287 5709
Fax: 02 6287 5709

Early Childhood Teachers Association (ECTA Inc.)

Queensland University of Technology
PO Box 84
Spring Hill Qld 4000
Tel: 07 3366 1288
Fax: 07 3366 1288
http://www.ecta.org.au

Primary English Teaching Association

PO Box 3106
Marrickville NSW 2204
Tel: 02 9565 1277
Fax: 02 9565 1070
email: info@peta.edu.au

Commonwealth Department of Education, Training and Youth Affairs (DETYA)
GPO Box 9880
Canberra ACT 2601
Tel: 02 6240 8111
Fax: 02 6240 7111
http://www.detya.gov.au

Curriculum Corporation
PO Box 177
Carlton Vic. 3053
Tel: 03 9207 9600
Fax: 03 9639 1616
email: sales@curriculum.edu.au

ACT

Department of Education and Training
PO Box 1584
Tuggeranong ACT 2901
Tel: 02 6207 5111
Fax: 02 6205 9333

Catholic Education Commission
Archdiocese of Canberra/Goulburn
PO Box 3317
Manuka ACT 2603
Tel: 02 6234 5455
Fax: 02 6234 5491

Association of Independent Schools of the ACT
42 Tyrell Circuit
Kaleen ACT 2617
Tel: 02 6241 2429
Fax: 02 6241 5923
email: aisact@ais.act.edu.au

NEW SOUTH WALES

Office of the Board of Studies (NSW)
GPO Box 5300
Sydney NSW 2001
Tel: 02 9367 8111
Fax: 02 937 8484
http://www.boardofstudies.nsw.edu.au

Department of Education and Training (DET)
35 Bridge Street
GPO Box 33
Sydney NSW 2001
Tel: 02 9561 8000
Fax: 02 9561 8759

Catholic Education Commission of NSW
PO Box A169
Sydney South NSW 2000
Tel: 02 9287 1555
Fax: 02 9264 6308

NORTHERN TERRITORY

Department of Education (NTDE)
GPO Box 4821
Darwin NT 0800
Tel: 08 8999 5606
Fax: 08 8999 5960
email: infocentre.ntde@nt.gov.au

Catholic Education Council
PO Box 219
Berrimah NT 0828
Tel: 08 8984 3833
Fax: 08 8947 1517

Association of Independent Schools of Northern Territory
GPO Box 2085
Darwin NT 0801
Tel: 08 8950 4511
Fax: 08 8952 2131
email: philipws@topend.com.au

QUEENSLAND

Education Queensland
PO Box 33, Albert Street
Brisbane Qld 4002
Tel: 07 3237 0111
Fax: 07 3229 0265
www.qed.qld.gov.au

Queensland School and Curriculum Council (QSCC)

PO Box 317 Albert Street
Brisbane Qld 4002
Tel: 07 3237 0794
Fax: 07 3227 1285
email: inquiries@qscc.qld.edu.au
www.qscc.qld.edu.au/qscc/qscc.html

Catholic Education Commission

GPO Box 2441
Brisbane Qld 4001
Tel: 07 3224 333
Fax: 07 3229 0907

Association of Independent Schools of Queensland

PO Box 957
Spring Hill Qld 4004
Tel: 07 3228 1515
Fax: 07 3228 1575
email: office@aisq.qld.edu.au

SOUTH AUSTRALIA

Department of Education, Training and Employment

GPO Box 1152
Adelaide SA 5001
Tel: 08 8226 1000
Fax: 08 8226 1234

South Australian Commission for Catholic Schools

PO Box 179
Torrensville Plaza SA 5031
Tel: 08 8301 6600
Fax: 08 8301 6611

South Australian Independent Schools Board

301 Unley Road
Malvern SA 5061
Tel: 08 8373 0755
Fax: 08 8373 1116
www.isb.sa.edu.au/

TASMANIA

Department of Education Tasmania
GPO Box 169B
Hobart Tas. 7001
Tel: 03 6233 8011
Fax: 03 6231 1576
www.tased.edu.au

Association of Independent Schools, Tasmania
Suite 15, Galleria Building
33 Salamanca Place
Hobart Tas. 7000
Tel: 03 6224 0125
Fax: 03 6224 0174
email: aist@tassie.net.au

Tasmanian Catholic Education Commission
PO Box 102
North Hobart Tas. 7002
Tel: 03 6231 1033
Fax: 03 6231 1793

VICTORIA

Department of Education, Employment and Training
PO Box 4367
Melbourne Vic. 3001
Tel: 03 9637 2000
Fax: 03 9637 2020
www.eduvic.vic.gov.au/

Board of Studies (Vic)
St Nicholas Place
15 Pelham Street
Carlton Vic. 3053
Tel: 03 9651 4300
Fax: 03 9651 4324
email: general@bos.vic.edu.edu.au

Association of Independent Schools Victoria
20 Garden Street
South Yarra Vic. 3141
PO Box 2138
Prahran 3181
Tel: 03 9825 7200
Fax: 03 9826 6066
www.ais.vic.edu.au/

Catholic Education Commission of Victoria
PO Box 3
East Melbourne Vic. 3002
Tel: 03 9267 0228
Fax: 03 9415 0325
www.cecv.melb.catholic.edu.au

WESTERN AUSTRALIA

Education Department of Western Australia
151 Royal Street
East Perth WA 6004
Tel: 08 9264 4111
Fax: 08 9264 5005
www.eddept.wa.edu.au/

Curriculum Council of Western Australia
27 Walters Drive
Osborne Park WA 6017
Tel: 08 9273 6300
Fax: 08 9273 6371
www.curriculum.wa.edu.au

Association of Independent Schools Western Australia
3/41 Walters Drive
Osborne Park WA 6017
Tel: 08 9244 2788
Fax: 08 9244 2786

Catholic Education Commission of Western Australia
PO Box 198
Leederville WA 6903
Tel: 08 9388 4388
Fax: 08 9381 3201

Glossary

ACER

Australian Council for Educational Research, est. 1930. This organisation conducts general research, develops tests and materials, and provides educational services.

allophone

One of the actual sounds that make up a phoneme. The actual sound of a phoneme may differ in speech according to its position in a word or the dialect in which it is spoken, e.g. the different sounds of /l/ in *lip* and *bill* and /k/ in *cup* and *cat*. In the second example the initial consonant is modified by the following vowel.

alphabetical writing system

A writing system in which the symbols represent the sounds of speech.

articulatory phonetics

The branch of phonetics that studies the production of speech sounds by the human vocal tract.

assessment

The process of describing and judging achievement on set tasks, against clear criteria.

authentic assessment

A selective collection of student work, teacher observations, and self-assessment that is used to show progress over time with regard to specific criteria.

benchmark

A point of reference from which quality or achievement is measured. National literacy and numeracy benchmarks are sets of descriptors that represent nationally agreed minimum levels of literacy and numeracy at a particular year level.

blend

The combining of two or three letter sounds so that each sound can be identified, e.g. *cl* in *clown* and *str* in *string*.

'bottom-up' view of reading

An approach to reading and learning to read that places emphasis on word recognition and the decoding of print. It is also described as a code-based or subskill approach.

chronotope

'Time-place'. Refers to the relationship in narrative between people and events on the one hand, and time and space on the other.

cloze test

A procedure in which readers provide words that have been omitted at systematic intervals or on the basis of function.

cohesion

Particular features that link different parts of a text.

cohesive ties

Connections within a text that help to develop unity. Also termed cohesive links, these ties operate within and across sentences. There are many types of cohesive ties, e.g. reference, substitution, ellipsis, conjunction.

collocation

Words that typically go together in a sequence (a faint hope, butt out), in associated pairs (bread and butter), or cluster around a topic (fish and chips; beach, surf, sand, sea).

conferencing

In the process approach to writing or reading, the opportunity for students to meet in 'conference' to discuss draft work or material being read.

criterion-referenced test

A test used to determine whether a student has mastered a particular skill or unit of instruction.

critical literacy

An approach to literacy that aims at revealing the hidden power relationships and ideological assumptions that underlie texts.

cultural literacy

(i)   Knowledge of the language and social structure within which we live;
(ii) awareness of the integrity of many different ways of thinking and acting.

cumulative assessment file

Collections of data that relate to a student's academic development.

decile

One of the parts of a distribution of scores, each of which contains one-tenth of the cases in the complete series.

diagnostic test

A test that determines a student's strengths and weaknesses from a set number of objectives.

digraph

A combination of two or more letters to form one speech sound, as in *bread*, *ship*.

diphthong

A blending of two vowel sounds that begins with the sound of the first vowel and glides into the other, as in the beginning of *ice*, *ale*, *old*, *oil*, *owl* and the end of *hear*, *chair*, *poor*.

directionality

In reading, the left to right and return sweep at the end of a line.

discourse

Communication of thought in speech or writing. In literature it refers to the process of telling the story, how story is told on the surface of the text.

discourse analysis

The study of continuous stretches of discourse or language longer than a sentence to analyse linguistic feature of its structure.

ESL

English as a Second Language; sometimes ESOL is preferred, i.e. English as a Second or Other Language, to denote that many people are already bilingual or trilingual.

etymology

The derivation of words from words or word elements.

evaluation

A value judgment made by estimating the worth of something.

field

Related words in a particular context, e.g. words associated with 'vegetables'. In functional grammar the field refers to the subject matter in a discourse.

focalisation

The positioning of readers and viewers to see and hear the events of the narrative and the thoughts and ideas of the characters.

formative evaluation

Evaluation that occurs during the progress of a program in order to give feedback for improvement.

Foundation handwriting

An approach to handwriting (common in NSW and ACT) whereby simple movements are repeated to form the shapes of letters. The letters can be joined to form cursive handwriting.

functional grammar

Grammar where the social function is central, based on the view of language as a process of social interaction and a communication of ideas. Sentences 'function' as commands, questions, and statements.

genre

In functional grammar, the description of a text in terms of the way it is structured to achieve a specific purpose. (See text-type.) It is a distinguishable category of text recognised by aspects such as subject matter and linguistic features.

grapheme

The written symbol of a particular phoneme.

graphological information

Visual information about letters, words, and punctuation in text.

graphophonic

Relating to the connections between sounds and letters in reading and spelling.

homonym

A word that is identical to another in pronunciation and spelling but has a different origin and meaning, e.g. *saw* (past tense of *see*) and *saw* (a cutting instrument). Can also include homophones, which sound the same but have different spelling and meaning, e.g. *fair* and *fare*, and homographs, which have the same spelling but differ in meaning and sometimes in pronunciation, e.g. *wind* (that blows) and *wind* (to wind up a clock).

hypertext

A set of semantic associations. An area of text on a web or CD-ROM page that acts as a link to a hyperlink.

hyperlink

An area of a web page or CD-ROM text or image that a user can click in order to go to another item or source of information.

ideogram (or ideograph)

A symbol used to represent a whole word or concept.

'invented' or 'temporary' spelling

Usually phonemic spelling used by a beginning writer attempting to spell a word.

implied reader

The person for whom a text appears to be written. Writers of children's literature compose their texts with the implicit knowledge that the person reading it will be a child.

indicator

A statement of the behaviour that students might display as they work towards the achievement of syllabus outcomes.

inferential meaning

The inferred meaning of a text. Often termed 'reading between the lines'.

inflection

A word ending that signifies grammatical meaning, e.g. *-s* (plural), *-ed* (past tense), and *-ing*.

intertextuality

Meaningful relationships and connections, overt and covert, that reach across, between, and beyond texts.

knowing readers

Readers who not only have all the skills they need to read but also read with depth, knowing how texts work, how significant the rewards of the reading experience are, and the value of persevering with difficult texts.

lexical
Relating to vocabulary.

lexicogrammatical
Relating to vocabulary (*lexis*) and grammar as closely related elements of language.

lingua franca
A language used to facilitate communication between people who have different first languages.

literacy
The ability to read and write; a synthesis of language, context, and thinking that shapes meaning.

literal meaning
The plain sense meaning of a text. Often termed 'reading the lines'.

logogram (logograph)
A symbol representing a word or phrase

metacognitive strategies
When applied to reading, the learning strategies that provide an overall plan for gaining meaning from text, such as changing reading speed, rereading parts of a text, asking oneself questions during reading, highlighting and summarising the text.

metalanguage
A language to describe language. Grammar is a metalanguage (adjective metalinguistic).

miscue analysis
The analysis of the oral reading errors (miscues)—graphophonic, syntactic, and semantic—that a student makes when reading a text, in order to develop improved strategies.

mode
In functional grammar, the channel of communication in a discourse, e.g. speech or writing.

morpheme
A meaning-bearing unit of language. 'Free' or 'unbound' morphemes are whole words in themselves, e.g. *boy*, or *rein* and *deer* in *reindeer*. 'Bound' morphemes are prefixes, suffixes, and inflections, e.g. *pre* in *prejudge*, *ly* in slow*ly*, and *s* in *boys*.

morphology
The study of structure in language.

narrative
A story. In literary theory it includes both the story (what is narrated) and the discourse (how it is narrated).

norm-referenced test
A test that allows an interpretation of an individual's test result by comparison with a group that is said to be the norm.

onset and rime
A form of segmentation of sounds in syllables. Onset is the initial consonant or consonant cluster in a syllable, e.g. *c-* in *cat*, *scr-* in *scratch*. Rime is that part of a syllable that contains a vowel and a final consonant, e.g. *-og* in *dog*.

orthography
The spelling system of a language.

outcomes
Specific statements of the results intended by a syllabus; goal statements of student achievements.

phone
A unique minimal segment of the stream of speech.

phoneme
The smallest unit of speech that distinguishes one word from another, e.g. the phonemes /s/ and /f/ in sat and fat. (See allophone.)

phonemic awareness
An understanding of the smallest sounds that make up oral language. It is characterised by a speaker's ability to hear, segment, and manipulate sounds in speech. Phonological awareness is a more general term that includes the ability to recognise syllables and other speech segments, such as onset and rime.

phonetics
The branch of linguistics dealing with speech sounds, their production, description, and classification. (See articulatory phonetics.)

phonics
An approach to teaching early reading, pronunciation, and spelling. Phonics refers to the relationship between written letters (graphemes) and spoken sounds (phonemes). Phonic analysis is a method of teaching word recognition by matching elements in writing with their corresponding sounds; phonic synthesis is the building up of words from the sounds within them.

phonology
The study of the sounds of language.

phonological information
Information about the sound system of language.

picaresque
In literature, especially the novel, relating to the adventures and wanderings of rogues or other colourful characters.

portfolios
Collections of students' work and observations that show significant aspects of development and achievement over time.

procedural texts
Texts that tell how something can be accomplished. Example: 'How to Make a Telephone Call'.

profiles
Lists of observed behaviour that map the desired development of a student.

readability
The level of difficulty of a particular piece of reading material.

reading
A process of literate thinking during which a reader brings meaning to and takes meaning from written text in a social and cultural context.

reading recovery
An early intervention program designed to improve the literacy skills of children who have made little progress in their first year of school.

redundancy
Having more information than we need. Redundancy in reading refers to additional information that helps a reader to predict.

register
Language appropriate for its audience, context, and purpose, e.g. colloquial, scholarly, legal. In sociolinguistics, the variety of language used in different social situations.

reliability
In assessment, the consistency of measurement, procedures, or results.

rhyme
A correspondence of sounds in two or more words, especially at the ends of lines of poetry, as in *found* and *pound*.

rime
See onset and rime.

root
The basic meaning-carrying element of a word, as *flex* in *inflexible* (i.e. un-bend-able).

running record
A record of the actual reading by a student of a particular piece of text.

saccades and fixations
Saccades or saccadic steps: the jumps a reader's eyes make when reading. Fixations: the stops or pauses that follow the saccades. A reader 'reads' during the fixations.

segmentation
The process of analysing speech into segments of discrete units of sound such as vowels or consonants.

semantics
The study of the meaning of words in language and how they change.

semiotics
The study of signs, focusing on the patterns of communication. Language is a sign system.

sight word
A word that is read 'on sight', as a whole, without being sounded out or analysed structurally, e.g. *said, the, was, through.*

sociolinguistic approach

The study of the ways in which language is used by societies in relation to class, ethnicity, gender, race, and social institutions.

standardised test

A test that has been given to various groups under uniform conditions in order to obtain norms against which the scores of other groups can be evaluated.

stanine

Contraction of 'standard of nine' in which a test population is divided into nine categories. An individual's score is given an integer from 1 to 9. The mean is 5, containing the middle 20 per cent. The bottom 4 per cent and the top 4 per cent are in the first and ninth classes.

story

A story emerges out of the events that take place, the actions the characters engage in, and the time and place or time-space.

subjectivity

Originally a psychoanalytical term: the developing knowledge of a sense of self.

summative assessment

Evaluation that occurs at the end of a unit or course of study, determining the extent of overall achievement according to identified learning outcomes. In contrast to formative assessment in which a student's progress is monitored or diagnostic assessment in which a student's particular strengths and weaknesses are discovered.

syllabary

A writing system in which the graphic symbols represent syllables.

syntax

The way words, phrases, and clauses are structured in sentences. In linguistics, the study of such structures.

taxonomy

Applied to education, a system of classifying educational objectives. Benjamin Bloom in the 1950s developed objectives for the cognitive domain.

tenor

In discourse, the relations among the participants in a language activity, particularly the level of formality. The style or manner in the variety of language.

text-type

Different genres in functional grammar such as recount, report, and narrative. (See genre.) Communication of meaning in various media that use language. Texts include written, spoken, and visual communication which can be identified. More or less synonymous with genre.

thesaurus

A book of words or phrases arranged by the meaning of words. Peter Mark Roget (1779–1869) produced a popular thesaurus.

'top-down' view of reading

An approach to reading and learning to read that emphasises the primary importance of meaning and what the reader brings to the text.

traditional grammar

The grammatical study (based originally on the grammar of Latin) of the structure of language, mostly within the sentence.

understory

A new term relating to the layers of themes and significance in children's literature texts. It gives narrative and thematic cohesion as well as points of connection to other texts.

validity

The extent to which a measurement tool does what it is intended to do.

visual literacy

The ability to read signs, images, pictures, perspectives, focalisation, shape, and form. It is also the ability to analyse the power of images in particular contexts.

Bibliography

Abbreviations

ACER	Australian Council for Educational Research
ALEA	Australian Literacy Educators' Association
ANU	Australian National University
DEETYA	Department of Employment, Education Training and Youth Affairs (Cwlth)
FILLM	Fédération Internationale des Langues et Litteratures Modernes
PETA	Primary English Teaching Association
SMH	*Sydney Morning Herald*
UNSW	University of New South Wales
UTS	University of Technology Sydney

General references and critical texts

Adams, M. J. 1990, *Beginning to read: Thinking and learning about print*, MIT Press, Cambridge, Mass.

Adams, M. J., and M. Bruck 1993, 'Word Recognition: The interface of educational policies and scientific research', *Reading and Writing: An Interdisciplinary Journal* 5: 113–39.

Anderson, J. 1985, 'Microcomputers and Reading'. In G. Winch and V. Hoogstad (eds), *Teaching Reading: A Language Experience*, Macmillan, Melbourne, 203–12.

Anderson, R. C., E. H. Hiebert, J. A. Scott and I. A. G. Wilkinson 1985, *Becoming a Nation of Readers: The report of the Commission on Reading*, Center for the Study of Reading, Champaign, Illinois.

Anderson-Inman, L. 1998, 'Electronic Text: literacy medium of the future', *Journal of Adolescent and Adult Literacy* 41(8): 678–82.

Anstey, M., and G. Bull 1996, *The Literacy Labyrinth*, Prentice Hall, Sydney.

Anstey, M., and G. Bull 2000, *Reading the Visual: Written and illustrated children's literature*, Harcourt, Sydney.

Australian Bureau of Statistics 1997, *Aspects of Literacy: Australia 1996*, 2 vols, AGPS, Canberra.

Australian Education Council 1994, *English—A Curriculum Profile for Australian Schools*, Curriculum Corporation, Melbourne.

Australian Language and Literacy Policy 1991, Companion volume to the Policy Paper, Australian Government Publishing Service, Canberra

Bakhtin, M. M. 1981, *The Dialogic Imagination*, ed. M. Holquist, transl. C. Emerson and M. Holquist, University of Texas Press, Texas.

Bakhtin, M. M. 1986, *Speech Genres and Other Late Essays*, transl. Vern W. McGee, ed. Caryl Emerson and Michael Holquist, University of Texas Press, Texas.

Bal, M. 1985, *Narratology: Introduction to the Theory of Narrative*, University of Toronto Press, Toronto.

Barrs, M. 1990, *Patterns of Learning*, Centre for Language in Primary Education, London.

Barthes, R. 1968. 'The Death of the Author'. In *Image-Music-Text* (1977), transl. Stephen Heath, Fontana/Collins, Glasgow.

Barthes, R. 1976, *The Pleasure of the Text*, transl. Richard Miller, Jonathan Cape, London.

Bean, W., and C. Bouffler, 1987, *Spell by Writing*, PETA, Sydney.

Bean, W., and C. Bouffler, 1997, *Spelling*, Eleanor Curtain Publishing, Melbourne.

Beard, R. 1998, *National Literacy Strategy: Review of Research and Other Related Evidence*, Department for Education and Employment, Sudbury, Suffolk, UK.

Benjamin, W. 1966, *Understanding Brecht*, Verso, London.

Benton, M. 1996, 'The Image of Childhood: Representations of the child in painting and literature, 1700–1900', *Children's Literature in Education* 27(1): 35–60.

Bettelheim, B. 1976, *The Uses of Enchantment: The meaning and importance of fairy tales*, Vintage, New York.

Bloom B. S. (ed.) 1956, *Taxonomy of Educational Objectives: The classification of educational goals*, Longmans, London.

Bloomfield, L. 1927, 'Literate and Illiterate Speech', *American Speech* 2(10): 432–9.

Board of Studies NSW 1998a, *English K–6 Syllabus*, Board of Studies NSW, Sydney.

Board of Studies NSW 1998b, *English K–6 Student Work Samples: Talking and Listening, Reading, Writing*, Board of Studies NSW, Sydney.

Bond, G., and R. Dykstra 1967, *Coordinating Center for First Grade Reading Instruction programs, Final Report*, US Department of Health, Education and Welfare, University of Minnesota Press, Minneapolis. (See also the reprint, with researchers' comments, *Reading Research Quarterly* (3)1, 1999.)

Bouffler, C. 1987, *Spelling It out to Parents*, PETA, Sydney.

Brian, J., and D. Cox 1998, *Leaves for Mr Walter*, Margaret Hamilton Books, Sydney.

Bruner, J. 1986, *Actual Minds, Possible Worlds*, Harvard University Press, Boston.

Bull, G. 1995, 'Children's Literature: using text to describe reality', *Australian Journal of Language and Literacy* 18(4): 259–69.

Bull, G., and M. Anstey (eds) 1996, *The Literacy Lexicon*, Prentice Hall, Sydney.

Bussis, A. M. 1982, 'Burn it at the Casket: Research, reading instruction, and children's learning of the first R.', *Phi Delta Kappa*, 64.

Butler, D. 1980, *Babies Need Books*, Bodley Head, London.

Butler, D. 1979, *Cushla and Her Books*, Hodder & Stoughton, London.

Cairney, T. H. 1991, *Other Worlds: The endless possibilities of literature*, Heinemann, Portsmouth, NH.

Cairney, T. H. 1995, *Pathways to Literacy*, Cassell, London.

Cairney, T. H. 1997, The role of the family in children's learning: Developing more effective partnerships between home and school, unpublished manuscript.

Cairney, T. H., and L. Munsie 1995, *Beyond Tokenism: Parents as partners in literacy*, Heinemann, Portsmouth, NH.

Calfee, R. C. 1994, E. H. Hiebert and P. Afflerbach (eds), *Authentic Reading Assessment: Practices and possibilities*, I. R. A, Newark, Delaware.

Calkins, L. M. 1983, *Lessons from a Child: On the teaching and learning of writing*, Heinemann Educational, Exeter, NH.

Cambourne, B. 1988, *The Whole Story*, Ashton Scholastic, Sydney.

Cambourne, B. 1999, 'What's the score on testing?', *Practically Primary* 4(1): 8–9.

Carney, E. 1994, *A Survey of Spelling*, Routledge, London.

Carpenter, H., and M. Prichard 1984, *The Oxford Companion to Children's Literature*, Oxford University Press, Oxford.

Catholic Education Office of Victoria 1990, 'Children's Literature and Second Language Acquistion', *Diversity* 8:1.

Chall, J. S. 1967, *Learning to Read: The great debate* (2nd edn 1983, 3rd edn 1996), McGraw-Hill, New York.

Chall, J. S. 1999, 'Some Thoughts on Reading Research: Revisiting the first-grade studies', *Reading Research Quarterly* 34(1): 8–10.

Chambers, A. 1993, *Tell Me: Children, reading and talk*, Thimble Press, Stroud, Glos., UK.

Chambers, A. 1985, *Booktalk*, Bodley Head, London.

Chapman, J. 1983, *Reading Development and Cohesion*, Heinemann, London.

Chatman, S. 1978, *Story and Discourse: Narrative structure in fiction and film*, Cornell University Press, Ithaca and London.

Chenfeld, M. D. 1987, *Teaching Language Arts Creatively*, 2nd edn, Harcourt Brace Jovanovich, New York.

Chomsky, N. 1965, Aspects of the Theory of Syntax, MIT Press, Cambridge Mass.

Christie, F. 1989, Curriculum Genres in Early Childhood Education: A case study in writing development. Unpublished PhD thesis, University of Sydney.

Christie, F., and J. R. Martin 1997, *Genre and Institutions: Social processes in the workplace and school*, Cassell, London.

Christie, F., and R. Misson (eds) 1998, *Literacy and Schooling*, Routledge, London.

Christie, F., and J. Rothery 1989, *Writing In Schools: A reader*, Deakin University Press, Geelong.

Christie, F., and J. Rothery 1990, 'Literacy in the curriculum: planning and assessment'. In F. Christie (ed.), *Literacy for a Changing World*, ACER, Melbourne, pp. 187–205.

Clark, M. M. 1976, *Young Fluent Readers*, Heinemann, London.

Clay, M. M. 1972, *The Early Detection of Reading Difficulties: A diagnostic survey*, Heinemann, Auckland.

Clay, M. M. 1979, *Reading: The Patterning of Complex Behaviour*, 2nd edn, Heinemann, Auckland.

Clay, M. M. 1991, *Becoming Literate: The construction of inner control*, Heinemann, Auckland.

Clay, M. M. 1993, *An Observation Survey of Early Literacy Achievement*, Heinemann, Auckland.

Clay, M. M. 1998, *By Different Paths to Common Outcomes*, Heinemann, Auckland.

Clay, M. M., and B. Tuck 1991, A *Study of Reading Recovery Subgroups: Including outcomes for children who did not satisfy discontinuing criteria*, Heinemann and University of Auckland, Auckland.

Clemmons, J., L. Laase, D. Cooper, N. Areglado and M. Dill 1993, *Portfolios in the Classroom, Grades 1–6*, Scholastic Professional Books, New York.

Collerson, J. 1988, *Writing for Life*, PETA, Sydney.

Collerson, J. 1997, *Grammar in Teaching*, PETA, Sydney.

Commonwealth Department of Education, Training and Youth Affairs 1998 (draft), *Assessing Literacy: Using Stage I outcomes* (Joint Project of Catholic Education Commission, Association of Independent Schools, Department of Education and Training NSW), Commonwealth of Australia, Canberra.

Cope, B., and M. Kalantzis 1993, *The Power of Literacy: A genre approach to the teaching of writing*, Falmer Press, London.

Cottee, K. 1989, *First Lady: A history-making solo voyage around the world*, Pan Books, Sydney.

CREArTA (International Journal of the Centre for Research and Education in the Arts, (CREA) UTS, 1(1) 2000.

Crossman, W. 2000, 'The End of Written Language', *SMH*, 1 January 2000, Sydney. Adapted from his forthcoming book, *Comspeak 2000: How talking computers will recreate an oral culture by the mid-21*st century.

Crystal, D. 1997, *English as a Global Village*, Cambridge University Press, Cambridge.

Curriculum Corporation 1994, *ESL Scales: A joint project of the States, Territories and the Commonwealth of Australia initiated by the Australian Education Council*, Curriculum Corporation, Melbourne.

Dale, E., and J. Chall 1948, 'A Formula for Predicting Readability', *Education Research Bulletin* 27: 1120.

Davidson, J. 1999, 'All Things in Moderation: a whole school approach to authentic assessment', *Practically Primary* 4(1): 18–19

Dawkins, R. 1996, *Climbing Mount Improbable*, Norton, New York.

Deakin University 1984, *Children Writing: A Reader*, Deakin University Press, Geelong, Vic.

De Bono, E. 1970, *Lateral Thinking: A textbook of creativity*, Ward Lock Educational, London.

Derewianka, B. 1991, *Exploring How Texts Work*, PETA, Sydney.

Derewianka, B. 1998, *A Grammar Companion for Primary Teachers*, PETA, Sydney.

Derrida, J. 1991, *Donner le Temps*, vol. 1, Galilee, Paris.

Dewey, J. 1971, *English Spelling: Roadblock to Reading*, Teachers College Press, Columbia University, New York.

Dickinson, P. 1986, 'Fantasy: The need for realism', *Children's Literature in Education* 17(1): 39–51.

Doonan, J. 1993, *Looking at Pictures in Picture Books*, Thimble Press, Stroud, Glos, UK.

Doonan, J. 1998, paper presented to Beyond the Riverbank Conference, University of Exeter.

Durkin, D. 1966, *Children Who Read Early*, Teachers' College Press, New York.

Education Department of Western Australia 1994a, *First Steps: Writing develpomental continuum*, Longman, Melbourne.

Education Department of Western Australia 1994a, *First Steps Reading Resource Book*, Longman, Melbourne.

Eichenbaum, B. 1998, 'Introduction to the Formal Method'. In Rivkin and Ryan, *Literary Theory*, pp. 8–16.

Ellyard, P. 1997, Australian College of Eduaction Conference, Cairns.

Emmitt, M. 1999, 'Authentic Assessment—what is it?' *Practically Primary*, 4(1): 5–7.

Ernst & Young 1998, Literacy, Education and Training. Their impact on the UK economy, mimeo. Quoted in R. Beard 1998, *National Literacy Strategy: Review of Research and other Related Evidence*, Department for Education and Employment, Sudbury, Suffolk, UK.

Estès, C. P. 1992, *Women who Run with the Wolves: Contacting the power of the Wild Woman*, Rider, London.

Fairclough, N. 1989, *Language and Power*, Longman, London.

Ferriero, E., and A. Teberosky 1982, *Literacy Before Schooling* (English edn), Heinemann, Portsmouth, NH.

Flesch, R. F. 1943, *Marks of Readable Style: A Study of Adult Education*, Teachers College Press, Columbia University.

Foucault, M. 1969, 'What is an Author?'. In M. Foucault, *Language, Counter-Memory, Practice: Selected Essays and Interviews*, Basil Blackwell, Oxford.

Freebody, P., and A. Luke 1990, 'Literacies Programs: Debates and demands in cultural context', *Prospect* 5: 7–16.

Freeman, L. 1998, *Phonemic/Phonological Awareness, Literacy Discussion Paper*, Department of Education and Training, NSW.

Freire, P. 1987, 'The Importance of the Act of Reading'. In C. Mitchell and K. Welert (eds), *Rewriting Literacy: Culture and the discourse of the other*, Bergin and Carbey, New York.

Frommer, A. 1988, *Hawaii on $50 a Day*, Macmillan Travel. World Book.

Fry, E. 1968, 'Readability Formula That Saves Time', *Journal of Reading* 11: 513–16; 575–8.

Gardner, H. 1983, *Frames of Mind: The theory of multiple intelligences*, London, Fontana.

Garner, A. 1976, *The Stone Book*, William Collins, London.

Gee, J. P. 1997, 'Literacy and Social Minds'. In Bull and Anstey, *The Literacy Lexicon*, pp. 5–14.

Gee, J. P., G. Hull and C. Lankshear 1996, *The New Work Order: Behind the language of the new capitalism*, Allen & Unwin, Sydney.

Genette, G. 1980, *Narrative Discourse: An essay in method*, Cornell University Press, Ithaca and London.

Gentry, J. R., and J. W. Gillet 1993, *Teaching Kids to Spell*, Heinemann, Portsmouth, NH.

Gibson, E. J. and H. Levin 1975, *The Psychology of Reading*, MIT Press, Cambridge, Mass.

Goodman, K. S. 1967, 'Reading : A psycholinguistic guessing game', *Journal of the Reading Specialist* 6: 126–35.

Goodman, K. S. 1973, 'Psycholinguistic Universals in the Reading Process'. In F. Smith, *Psycholinguistics and Reading*, Holt, Reinhart & Winston, New York, pp. 21–7.

Goodman, K. S. 1986, *What's Whole in Whole Language?*, Heinemann, Portsmouth NH.

Goodman, Y. 1997, 'Reading Diagnosis—qualitative or quantitative?', *The Reading Teacher* 50(7): 534–8.

Goodman, Y. M., and C. L. Burke 1972, *Reading Miscue Inventory Manual: Procedure for diagnosis and evaluation*, Macmillan, New York.

Graves, D. 1983, *Writing: Teachers and children at work*, Heinemann, Portsmouth, NH.

Graves, D. 1994, *A Fresh Look At Writing*, Heinemann, Portsmouth, NH.

Gunew, S. 1985, 'Migrant Women Writers: Who's on whose margins"'. In C. Ferrier (ed.), *Gender, Politics and Fiction: Twentieth century australian womens' novels*, University of Queensland Press, Brisbane, pp. 163–78.

Habermas, J. 1981, *The Theory of Communicative Action*, vol. 1. Beacon Press, Boston.

Halliday, M. A. K. 1979, 'Differences between Spoken and Written Language: Some implications for library teaching'. In G. Page, J. Elkins and B. O'Connor (eds), *Communication Through Reading: Proceedings of the 4th ARA Conference* Australian Reading Association, Adelaide, pp. 35–52.

Halliday, M. A. K. 1985a, *An Introduction to Functional Grammar*, Edward Arnold, London.

Halliday, M. A. K. 1985b, *Spoken and Written Language*, Deakin University Press, Melbourne.

Halliday, M. A. K. 1986, 'Points from Speakers'. In Walshe et al. (eds), *Writing and Learning in Australia*, pp. 5–6.

Halliday, M. A. K., and R. Hasan 1976, *Cohesion in English*, Longman, London.

Hammel, F., and S. Levey 1988, *Frommer's Hawaii On $50 A Day*, Prentice Hall Press, New York.

Hammond, J. 1996, 'Reading Knowledge about Language and Genre Theory'. In Bull and Anstey, *The Literacy Lexicon*, pp. 207–20.

Heath, S. B. 1983, *Ways with Words: Language, life and work in communities and classroom*, Cambridge University Press, Cambridge.

Heidegger, M. 1968, *An Introduction to Metaphysics*, transl. Michael Heim, Yale University Press, New Haven.

Ho, C. 2000, 'A log-on beats a show-up for many tertiary students', *SMH*, 11 January.

Holdaway, D. 1979, *The Foundations of Literacy*, Scholastic Australia, Gosford, NSW.

Holliday, R. 1988, 'Handwriting: handwriting and the learner'. In J. Murray and F. Smith (eds), *Language Arts and the Learner*, Macmillan, Melbourne, pp. 98–124.

Hollindale, P. 1995, 'Children's Literature in an Age of Multiple Literacies', *Australian Journal of Language and Literacy* 18(4): 249–58.

Hollindale, P. 1997 *Signs of Childness in Children's Books*, Thimble Press, Stroud, Glos., UK.

Hooton, J. 1990, *Stories of Herself When Young: Autobiographies of Australian women*, Oxford University Press, Melbourne.

Hourihan, M. 1997, *Deconstructing the Hero*, Routledge, New York.

Hunt, P. 1995, *Children's Literature: An illustrated history*, Oxford University Press, Oxford and New York.

International Reading Association 1998, *Phonemic Awareness and the Teaching of Reading*, IRA, Newark, Del.

Iser, W. 1980, *The Act of Reading: A theory of aesthetic response*, Johns Hopkins University Press, London.

Jacobson, R. 1998, 'Two Aspects of Language'. In Rivkin and Ryan, *Literary Theory*, pp. 91–5.

Johnston, R. R. 1995, 'Of Dialogue and Desire: Children's literature and the needs of the reluctant L2 reader', *Australian Journal of Language and Literacy* 18(4): 293–303.

Johnston, R. R. 1996, 'Connecting and Community: How to encourage your child to become a reader'. In *Real Books for Real Kids*, Australian School Library Association NSW Inc., Parramatta, NSW, pp. 2–10.

Johnston, R. R. 1997, 'Children's Literature: The missing link?', *The Literature Base* 8(3): 4–11.

Johnston, R. R. 1998a, 'Thisness and Everydayness in Children's Literature: The "being-in-the-world proposed by the text"', *Papers* 8(1): 25–35.

Johnston, R. R. 1998b, 'Time-space: History as palimpsest and *myse-en-abyme* in children's literature', *Orana* (Australian Library and Information Association Journal): 18–24.

Johnston, R. R. 2000, 'The Literacy of the Imagination', *Bookbird* 38(1): 25–30.

Johnston, R. S. 1998, 'The Case for Orthographic Knowledge: A response to Scholes 1998, the case against phonemic awareness', *Journal of Research in Reading* 21(3): 195–200.

Just, M. A., and P. A. Carpenter 1987, *The Psychology of Reading and Language Comprehension*, Allyn & Bacon, Boston.

Kilgour, G. 1998, *The Evolution of the Book*, Oxford University Press, New York.

Kolers, P. A., H. Levin and J. P. Williams (eds) 1970, *Basic Studies in Reading*, Basic Books, Inc., New York. Reprinted as P. A. Kolers, 'Three Studies in Reading'. In F. Smith (ed.), *Psycholinguistics and Reading*, Holt Reinhart & Winston, New York, 1973, pp. 28–50.

Kress, G. 1982, *Learning to Write*, Routledge & Kegan Paul, London.

Kress, G. 1988, *Communication and Culture: An introduction*, UNSW Press, Sydney.

Kushner, D. 1980, *The Violin-Maker's Gift*, Macmillan of Canada, Toronto.

Kushner, E. 1996, 'Liberating Children's Imagination'. Plenary paper, XX International Congress, FILLM, Regensburg, Germany.

Lanham, R. A. 1993, *The Electronic Word: Democracy, technology and the arts*, University of Chicago Press, Chicago.

Lankshear, C. 1996, 'Language and Cultural Process'. In Bull and Anstey, *The Literacy Lexicon*, pp. 17–27.

Lewis, A. 1992, *Writing*, Addison-Wesley, Reading, Mass.

Ljungdahl, L. 1999, 'Teachers' Choices and Children's Literature', *TESOL in Context* 9(1): 22–6.

Luke, A. 1993, 'The Social Construction of Literacy in the Primary School'. In Len Unsworth (ed.), *Literacy Learning and Teaching*, Macmillan, Melbourne, pp. 3–53.

Luke, C. 1996, 'Reading Gender and Culture in Media Discourses and Texts'. In Bull and Anstey, *The Literacy Lexicon*, pp. 177–89.

Manguel, A. 1997, *A History of Reading*, HarperCollins, London.

Martin, J. R. 1984, 'Language, Register and Genre'. In F. Christie and J. Rothery (eds), *Children Writing: A Reader*, Deakin University Press, Geelong, Vic., pp. 21–9.

Martin, J. R. 1992, *English Text: System and structure*, John Benjamins, Amsterdam.

Martin, J. R., and J. Rothery 1981, 'Writing Project 1 & 2', Linguistics Department, University of Sydney.

Martin, J. R., and J. Rothery 1990, 'Literacy for a Lifetime', Department of Linguistics, University of Sydney.

Martin, W. 1986, *Recent Theories of Narrative*, Cornell University Press, Ithaca and London.

Masters, G. 1991, *Assessing Achievement in Australian Schools. A discussion paper prepared for the National Industry Education Forum*, National Industry Education Forum, Melbourne.

Masters, G. N., and M. Forster 1996, *Developmental Assessment: Assessment resource kit*, ACER, Melbourne.

Masters, G. N., and M. Forster 1997a, *Literacy Standards in Australia*, Commonwealth of Australia, Canberra.

Masters, G. N., and M. Forster 1997b, *Mapping Literacy Achievement: Results of the 1996 National School English Literacy Survey*, DEETYA, Canberra.

Meek, M. 1982, *Learning to Read*, Bodley Head, London.

Meek, M. 1988, *How Texts Teach What Readers Learn*, Thimble Press, Stroud, UK. In association with PETA, Sydney.

Meek, M. 1991, *On Being Literate*, Bodley Head, London.

Merleau-Ponty, M. 1986, *Phenomenology of Perception*, Routledge & Kegan Paul, London [1962].

Moni, K., C. van Krayenoord and C. Baker 1999, 'English teachers' Perceptions of Literacy Assessment in the First Year of Secondary School', *Australian Journal of Language and Literacy* 22(1): 26–39.

Morley-Warner, T. 2000, *Academic Writing is …*, CREA Publications, UTS, Sydney.

Mulvaney, D. J. 1987, 'The end of the beginning: 6,000 years ago to 1788'. In D. J. Mulvaney and J. Peter White (eds), *Australians to 1788*, Fairfax, Syme & Weldon, Assoc. Sydney, pp. 75–114.

Mudd, N. 1997, *The Power of Words*, UK Reading Association, Royston.

Muecke, S. 1999, 'The Sacred in History', *Humanities Research*, Humanities Research Centre, ANU, Canberra, pp. 27–37.

Muspratt, S., A. Luke and P. Freebody (eds) 1997, *Constructing Critical Literacies: Teaching and learning textual practice*, Allen & Unwin, Sydney.

Nikolajeva, M. 1988, *The Magic Code: The Use of Magical Patterns in Fantasy for Children*, Almqvist & Wiksell International, Stockholm.

Nikolajeva, M. 1996a, *Children's Literature Comes of Age: Towards a new aesthetic*, Garland Publishing, New York.

Nikolajeva, M. 1996b, 'Exit Children's Literature?' Plenary paper, XX International Congress, FILLM, Regensburg, Germany.

Nikolajeva, M. 2000, *From Mythic to Linear: Time in children's literature*, Children's Literature Association and Scarecrow Press, London.

Nodelman, P. 1996, *Words About Pictures*, University of Georgia Press, Athens and London.

Nodelman, P. 1996, *The Pleasures of Children's Literature*, 2nd edn, Longman Publishers, White Plains, NY [1992].

NSW Department of Education and Training 1997, *Teaching Reading: A K–6 Framework*, Department of Education and Training, Sydney.

NSW Department of Education and Training 1998a, *State Literacy Strategy: Teaching spelling K–6*, Department of Education and Training, Sydney.

NSW Department of Education and Training 1998b, *English K–6: Student work samples*, Department of Education and Training, Sydney.

NSW Department of Education and Training 1999, *Literacy Strategy Evaluation 1997 and 1998*, Department of Education and Training, Sydney.

NSW Department of School Education 1994, *Step by Step Booklist*, Curriculum Directorate, Sydney.

Oakhill, J., and R. Beard (eds) 1999, *Reading Development and the Teaching of Reading: A psychological perspective*, Blackwell, Oxford.

Olinder, B. (ed.), 1984, *A Sense of Place*, Gothenburg University Press, Gothenburg.

Olsen, D. R. 1977, 'From Utterance to Text: The bias of language in speech and writing', *Harvard Educational Review* 47: 257–81.

O'Malley, M., and L. Valdez Pierce 1996, *Authentic Assessment for English Language Learners: Practical approaches for teachers*, Addison-Wesley Publishing Co., USA.

Palous, R. 1995, 'The Social and Political Vocation of the University in the Global Age'. In T. Schuller (ed.), *The Changing University*, Open University Press, Buckingham, UK, pp. 176–8.

Parry, J., and D. Hornsby 1985, *Write On: A conference approach to writing*, Martin Educational, Sydney.

Partridge, E. 1953, *You Have a Point There*, Hamish Hamilton, London.

Perfetti, C. A. 1995, 'Cognitive Research can Inform Reading Education', *Journal of Research in Reading* 18(2): 106–15.

Peterson, B. 1988, *Characteristics of Texts That Support Beginning Readers*, Ohio State University, Columbus, Ohio.

Peterson, B. 1991, 'Selecting Books for Beginning Readers'. In D. De Ford, C. Lyons and G. Pinnell, *Bridges to Literacy: Learning from Reading Recovery*, Heinemann, Portsmouth, NH, pp. 119–47.

Pinnell, G. S., and I. G. Fountas 1998, *Word Matters: Teaching phonics and spelling in the reading/writing classroom*, Heinemann, Portsmouth, NH.

Popper, K. 1976, *Unended Quest: An intellectual autobiography*, Fontana, New York.

Potter, S. 1960, *Modern Linguistics*, Andre Deutsch, London.

Protheroe, P. 1992, *Vexed Texts: How Childrens's Picture Books Promote Illiteracy*, The Book Guild Ltd, Sussex, UK.

Pullman, P. 1989, 'Invisible pictures', *Signal 60* September:160–86.

Raphael, T. E., and F. B. Boyd 1997, 'When Readers Write'. In S. I. McMahon and T. E. Raphael (eds) with V. Goatley and L. Pardo, *The Book Club Connection: Literacy learning and classroom talk*, Teachers College Press, Columbia University.

Report of the Literacy Taskforce: A report prepared for the Minister of Education 1999, New Zealand.

Richards, I. A. 1969, *Practical Criticism: A study of literary judgment*, Harcourt, Brace and World, New York [1929].

Ricoeur, P. 1985, *Time and Narrative*, transl. Kathleen McLauglin and David Pellauer, University of Chicago Press, Chicago.

Rivkin, J., and M. Ryan 1998, *Literary Theory: An anthology*, Blackwell, Oxford.

Rose, Ellen Cronan 1983, 'Through the Looking Glass: When women tell fairy tales'. In E. Abel, M. Hirsch and E. Langland (eds), *The Voyage In: Fictions of female development*, University Press of New England, Dartmouth, New England, pp. 209–27.

Rosen, C., and H. Rosen 1973, *The Language of Primary School Children*, Penguin Books, Harmondsworth.

Rosencrans, G. 1998, *The Spelling Book: Teaching children how to spell, not what to spell*, International Reading Association, Newark, Delaware.

Sainsbury, M. 1998, *Evaluation of the National Literacy Strategy: Summary REPORT* National Foundation for Educational Research, Slough, UK.

Sale, C. 1995, *Demystifying Reading Recovery*, Primary English Teaching Association, Sydney.

Saljo, R. 1979, in F. Marton, D. Hounsel and N. Entwhistle (eds), *The Experience of Learning,* Scottish University Press, Edinburgh.

Saxby M. 1997, *Books in the Life of a Child*, Macmillan Education Australia, Melbourne.

Scholes, R. J. 1998, 'The case against phonemic awareness', *Journal of Research in Reading* 21(3): 177–88.

Schools Council, National Board of Employment, Education and Training 1995, *The Elements of Successful Student Outcomes: Views from upper primary classroom teachers*, Commissioned Report No. 41, Price Waterhouse, December.

Sell, R. 1996, 'Literary and Language Education in the mediation of Cultural Difference'. Plenary paper, XX International Congress, FILLM, Regensburg, Germany.

Shotter, J. 1993, *Cultural Politics of Everyday Life*, Open University Press, Buckingham.

Sinclair, N. 1999, comment in Master of Arts in Children's Literature and Literacy class at UTS.

Smith, F. 1973, 'Decoding: The Great Fallacy'. In F. Smith (ed.), *Psycholinguistics and Reading*, Holt Reinhart & Winston, New York, pp. 70–83.

Smith, F. 1978, *Reading*, Cambridge University Press, Cambridge.

Smith, F. 1982, *Writing and the Writer*, Holt, Reinhart & Winston, New York.

Smith, N. B. 1969, 'The many faces of reading comprehension', *The Reading Teacher* 23(3): 249–59.

Snow, C. E., M. S. Burns and P. Griffin (eds) 1998, *Preventing Reading Difficulties in Young Children*, Commission on Behavioural and Social Sciences and Education, National Research Council, National Academy Press, Washington DC.

Sollat, K. 1997, 'The Boundaries of Fantasy in German Children's Literature' *Bookbird* 35(4): 6–11.

Spache, G. 1953, 'A New Readability Formula for Prime Grade Reading Materials', *Elementary School Journal* 53: 410–13.

Stanovich, K. E. 1994, 'Romance and reality', *The Reading Teacher* 47(4): 280–91.

Stanovich, K. E., and J. Paula 1995, 'How Research might Inform the Debate about Early Reading Acquisition', *Journal of Research in Reading* 18(2): 87–105.

Stephens, J. 1992, *Language and Ideology in Children's Fiction*, Longman, London and New York.

Stewart Dore, N. 1986, *Writing and Reading to Lear*, PETA, Sydney.

Stoodt, B., L. Amspaugh and J. Hunt 1996, *Children's Literature*, Macmillan Education, Melbourne.

Stuart, M. 1998, 'Let the Emperor Retain his Underclothes: A response to Scholes 1998, The case against phonemic awareness', *Journal of Research in Reading* 21(3): 189–94.

'*The National Literacy Project* 1998, an HMI Evaluation', Office for Standards in Education, London.

Tierney, R. J., M. A. Carter and L. E. Desai 1991, *Portfolio Assessment in the Reading-Writing Classroom*, Christopher-Gordon, Norwood, Mass.

Treiman, R., and A. Zukowski 1996, 'Children's Sensitivity to Syllables, Onsets, Rimes and Phonemes', *Journal of Experimental Child Psychology* 61: 193–215.

Tucker, E. 1986. 'Conference/How To?'. In Walshe et al., *Writing and Learning in Australia*, pp. 196–8.

Turner, M. 1996, *The Literary Mind*, Oxford University Press, New York.

Valencia, S. 1990, 'A Portfolio Approach to Classroom Reading Assessment: the Whys, Whats, and Hows', *The Reading Teacher* 43(4): 338–40.

Valencia, X. W. 1991, 'Portfolios: Panacea or Pandora's Box?'. In F. L. Finch (ed.), *Educational Performance Assessment*, Riverside Publishing Co., Chicago, pp. 33–46.

Van Krayenoord, C. 1996, 'Literacy Assessment'. In Bull and Anstey, *The Literacy Lexicon*, pp. 237–47.

Venezky, R. L. 1967, 'English Orthography: Its graphical structure and its relation to sound', *Reading Research Quarterly* 2: 75–106.

Vygotsky, L. S. 1978, *Mind in Society*, Harvard University Press, Harvard.

Wallace, C. 1988, *Learning to Read in a Multicultural Society*, Prentice Hall, Hemel Hempstead, UK.

Walshe, R. D., P. March and D. Jensen (eds) 1986, *Writing and Learning in Australia*, Oxford and Dellasta, Melbourne.

Warner, M. 1994, *From the Beast to the Blonde*, Chatto & Windus, London.

Waugh, P. 1997, *Revolutions of the Word*, Hodder Headline, Sydney.

Webster, R. 1990, *Studying Literary Theory*, Edward Arnold, London.

Wilkinson, A., G. P. Barnsley, P. Hanna and M. Swan 1980, *Assessing Language Development* (Oxford Studies in Education), Oxford University Press, Oxford.

Wille, C. 1996, *Matching Books to Children*, PETA, Sydney.

Williams, E. 1977, *Assignments in Punctuation and Spelling*, Edward Arnold, London.

Winch, G. 1988, 'Literature: Its place in learning to read'. In A. Hanzl (ed.), *Literature: A focus for language learning*, Australian Reading Association, Melbourne, pp. 3–13.

Winch, G. 1991, 'The Light in the Eye: On good books for children'. In M. Saxby and G. Winch (eds), *Give Them Wings: The experience of children's literature*, 2nd edn, Macmillan of Australia, Melbourne, pp. 19–25.

Winch, G., and G. Blaxell 1992, *Spell Well, Teacher Resource Book 1*, Horwitz Grahame, Sydney.

Winch, G., and G. Blaxell 1999, *The Primary Grammar Handbook: Traditional and functional grammar, punctuation and usage*, rev. edn, Horwitz Martin, Sydney.

Winch, G., and B. Poston-Anderson 1993, *Now For a Story: Sharing stories with young children*, Phoenix Education, Melbourne.

Winch, J. 1999, The Third Space. Unpublished Masters Thesis, UTS.

World Book Encyclopaedia, 1986 (edition), World Book, Inc.,Chicago.

Wray, D., and J. Medwell 1998, *Teaching English in Primary Schools*, Letts Educational, London.

Wycoff, J. 1991, *Mindmapping: your personal guide to exploring creativity and problem-solving*, Berkley Books, New York.

Zipes, J. 1979, *Breaking the Magic Spell: Radical theories of folk and fairy tales*, Heinemann, London.

Zipes, J. 1987, transl. *The Complete Fairy Tales of the Brothers Grimm*, Bantam, New York.

Zipes, J. 1994, *Fairy Tale as Myth*, University Press of Kentucky, Lexington, Kentucky

Children's books

Abdullah, I. 1992, *As I Grew Older*, Omnibus Books, Adelaide.

Abdullah, I. 1994, *Tucker*, Omnibus Books, Adelaide.

Ada, A. F., and L. Tryon 1998, *Yours Truly, Goldilocks*, Atheneum Books, New York.

Agard, J., and G. Nichols (eds) 1994, *A Caribbean Dozen*, Walker Books, London.

Ahlberg, J. and A. 1981, *Peepo*, Kestrel Books, London.

Ahlberg, J. and A. 1989, *Each Peach Pear Plum*, Puffin, London [1978].

Allen, P. 1993, *Bertie and the Bear*, Nelson, Melbourne.

Angelou, M. 1994, *My Painted House, My Friendly Chicken, and Me*, Bodley Head, London.

Applegate, C., and D. Huxley 2000, *Rain Dance*, Margaret Hamilton Books, Sydney.

Baillie, A. 1997, *Secrets of Walden Rising*, Penguin, Melbourne.

Baillie, A., and J. Tanner 1991, *Drac and the Gremlin*, Penguin Books, Melbourne [1988].

Baker, J. 1987, *Where the Forest Meets the Sea*, Julia MacRae Books, Sydney.

Baker, J. 1992, *Window*, Red Fox, London

Baker, J. 1995, *The Story of Rosy Dock*, Random House, Sydney.

Baker, J. 2000, *The Hidden Forest*, Walker Books, London.

Bantock, N. 1997a, *Ceremony of Innocence* (computer optical disk), Real World Multimedia, UK.

Bantock, N. 1997b, *Griffin and Sabine: An extraordinary correspondence*, Pan Macmillan Australia.

Bantock, N. 1992, *Sabine's Notebook: In which the extraordinary correspondence of Griffin continues*, Pan Macmillan Australia.

Bantock, N. 1993, *The Golden Mean: In which the extraordinary correspondence of Griffin and Sabine concludes*, Pan Macmillan Australia.

Banyai, I. 1995, *Zoom*, Viking, New York.

Barbalet, M., and J. Tanner 1994, *The Wolf*, Penguin, Melbourne.

Barber, A. 1994, *The Enchanter's Daughter*, Farr, Straus & Giroux, New York.

Bradbury, P. 1984, *One-Eyed Cat*, Author, New York.

Brian, J., and D. Cox 1998, *Leaves for Mr Walter*, Margaret Hamilton Books, Sydney.

Browne, A. 1981, *Hansel and Gretel*, Julia MacCrae Books, London.

Browne, A. 1986, *Piggybook*, Julia MacRae Books, London.

Browne, A. 1992, *Zoo*, Red Fox, London.

Browne, A. 1999, *Voices in the Park*, Transworld, London.

Burningham, J. 1977, *Come Away from the Water, Shirley*, Jonathon Cape, London.

Burningham, J. 1996, *Cloudland*, Jonathan Cape, London.

Carr, R. V., and A. James 1996, *The Butterfly*, Random House, Sydney.

Caswell, B. 1994, *Lisdalia*, University of Queensland Press, Brisbane.

Caswell, B., and D. Phu An Chiem 1997, *Only the Heart*, University of Queensland Press, Brisbane.

Cole, B. 1986, *Princess Smartypants*, G. P. Putnam's Sons, New York.

Cole, B. 1987, *Prince Cinders*, G. P. Putnam's Sons, New York.

Crew, G., and S. Tan 1999, *Memorial*, Thomas C. Lothian, Melbourne.

Dahl, R. 1997, *George's Marvellous Medicine*, illus. Quentin Blake, Puffin Books, Harmondsworth.

Dahl, R. 1984, *The BFG*, illus. Quentin Blake, Puffin Books in association with Cape, Harmondsworth.

Disher, G. 1991, *The Bamboo Flute*, HarperCollins, Sydney.

Farmer, N. *The Ear, The Eye and The Arm: A 21st Century Adventure Story*, Puffin, London.

Fine, A. 1989, *Bill's New Frock*, Mammoth Books, London.

Fox, M. *Possum Magic*, Omnibus Books, Adelaide.

Fox, M. 1984, *Wilfred Gordon McDonald Partridge*, Omnibus Books, Adelaide.

Fox, M., and J. Dyer 1993, *Time for Bed*, Omnibus Books, Adelaide.

French, F. 1986, *Snow White in New York*, Oxford University Press, London.

Gaarder, J. 1995, *Sophie's World*, Phoenix House, London.

Gleeson, L., and A. Greder 1999, *The Great Bear*, Scholastic Australia, Gosford, NSW.

Gleeson, L. 1984, *Eleanor, Elizabeth*, Angus & Robertson, Sydney.

Gleeson, L. 1987, *I am Susannah*, Angus & Robertson, Sydney.

Gleeson, L. 1994, *Skating on Sand*, Penguin, Melbourne.

Gleeson, L, 1999, *Hannah and the Tomorrow Room*, Penguin, Melbourne.

Gleeson, L., and C. Smith 1992, *Where's Mum?* Omnibus Books, Adelaide.

Gwynne, P. 1999, *Deadly Unna*, Penguin, Melbourne.

Harlen, J., and E. Quay 1998, *Champions*, Random House, Sydney.

Hartnett, S. 1994 *Wilful Blue*, Viking, Melbourne.

Hartnett, S. 1995, *Sleeping Dogs*, Penguin, Melbourne.

Hashmi, K., and F. Marshall 1998, *You and Me, Murrawee*, Viking, Melbourne.

Hathorn, L., and G. Rogers 1994, *Way Home*, Random House, Sydney.

Hathorn, L., and P. Gouldthorpe 1995, *The Wonder Thing*, Viking/Penguin Books Australia.

Hill, A. 1994, *The Burnt Stick*, Viking, Melbourne.

Hill, S., and Barrett, A. 1993, *Beware, Beware*, Walker Books, London.

Howes, J., and R. Harvey 1998, *Islands in My Garden*, Roland Harvey Books, Vic.

Hughes, S. 1973, *Lucy and Tom Go to School*, Gollancz, London.

Hughes, S. 1988, *Out and About*, Walker Books, London.

Hutchins, P. 1968, *Rosie's Walk*, Bodley Head, London.

Hutchins, P. 1991, *Tidy Titch*, Julia MacCrae Books, London.

Isadora, R.1991, *At the Crossroads*, Red Fox, London.

Jenkins, M., and S. Shields 1997, *Chameleons are Cool*, Walker Books, London.

Jennings, P. 1993, *Uncovered!*, Puffin Books, Ringwood, Vic.

Jennings, P., and J. Tanner 1994, *The Fisherman and the Theefyspray*, Penguin, Melbourne.

Killeen, G., F. Partridge and F. Dubuc 1998, *Cherry Pie*, Random House, Sydney.

Klein, R. 1984, *Hating Alison Ashley*, Penguin, Melbourne.

Klein, R. 1991, *All in the Blue Unclouded Weather*, Puffin, Melbourne.

L'Engle, M. 1962, *A Wrinkle in Time*, Longman, London.

Loh, M. 1985, *The Kinder Hat*, Hyland House, Melbourne.

Maloney, J. 1993, *Dougy*, University of Queensland Press, Brisbane.

Marsden, J. 1994, *Tomorrow, When the War Began*, Pan Macmillan, Sydney.

Marshal, V. and B. Tester 1988, *Bernard was a Bikie*, Ashton Scholastic, Gosford NSW.

Mayne, W. 1987, *Mousewing*, Walker Books, London.

McBratney, S. 1994, *Guess How Much I Love You*, Walker Books, London.

McKee, D. 1980, *Not Now, Bernard*, Red Fox, London.

Meeks, Arone R. 1991, *Enora and the Black Crane*, Scholastic Australia, Gosford, NSW.

Montgomery, L. M. (1972) *Anne of Green Gables*, Peacock Books, London [1908].

Morgan, S. 1997 *The Flying Emu and Other Stories*, Puffin Books Australia [1992].

Morimoto, J. 1997, *The Two Bullies*, Random House, Sydney

Mullins, P. 1993, *V is for Vanishing: An Alphabet of Endangered Animals*, Margaret Hamilton Books, Sydney.

Munsch, R., and M. Marchenko 1980, *The Paper Bag Princess*, Annick Press, Toronto.

Naidoo, B. 1995, *No Turning Back*, Viking, London.

Nodelman, P. 1996, *Alice Falls Apart*, Bain & Cox, Winnipeg.

Noon, S., and A. Willard 1998, *A Street Through Time: A 12,000 Year Journey Along the Same Street*, Dorling-Kindersley, London.

Norman, L. 1992, *The Paddock*, Random House, Sydney.

Ottley, M. 1998, *Mrs Millie's Painting*, Hodder Headline, Sydney.

Overend, J., and J. Vivas 1999, *Hello Baby*, ABC Books, Sydney.

Park, R. 1980, *Playing Beatie Bow*, Penguin, Melbourne.

Paulsen, G. 1998, *The Transall Saga*, Delacorte, New York.

Perversi, M., and R. Brooks 1997, *Henry's Bed*, Viking, Melbourne.

Pohl, P. 1991, *Johnny, My Friend*, transl. Laurie Thompson, Turton & Chambers, Stroud, UK [1985].

Poole, J., and A. Barrett 1993, *Snow-White*, Red Fox, London [1991].

Price, S. 1998, *The Sterkarm Handshake*, Scholastic Press, London.

Riddle, T. 1996, *The Tip at the End of the Street*, HarperCollins, Sydney.

Rowan, K., and K. McEwen 1988, *I Know How We Fight Germs*, Walker Books, London.

Rowling, J. K. 1997, *Harry Potter and the Philosopher's Stone*, Bloomsbury, London.

Rubinstein, G. 1989, *Skymaze*, Omnibus/Puffin Book, Ringwood, Vic.

Russell, E. 2000, *A is for Aunty*, ABC Books, Sydney.

Scieska, J., and S. Johnson 1991, *The Frog Prince Continued*, Viking, New York.

Scieska, J., and L. Smith 1992, *The Stinky Cheeseman and Other Fairly Stupid Tales*, Puffin, London.

Sendak, M. 1992, *Where the Wild Things Are*, HarperCollins, London [1963].

Sendak, M. 1993, *Outside Over There*, HarperCollins, London.

Seuss, Dr., S. Johnson and L. Fancher 1998, *My Many Coloured Days*, Hutchinson, London.

Torres, P. 1994, *Jalygurr: Aussie Animal Rhymes*, Magabala Books, Broome, WA [1988].

Utemorrah, D., and P. Torres 1990, *Do Not Go Around the Edges*, Magabala Books, Broome, WA.

Voake, C. 1997, *Ginger*, Walker Books, London.

Waddell, M., and P. Benson 1986, *The Tough Princess*, Philomel Books, New York.

Waddell, M., and P. Benson 1992, *Owl Babies*, Walker Books, London.

Wagner, J., and R. Brooks 1977, *John Brown, Rose and the Midnight Cat*, Puffin, London.

Wagner, J., and R. Roennfeldt 1995, *The Werewolf Knight*, Random House, Sydney.

Walker, K., and D. Cox 1994, *Our Excursion*, Omnibus Books, Adelaide.

Wells, R. 1981, *Timothy Goes to School*, Dial, New York.

Wells, R. 1996, *Edward's First Day at School*, Walker Books, London.

Wheatley, N., and D. Rawlins 1987, *My Place*, Longman, Melbourne.

White, E. B. 1952, *Charlotte's Web*, Harper & Row, New York.

Wild, M., and R. Brooks 2000, *Fox*, Allen & Unwin, Sydney.

Wild, M., and J. Vivas 1991, *Let the Celebrations Begin*, Omnibus Books, Adelaide.

Wilde, O. 1977, *The Happy Prince and Other Stories*, Puffin, Pandora's Books Ltd, Harmondsworth.

Wilde, O. 1979, *The Selfish Giant*, Evans Bros, London.

Williamson, J., and G. Singleton 1988, *Christmas in Australia*, Ashton Scholastic, Sydney.

Wilson, J. 1992, *The Suitcase Kid*, Corgi Yearling, London.

Winch, G. 1985, *Samantha Seagull's Sandals*, Childerset, Adelaide.

Winch, G. 1989, 'Me Moving'. In *Words Come Out to Play*, Rigby, Melbourne, pp. 10–11.

Winch, G., and G. Blaxell 1996, *Danny Dolphin's Nose*, Blake Education, Sydney.

Winch, G., and G. Blaxell 1997, *Sal and Sam on the Farm*, Blake Education, Sydney.

Winton, T. 1993, *Lockie Leonard: Human Torpedo*, Puffin Books, Ringwood, Vic.

Yashima, T. 1983, *Crow Boy*, Puffin, New York.

Yolan, J., and L. Baker 1991, *All Those Secrets of the World*, Little, Brown & Co., Boston.

Zamorano, A., and J. Vivas 1996, *Let's Eat!* Omnibus Books, Adelaide.

Zurbo, M. 1997, *Idiot Pride*, Penguin, Melbourne.

Further reading

Chapter 1

Further reading for this chapter and others in the Reading and Writing sections should include key journals on literacy such as the *Australian Journal of Language and Literacy* (ALEA), *Practically Primary* (PETA), *Reading Research Quarterly* (IRA), *The Reading Teacher* (IRA), *Journal of Research in Reading* (UK Reading Association). These associations also publish specialist monographs on important literacy topics. Readings from relevant web sites are also to be included (see appendices).

Anstey, M., and G. Bull (eds) 1996, *The Literacy Labyrinth*, Prentice Hall, Sydney.

Cambourne, B. 1988, *The Whole Story*, Ashton, Sydney.

Holdaway, D. 1979, *The Foundations of Literacy*, Scholastic Australia, Gosford, NSW.

Smith, F. 1971, *Understanding Reading*, Holt Rinehart & Winston, New York.

Smith, F. 1973, *Psycholinguistics and Reading*, Holt, Rinehart & Winston, New York.

Chapter 2

Clay, M. M. 1991, *Becoming Literate: The construction of inner control*, Heinemann, Auckland.

Clay, M. M. 1998, *By Different Paths to Common Outcomes*, Heinemann, Auckland.

Meek, M. 1982, *Learning to Read*, Bodley Head, London.

Meek, M. 1988, *How Texts Teach What Readers Learn*, Thimble Press, Stroud, UK. In association with PETA, Sydney.

Meek, M. 1991, *On Being Literate*, Bodley Head, London.

Winch, G., and V. Hoogstad (eds) 1985, *Teaching Reading: A language experience*, 2nd edn, Macmillan, Melbourne.

Chapter 3

Anstey, M., and G. Bull (eds) 1996, *The Literacy Labyrinth*, Prentice Hall, Sydney.

Singer, H., and R. Ruddell (eds) 1985, *Theoretical Models and Processes of Reading*, 3rd edn, International Reading Association, Newark, Delaware.

Unsworth, L. (ed.) 1993, *Literacy Learning and Teaching: Language as social practice in the primary school*, Macmillan, Melbourne.

Chapter 4

Department of Education and Children's Services 1997, *Early Literacy Practices and Possibilities*, Adelaide.

Education Department of Western Australia 1994, *First Steps*, Longman, Melbourne.

Hill, S. 1997, 'Perspectives on early literacy and home–school connections', *Australian Journal of Language and Literacy* 20(4): 263–79.

Morrow, L. 1993, *Literacy Development in the Early Years: Helping children read and write*, Allyn & Bacon, Needham Heights, MA.

Chapters 5 and 6

Students are advised to consult the current curriculum and support documents relating to the teaching of literacy and reading in their state or territory.

Chapter 7

Clay, M. 1993, *Reading Recovery: A guidebook for teachers in training*, Heinemann, Auckland.

Derewianka, Beverly (ed.) 1992, *Language Assessment in Primary Classrooms*, Harcourt Brace Jovanovich, Sydney.

Students should read the curriculum documents relating to assessment in their state or territory. They should also observe the various approaches to assessing and monitoring reading development in particular schools during practicum.

Chapter 8

Students should read the various approaches to the Literacy Block or Literacy Session advocated by state or territory documents. As noted in the chapter, such practices vary considerably but all stress a dedicated period of time to be set aside for literacy learning in the school curriculum. Observation should be made of schools that operate or are developing a literacy session in their programs.

Chapter 9

Czerniewska, P. 1992, *Learning About Writing*, Blackwell, Oxford.

Darder, A. 1991, *Culture and Power in the Classroom: a critical foundation for bicultural education*, Bergin & Garvey, New York.

Gee, P. 1996, *Social Linguistics and Literacies: Ideology in discourses*, 2nd edn, Falmer Press, London.

Johnson, P. 1995, *Children Making Books*, Reading: Reading and Language Information Centre, University of Reading.

Knobel, M. 1998, *Everyday Literacies: Students, discourses, and social practices*, Peter Lang, New York.

Kress, G. 1997, *Before Writing: Rethinking the paths to literacy*, Routledge, London.

Luke, A. 1993, 'The Social Construction of Literacy in the Primary School'. In Len Unsworth (ed.), *Literacy Learning and Teaching: Language as social practice in the primary school*, Macmillan, Melbourne, pp. 3–53.

Chapter 11

Christie, F., and J. Rothery 1989, *Children Writing: A Reader*, Deakin University Press, Geelong, Vic.

Derewianka, B. 1990, *Exploring How Texts Work*, PETA, Sydney.

Graham, L. 1995, *Writing Development: A framework*, Schools Advisory Service, London Borough of Croydon, Croydon, UK.

Graves, D. 1994, *A Fresh Look At Writing*, Heinemann, Portsmouth, NH.

Kroll, B. M., and G. Wells 1983, *Explorations in the Development of Writing Theory*, Research and Practice, Wiley, Chichester, UK.

Wilde, J. 1993, *A Door Opens: Writing In Fifth Grade*, Heinemann, Portsmouth, NH.

Chapter 12

Knobel, M., and A. Healy (eds) 1998, *Critical Literacies in the Primary Classroom*, PETA, Sydney.

Luke, C. 1997, *Technological Literacy*, Adult Literacy Research Network, Language Australia, Melbourne.

Neuman, S. B., and K. A. Roskos (eds) 1998, *Children Achieving: Best practices in early literacy*, International Reading Association, Newark, Delaware.

Potter, W. J. 1998, *Media Literacy*, Sage Publications, Thousand Oaks.

Tyner, K. R. 1998, *Literacy in a Digital World: Teaching and learning in the age of information*, L. Erlbaum Assoc., Mahwah, NJ.

Chapter 13

Bean, W., and C. Bouffler 1987, *Spell by Writing*, PETA, Sydney.

Bolton, F., and D. Snowball 1993, *Teaching Spelling: a practical resource*, Nelson Australia, Melbourne.

Bouffler, C. 1997, 'They don't teach spelling anymore—or do they?', *Australian Journal of Language and Literacy* 20(2): 140–7.

Department of Education and Student Services, South Australia 1997, *Spellings from Beginnings to Independence*, Darlington Materials Development Centre, Seacombe Gardens, SA.

Fresch, M., and A. Wheaton 1997, 'Sort, Search and Discover: Spelling in the Student-centred Classroom', *The Reading Teacher* 51(1): 20–30.

Heald-Taylor, B. G. 1998, 'Three Paradigms of Spelling Instruction in Grades 3 to 6', *The Reading Teacher* 51(5): 404–13.

Nightingale, G., and P. Nightingale, P. 1985, *Foundation Handwriting*, Martin Educational, Cammeray. [Series of 7 books from Kindergarten to Year 6]

Shepherd, J. 1994, *Spell It Out! Success with spelling*, Oxford University Press, Melbourne.

Westwood, P. 1994, 'Issues in spelling instruction', *Special Education Perspectives* 3(1): 31–44.

Chapter 14

Bull, G., and M. Anstey (eds) 1996, *The Literacy Lexicon*, Prentice Hall, Sydney.

Cambourne, B. 1995, 'Towards an educationally relevant theory of literacy leaning: twenty years of inquiry', *The Reading Teacher* 49(3): 182–90.

Collerson, J. 1994, *English Grammar: A functional approach*, PETA, Sydney.

Eggins, S. 1994, *An Introduction to Systemic Functional Linguistics*, Cassell, London.

Graham, J., and K. Alison (eds) 1998, *Writing Under Control: Teaching writing in the primary school*, Centre for Language Education and Research, David Fulton in association with Roehampton Institute, London.

Luke, A., and P. Gilbert (eds) 1993, *Literacy in Contexts*, Allen & Unwin, Sydney.

Chapter 15

Breen, M. P., C. Barratt-Pugh, B. Derewianka, H. House, C. Hudson, T. Lumley and M. Rohl 1997, *Profiling ESL Children: How teachers interpret and use national and state assessment frameworks*, DEETYA, Canberra.

Brindley, G., and G. Wigglesworth 1997, *Access: Issues in language test design and delivery*, National Centre for English Language Teaching and Research, Macquarie University, Sydney.

Cairney, T. H. 1995, *Pathways to Literacy*, Cassell, London.

Derewianka, B. (ed.) 1992, *Language Assessment in Primary Classrooms*, Harcourt Brace Jovanovich, Sydney.

Chapter 17

Klein, C. 1988, *A Space for Delight*, Erewhon, Sydney.

McCourt, F. 1998, *Angela's Ashes*, HarperCollins, London [1996].

Chapter 18

Grisham, J. 1999, *The Testament*, Century, London.

Koch, C. 1988, *Highways to a War*, Minerva, Melbourne.

Chapter 19

Calvin and Hobbes cartoon series.

Frank, A. 1963, *Anne Frank: The diary of a young girl*, Washington Square Press, USA.

Guterson, D. 1995, *Snow Falling on Cedars*, Bloomsbury, London.

Kovic, R. 1996, *Born on the Fourth of July*, Pocket Books, New York [1976].

Malouf, D. 1978, *An Imaginary Life*, Chatto & Windus, London.

Morrison, T. 1997, *Beloved*, Vintage/Random House, London [1987].

Chapter 21

Bail, M.1998, *Eucalyptus*, Text, Melbourne.

Chapter 25

Morgan, S. 1987, *My Place*, Fremantle Arts Centre Press, Fremantle, WA.

Ward, G. 1987, *Wandering Girl*, Magabala Books, Brooke, WA.

Answers to the tiny test (page 34).

3; 4; 3; 2.

1; 3; 4; 2.

Name and Title Index

This index includes names of authors discussed in the text and titles of films and children's books. References to figures are suffixed with an f.

Subject and Organisation Index

This index covers subjects, organisations and glossary entries. References to illustrations are italicised. References to activities and tasks are suffixed with an a; figures are suffixed with an f.